ORIGINS, ANCESTRY AND ALLIANCE

EXPLORATIONS IN AUSTRONESIAN ETHNOGRAPHY

ORIGINS, ANCESTRY AND ALLIANCE

EXPLORATIONS IN AUSTRONESIAN ETHNOGRAPHY

Edited by James J. Fox and Clifford Sather

A publication of the Department of Anthropology
as part of the Comparative Austronesian Project,
Research School of Pacific Studies
The Australian National University
Canberra ACT Australia

ANU
THE AUSTRALIAN NATIONAL UNIVERSITY

E PRESS

ANU
E PRESS

Published by ANU E Press
The Australian National University
Canberra ACT 0200, Australia
Email: anuepress@anu.edu.au
Web: http://epress.anu.edu.au

Previously published in Australia by the Department of Anthropology in association
with the Comparative Austronesian Project, Research School of Pacific Studies, The
Australian National University, Canberra 1996.

National Library of Australia
Cataloguing-in-Publication entry

Origins, Ancestry and Alliance:
explorations in Austronesian ethnography.

Bibliography.
ISBN 0 7315 2432 2 (print)
ISBN 1 920942 87 4 (online)

1. Ethnography - Islands of the Pacific. 2. Ethnography - Asia, South
East. 3. Kinship - Islands of the Pacific. 4. Kinship - Asia, South East.
5. Islands of the Pacific - Social life and customs. 6. Asia, South East -
Social life and customs. I. Fox, James J., 1940- . II. Sather, Clifford,
1938- . III. Australian National University. Dept of Anthropology.
IV. Comparative Austronesian Project.

305.899

Typesetting by Norma Chin; drawings by Robert Nee/Neville Minch
Cover design by Griffiths & Young Design/Bronwyn Dillon

Table of Contents

Acknowledgements

This volume has been a long time in preparation. As a result, acknowledgement and thanks are due to the patience and forbearance of those contributors who waited for their papers to appear while this volume slowly took shape and then took its place in the queue for publication. A majority of the papers in the volume were initially presented at a conference of the Comparative Austronesian Project. For the organization of that conference and of the project in general, we wish to thank Annegret Schemberg for her efforts and enthusiasm.

The cover of this volume was designed by Bronwyn Dillon of Griffiths & Young Design Pty Ltd. The textile that forms the background is a man's cloth of the Atoni Pah Meto of west Timor. The *ikat* centre of this cloth consists of anthropomorphic figures arranged in a succession of sizes, thus forming a kind of ancestral chain. The cloth is composed of a central warp *ikat* with multicoloured borders of woven cotton thread, each with a supplementary *ikat* stripe. The photograph on the front cover shows a recitation of origins among the Atoni. This photograph was taken in the central village of the Nabuasa clan in the mountains of southwestern Timor at a ceremony in which a high-ranking member of a branch of the clan, which had migrated from the centre generations earlier, returned to request a recitation of the chant that recounts the origin and migration of the Nabuasa clan. In the photograph, a woman holds a betel nut offering basket to the side of the main chanter. For reproduction of the textile, we wish to thank the National Gallery of Australia and the former curator of Asian textiles, Robyn Maxwell, who now teaches in the Department of Art History at The Australian National University. The photograph is from the private collection of the editor, James J. Fox. Figures and cartography in the volume were done by Robert Nee and Neville Minch of the Cartography Unit of the Research School of Pacific and Asian Studies.

As editors, we wish to express our particular thanks to Norma Chin for her considerable and unstinting effort in producing this volume. She has carried out deft copy-editing of individual papers, careful proofreading, the arrangement and formatting of the volume and the exacting preparation of the index. Since she also edited *The Austronesians*, she has provided vital editorial continuity to the series. We are particularly indebted to her for her skill, efficiency and determination to produce a volume that would be of scholarly value and of general interest.

James J. Fox
Clifford Sather

April 1996

Chapter 1. Introduction

James J. Fox

This is the third in a series of volumes produced in the Departme of Anthropology from the work of the Comparative Austronesian Project.[1] The first of these volumes examined the comparative design of Austronesian houses and related these spatial forms to the social and ritual practices of their resident groups. The second volume provided a general survey of the Austronesians focusing on their common origins and historical transformations. This third volume explores indigenous Austronesian ideas of origin, ancestry and alliance and considers the comparative significance of these ideas in social practice. As a collection, these papers offer a variety of perspectives across a range of societies of the Austronesian-speaking world from insular Southeast Asia to the islands of the Pacific.

The Comparative Austronesian Project

The Comparative Austronesian Project was originally prompted by a recognition that on virtually every area of the Austronesian-speaking world, there had been a considerable increase in significant research. As a consequence of the development of this research, there had also occurred a "localization" of interests and a proliferation of different modes of analysis to deal with what, from a comparative perspective, could reasonably be considered as similar questions.

Many regional specialists seemed no longer aware of important work being done by other Austronesian specialists. Thus researchers in Indonesia, in the Philippines, in Melanesia, in Micronesia and the Pacific islands had each developed their own research concerns. Many of these research concerns reflected the interests of previous research that had been based on established traditions of inquiry within each area. Moreover, for a large area such as Indonesia, there was even greater "localization" of interests with specialization tending to foster a focus on specific islands or subregions, with a deep bifurcation between the eastern and western halves of the archipelago.

Yet, at the same time, a great deal of comparative linguistic research had clarified internal relationships within the Austronesian language family and archaeologists had begun to trace the Austronesian expansion along lines indicated by the linguistic evidence. The possibilities for comparative research within an Austronesian framework had never been better.

It was the intention, therefore, of the Comparative Austronesian Project to bring together researchers from different parts of the Austronesian-speaking world to initiate discussions on comparative issues. The Project was conceived of as broadly interdisciplinary. It endeavoured to involve archaeologists, linguists, anthropologists and historians in this common discussion of related comparative concerns. For a period from 1989 to 1991, the Comparative Austronesian Project was given formal project status within the then Research School of Pacific Studies. Since this period and as a result of the Project, comparative Austronesian studies have been recognized as a continuing focus of research within the renamed Research School of Pacific and Asian Studies.

Origins, Ancestry and Alliance

The papers in this volume were originally presented in a marathon six-day conference (25-30 January 1990) on issues of "Hierarchy, Ancestry and Alliance" held in Canberra and the University's property at Kioloa on the south coast of Australia, offering participants a fine view of the Pacific Ocean for the concluding sessions of the conference. The conference produced a total of twenty-nine papers. From these papers, one set dealing specifically with ideas of hierarchy was selected to form the volume, *Transformations of Hierarchy*, edited by Margaret Jolly and Mark S. Mosko (1994). A second set of papers also concerned with hierarchy and precedence but equally concerned with ideas of origins, ancestry and alliance was selected to form this present volume. A majority of the papers in this volume are based on presentations at the conference but they have been revised, rewritten and, in several cases, substantially expanded as this volume has proceeded toward publication.

A feature of this second set of papers is its coverage of a diverse range of Austronesian societies ranging from Malaysia, Indonesia and the Philippines to Micronesia and central Polynesia. Although each paper presents a specific case or cases, the volume, as a whole, has been framed to highlight possibilities of comparison among societies that might otherwise be considered within separate different regional settings. Discussion of issues of hierarchy — rank, stratification and status — as well as issues of equality figure prominently in all of the papers. A principal concern is to examine how hierarchy and equality are created, imagined and maintained by reference to ideas of origin and ancestry as a "founding" ideology in Austronesian societies.

To explore these ideas also requires attention to history. Indeed an historical perspective is essential to the comparative effort. The expression of fundamental conceptions that constitute the basis by which these societies are defined as Austronesian is made evident in their history.

The Austronesian Language Context

Comparisons among the Austronesian-speaking peoples have a long history (see Jolly and Mosko 1994:1-18; Bellwood, Fox and Tryon 1995:1-16). By definition, all such "Austronesian" comparisons must, either implicitly or explicitly, be carried out in reference to some understanding of the Austronesian language family. Linguistic relations among Austronesian languages point to relations of historical derivation, often of a time depth that provides a perspective for comparison. It is, for example, of comparative significance to recognize that although Palau (or Belau) is located in Micronesia, the language of its population is classified as a Western Malayo-Polynesian language. Many of the fundamental features of Belau culture may thus bear a closer resemblance to cultures far to the west than to those of many of their own nearer neighbours (see Fox 1992, 1995a:42-45).

There are by present reckoning roughly 1200 Austronesian languages, of which all but about 14 form part of the Malayo-Polynesian subgroup (see Ross 1995; Tryon 1995). In recent years, as historical linguistic research has developed, our understanding of linguistic relationships within this large family has been vastly enhanced. In the process, earlier suppositions about higher order relationships among these languages have been re-examined and, in some cases, called into question. As a result, there are many issues of linguistic classification that are currently the subject of considerable debate (see Ross 1995 for an extensive examination of a variety of current issues in Austronesian linguistics).

Present uncertainties have much to do with the nature of the Austronesian expansion and the consequences of constructing the Austronesian family tree to represent this expansion (Ross 1995:45-55). The schematic representation of the diversification of Austronesian languages has generally relied upon a "rightsided" branching to denote a group of speakers that has separated itself and migrated from another settled population. While this migration may constitute a clear separation from a parent language, it gives no indication of the status of the language or dialects of the "stay-at-home" population. If the separating language were part of a dialect chain, then the historical break produced by the migrating group may be easier to identify as a distinctive linguistic occurrence than the differentiation that may occur among localized communities whose dialects slowly diverge, in diverse ways, over a long period of time.

Thus, for example, in terms of the primary separation that occurred within the Austronesian family, it is reasonable to inquire whether the various Austronesian languages of Taiwan — such as Atayal, Rukai and Paiwan — were part of one or more Formosan dialect linkages (Ross 1995:45-49). Similarly but for even more complex reasons, as both Blust (1985) and Ross (1995:72) have noted, the languages assigned to Western Malayo-Polynesian may not all form a single subgroup. And if this is true of the Western Malayo-Polynesian languages, the unity of so-called Central Malayo-Polynesian subgroups is even more questionable.

In a situation where so much historical linguistic research is underway, it is useful to continue to draw provisional schematic representations of the

Austronesian language family as Tryon has done for the *Comparative Austronesian Dictionary* (1995:22-28) and at the same time to draw up lists of Austronesian language groupings within provisional subgroups for further consideration as Ross has done in his sequel commentary on Tryon's classification (1995). These different perspectives provide both a specific and a general structure that can (and will) be subjected to modification as research progresses.

The papers in this volume may be taken to present a broad cross-section of Austronesian societies whose separation can be interpreted to represent a dispersal over a period of some 3000 to 4000 years. The arrangement of papers in the volume is explicitly intended to achieve a rough balance in coverage across the Austronesian- (or more accurately, the Malayo-Polynesian-) speaking world and at the same time to highlight similarities (and differences) among larger linguistic subgroups.

In terms of the present provisional classification of Austronesian languages, the societies discussed in this volume belong to three large subgroupings: Western, Central and Eastern Malayo-Polynesian, which also represent a broad regional distribution of these languages. The Iban, the Mandaya, the Makassarese and both the Tausug and the Sama-Bajau are groups whose languages would be classified as Western Malayo-Polynesian. Similarly the various related languages of the Timor area, the languages of Sikka and Tana 'Ai, that of Palu'é, Buru and that of the Mayawo of Damer would all be classified within Central Malayo-Polynesian, even though the differences among these languages is considerable. Finally Rarotongan in the Cook Islands, the language of Satawal in the Caroline Islands and Tongan all belong to Eastern Malayo-Polynesian. In terms of Ross's classification (1995:74-94), this range of languages includes at least four distinct language groups in both the Western and Central Malayo-Polynesian subgroups and at least two in Eastern-Malayo-Polynesian. The extent to which similarities are discernible across this range of societies may be indicative of the sharing of fundamental cultural conceptions that constitute some of the epistemic ideas of the Austronesians.

The Discourse on Origins Among the Austronesians

One of the perennial preoccupations in Austronesian studies has been with tracing the origins of the Austronesians. Archaeologists, linguists and historians have all been concerned with this task. A less prominent concern has been to examine indigenous ideas of origin and how they function within Austronesian societies.

Ideas of origin are themselves a matter of concern in most Austronesian societies and hence a suitable subject for investigation. However, such indigenous ideas of origin involve a complex array of notions. Conceptions of ancestry are invariably important but rarely is ancestry alone a sufficient and exclusive criterion for defining origins. Recourse to notions of place is also critical in identifying persons and groups, and thus in tracing origins. Similarly, alliance, defined in the broad sense of relations of persons and groups to one another, is also an important element in defining origins. Together all of these notions imply an attitude to the past: that it is knowable and that such knowledge is of value, that what happened in the past has set a pattern for the present, and that it is essential to have access to the past in attempts to order the present. Origins may be conceived of as multiple and access to them may be provided by diverse means. Dreaming, contact with spirits, the recitation of formulaic wisdom, the witness of the elders, or the presentation of sacred objects as evidence of links to the past may each provide forms of access to the past.

Considered comparatively, ideas of origin may vary significantly among Austronesian populations but these ideas generally rely upon a combination of elements often phrased in terms of common metaphors based on recognizable cognate expressions. It is this discourse on origins that is distinctively Austronesian.

It is possible, in linguistic terms, to trace the use of cognate terms among different groups but much more is involved in this discourse. Frequently similar metaphors of origin persist even where the terms used in these metaphors are unrelated. Fictitious etymologies are also frequently devised and elaborated to support narrative claims about origin within this discourse. It is therefore not just a general concern with origins that is significant but a rich and complex discourse by which "origin structures" are created and disputed that is of primary interest. It is this discourse on origins and its relationship to social practice that is a focus of this volume.

Idioms in the Discourse on Origins

Austronesian discourse on origins is based both on a semantics of recognizable cognate terms and on a variety of similar metaphoric idioms. The combination of similar idioms and common metaphors, often bolstered by recourse to folk etymologies, is discernible in various papers in this volume.

Sather provides an excellent example of this usage in his discussion of the Iban understanding of the concept of *pun*. *Pun* means "source, basis, origin, or cause". Quoting Freeman, he notes that its root meaning "is that of stem, as of a tree, from which development of any activity springs". *Pun* may thus describe a person who initiates an action, such as a *pun bejelai*, who organizes and leads an expedition, but it may also apply to the founder of a family, *pun bilik*, the originator of a house, *pun rumah*, or the main line of a genealogy, *pun tusut*. These usages all imply a focus of reference, a point of initiation and a locus of continuity. As such they evoke an entire epistemology of origins. It is within these terms that Sather is able to differentiate between equality and hierarchy in Iban social practice.

The term, *pun*, derives from proto-Malayo-Polynesian (PMP) * *puqun*: "tree, trunk, base, source" and is one of a number of terms in Austronesian discourse on origins. The metaphoric linkage of "origin" and "cause" with the "base", "trunk" or "(tap)-root" of a tree and the implied sense of growth that derives from this botanic idiom may also be applied to life in general and to social life in particular. For examines reflexes of * *puqun (fun, pun, hun, un)* in six societies of the Timor area, taking this term for origin as a "marker" to distinguish "progenitor lines" in each society and to point to the social transformations these lines have undergone from one society to another. As an essay in regional comparison, the paper considers alternative possibilities for viewing groups in relation to their "origin structures".

The occurrence of reflexes of * *puqun* as a botanic origin category is common and wide-spread in both Western and Central Malayo-Polynesian languages (see Adelaar 1992:48; Fox 1980:14; Sugishima 1994:156) but it is by no means the only term that links origins to a base, trunk or root. Thus, in Madagascar, among different Malagasy-speaking populations, *fotora* ("trunk") or *fototra* ("origin root") as in the expression, *fotoran'razan'ay* ("root of our ancestors") figures prominently in the identification of origins (see Feeley-Harnik 1991:132-137; Thomas 1994:9). The equivalent terms among the Karo Batak would be *benakayu*; among the Minangkabau, *pangkalan*; among the Javanese and Balinese, *wit (kawitan)*; among the Tontemboan of Minahasa, *tu'ur* (see Graafland 1898,I:215; Schwarz 1908:553); or as in the case of Bislama, the pidgin of Vanuatu, where the term *stamba*, "root-place" (from English, stump) is used, this botanic term may derive from an outside source (Bonnemaison 1985:41).

It is possible also to identify reflexes of other origin categories that can be traced back to and reconstructed as proto-Malayo-Polynesian. Besides * *puqun*, reflexes of * *t-u(m)pu* (or * *epu*), "ancestor, master, second generation relative", and * *tu(m)buq*, "growth", figure prominently in metaphoric statements about origins (Fox 1995a:36). Together these reflexes interrelate the notions of origin as "trunk", as "ancestor" and as "growth". Such reflexes may be used in various combinations. The Kedang of Lembata, for example, combine a reflex of * *epu* with a term for trunk, *puén*, to designate the affinal position of the mother's brother (*epu puén*) (Barnes 1980:79). The neighbouring Lamaholot utilize a different combination to a similar end by combining the term *belaké*, "wife-giver", with *pukén*, to identify the "stem or source wife-giver" (*belaké pukén*) while relying on *opu* as a reciprocal of *belaké* to designate wife-taking affines (Graham 1994:346-352). In the Pacific, reflexes of * *tu(m)buq* and * *t-u(m)pu* combine, in various forms, to create a semantics of origins. Writing on ideas about ancestors (*tipuna, tupuna*) among Maori, Ann Salmond has examined the semantic use of such terms as *tupu*, "generative force with an individual growth, bud, shoot" and the related term, *puu*, which, in Maori, has come to mean "origin, cause, source, root of a tree or plant, heart, centre, main stock of a kin group" to argue that "plant growth and the growth of human beings are often held parallel in the semantic patterns of the Maori lexicon" (1991:344).

Lewis takes up this discussion of origin structures and examines the differences between progenitor and progenitrix lines in Sikka and Tana 'Ai. In these societies, the term for source or trunk is *pu'an/puang*. Similarly, Grimes considers the way in which people of the island of Buru "express ideas of origin and cause using metaphors based on the imagery of a living plant or tree". The word for trunk and root in Buru is *lahin* and among the population of the island, all things grow, develop and are traced from root (*lahir*) to tips (*luken*).

Biersack examines the concept of origin in Tonga focusing in particular on the Tu'i Tonga as the *tefito*, or original "root" of society. Cognates of the word, *tefito*, also figure prominently in other Pacific island societies and are referred to in some of the classic ethnographies of the region. In his *Tikopia-English Dictionary* (1985:466-467), Firth reports that *tafito* means "base, basis, origin, reason, cause". *Tafito* is the principal term used to identify social or ancestral origin and can also refer to a person who is a principal figure in any formal proceeding or a major participant in an exchange transaction. According to Firth, the notion of *tafito* that applies to ritual officiants takes its reference from the gods:

> Each god was regarded as having his basis (*tafito*) in a special ritual officiant, who himself might have several titles (*rau*) by which he addresses the god in different contexts: by his temple in Uta; in his canoe yard; for curing illness. Like the botanical principle of postulating the origin of a species near where most of its varieties are found, the "owner" of a god often has more titles than other men do … (Firth 1970:144).

Thus, in Tikopia as in Tonga, the notion of origin has direct relevance to a system of titles. It is also relevant to a sacred geography that identifies places where rituals are performed. From the term *tafito* are derived the word *tafitoanga* ("place of origin") and *tafito-ranga* ("beginning") (see Fox 1995a:45-47 for a further discussion of these and other terms in the epistemology of Tikopian ideas of origins).

Another critically important term for designating origins in many Polynesian societies is *tumu* (Hawaiian: *kumu*), which carries a similar configuration of botanic meanings. In Rarotongan, for example, *tumu* signifies "foundation, root, cause, origin, source, that which introduces, the reason or cause of anything; the trunk or the main part of anything from which something springs or is made, created or fashioned". *Tumu* thus forms the base for a variety of other crucial terms: *tumu-enua* ("chief" or "leader"), *tumu-karakia* ("principal priest") or *tumu-emu* ("leading part of a recitative") (Savage 1962:413).

Siikala, in his paper, refers to the tracing of origins among the Cook Islanders through path and genealogy as "expressions of the same process, the extension of the ancestral *tumu* in space and time". In his monographic exposition of indigenous ideas of origin, 'Akatokamanāva, Siikala (1991) has provided a much more extended examination of these notions of *tumu* and in particular of the Cook Islanders' genealogical conceptions of the "origin of all things" from Atea and Papa-i-te-'itinga through their child, Te Tumu.

All these various distinctive botanic metaphors that combine notions of growth and succession, of derivation, division and differentiation are relied upon for heuristic purposes: to trace and distinguish features of social and religious life. Reliance on such botanical analogies is in no way unique to the Austronesians. In *Biological Metaphor and Cladistic Classification* (1987), Hoenigswald and Wiener have assembled a remarkable collection of essays that chart the use of botanical metaphors in the history of western sciences from the ancient Greeks to modern taxonomists who are concerned with the rigorous methodologies of what is referred to as "phylogenetic systematics" or "cladistics". In this respect, it is evident that ancient Greek thinkers were as much concerned with the processes of change and the origin of things as are many Austronesians and that they relied on similar organismic analogies and on their own forms of folk etymologizing — Plato's primordial words: *prōta onomata* — to intuit and articulate relationships (see Percival 1987). Austronesian concerns with origins and all the varied discourse on such origins may thus be viewed as particular articulation of a near universal orientation to the world.

A common effect of the variety of Austronesian botanic metaphors is to give physical representation to temporal processes. As is reiterated by contributors to this volume, these metaphors conflate temporal and spatial modes of comprehension. This relates to the analytical notion of precedence that is developed throughout this volume. As is implied by the term, precedence connotes a priority in time but also a priority of position, rank or status. This double aspect is crucial to an understanding of this notion.

During the course of the Comparative Austronesian Project, precedence was the subject of much discussion. There was a "working paper" on precedence (Fox 1990) which was eventually published in a somewhat revised form (Fox 1994), but more importantly there were a number of detailed ethnographies that developed ideas of precedence in specific Austronesian societies. The publication of Lewis's *People of the Source* (1988) provided the first extended use of precedence in a study of an eastern Indonesian society. This was followed by a succession of other equally important theses that utilized ideas of precedence: McWilliam on the mountain Timorese (1989); Graham on Lewotala in east Flores

(1991); Vischer on the population of Palu'é of Flores (1992), Grimes on Buru (1990, 1993) and Reuter on Sumatra (1993).[2]

All of this work was as much directed to the practice of precedence as to the language of precedence. One concern was to distinguish precedence from hierarchy. Whereas it is theoretically possible to conceive of precedence as either coincident with or supportive of hierarchy, the focus of most of these initial studies of precedence was on the continuous positioning among groups and individuals, using a variety of mixed criteria, to argue for their place within society. The concern was more with competition and contention; the creation of orders of precedence that were subject to dispute and revision; and with the possibilities of a variety of outcomes locally in different groups within similar cultural contexts. It is these ideas of precedence as discourse and practice that are also considered in various papers in this volume.

Precedence as Discourse and Practice

Bellwood initiates the discussion of origins in relation to practice by pointing to the critical importance of what he calls a "founder-focused ideology". This ideology includes reverence for ancestral founders, the naming of groups after them, and the ranking of positions in relation to such founders by which rights to land, labour and ritual prerogatives are derived. The general ascription of genealogically based rank in turn contributes to what Bellwood terms "founder rank enhancement" by which junior members of society are propelled to move out to establish their own senior founding position elsewhere, thus providing a strong motivation for exploration and expansion. This model, which Bellwood sketches, is concerned not just with single founders but "with successive and multiple founders" whose existence admits of a great variety of possibilities for tracing origins. History and its representation are crucial factors for this model and the complexity of cases to which it may apply.

Recognition of this complexity is Siikala's starting point in his examination of chiefly relations among the island polities of 'Atiu, Ma'uke and Mitiaro in the Southern Cook Islands. Although the origin narratives of the Cook Islanders recount relations among the islands based on an opposition between elder and younger, which also distinguishes between gods and humans, a whole set of other oppositions involving gender and marriage are brought into play to support internal claims to succession among the chiefly lines on the different islands. Because islands have separate gender identities, a claim to succession on one island is based on the reverse criterion of a claim to succession on another.

In his succinct analysis of the complexity of relations among founders, Siikala also presents another epistemic theme among Austronesians: the tracing of relations by means of the notion of "path". In such a notion, genealogy and journey merge — as do place and person in many Austronesian societies — to create both a spatial and a temporal narrative of social relationships. In this narrative, as Siikala notes, "precedence is determined in a recursive way, creating an overall hierarchy".

In his paper, Sudo continues the consideration of origins in an examination of claims of origin among the matriclans of Satawal in the Caroline Islands of Micronesia. The paper examines relationships among successive and multiple founders. Of Satawal's eight clans, three are regarded as first settlers and are thereby accorded chiefly status; four clans are considered to be later arrivals and are thus accorded commoner status. One clan, although distinguished as the earliest of all the founder clans, is said to have surrendered its rights to the first of the chiefly clan. These relations encapsulate an order of precedence that acknowledges the transference of superiority from an autochthonous group to groups of incoming settlers. This same theme, in innumerable variants, is a recurrent founding myth for many Austronesian status groups (Sahlins 1985; Fox 1995b).

Sudo examines the complexities involved in these founder relations including claims to migrations from different directions, local and more distant tribute relations, an allocation of rights to the produce of land and sea. In Sudo's discussion, as in Siikala's, the idea of alternative modes of arguing rights, which are those of precedence, are indicated as a vital factor in determining local rank and status.

The papers by Sather and Yengoyan form a valuable pair in that both are concerned with societies that are characterized as egalitarian. As Sather shows, the value placed on autonomy and equality among the Iban do not preclude the pursuit of prestige and renown by enterprising individuals. As Freeman has phrased it: "… an individual had to be the source (*pun*) of his own achievement (1981:38). Nor do these values preclude the concrete representation of "an idealized world of precedence" in the alignment of visitors and hosts at ritual performances in a longhouse.

Yengoyan makes similar observations in regard to the Mandaya of Mindanao among whom precedence derives from a remembered past, while egalitarian values dominate domestic life. Formerly organized into territorial groups around a war leader known as *bagani*, the Mandaya required that each *bagani* who succeeded to authority had yet to prove himself by personal valour and daring achievements. The selection of all *bagani* was subject to popular scrutiny and physical confirmation. In contemporary communities where differences are minimized, the places associated with the origins and heroic actions of this *bagani* complex still provide "the emotional sustenance to what the Mandaya consider as their past".

The subsequent four papers in the volume form a closely related set of essays that reflect shared understandings of notions of origin and their relation to the practice of precedence in a number of different societies in eastern Indonesia. The papers by Fox and Lewis are broadly comparative and concerned with a reexamination of ideas of alliance. Instead of focusing on exchange *per se*, Fox considers the "giving of life" implied by the kinship categories and botanic metaphors of origin that identify groups that exchange either women or men in various societies of the Timor area and on Flores. Instead of the categories of wife-giver/wife-taker, he adopts the terms progenitor/progeny (or progenitrix/progeny in the case of maternal groups that exchange males) to approximate, at an analytic level, an understanding of local native categories. He then examines the differences among progenitor or progenitrix lines in the various different societies as possible transformations within recognizable bounds. Lewis takes up Fox's final case, that of the Ata Tana 'Ai, and considers in detail the internal precedence of its progenitrix lines. From this vantage point, he then compares the two closely related societies of the Ata Tana 'Ai and of Sikka, particularly in relation to the delegation of authority. In his analysis, he emphasizes the dynamism and fluidity of relationships and their representations as ordered by precedence.

Following on from Lewis's paper, Vischer examines contestation in the order of precedence for the performance of ceremonies that both link and differentiate domains on the island of Palu'é, located off the northern coast of Flores. From among 14 small domains, Vischer focuses on a group of three domains whose relationship to one another is likened to the "three hearth stones" that support a single pot. Each of these domains has its own perception of its relationship to the other two based on categorical oppositions to one another. Successful performance of the major water buffalo sacrifice in one has the potential to alter this perceived relationship. With this as background, Vischer examines the specific performance of the all-important water buffalo sacrifice by one domain, Ko'a, and assesses its outcome internally as well as between the domains. The paper is a model of an event-oriented analysis of shifting precedence.

Finally, in this set of four papers, Grimes examines the remarkable configuration of origin structures on the island of Buru. Among the indigenous population of Buru, different houses or house circles (*hum lolin*) are comprised of several generations of related agnatic kin. Houses, in turn, make up a *noro*, which are the basic constituent units of Buru society. Unlike the cases discussed by Fox and Lewis, where precedence is applied both internally within house groups and also between allied "life-giving" groups, on Buru relations between the houses of a *noro* are structured on precedence based on temporal establishment. Relations between individuals within houses are structured on precedence based on relative age, but no precedence is recognized based upon marriage alliance, despite a discourse that conceives of the giving of women as the giving of life. Thus, what Grimes shows clearly is that similar forms of discourse on origins do not necessarily translate into similar practices of precedence.

Origin Narratives and Historical Formations

Pannell's paper, which is also focused on a society in eastern Indonesia — the population of the village of Amaya on the island of Damer — examines the politics of precedence within the village structures of a modernizing bureaucratic administration. The focus in this paper, as Pannell phrases it, is on "the conjunction of local origin narratives with the logic and practices of the Indonesian state". Features discussed in other papers — the multiple origins of groups, their social categorization as indigenous versus immigrant groups, and the contestation of precedence — are also discussed in this paper but they are given new significance in the efforts of local officials to appropriate these traditions to support their authority. The paper is a salient reminder that such appropriations have been a continuing process among the Austronesians.

The three concluding papers in the volume take up these historical themes directly. Biersack's essay is an extended examination of the Tongan origin structure that has as its "root" the Tu'i Tonga, covering succession within this title system over a period of more than 150 years. Biersack distinguishes between two ranking schemes and carefully analyses the way in which rivals strove to gain precedence resulting in the eventual ascendancy of juniors over seniors. As another appropriate historical case, Bulbeck presents a meticulous analysis of the politics of marriage in the Makassar kingdom of Gowa during the sixteenth and seventeenth centuries and of the political manoeuvring based on marriage that ultimately determined succession to positions within the interrelated title systems of Gowa and Tallok. The two cases can be usefully compared since sociologically they both involve processes of apical demotion combined with competition for succession by agnatic legitimation that remains open to alternative forms of succession through cognatic relationships.

Where historical records are available, it is evident that Austronesian origin structures are by no means timeless nor are they as transparent as their justifying narratives purport to claim. The final paper in the volume makes this abundantly clear in its analysis of another area of status complexity within the Austronesian world, that of the Sulu Archipelago. Frake compares the perceptions and pretensions of the Tausug of Jolo Island and of the Subanum of the mountains of Zamboanga with those of various Samalan-speakers, some of whom have distinguished themselves, generally by their reputations for banditry or piracy or by being land-based cultivators, as not part of the general boat-dwelling Sama population. In this complex mix of differently identified ethnic groups, the Tausug claim pre-eminence as the original inhabitants of Jolo Island who have attracted the Sama population as immigrants. Yet linguistically, Tausug appears to be the intrusive group whose language is most closely related to the languages of the central Philippines whereas the Samalan language would appear to have greater antiquity within the Sulu Archipelago. The case makes a valuable conclusion by pointing, once again, to the need to differentiate between the study of indigenous ideas of origin and how they are used in the structuring of Austronesian societies and the study of Austronesian origins that are gradually being pieced together through historical and linguistic research. Both have a part to play in our understanding of the Austronesians.

Bibliography

Adelaar, K. Alexander

1992   *Proto-Malayic: the reconstruction of its phonology and parts of its lexicon and morphology*. Pacific Linguistics Series C-119. Canberra: Department of Linguistics, Research School of Pacific Studies, The Australian National University.

Barnes, Robert H.

1980   Concordance, structure, and variation: Considerations of alliance in Kedang. In J.J. Fox (ed.) *The flow of life: essays on Eastern Indonesia*, pp.68-97. Cambridge, MA: Harvard University Press.

Bellwood, Peter, James J. Fox and Darrell T. Tryon (eds)

1995   *The Austronesians: historical and comparative perspectives*. Canberra: Department of Anthropology, Research School of Pacific and Asian Studies.

Blust, Robert A.

1985   The Austronesian homeland: a linguistic perspective. *Asian Perspectives* 26:45-67.

Bonnemaison, Joël

1985 The tree and the canoe: roots and mobility in Vanuatu society. In *Mobility and Identity in the Island Pacific, Special Issue of Pacific Viewpoint* 26(1):30-62.

Feeley-Harnik, Gillian

1991   Finding memories in Madagascar. In S. Küchler and W. Melion (eds) *Images of memory: on remembering and representation*, pp.121-140. Washington, DC: Smithsonian Institution Press.

Firth, Raymond

1970   Spirit patterns and the social structure. In R. Firth, *Rank and religion in Tikopia*, pp.128-166. London: George Allen and Unwin.

1985   *Tikopia-English dictionary*. Auckland: Auckland University Press.

Fox, James J.

1980   Models and metaphors: comparative research in Eastern Indonesia. In J.J. Fox (ed.) *The flow of life: essays on Eastern Indonesia*, pp.327-333. Cambridge, MA: Harvard University Press.

1990   Hierarchy and precedence. Working Paper No. 3. Comparative Austronesian Project, Department of Anthropology, Research School of Pacific Studies, Canberra.

1992   Origin and order in a Micronesian society: a comparative assessment of two books on Palau. *Canberra Anthropology* 15(1):75-86.

1994   Reflections on "Hierarchy" and "Precedence". In M. Jolly and M. Mosko (eds) *Special Issue of History and Anthropology. Transformations of hierarchy: structure, history and horizon in the Austronesian world*, 7(1-4):87-108. Chur and Reading: Harwood Academic Publishers.

1995a   Origin structures and systems of precedence in the comparative study of Austronesian societies. In P. J. K. Li, Cheng-hwa Tsang, Ying-kuei Huang, Dah-an Ho and Chiu-yu Tseng (eds) *Austronesian studies relating to Taiwan*, pp.27-57. Symposium Series of the Institute of History & Philology: Academia Sinica 3. Taipei.

1995b   Installing the "outsider" inside: an exploration of an Austronesian culture theme and its social significance. Unpublished paper. First Conference for the European Association for South-East Asian Studies. Leiden 29 June - 1 July, 1995.

Freeman, Derek

1981   *Some reflections on the nature of Iban society*. An Occasional Paper, Department of Anthropology. Canberra: Research School of Pacific Studies.

Graafland, N.

1898   De Minahassa: Haar verleden en haar tegenwoordige toestand. Haarlem: Bohn.

Graham, Penelope

1991   To follow the blood: the path of life in a domain of eastern Flores, Indonesia. Unpublished PhD thesis. Canberra: The Australian National University.

1994   Alliance against hierarchy: affinal distinctions and sovereign rights in eastern Flores, Indonesia. In M. Jolly and M.S. Mosko (eds) *Transformations of hierarchy: structure, history and horizon in the Austronesian world, Special Issue of History and Anthropology* 7(1-4):339-362. Chur and Reading: Harwood Academic Publishers.

Grimes, Barbara

1990   The return of the bride: affiliation and alliance on Buru. Unpublished MA thesis. Canberra: The Australian National University.

1993   The pursuit of prosperity and blessing: social life and symbolic action on Buru Island, Eastern Indonesia. Unpublished PhD thesis. Canberra: The Australian National University.

Hoenigswald, Henry M. and Linda F. Wiener

1987   *Biological metaphor and cladistic classification: an interdisciplinary perspective*. Philadelphia: University of Pennsylvania.

Jolly, Margaret and Mark S. Mosko (eds)

1994   *Transformations of hierarchy: structure, history and horizon in the Austronesian world. History and Anthropology*. Vol. 7. Chur and Reading: Harwood Academic Publishers.

Lewis, E. Douglas

1988   People of the source: the social and ceremonial order of Tana Wai Brama on Flores. *Verhandelingen van het Koninklijk Instituut voor Taal-, Land- en Volkenkunde* 135. Dordrecht: Floris.

McWilliam, Andrew

1989   Narrating the gate and the path: place and precedence in southwest Timor. Unpublished PhD thesis. Canberra: The Australian National University.

Percival, W. Keith

1987   Biological analogy in the study of language before the advent of comparative grammar. In H.M. Hoenigswald and L.F. Wiener (eds) *Biological metaphor and cladistic classification: an interdisciplinary perspective*, pp.3-37. Philadelphia: University of Pennsylvania.

Reuter, Thomas

1993   Precedence in Sumatra: an analysis of the construction of status in affinal relations and origin groups. *Bijdragen tot de Taal-, Land- en Volkenkunde* 148:489-520.

1996   Custodians of the sacred mountains: the ritual domains of highland Bali. Unpublished PhD thesis. Canberra: The Australian National University.

Ross, Malcolm D.

1995   Some current issues in Austronesian linguistics. In D. Tryon (ed.) *Comparative Austronesian dictionary: an introduction to Austronesian studies*, pp.45-120. Berlin: Mouton de Gruyter.

Sahlins, Marshall

1985   The stranger-king; or, Dumézil among the Fijians. In *Islands of history*, pp.73-103. Chicago: The University of Chicago Press.

Salmond, Ann

1991   Tipuna-ancestors: aspects of Maori cognatic descent. In Andrew Pawley (ed.) *Man and a half: essays in Pacific anthropology and ethnobotany in honour of Ralph Bulmer*, pp.343-356. Auckland: The Polynesian Society.

Savage, Stephen

1962   *A dictionary of the Maori language of Rarotonga*. Wellington: The Department of Island Territories.

Schwarz, J.A.T.

1908   *Tontemboansch-Nederlandsch Woordenboek*. Leiden: Brill.

Siikala, Jukka

1991   '*Akatokamanāva: myth, history and society in the Southern Cook Islands*. Auckland: The Polynesian Society in association with The Finnish Anthropological Society.

Sugishima, Takashi

1994   Double descent, alliance, and botanical metaphors among the Lionese of central Flores. *Bijdragen tot de Taal-, Lande- en Volkenkunde* 150:146-170.

Thomas, Philip

1994 The water that blesses, the river that flows: origins, roots, and attachment to place among the Temanambondro of southeast Madagascar. Unpublished MS.

Tryon, Darrell T.

1995   The Austronesian languages. In D. Tryon (ed) *Comparative Austronesian dictionary: an introduction to Austronesian studies*, pp.5-44. Berlin: Mouton de Gruyter.

Vischer, Michael

1992   Children of the black patola stone: origin structures in a domain on Palu'é Island, Eastern Indonesia. Unpublished PhD thesis. Canberra: The Australian National University.

Notes

[1] This trilogy of volumes represents only part of a larger collection of studies produced by the Comparative Austronesian Project. These include:

Spriggs, Matthew (ed.)

Lapita design, form and composition. Proceedings of the Lapita Design Workshop. Canberra: Department of Prehistory, Research School of Pacific Studies (1990).

Pawley, Andrew and Malcolm Ross (eds)

Austronesian terminologies: continuity and change. Pacific Linguistics Series C No. 127. Canberra: Department of Linguistics, Research School of Pacific Studies, The Australian National University (1994).

Tryon, Darrell (ed.)

Comparative Austronesian dictionary. 4 vols. Berlin: Mouton de Gruyter (1994).

Jolly, Margaret and Mark S. Mosko (eds)

Transformations of hierarchy: structure, history and horizon in the Austronesian world. Special Issue of History and Anthropology. Chur and Reading: Harwood Academic Publishers (1994).

[2] Reuter was a vacation scholar in the Department of Anthropology while preparing his Honours thesis under Dr E.D. Lewis's direction at Melbourne. His thesis is summarized in his 1993 paper. He later joined the Department and wrote an ethnography of the Bali Aga (1996) which also examines origins and precedence among this mountain population.

Chapter 2. Hierarchy, Founder Ideology and Austronesian Expansion[1]

Peter Bellwood

Introduction

Is it possible to correlate the earliest colonizing movements of Austronesian-speaking peoples into Taiwan, the Philippines, Vietnam, Malaysia, Indonesia and the myriad islands of Oceania[2] with the existence of a hereditary élite stratum of society? How far back in time can such élites be traced and can their genesis be related in any way to the colonization process itself? And how were the social systems of the earliest Austronesian groups, especially in Melanesia, affected by contact with pre-existing societies, perhaps similar in terms of economy and technology but fundamentally different in terms of social ideology?

The literature on aspects of prehistoric Austronesian social hierarchy is very large,[3] so in this paper I will focus only on three relatively fundamental topics of enquiry. The first is to document available opinion about the prehistory of rank in its various forms in the early centuries of Austronesian expansion, before approximately 3000 years ago. One of my contentions here is that some degree of perspective on the early history of hierarchy, particularly in the Austronesian-speaking parts of Oceania, can be achieved if one discards the engrained habit of regarding "Melanesians" as a single anthropological entity with respect to other Oceanic peoples such as Polynesians. Many other writers share my misgivings about this (e.g. Douglas 1979; Lilley 1986; Thomas 1989), but few have taken what appears to me to be the obvious approach from a historical-linguistic perspective. This is to focus instead on the fundamental differences that divide the societies of the Austronesian- and the Papuan-speaking populations of western Oceania.

The second topic of enquiry revolves around the widespread occurrence of a "founder-focused ideology" in a great many of the ethnographic Austronesian societies of Island Southeast Asia and Oceania. Founders very frequently tend to be revered by their descendants, and one aspect of this ideology in the societies of eastern Indonesia, Micronesia and Melanesia is that greater status (often of a ritual or sacerdotal nature) is allocated within a community to those who descend from earlier rather than later kin group founders.

The third topic of enquiry follows on from the second. Did the existence of a founder-focused ideology have any influence or causal role in determining the rate and vast extent of Austronesian expansion? To answer this question I focus on "founder rank enhancement", a process whereby junior founders moving into relative or absolute isolation (such as a new island, previously inhabited or not) could establish senior lines, aggrandize their resources, and attempt to ensure methods of genealogical inheritance which would retain privileges for their descendants. *Separation*, in short, could have given founders opportunities for aggrandizement of their own and their descendants' statuses that they might not have had at home. This kind of aggrandizement operated under conditions of foundership in empty territories as well as through successful intrusion by foreigners into existing ruling élites, as seems to have happened occasionally in certain Oceanic islands. In addition, I will suggest that this type of enhancement was correlated in some parts of Austronesia (especially Micronesia and Polynesia) with continuous tendencies through space and time towards a development of greater structural dependence on inherited forms of leadership.

Early Austronesian Ranking: The Evidence

The most persuasive evidence for the presence of some form of institutionalized inequality in early Austronesian societies comes from comparative linguistics. For the oldest linguistic stages we have the reconstructions of Blust (1980), who offers Proto-Austronesian * *Rumaq* ("house") as a descent group and Proto-Malayo-Polynesian * *datu* (after Dempwolff) with four possible components of meaning: 1) political leader, chief; 2) priest; 3) aristocrat, noble; and 4) ancestor, grandfather, elder. This range of meaning is admittedly rather wide, and Blust suggests that the * *datu* "probably was a lineage- (or clan-) linked official" (Blust 1980:217). Some such reconstruction is supported by the existence of the term *ratu* in Javanese inscriptions before about AD 800, seemingly referring here to the head of a district polity (*watek*) (Christie 1983). The presence of *ratu* meaning "high-ranking man" as far away as Fiji is worthy of note, but it also appears that a *rato* title in west Sumba today can be earned by a wealthy man able to raise the manpower and wealth to construct a megalithic grave before his death (Hoskins 1986). So the original meaning of * *datu* still presumably floats somewhere in a hazy zone of authority, unspecified as to ascription or achievement.

The more specific claim that Proto-Oceanic (POc) (the ancestor of all Oceanic Austronesian languages except for some of western Micronesia) had terms associated with hereditary chieftainship has been developed by Pawley (1982; see also Pawley 1981; Pawley and Green 1984:132). He has reconstructed POc * *qa-lapa(s)* as "chief, senior person of a descent group", and * *qa-diki* as "first-born son of a chief" (the particle * *qa* marked a proper name or title). Only * *qa-diki* continued into Proto-Polynesian, where as * *qariki* it took on the meaning formerly ascribed to * *qa-lapa(s)*. The reflexes of * *qariki* have the meaning of hereditary chief in most modern Polynesian languages, whereas reflexes of the two original Proto-Oceanic terms have been retained in the Arosi and Bauro languages of San Cristobal in the Solomons (Pawley 1982).

The reconstructions of Pawley have more recently been examined by Lichtenberk (1986), who takes a more cautious position on the question of hereditary rank. He suggests that Pawley's Proto-Oceanic reconstructions should be modified to * ta-la(m)pat (lit. "great man") for an unspecified type of leader, and * qa-adiki for "oldest child". Lichtenberk believes that the linguistic evidence is indeterminate as regards the presence of hereditary leaders in Proto-Oceanic society. However, it is hard to avoid the conclusion from other comparative anthropological and linguistic observations that the likelihood of their presence at this time is very high (Koskinen 1960). Indeed, the term lapan, presumably a reflex of POc * ta-la(m)pat, is still used today to refer to a hereditary leader in the Admiralty Islands (Otto 1994:225).

In chronological terms these Proto-Oceanic reconstructions refer to the period around 1500 BC when the Lapita culture was undergoing its rapid expansion from the Bismarck Archipelago into Island Melanesia and ultimately, by at least 1000 BC, western Polynesia. Whether Austronesian societies had hereditary leaders before this time is a moot point, and one to which I will return.

Non-linguistic perspectives

For the earliest stages of Austronesian expansion in Island Southeast Asia the archaeological record relevant to social hierarchy is too sparse to merit consideration. However, as I have indicated above, I am willing to accept from the linguistic evidence that genealogically-based ranking, presumably of individuals within descent groups and also of the descent groups themselves within the larger confines of their societies, was present in Austronesian western Oceania by 3500 years ago.[4]

But were Austronesian societies ranked in this way long before the settlement of Oceania, or did hierarchy develop during the actual process of geographical expansion from older non-hereditary forms of leadership? How are we to interpret the evidence that non-hereditary leadership evolved in parts of western Melanesia, contrary to certain modern evolutionary beliefs, out of former hereditary chiefdoms (Pawley 1981)? And where do the Papuan-speakers, descendants of the original settlers of western Melanesia and always the dominant population in New Guinea, fit into the overall trajectory? The Papuan-speakers, after all, are excellent exponents of the view that leadership can be splendid and highly visible and yet have no hereditary component whatsoever.

These are complex and important questions. In order to answer them it is necessary to examine the question of non-hereditary leadership in western Melanesia, particularly the institution of the "big man", a type of leadership currently being intensively examined by many anthropologists in New Guinea and adjacent islands. As many have asked (Schwartz 1963; Friedman 1982:183; Hayden 1983), if big men (or their "great man" counterparts in the sense of Godelier (1986)[5]) represent the forebears of hereditary chiefs, then why have they not developed into the latter amongst the densely populated, highly competitive and often strongly inegalitarian Papuan-speaking societies of the New Guinea Highlands? This line of questioning suggests that big men and hereditary chiefs are the results of quite different evolutionary trajectories, rather than successive stages of a hypothetical trend towards fully fledged hereditary aristocracy. In addition, the important question arises of why, if ancestral Proto-Oceanic leaders were hereditary chiefs, so many western Melanesian Austronesian societies should have non-hereditary forms of leadership today.

One answer to this latter question, associated with the writings of Friedman (1981, 1982) and Pawley (1981), is that the relatively egalitarian social systems of Austronesian western Melanesia owe their existence to a kind of "devolution", a process which Friedman explains as due to an increasing density of trade networks over time giving fewer opportunities for chiefly prestige-good monopoly. His basic view, without the emphasis on trade, is paralleled by that of Liep (1991), who suggests that an original type of hierarchical society introduced by Austronesian settlers into the Massim region of western Melanesia has been deconstituted there into a series of small-scale big or great man systems. Some of these systems have continuing hereditary components in the transmission of ritual skills but they lack a distinctive chiefly stratum, except in the Trobriands where aspects of the earlier hierarchical format survive.

Neither Friedman nor Liep give reasons for this deconstitution of former hierarchy in western Melanesia, and increasing trade density is surely an epiphenomenon reflecting other more fundamental socio-economic changes. The question remains why such deconstitution should have occurred so widely in western Melanesia when it appears to be relatively uncommon on this scale elsewhere in Austronesia. The answer may lie with the prior Papuan-speaking settlers of the region.

Basically, there appears to be a major, deep-seated and probably crucial distinction between the Papuan and the Austronesian societies of Melanesia when they are taken as wholes (ignoring the occasional cases of indeterminacy due to intensive historical contact). The big or great man Papuan systems seem to lack totally any concept of genealogically-based ranking, whether of persons or descent groups, whereas those of the Austronesian-speaking groups often do retain some degree of hereditary transmission of ritual statuses and even a ranking of descent groups by genealogical criteria such as the birth-order of founders. It is my suspicion that a great deal of the deconstitution of chieftainship postulated for Melanesia may be due to the results of strong influence and even cultural take-over by Papuan-speakers of Austronesian social networks (as also suggested by Pawley 1982:46-47), but this process has generally not entirely effaced the prior traces of hereditary rank order amongst the latter.

Although my forays into the literature on the anthropology of Papuan-speaking societies have been rather restricted, I cannot help but notice everywhere the almost total lack of commitment to principles of ascribed ranking. True, some authors have claimed an incipient presence (e.g. Harrison (1987) for the Sepik River Manambu, and Golson (1982) for the Hagen area immediately prior to European contact), but in no case does the ascription seem to have developed a permanent historical existence, unlike the situation amongst many Austronesian-speaking groups in Melanesia. The general lack of concern amongst Papuan-speaking societies with descent and ascription of rank, whether of individuals or clans, and their focus on synchronic affinal and residence ties rather than the diachronic threads of birth and consanguinity, have been clearly expressed by many authors who have explicitly discussed Papuan-speaking societies rather than Melanesians in general (e.g. Brown 1978:186-187; Foley 1986). As Brown states of the Chimbu:

> Chimbu concern for the present is indicated in the patterns of social relations and the absence of genealogical recall. Ties are more common with affines than with kin, and adopted members are not distinguished from birth members of groups ... There are no ever-enduring clan and tribe ties ... Tribes are made up of local alliances, and migrating groups form new alliances (Brown 1972:7).

An even more explicit statement that incorporates some comparative historical reconstruction for New Guinea/Papuan-speaking groups is that of Rubel and Rosman (1978:320-323), although these authors never in fact refer to the linguistic backgrounds of their sample of societies. Their "prototypical structure" for a New Guinea society includes patrilineal descent with a tendency towards virilocal postmarital residence, politically autonomous residential units, formal inter-group exchange patterns involving women and ceremonial feasts, political leadership of the big man type, ritual separation of men and women, and a high significance for male initiation ceremonies. Although this reconstruction is somewhat timeless and placeless, it does hint at the kind of social landscape that might have confronted the initial Austronesian settlers of Melanesia. Taken as a whole, the archaeological and comparative anthropological evidence indicates that some Papuan-speaking societies had evolved dense population networks based on intensive agriculture (Golson 1981) or increasingly efficient forms of exchange, long before the arrival in the region of Austronesian-speakers. In doing so they maintained their ancestral forms of society that allowed the inevitable pressures for inequality to be channelled into non-heritable patterns of leadership and domination. Large and dense populations in this region, contrary to certain cultural-materialist perspectives, did not produce hereditary chiefs.

But why does the Papuan influence on Austronesian societies in western Melanesia seem to have been so pervasive? It seems quite likely that many of the Austronesian peoples of western Melanesia, in terms of genetic research (see Stoneking *et al.* (1990) and the various discussions in Hill and Serjeantson (1989)), reflect a very high degree of biological input from non-Asian, indigenous Melanesian sources. This input might have been due to continuous intermarriage or even conquest; the finer social details will probably always escape us. The overall result, however, was that some groups of essentially non-Austronesian (presumably ancestral Papuan) linguistic stock transferred their linguistic affiliations to the homogeneous and widely-understood Oceanic Austronesian languages which were being spread rapidly through Melanesia by Lapita colonization around 1500 BC (Bellwood 1989; Pawley 1981; Pawley and Green 1984). As Ross (1988, 1989) has recently noted, the western Melanesian Oceanic languages, which extend from New Guinea to as far east as the southeastern Solomons, show evidence for major interaction with Papuan languages. Furthermore, the Meso-Melanesian languages of the Bismarcks and Solomons, which reveal especially strong traces of such Papuan interaction, have apparently expanded through an area previously occupied (during Lapita times?) by speakers of Central/Eastern Oceanic languages.

From the viewpoint of the coastal Papuan-speakers of the period of Lapita expansion, what better way perhaps to gain some of the advantages of access to a widespread trade network than to learn a language (such as Proto-Oceanic or one of its immediate descendants such as Proto-Central/Eastern Oceanic) which might have been spoken, with only dialectal differentiation, by hundreds of communities spread over thousands of square kilometres of Melanesia — an ethnolinguistic situation that is almost impossible to imagine from the state of diversity in the same region today? Of course, two-way contact between many geographically-contiguous Papuan and Austronesian groups has undoubtedly characterized western Melanesian prehistory continuously during the past 3000 years. But I suspect that a very strong burst of interaction, more Papuan to Austronesian in terms of gene flow but perhaps reversed in terms of language and voyaging technology, occurred right at the start of the Austronesian colonization period.

Having presented a historical stance on the issue of non-hereditary ranking in Austronesian-speaking Melanesia, one that sees the big or great man as in part a transfer from Papuan ideology, I can now return to the issue of ascribed ranking in early Austronesian societies. Were hereditary chiefs a part of the Austronesian social landscape before Proto-Oceanic times, or did they develop purely as an effect of the process of island to island colonization? Are the nonhereditary Austronesian leaders of western Melanesia purely a product of "Papuanization", or are there other ingredients derived from the Austronesian expansion process itself?

Founder-Focused Ideology Among Austronesian-Speakers

> Tikopia estimation … rates autochthonous origin as the most worthy and immigrant origin as the lowest … In Tikopia theory, priority of origins gives status and power (Firth 1961:178).

Despite the unimportance of ascribed rank in many Austronesian societies in Island Southeast Asia and Melanesia, certain features of rank-focused ideology nevertheless stand out as being very widespread in the Austronesian world as a whole. These include a reverence for kin-group founders extending to ultimate deification in some cases, a common practice of naming kin-groups after such founders, and a ranking of status positions by descent, often primogenitural (but not always patrilineal), from them. High rank derived from genealogical closeness to an important founder would also give access to the economic rights usually associated with chiefs: stewardship over land, rights to demand labour and services from other kin-group members, and in some cases polygynous marriages. Most kin-groups obviously recognize successive and multiple founders rather than just one, but often the highest traditional rank is held by the descendants of the first founders and the lineages founded by later arrivals have lesser ritual statuses.

Political contestation, of course, has often allowed younger or intrusive lines, autochthonous or foreign, to acquire considerable authority, to the extent that many societies have dualistic chiefly structures or "stranger king" myths about leadership (Sahlins 1985; and see also Hanlon (1988) on Pohnpei). Nevertheless, despite all such ramifications of rank and aristocracy there does seem to be a common set of principles found right across Austronesia based on what I will term a "founder-focused ideology". One of these principles, which I will identify specifically as "founder rank enhancement", was, I believe, an integral part of the phenomenon of Austronesian expansion.

Founder-Focused Ideology: Some Instances

If attention is turned first to the Southeast Asian portion of the Austronesian world, it is apparent that founders and their closest descendants frequently hold central positions of rank.[6] A comparative survey of forms of ranking in traditional Austronesian societies across Indonesia has recently been presented by Slamet-Velsink, who suggests (Slamet-Velsink 1986:246) that:

> As to the tribal societies hitherto treated [mainly Nias, Batak, Ngada, East Sumba, Flores, Timor and Sa'dan Toraja], I think that they may all be called ranked, since they are all marked by differences in status at

least between older and younger branches of a "house" or clan, and between core villagers considered to be the descendants of the village founders and later arrived co-inhabitants of the same village or area ...

This kind of ranking according to founder order seems to be particularly common in the societies of Nusa Tenggara. Forth (1981), for instance, describes it for Rindi, East Sumba, where founder clans have rights of land stewardship and maintain these rights even if secular power is taken from them. Perhaps the most striking description of such a system is that by Lewis (1988:51-60) for the Tana 'Ai domain of Tana Wai Brama in eastern Flores. The founding or source clan (called Ipir Wai Brama) of this domain was founded by two brothers with their male and female followers, according to a tradition translated as "The spread of the people through the firmament for empty land". The members of this source clan have rights of precedence within the social system, and the domain leader termed "The Source of the Domain" inherits his role matrilineally (from mother's brother to sister's son) from the elder of the two brothers:

> The Source of the Domain (*tana pu'an*) is heir to the earth of Tana Wai Brama by virtue of membership in the clan that first settled his domain (*tana*) and his descent from the elder of the founding brothers of that clan. It is from the precedence of his clan, which is related in the histories, that his status in the community is derived (Lewis 1988:71).

The descendants of the younger brother hold positions of political and secular authority, thus forming a dualistic status hierarchy similar to that found in many other parts of Austronesia. In addition, the clan Ipir Wai Brama retains ritual rights to and authority over all the lands of the domain. Founders who arrived subsequently to the ancestors of the source clan were given land by it and integrated into a single ritual system under Ipir stewardship. The clans that descend from these later founders are ideally ranked in descending status, the more recent the founder the lower the rank. As Lewis (1988:81) stresses, sequence is a principle that orders much of the social and religious life of the Tana 'Ai.

Within Oceania there are also many instances to be found amongst the societies of Melanesia and Micronesia of founder-focused ideology, together with clan ranking by founder chronological order. Sudo (this volume) gives an excellent example of the traditional ranking of matrilineal clans on Satawal (Carolines) according to sequence of founder arrival, despite the fact that the original founder clan has since been demoted owing to an unfortunate choice of marriage alliance. Elsewhere in Micronesia traces of clan ranking by founder order appear to be almost universal if one collates the observations and surmises of authors such as Oliver (1989) for Micronesia generally, Lingenfelter (1975:90) for Yap, Lessa (1966:27) for Ulithi, and Alkire for the central Carolines ("the Carolinean explanation of chiefly status emphasizes seniority of settlement on the particular island" [Alkire 1977:47]).

Given the complex prehistory of Melanesia already alluded to above, it need hardly be stressed that founder-focused ideologies and ascribed ranks are obviously very discontinuous in their distributions. Among the Mekeo of coastal Papua, however (Hau'ofa 1971; Mosko 1985:112-114), chiefly titles descend primogeniturally within subclans which are ranked in terms of "prior residence, original land ownership, on the nature of other historical relationships among the subclans themselves, and often on numerical strength" (Hau'ofa 1971:166). In New Caledonia, genealogical seniority (but not necessarily political power) is held by the descendants of original settler clans (Douglas 1979:18), and the same seems to have applied originally in Manus (Otto 1994). Young's observations for the Kalauna community on Goodenough Island also seem relevant here:

> *Atuaha* [ceremonial stone structures] are built by the men, generally a group of brothers, who settle a new hamlet. They name the *atuaha* and henceforth that name may be given to the hamlet. Subsequently, as the patrilineage (*unuma*) expands, it segments and the junior portion will establish its separate identity by building a new *atuaha* … The original settlers have the status of "elder brothers" to more recent arrivals as well as to junior lines of their own descent group, and they should provide the leader of the hamlet (Young 1971:22).

A classification of the descendants of the first settlers of a neighbourhood as "elder brothers" also seems to be characteristic of other Austronesian societies in western Melanesia, as amongst the Wamira people of Milne Bay (Kahn 1990:56).

In Polynesia, the richness of tradition about founders has fuelled anthropological debate for over a century. As noted by Buck (1932:16):

> most Polynesians recognise the ancestral migrations to the islands they now occupy. The traditional history gives the names of the progenitors who came from another land and usually gives such details as the name of the canoe, the names of those who accompanied him and anything of note that was brought.[7]

There are in Polynesia, however, few clear cases of ranking between kin groups relating directly to the chronological order of their founders, and I suspect this general absence may be due to the optative and non-segmentary methods of kin group recruitment and expansion characteristic of the region. The patrilineages of Tikopia are of course an exception here, as described by Firth (1961) and illustrated in the above quotation (page 24).

In the more stratified societies of Polynesia the patterning of founder-focused ideology has frequently been made more complex by a dualistic separation between political power and the ritual status derived by descent from an original, or at least more ancient, founder (e.g. Gunson (1979) for western Polynesia, especially Tonga). Developments of this type are certainly not unique to Polynesia and occur in many of the hierarchical social systems of other Oceanic islands, such as Fiji (Sahlins 1985), Rotuma (Howard 1985) and Pohnpei (Hanlon 1988). However, despite these complications due to the usurpation of rank from original founder lines, the elements of founder-focused ideology still occur so widely in Austronesia that one may suspect them of having a high antiquity and possibly of having played a major role in the Austronesian expansion process itself. Some time and place parameters of this expansion now require to be discussed, before moving finally to the process of founder rank enhancement.

Initial Austronesian Expansion: Some Parameters

The Austronesian expansion ultimately extended well over half way round the world, mainly in tropical latitudes, from Madagascar to Easter Island. In its western regions it intruded into a far more complex pre-existing social landscape than did those pioneer navigators who settled the empty islands of Remote Oceania beyond the Solomons (Green 1991). There is a large quantity of linguistic and archaeological information that relates to early Austronesian expansion, and readers are referred to fuller sources (Bellwood 1985, 1989, 1991, 1992; Blust 1988; Ross 1989; Spriggs 1989). I list some major relevant observations.

Dated archaeological assemblages that can be related to Austronesian proto-language inventories (Blust 1976; Pawley and Green 1984; Bellwood 1985:102-129) suggest that Austronesian expansion moved from Taiwan, through the coastal Philippines, into Sulawesi and towards coastal New Guinea between about 3000 and 2000 BC. This represents a hypothetical average rate of "as the crow flies" colonization of perhaps three km per annum, or 75 km per 25-year generation. The rate after about 1500 BC within Melanesia and western Polynesia was apparently much faster; the Lapita culture achieved a distribution from the Admiralties to Samoa within about 300 years (Kirch and Hunt 1988), representing an average of about 13 km per annum, or 325 km per 25-year generation. Obviously the real rate of coastal colonization was much slower than that across sea, but these average rates still give some idea of relative speeds in different areas. The spread into Polynesia might have been equally as rapid as that of Lapita according to the navigational calculations of Irwin (1989), although central Polynesian island groups such as the Cooks and Societies have not yet produced direct archaeological evidence for settlement contemporary with Lapita.

The overall archaeological and linguistic records also suggest that the process of Austronesian expansion can be divided into three roughly-defined geographical units in terms of the pre-existing social landscapes with which Austronesian colonists had to contend. These are a) from Taiwan through the Philippines and Indonesia — pre-existing low density foragers; b) western

Melanesia, Vietnam and Peninsular Malaysia — pre-existing agriculturalists or intensive foragers with high population densities; and c) Remote Oceania and Madagascar — no attested pre-existing human populations at all. Since Melanesia is central to the issues discussed in the presence here of an apparently independent transition to agriculture, especially in the New Guinea Highlands (Golson 1981), but with presumed lowland repercussions, is worthy of emphasis. The rapidity of the Austronesian (Lapita) spread from the Bismarck Archipelago into Remote Oceania may thus be related to the presence of high density prior occupation in many parts of western Melanesia.

Early Austronesian expansion, like that of the Indo-European and Bantoid language speakers, was thus quite a rapid phenomenon when placed in perspective against overall human ethnolinguistic prehistory. In the Austronesian case the archaeological record for Island Southeast Asia and Oceanic Lapita suggests strongly that founders moved onwards to new regions after good coastal locations were occupied, before any major attempts to colonize island interiors. Population pressure alone is thus not an acceptable sole reason for early Austronesian expansion. More feasible ecological and techno-economic reasons which might have contributed to the expansion, especially in its earlier phases, include continuous population growth and fissioning due to the possession of an agricultural economic base; the inherent ability of an agricultural economy to be transported and to support colonizing founder populations; the possession of skilled canoe and navigational technology; a search for prestige goods;[8] and predilections for special environments such as swamplands for rice and taro or good fishing lagoons.[9] One purpose here, however, is to suggest that this list, while of undisputed validity, probably lacks an essential component in the sphere of ideology.

Founder Rank Enhancement and its Possible Significance

> It may also be that now and then ambitious younger sons of chiefs, discontented at not being able to attain a higher rank within the community, organized expeditions and left home in order to acquire new lands and there found their own chiefdoms (Akerblom 1968:92-93).

So far, I have reviewed some of the sources of evidence that relate, however shakily, to the prehistory of hierarchy in Austronesia. I am inclined to push back some form of hierarchy, probably hereditary, to at least Proto-Oceanic and perhaps even Proto-Malayo-Polynesian times. Proto-Austronesian, however, still seems to elude the comparativist on such matters. It is now necessary to ask if, and how, founder-focused ideologies of rank, especially through principles of founder rank enhancement, might have influenced the course of Austronesian expansion.

Reasons for individual episodes of Austronesian colonization would, of course, have been many. One thing is certain, however; inter-island colonizations over large distances must have been intentional if they were to be successful, owing to the need to carry a human population with a capacity for reproduction and viable stocks of domestic animals and plants. Current reconstructions of Oceanic canoe and navigational technologies (Gladwin 1970; Lewis 1972; Feinberg 1988; Irwin 1989, 1992) render an undue reliance on unplanned drifting rather unnecessary.

The initial movements of pre-Austronesian-speakers, along the coastlines of southern China and into Taiwan, might have been simply the result of a gradual increase of population consequent upon the development of rice cultivation in southern China between 8500 and 5000 years ago. The Austronesian language family, like those of most other major populations with long histories of agriculture (Papuan, Austroasiatic, Sino-Tibetan, Thai-Kadai (Tai Kadai or Daic), Elamo-Dravidian, Afro-Asiatic, Indo-European, Nilo-Saharan, Niger-Kordofanian) thus commenced its expansion, according to linguistic reconstructions based on patterns of diversity, in a region where agriculture developed in a primary sense from a previous foraging baseline (i.e. without diffusion from an external source). The gradient of population density between cultivators and foragers, even if only slight, would have been sufficient to commence the process, as I have discussed elsewhere (Bellwood 1991).

As the process of expansion continued, however, and as Austronesians moved towards increasing opportunities for isolation in the island worlds of Southeast Asia and Oceania, the process of founder rank enhancement would have come increasingly into play. It matters little whether Initial Austronesians had hereditary or non-hereditary systems of leadership before the expansion process began. The founder rank enhancement process itself would have been reinforced by constant repetition as colonizers moved ever onwards, and in return it would have stimulated, by direct feedback, more colonization.

What were the main advantages in being a founder? We can see that founders in many Austronesian societies were (and often still are) revered by their descendants and provided with enduring fame. Their descendants have also fared well; they occupy positions of high rank in many aspects of social life and clearly have some major advantages in the overall strategies of acquiring land and material goods. We also need to consider that most founders would know of the successes of predecessors, and the more recent the founders the more the successes behind them. In other words, the initial settlers of New Zealand about 1000 years ago would have been heirs to perhaps 3000 years of successful Austronesian expansion, much doubtless recorded in detail in their traditions.

On the material side, the first founder and his/her followers to reach a new territory or island would have had free access to all resources. They would have been able to choose the best dwelling, agricultural and fishing locations, and they would have had moral rights to claim and mark these against the encroachments of later comers (who presumably would also have been much smaller in numbers in most cases). Naturally, any founder would wish his/her descendants to maintain such rights and privileges, and one obvious way to ensure this, especially in a period of rapid follow-up founder competition (such as might have occurred frequently during the process of Lapita expansion), would be to promote an ideology whereby the offices that gave the needed control over resources should be transmitted within a family or lineage, rather than simply laid open to free contestation in big man style. Enter, no doubt gradually and not without some resistance, the ideology of primogenitural inheritance?[10]

From a more diachronic viewpoint it is not difficult to see how continuous founder events, stacked one upon the other into the depths of Austronesian memory and enshrined in ritual chants, would reinforce the worldly status of founders and their direct descendants. They would also reinforce their access to the best of those material resources (including prestige goods) which theory dictates they should have monopolized in order to enhance or aggrandize their statuses. In short, founders had a head start whenever they discovered a new territory, and their descendants knew how to keep the head start within the family, at least until other forces out of their control (fluctuations in population numbers or successful invasion, for instance) overwhelmed them.

Some care, however, is needed with the founder rank enhancement principle as offered so far. In the discussion I have been careful to stress the concept of *new* territory, rather than simple fission within an already-settled area. Most founder movements would have been highly local events, like those described in the quotation from Michael Young for Goodenough Island given above at p.26. In these local circumstances founders might have found it hard to enhance rank, especially if they belonged, as many surely did, to junior lines in the parent community. The aim for a really ambitious young man of a junior line might perhaps have been to remove himself and his followers as far as possible from his home settlement in order to convert himself and his descendants into a *senior* line without interference. What better way to do this than to find another island, or at the very least a piece of good land far removed from home? *Spatial* separation thus becomes a factor of importance in the equation.[11]

It is when the concept of moving to another island comes in that another variable enters the equation — the sea-going canoe capable of carrying viable populations of humans, plants and animals. As Hayden (1983) has stressed, the construction and manning of a large canoe needs manpower, and this may mean that founders who successfully undertook long voyages, such as many of those necessary to colonize Oceania, would already have belonged to a stratum of the homeland society which might well have had élite privileges. In other words, the need to build and man a canoe would have selected for founders those of relatively high rank, and it is rather irrelevant here if that rank in early stages was ascribed or achieved. A strong chain of authority on a voyaging canoe could have meant the difference between success and failure, as anyone will realise after reading Finney's entertaining account (Finney 1979) of the experimental Hokule's voyage from the Hawaiian Islands to Tahiti in 1976.

If we imagine the founder process occurring into relative or complete isolation time and time again over a period of four millennia, with each major ocean crossing selecting for a leader with at least a better than average access to wealth and manpower and giving that leader a pristine new laboratory in which to enhance his own rank and that of his descendants, then it may not be hard to understand why so many anthropologists have commented on the general west to east gradient in the occurrence of ascribed ranking in Oceania. The big and great men in western Melanesian Austronesian societies may reflect some degree of Papuan assimilation, and if Austronesians had not undergone this experience we might expect ascribed rank to have been more common in this region. But this may not be the only reason for the gradient; the ancestors of the Polynesians and Micronesians, after all, presumably went through more founder enhancing events than anyone else.

In addition, it is worth reflecting that there might also have been a similar gradient, now masked by Indic and Islamic influences, from Taiwan, the Philippines, Borneo, and Sulawesi down into the Malay world, the Sunda islands of Java and Bali, and Nusa Tenggara. This was also an axis of Austronesian colonization, and my overall reading of the literature suggests to me that traditional societies tended to rely more on ascribed ranking in the south (e.g. Java, Bali and Nusa Tenggara) than in many parts of the Philippines and Borneo, where many societies have probably retained stable forms of non-hereditary leadership since initial Austronesian colonization occurred. Clearly, one would not wish to explain the differences between Maori and Hawaiian society, or between the Kayan, the Iban and the Balinese, purely on the basis of the number of decisive founder events in their respective histories. Factors of ecology, production, circumscription (Kirch 1988a) and even perhaps free-thinking ideology surely had roles to play as well, as in all societies, not to mention the influences of India and Islam. But there is something attractive about the concept of a founder event that leads to a complete separation between a homeland and a daughter settlement. After all, this is precisely how many biologists would explain the process of speciation in living organisms. Perhaps small human founder groups in isolation can produce massive cultural changes, just as, if given far longer spans of time, their animal cousins can create species.

Some Afterthoughts

The processes of founder rank enhancement did not only operate when founders settled empty lands or islands. Indeed, the importance of secondary invaders from without has bulked large in recent writings on Pacific anthropology. In many islands an original founder-focused ideology of rank was clearly replaced by an invader-focused one (Howard 1985; Sahlins 1985; Hanlon 1988), although as Sahlins himself points out these stranger king myths probably reflect "indigenous schemes of cosmological proportions" (Sahlins 1985:76) rather than any necessary historical process of conquest by true foreigners. Nevertheless, in the few instances where conquest by true foreigners does appear to have occurred (and the examples discussed by Sahlins and Howard may not be within this category), these foreigners clearly managed to aggrandize their rank rather spectacularly in the process of separation from their homeland community.

Two examples of this would appear to be recorded archaeologically. The most striking must surely be the huge Nan Madol élite dwelling and sacred complex on Pohnpei, established by the immigrant Saudeleur dynasty after its two founders arrived from an island to the west between AD 1000 and 1200 (Hanlon 1988:9; Morgan 1988). In mortuary terms, however, the accolade surely goes to Roy Mata, whose rather gruesome burial complex (c.AD 1250) was committed to the afterlife on a small island off the western coast of Efate in central Vanuatu. As recounted by the excavator (Garanger 1972), Efate traditions record Roy Mata and his followers as emigrants into the region, possibly from the south, although the direction is uncertain. I have summarized the main elements of the burial complex as follows (Bellwood 1978:270):

> The body of a man, who can hardly be any other than Roy Mata himself, was found extended on its back in a pit which also contained, to his left, a man and woman side by side, to his right a single male, and across the feet of these four parallel bodies, a young girl … The pit was marked on the ground surface by two large slabs of stone … Around it were slightly shallower burials of 35 individuals, of which 22 comprised men and women buried together in pairs … In Garanger's words, the women "seemed always to be seeking the protection of their companion, clasping him by the neck, waist or arm, with their legs frequently interwoven with those of the man, and their fingers and toes clenched" … it seems that the men may have been stupefied with kava before burial, while the women were in many cases buried alive and conscious.

Not only was Roy Mata both a founder and an invader according to tradition, but his burial extravaganza, worthy of a Sumerian or Shang Chinese king, is totally without precedent in the anthropological and archaeological records of Oceania. We may never know just why he was considered worthy of human sacrifice on such a scale, but there is little doubt that Roy Mata owed much of his "success" (if we can call it that) to foundership, a success which might have been denied to him were he just another locally-born man of charisma.

References

Akerblom, K.

1968   *Astronomy and navigation in Polynesia and Micronesia*. Stockholm: Ethnographical Museum.

Alkire, W.H.

1977   *An introduction to the peoples and cultures of Micronesia*. Menlo Park: Cummings.

Bellwood, P.

1978   *Man's conquest of the Pacific*. Auckland: Collins.

1985   *Prehistory of the Indo-Malaysian Archipelago*. Sydney: Academic Press.

1989   The colonization of the Pacific: some current hypotheses. In A.V.S. Hill and S.W. Serjeantson (eds) *The colonization of the Pacific: a genetic trail*, pp.1-59. Oxford: Oxford University Press.

1991   The Austronesian dispersal and the origins of languages. *Scientific American* 265(1):70-75.

1992   Southeast Asia before history. In N. Tarling (ed.) *The Cambridge history of Southeast Asia*, pp.55-136. Cambridge: Cambridge University Press.

Bellwood, P. and P. Koon

1989   Lapita colonists leave boats unburned! *Antiquity* 63:613-622.

Blust, R.A.

1976   Austronesian culture history: some linguistic inferences and their relations to the archaeological record. *World Archaeology* 8:19-43.

1980   Early Austronesian social organisation: the evidence of language. *Current Anthropology* 21:205-247.

1988   The Austronesian homeland: a linguistic perspective. *Asian Perspectives* 26:45-67.

Brown, P.

1972   *The Chimbu*. Cambridge, MA: Schenkman.

1978   *Highland peoples of New Guinea*. Cambridge: Cambridge University Press.

Buck, P.

1932   *Ethnology of Tongareva*. Honolulu: Bishop Museum Bulletin 92.

Christie, J.W.

1983   Raja and Rama: the classical state in early Java. In L. Gesick (ed.) *Centers, symbols and hierarchies: essays on the classical states of Southeast Asia*, pp.9-44. New Haven, CT: Yale University Press.

Douglas, B.

1979   Rank, power, authority: a reassessment of traditional leadership in South Pacific societies. *Journal of Pacific History* 14:2-27.

Dove, M.R.

1985   *Swidden agriculture in Indonesia*. Berlin: Mouton.

Feinberg, R.

1988   *Polynesian seafaring and navigation*. Kent, OH: Kent State University Press.

Finney, B.

1979   *Hokule'a*. New York: Dodd, Mead.

Firth, R.

1961   *History and traditions of Tikopia*. Wellington: The Polynesian Society.

Foley, R.

1986   *The Papuan languages of New Guinea*. Cambridge: Cambridge University Press.

Forth, G.R.

1981   *Rindi*. The Hague: Nijhoff.

Freeman, D.

1981   *Some reflections on the nature of Iban society*. Canberra: Department of Anthropology, Research School of Pacific Studies, The Australian National University.

Friedman, J.

1981   Notes on structure and history in Oceania. *Folk* 23:275-295.

1982   Catastrophe and continuity in social evolution. In C. Renfrew, M.J. Rowlands and B.A. Segraves (eds) *Theory and explanation in archaeology*, pp.175-196. New York: Academic Press.

Garanger, J.

1972   *Archéologie des Nouvelles Hébrides: contribution a la connaissance des iles du Centre*. Paris: ORSTOM [Centre Nationale de la Recherche Scientifique et Technique Outre-Mer].

Gladwin, T.

1970   *East is a big bird: navigation and logic on Puluwat Atoll*. Cambridge, MA: Harvard University Press.

Godelier, M.

1986   *The making of great men: male power and domination among New Guinea Baruya*. [Originally *Production des grands hommes*.] Cambridge: Cambridge University Press.

Golson, J.

1981   New Guinea agricultural history: a case study. In D. Denoon and C. Snowden (eds) *A time to plant and a time to uproot*, pp.55-64. Port Moresby: Institute of Papua New Guinea Studies.

1982 The Ipomoean revolution revisited; society and sweet potato in the upper Wahgi valley. In A. Strathern (ed.) *Inequality in New Guinea Highland societies*, pp.109-136. Cambridge: Cambridge University Press.

Green, R.C.

1991 Near and remote Oceania: disestablishing "Melanesia" in culture history. In A.K. Pawley (ed.) *Man and a half: essays in Pacific anthropology and ethnobiology in honour of Ralph Bulmer*, pp.491-502. Auckland: The Polynesian Society.

Gunson, N.

1979   The *hau* concept of leadership in Western Polynesia. *Journal of Pacific History* 14:28-49.

Hanlon, D.

1988   *Upon a stone altar*. Honolulu: University of Hawaii Press.

Harrison, S.

1987   Cultural efflorescence and political evolution on the Sepik River. *American Ethnologist* 14:491-507.

Hau'ofa, E.

1971   Mekeo chieftainship. *Journal of the Polynesian Society* 80:152-169.

Hayden, B.

1983   Social characteristics of early Austronesian colonisers. *Bulletin of the Indo-Pacific Prehistory Association* 4:123-134.

Hill, A.V.S. and S.W. Serjeantson (eds)

1989   *The colonization of the Pacific: a genetic trail*. Oxford: Oxford University Press.

Hoskins, J.A.

1986   So my name shall live. *Bijdragen tot de Taal-, Land- en Volkenkunde* 142:31-51.

Howard, A.

1985   History, myth and Polynesian chieftainship: the case of Rotuman kings. In A. Hooper and J. Huntsman (eds) *Transformations of Polynesian culture*, pp.39-78. Auckland: The Polynesian Society.

Irwin, G.J.

1989   Against, across and down the wind. *Journal of the Polynesian Society* 98:167-206.

1992   *The prehistoric exploration and colonization of the Pacific.* Cambridge: Cambridge University Press.

Kahn, M.

1990   Stone-faced ancestors. *Ethnology* 29:51-66.

King, V.T.

1975-76   Migration, warfare and culture contact in Borneo: a critique of ecological analysis. *Oceania* 46:306-327.

1978   Introduction. In V.T. King (ed.) *Essays on Borneo societies*, pp.1-36. Oxford: Oxford University Press.

Kirch, P.V.

1988a   Circumscription theory and sociopolitical evolution in Polynesia. *American Behavioral Scientist* 31:416-427.

1988b   Long-distance exchange and island colonization: the Lapita case. *Norwegian Archaeological Review* 21:103-117.

Kirch, P.V. and T.L. Hunt (eds)

1988   *Archaeology of the Lapita cultural complex: a critical review.* Seattle: Burke Museum.

Koskinen, A.A.

1960   *Ariki the first-born.* Helsinki: FF Communications 181.

1963   *Linking of symbols: Polynesian patterns 1.* Helsinki: Finnish Society for Missionary Research.

Lederman, R.

1990   Big men, large and small? *Ethnology* 29:3-16.

Lepowski, M.

1990   Big men, big women and cultural autonomy. *Ethnology* 29:35-50.

Lessa, W.A.

1966   *Ulithi: a Micronesian design for living*. New York: Holt, Rinehart and Winston.

Lewis, D.

1972   *We, the navigators*. Canberra: The Australian National University Press.

Lewis, E.D.

1988   *People of the source*. Dordrecht: Foris.

Lichtenberk, F.

1986   Leadership in Proto-Oceanic society: linguistic evidence. *Journal of the Polynesian Society* 95:341-356.

Liep, J.

1991   Great man, big man, chief: a triangulation of the Massim. In M. Godelier and M. Strathern (eds) *Big men and great men: personifications of power in Melanesia*, pp.28-47. Cambridge: Cambridge University Press.

Lilley, I.

1986   Chiefs without chiefdoms. *Archaeology in Oceania* 20:60-65.

Lingenfelter, S.G.

1975   *Yap: political leadership and culture change in an island society*. Honolulu: University of Hawaii Press.

McKinley, R.

1978   Pioneer expansion, assimilation and the foundations of ethnic unity among the Iban. *Sarawak Museum Journal* 47:15-27.

Morgan, W.N.

1988   *Prehistoric architecture in Micronesia*. Austin: University of Texas Press.

Mosko, M.

1985   *Quadripartite structures*. Cambridge: Cambridge University Press.

O'Connor, R.A.

1983   *A theory of indigenous Southeast Asian urbanism*. Singapore: Institute of Southeast Asian Studies.

Oliver, D.

1989   *Oceania*. 2 vols. Honolulu: University of Hawaii Press.

Otto, Ton

1994   Feasting and fighting: rank and power in pre-colonial Baluan. In M. Jolly and M. Mosko (eds) *Transformations of hierarchy: structure, history and horizon in the Austronesian world. Special Issue of History of Anthro-*

pology 7(1-4):223-239. Chur and Reading: Harwood Academic Publishers.

Pawley, A.K.

1981 Melanesian diversity and Polynesian homogeneity: a unified explanation for language. In K. Hollyman and A.K. Pawley (eds) *Studies in Pacific languages and cultures*, pp.269-309. Auckland: Linguistic Society of New Zealand.

1982 Rubbish-man commoner, big-man chief? In J. Siikala (ed.) *Oceanic studies: essays in honour of Aarne A. Koskinen*, pp.33-52. Helsinki: Finnish Anthropological Society.

Pawley, A.K. and R. Green

1984 The Proto-Oceanic language community. *Journal of Pacific History* 19:123-146.

Ross, M.

1988 *Proto Oceanic and the Austronesian languages of western Melanesia*. Pacific Linguistics Series C No. 98. Canberra: Department of Linguistics, Research School of Pacific Studies, The Australian National University.

1989 Early Oceanic linguistic prehistory. *Journal of Pacific History* 24:135-149.

Rubel, P.G. and A. Rosman

1978 *Your own pigs you may not eat*. Canberra: The Australian National University Press.

Sahlins, M.D.

1985 The stranger king, or Dumézil among the Fijians. In M. Sahlins (ed.) *Islands of history*, pp.73-103. Chicago: University of Chicago Press.

Schwartz, T.

1963 Systems of areal integration. *Anthropological Forum* 1:56-97.

Slamet-Velsink, I.

1986 *Emerging hierarchies*. Leiden: University of Leiden.

Specht, J., R. Fullagar, R. Torrence and N. Baker

1988 Prehistoric obsidian exchange in Melanesia: a perspective from the Talasea sources. *Australian Archaeology* 27:3-16.

Spriggs, M.

1989 The dating of the Island Southeast Asian Neolithic. *Antiquity* 63:587-613.

Spriggs, M. and S. Wickler

1989   Archaeological research on Erromango. *Bulletin of the Indo-Pacific Prehistory Association* 9:68-91.

Stoneking, M., L.B. Jorde, K. Bhatia and A.C. Wilson

1990   Geographic variation in human mitochondrial DNA from Papua New Guinea. *Genetics* 124:717-733.

Thomas, N.

1989   The force of ethnology. *Current Anthropology* 30:27-42.

Thomas, S.D.

1987   *The last navigator*. London: Hutchinson.

Wheatley, P.

1983   *Nagara and commandery: origins of the Southeast Asian urban traditions.* Chicago: University of Chicago, Department of Geography Research Paper 207-208.

Wolters, O.W.

1982   *History, culture, and region in Southeast Asian perspectives.* Singapore: Institute of Southeast Asian Studies.

Young, M.W.

1971   *Fighting with food.* Cambridge: Cambridge University Press.

Notes

[1] This was a difficult paper for a prehistorian to write, but as a migrant myself I have some personal experience of what I hope has been founder rank enhancement. I would like to thank James Fox, Roger Keesing, John Liep, Andrew Pawley, Clifford Sather and Matthew Spriggs for commenting on the manuscript in draft form. They have all given me useful information and references that I might otherwise have missed.

[2] I exclude Madagascar from consideration in this paper, although hopefully some of my conclusions could still apply to the settlement of this island.

[3] Much of the archaeological literature on prehistoric Austronesian ranking is not discussed in detail in this article since it relates to late or terminal prehistory rather than to the early phases of Austronesian expansion with which I am primarily concerned.

[4] This is not to deny the importance of individual achievement in the quest for leadership, as in all human societies. This paper is concerned with general trends rather than specific historical situations.

[5] In this section I do not wish to discuss further the distinction between so-called "great man" and "big man" types of leadership, a distinction dealt with in great detail recently by many anthropologists working in Melanesia and one which seems to operate within both Austronesian- and Papuan-speaking societies (Lederman 1990; Lepowski 1990).

[6] The wide occurrence of patterns of ascribed rank in Island Southeast Asia tends to negate the claims of historians such as O'Connor (1983) and Wolters (1982) that pre-Indic leadership in those regions later Indianized was of a rather unspecified big man type. Wheatley (1983), with his pre-Indic "chiefdoms" subsequently promoted to state-like polities by the identification of their leaders with Siva, is perhaps closer to the mark.

[7] Another aspect of a concern with canoe-borne founders might also have been the common practice of symbolizing kin-groups as canoes, as in New Zealand, Tahiti or the Cook Islands (Koskinen 1963:31),

or, more distantly, in southern Vanuatu (Spriggs and Wickler 1989) and central Micronesia (Thomas 1987:59 for Satawal).

[8] Hayden (1983), following Friedman (1981, 1982) has suggested that a demand for prestige goods by a Lapita élite led to a dispersal of traders looking for new sources of supply. Hayden's view has been supported by Kirch (1988b), who has specified the Lapita prestige good system in terms of actual artefact types in shell, stone and pottery. However, while I am willing to agree that a search for new supplies of exotic raw materials might have contributed something to the rapidity of the Lapita dispersal within Melanesia and western Polynesia, materials such as shells or potting clays are common in many environments and their supply seems rather an unconvincing cause for fully-stocked voyages of exploration into the unknown. Although obsidian has very localized geographical sources, the finding of 188 chips of this material, some from a New Britain source 3000 kilometres to the east, in a midden of discarded shells, fish bones, stone tools and other debitage at the Bukit Tengkorak site in Sabah (Bellwood and Koon 1989) suggests that it was hardly an item of great prestige (as opposed to utilitarian) value (Specht *et al.* [1988] also doubt its function as a prestige good in New Britain). A desire for exotic valuables alone thus seems unlikely to have fuelled the whole process of Austronesian expansion, even though the early archaeological record of virtually all Oceanic communities, including eastern Polynesians, contains elaborate artefacts of shell, whale teeth, bone and stone which might have functioned to reinforce the visible status of hereditary chiefs.

[9] The phenomenon of recent Iban expansion, evidently mainly for reasons of prestige and headhunting rather than a need for new agricultural land (King 1975-76; McKinley 1978), may at first sight seem relevant as a parallel for early Austronesian expansion. However, two factors make this unlikely; first the free availability amongst the Iban of iron tools, and second the lack of evidence for any such rapid agricultural spread in prehistoric times into an area of truly equatorial and perhumid rainforest. Early Austronesian colonists were almost certainly coastal and inter-island in orientation and were, of course, only supplied with stone tools.

[10] Some may ask why the process of founder rank enhancement as here described does not appear to have influenced the Papuan-speaking peoples if, as I suggest, they took over parts of an Austronesian social network from about 3500 years ago. As the primary inhabitants of some very large landmasses (including New Guinea) perhaps they did not need to make any major or sustained long distance moves. In addition, with certain marked exceptions (such as the Mailu), the Papuan-speaking peoples seem not to have adopted many maritime skills.

[11] The anthropologically-renowned expansions of the egalitarian Iban of Sarawak (Freeman 1981) have clearly not led to any obvious development of ranking within Iban society, and indeed the most recent migrants seem to be the most egalitarian, as King has pointed out (1978:32). Perhaps this situation reflects continuous contact with homeland communities, thus offering few opportunities to those who might have wished to place their privileges as founders of a new community on a hereditary footing. However, amongst the nearby Kantu of Kalimantan it appears that founders are able to accumulate considerable wealth and prestige (Dove 1985:13).

Chapter 3. The Elder and the Younger — Foreign and Autochthonous Origin and Hierarchy in the Cook Islands

Jukka Siikala

In Principle, Everything is so Simple

For quite some time the Polynesian hierarchical systems seemed to be so simple. They were formed through chiefly lineages, in which a system of primogeniture reigned. Those, who were genealogically closest to the gods were also socially superior, and this divinely derived superiority was inherited from first born to first born (Koskinen 1960; Sahlins 1958). This normative notion of early anthropological literature has found its way to the islands through the literary interpretations of western anthropologists to such a degree that it has been constantly recollected in the field. But the origin of this kind of account cannot be found in anthropological interpretations only. In the Cook Islands one of the most important literary sources for the people of their own culture is "The Genealogy of the Kings of Rarotonga and Mangaia", published by W.W. Gill in 1890. It is a compilation which attempts to link together all the fragments of genealogical information Gill was able to collect during his long stay as a missionary in the islands. It can be regarded as one of the prototype interpretations of its kind, quickly followed by a number of genealogical accounts of the history of the archipelago.

The interest behind these accounts was historical. They represented an attempt to reconstruct the past movements of people and "tribes" from one island to another. The use of genealogies for this kind of purpose was based on the presupposition of a normative patrilineal succession. It was this succession which was the basis of the linkages between different genealogical fragments and thus in fact complete historical reconstruction. Interestingly enough, the Europeans first systematically interested in genealogies were colonial officials occupied in the first great task of their administration: the organization of land rights. The normative legitimating power of the genealogies increased with this help from outsiders, which explains the later interest of the islanders in their "complete" genealogies.

Of course in Bourdieuan outward oriented discussion emphasizing the normative aspect of culture, it is easiest to explain the intricacies of a social system in simplified, normative terms (Bourdieu 1977:18). This simplification, however, decreased the number of the legitimating and hierarchy-establishing qualities in a significant way. Relative age and genealogical proximity are of course, legalistic arguments, but culturally genealogies contain much more, and the legitimation of a hierarchy is dependent on a much wider scale of qualities.

Although in principle a simple distinction, the elder/younger — the basis of seniority — opposition has been the subject of refined analysis. The discussion about the relationship between the elder and the younger has culminated in the opposition between prescription and performance, "historylessness" and historical character of the society. This is especially emphasized by Valerio Valeri (1990). In his comparison of Hawaiian and Tongan societies he found in Tonga "a refusal to tolerate (or perhaps acknowledge) hierarchical ambiguities in the elder/younger relationship" (Valeri 1990). According to his interpretation this is in total contrast to the Hawaiian situation, where history enters the chiefly rivalry in a more direct way. There the younger person can take possession of a chiefly position without being transformed into a senior person, which is what happened in the mythical case of 'Aho'eitu in Tonga. After the heavenly inversion, the younger brothers of Hau do not, according to Valeri, even dream of taking the position of Tu'i Tonga. The stable Tongan normative system thus negates history, and reproduces the mythical transcendent situation again and again. To this he sees the Hawaiian system standing in complete contrast. There the younger brother can be a chief as *younger* and does not need to be transformed into a senior brother.

The Hawaiian chiefly system is immanent, not transcendent; unstable, not stable and, accordingly, the systems of legitimation in these societies must correspondingly stand in opposition to each other. In Tonga it is the genealogy; in Hawaii the historical performance of the king which forms the basis of the legitimation of his position. Tonga thus seems to correspond to the ideal-typical image of early anthropology.

Aletta Biersack has complicated this situation with her emphasis on the Tongan distinction between "blood" and "garland". The garland is the title, which, according to her interpretation, can be acquired as well as inherited. In the famous case of Tupou I the ability of the Tongan Hau to dream and even take the position of Tu'i Tonga was well manifested (Biersack 1990). Valeri's notion about the historyless Tongans and the historical Hawaiians is thus a normative image based on the prevailing mode of political ideology in the islands. This structural difference is of course an important one, but structures apart, both societies seem to be historical, and have been able to produce new political constellations even against the rules or ideological norms. The stereotypic reproduction is not the predominant mode of historical reproduction even in Tonga.

In all their complexity the Polynesian hierarchical systems cannot be fully comprehended by uncomplicated models. The number of possible opposing factors acting as hierarchy-generating operators has been and still is very large. The more complex versions of the normative system promoted and made famous by, for example, Marshall Sahlins (1981) add to the principal distinctions of human/divine, younger/elder the third pair: foreign/autochthonous. According to Sahlins, the power is from abroad; it is foreign to the people and the society, and thus transcends the limits of ordinary human beings. The foreignness of the power, however, requires the creation of a bond between the power and the people, and thus marriage and gender distinctions begin to play an important role. It is possible to go still further, and look for differences in foreign power and different kinds of relations between this foreigner and the people of the land. Highly stratified and politically relatively unified Hawaii and Tonga, with the focus of their political life in the relationship between chiefs and the people, blur the distinctions between, for example, the different islands and the systematic qualitative differences which the people themselves attribute to these. With this in mind, I will in the following look into the hierarchical relationships in the southern Cook Islands and the interplay of genealogical and other cultural operators.

Ngaputoru

Origin

The three islands of 'Atiu, Ma'uke and Mitiaro form one of the local polities which can be regarded as having had some degree of internal political coherence in the form of overarching chiefly authority at the beginning of colonial contacts (Siikala 1990). This unity of the Ngaputoru group is emphasized also in the historical narrative accounts — mythical in nature — about the origin of both the islands and their populations. These origin narratives establish a connection between divine and human worlds, but at the same time they also reveal the same transcendent reversal of the younger/elder relationship as the myth of 'Aho'eitu. The origin narratives of both 'Atiu and Ma'uke tell about the migration of the original founding chiefs from Avaiki. Typical to these heroic figures on both islands is that they were renegades, younger brothers who had to leave their original home island because of a lack of land or because of a defeat in a fight. Their travel from the transcendent Avaiki, however, transforms them into chiefs who are able to establish their own reigns on the new islands they now occupy.

In the case of 'Atiu, historically the dominant of the islands, the origin of the population is claimed to descend from *Tura*. The historical narrative about Tura gives a clear picture of his genealogical position:

> Ina-tokoai-kura lived with her husband, who was Tangaroa. He was called Tangaroa because he was a god and he was said to be a bird. This is why our island is called Enuamanu. Some say differently, but this is

mine. Ina-tokoai-kura lived with her husband Tangaroa, and they had their children, whose names were 'Atiu Mua, whom some people say is Mariri, the first was 'Atiu Mua, the second was 'Atiu Nui and the third was 'Atiu Iti. 'Atiu Mua had two children, Papa and Tuariki. 'Atiu Nui had a son, Mariri, this was 'Atiu Nui's second child. 'Atiu Iti, Ina-tokoai-kura's third child by Tangaroa, had Tura Ariki.

The genealogy of Tura looks as follows:

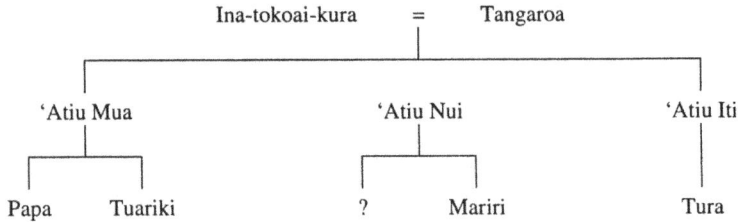

```
                  Ina-tokoai-kura    =    Tangaroa
          ┌──────────────────────────────┼──────────────────────────┐
          │                               │                          │
      'Atiu Mua                       'Atiu Nui                   'Atiu Iti
        │                              │                             │
    ┌───┴───┐                     ┌────┴────┐                        │
    │       │                     │         │                        │
  Papa   Tuariki                  ?       Mariri                    Tura
```

'Atiu Iti thus seems to be the youngest of the three sons of the shade of a woman, Ina-tokoai-kura and Tangaroa, who was said to be a god and a bird. And from this youngest grandchild the population descends. The other two, 'Atiu Mua and 'Atiu Nui (also known as 'Atiu Muri) gave birth to other significant descendants, among whom Tura also stands in a *teina-tuakana*-relationship. 'Atiu Mua is said to have given birth to Papa, who is the earth. 'Atiu Nui's descendant is in turn Mariri, to whom the bird-motif is also attached. He is known by the name Mariri-tutu-a-manu, Mariri-the-image-of-a-bird.

There seems so to be a system prevailing in this account. The human beings are the younger brothers, and the elder ones remind us more of gods; they are connected through their superior abilities, for example, to fly like Tangaroa. It is the youngest of the whole genealogical structure, Tura, who has to leave the supernatural homeland and go to look for an island for himself. The arrival of the canoe of Tura at 'Atiu from Avaiki marks the beginning of the population there.

The origin of the Ma'uke population is similarly narrated in a migration myth, according to which Avaiki was filled with blood, and the tribes there were at war with each other. The son of Tangaroa had to leave the island and travel to look for another island to live on. The origin of the Ma'uke population is thus also divine, but however from the side of the loser in war. The people originate from those who are not able to secure a place for themselves in Avaiki, which is thus left to the gods alone.

In both cases the origin is not through the paramount lines, but through the younger and losing ones. The transcendent character of the origin leaves the elder lines in Avaiki and gives them more of the attributes of the gods, while it transforms the younger ones into chiefly human beings through their travels. In this respect the Ngaputoru situation is structurally homologous to the Tongan

'Aho'eitu case. The overall situation leads, however, to different conclusions. The third island of the group, Mitiaro, has to thank both for its soil and for its population of the other two islands. The soil was transferred by gods and spirits from 'Atiu and Ma'uke to Mitiaro to make it inhabitable, and in a similar way the descendants of 'Atiu and Ma'uke populated the island. Mitiaro thus falls totally in a youngest-descendant category in the polity of Ngaputoru. The parents of this descendant are 'Atiu and Ma'uke, which have gender values attached to them. 'Atiu is the male, and thus father; and Ma'uke is the female and mother. Hierarchically significant distinctions in this island polity are accordingly the positional distinctions between the members of a nuclear family which are used as a metaphor for the whole political system. The elder/younger opposition plays a role in the origin narratives as a marker between gods and humans, the markers of the political hierarchy are the gender values and parent/child relationships. If we look at the origin narratives from the point of view of their politically significant end-result, this is the whole significance of these. Through their mutual relationships the islands acquire their qualities, and these qualities in turn determine each island's hierarchical position.

Genealogy or Genealogies: Path and Birth

Path

The origin narratives which at the same time tell both about the migration of the original ancestors from the mythical homeland to the present day islands and give their genealogies, create the qualitatively separate island populations. The role of the resulting genealogical accounts consequently is not only to provide a genealogical link to the ancestor, or even to his divine forefathers, but to convey the qualities connected to the ancestor in question. This in turn can ensue in several ways, and accordingly there has to be several kinds of genealogies.

The genealogical representation of the present day population on the islands is a complex one. We do not have a simple distinction between historical narratives and uniform genealogical accounts, and even the genealogies are of varied kinds. My argument is that we have to make a clear distinction between genealogical information on the basis by which we as anthropologists are able to construct extremely encompassing genealogies and different genres of genealogies as they are used and recited on the islands. The politically significant ones are these genres, and not the possible sum of information in our notebooks. To draw conclusions based on comprehensive reconstructions in the way of the early anthropologists and colonial administrators is, of course, a legitimate pursuit. What is not tenable, however, is to claim that these kinds of conclusions are based on local genealogical representations of the society. For this purpose one has to look for the genealogies as they are really used.

Visually and logically, the simplest kind of genealogy is a straight list. It begins with the name of one of the founding ancestors, lists all the intermediating ancestors, and ends with the individual whose ascent is being represented. The term used for such a genealogy is *ara*, the road or the path. To give an example from a Ma'ukean familybook, one *ara* reads:

Te ara is Koumu (The road of Koumu)

Tekeunui

Tekeumaina

Upokonui

Teenui

Tekatake

Atiuru Upoko

Utatakienua

Oe

Utaavarau

Tangaavarau

Koumu

Koumu's road to an ancestor called Tekeunui is thus represented with the help of a list of names which is claimed to be a genealogy. Te Rangi Hiroa describes this kind of genealogy in Tongareva: "a particular line of descent from a specified ancestor is called *ara* (a path) ... A person who is descended from more than one member of that family has more than one path (*ara*) to [a specified ancestor] and in a recital runs them down in order of seniority" (Buck 1932). In the Cook Islands, especially in the minute books of the land court, numerous examples are to be found in which an individual's "path" to a common ancestor is given through a number of different "paths". This is especially important in the case of candidates for a chiefly title. A combination of several paths can be claimed to provide a candidate with a stronger case, and the production of these combinations naturally requires more comprehensive genealogical knowledge, too. Rongomatane Ngakaara presented five versions of his genealogy as "different paths" in an argument over his chiefly position to the Land and Titles Court in 1903 and all of them were recorded as "genealogies of Rongomatane through different lines of ancestry".

The interesting point in these chiefly paths is the way in which they combine the ascent to different original ancestors. So we have a picture in which the three chiefs of the islands construct their paths to the two ancestors of their own island.

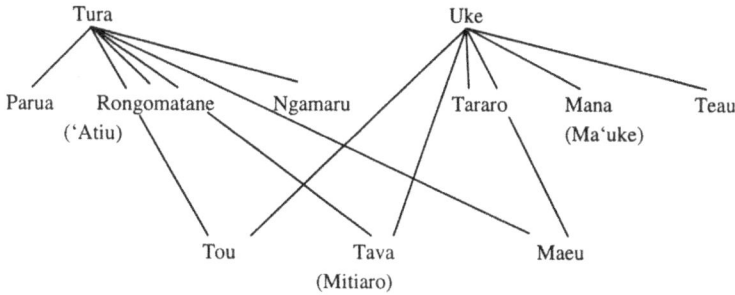

The paths give a clear image of the independent origin of 'Atiu and Ma'uke. Only Mitiaro seems to be dependent. The paths lead, however, also to the ancestors of the neighbouring islands. These paths can be used as supporting evidence for a chiefly candidate's claims. Alone, the connections to "wrong" ancestors are not sufficient; on the contrary, vague links to the ancestor of one's own island and strong links to the ancestor of the neighbouring island can be used as counter argument. In the case of 'Atiu and Ma'uke the autochthonous origin of chiefly titles is a rule. As Tura is the hierarchical descendant of the 'Atiu chiefs, so Uke is his Ma'uke counterpart and they are the end points of the paths of the genealogies of their islands.

The *ara* form of genealogy seems to correspond closely to the western concept of descent. The focus of the paths is not, however, unilineal descent, but ascent, and the path can, in fact, not be directly translated into inheritance rights, although this legalistic reinterpretation of paths of ascent as lines of descent is now the norm, according to which the people in the Cook Islands have adapted their own interpretation of their genealogical data. The connotations of *ara* have begun to deviate even from the Tikopian ones described by Raymond Firth. During the ritual of the sacred canoes in generally patrilineal Tikopia, *ara* is a term used to refer to the relationship between mother's father and daughter's son, between Kafika and Taumako clans (Firth 1967:135, see also Hooper 1981:19). In eastern Polynesian languages *ara* alludes to progeny and birth in general, without any patrilineal connotations (see Koskinen 1963:68-69).

Birth

The path is not, however, sufficient even at the level of a formalized representation to account for the continuation of life on an island. As important as the path is, birth and marriage ties begin to play havoc in the minimalism of name list genealogies (see also McKinnon 1990). The single path multiplies itself, and the possibilities of choice and the political pragmatism connected with the preferences become central. At the same time all the connotations of the path become clear, adding further arguments against the legalistic descent-line interpretation of *ara*.

In addition to the simple "path" form of genealogy, there is another formalized mode of genealogical recitation and, since the coming of missionaries at the beginning of the last century, also writing. This more complex form is not a single path, but a combination of generations and marriages. It is produced patrilineally around the expressions "so and so *no'o ki te vaine so and so, anau tana* ..." ("so and so lived with the woman so and so and so and so was born to them") and the result is a genealogy called *papa'anga*. The term refers to layers or growth as does its synonym *tupu'anga*. The addition is a minor one, but it brings a totally new dimension to genealogy: marriage ties. In the simple path mode the sex of the generations is insignificant. In my calculations I have found that about 30 per cent of the names mentioned in the "paths" of the chiefs are female, but the sex is never mentioned. First the *no'o ki te vaine* ... *anau tana* mode of genealogical representation gives some patrilineal emphasis to the genealogies (if it is not expressed in the form *no'o ki te tane*, lived with a man ...).

In the political context of Ngaputoru marriage ties and thus reproductive ability play an important role. The origin narratives do give an asymmetric image of these abilities to the first generations. Uke finds a wife on his journey to the new island of Ma'uke. In a significant manner this wife is not a virgin; on the contrary, she is a wife of a warrior whom Uke kills in a fight. Uke's wife also has a son from the killed warrior, and this son becomes the husband for Uke's first born daughter. Uke thus brings to his island all the prerequisites for society: edible plants, rituals, wife, and husband for his future daughter. On 'Atiu in turn, Tura comes alone and has no wife. Accordingly, 'Atiu has to rely on Ma'uke for female reproductive powers, and Tura has to marry the second born daughter of Uke. Thus Ma'uke's position is an ambivalent one: on the one hand, the island is more complete, and thus hierarchically above 'Atiu; however, in the context of Ngaputoru politics it acquires the status of a tributary wife-giver, and thus becomes hierarchically below 'Atiu. The genealogical situation between the islands begins to look like this:

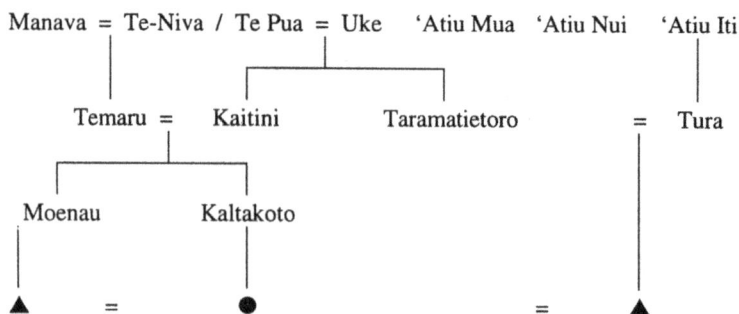

Figure. 1. Genealogical connections of Ma'uke and 'Atiu.

According to this genealogical construction Moenau seems to be the representative of the senior line on Ma'uke. He also appears on all the genealogies of the Ma'uke chiefs in a prominent position. The two marriage ties around the daughters of the younger Ma'ukean line represent the decisive alliances, which finally determined the power on the island. The intermarriage of the chiefly lines of both islands, however, creates a situation in which all three chiefs of both islands have paths to both of the mythical ancestors, both to Uke and to Tura.

Path and birth combined

Marriage, although clear on the level of genealogical representation, is not so systematic in the Ngaputoru context after all. The genealogies give reason to wife-giver/wife-taker analysis and to the consequent emergence of hierarchical levels. In fact, marriages are not transactions connected with social prestations, gift-exchange, etc. The significant way of "living with a woman" (*no'o ki te vaine*) in the historical narratives is to visit a woman secretly, possibly a wife of somebody else, and have offspring. The recurring feature of the narrative accounts about the deeds of the heroic chiefs in the Cook Islands is that the chiefs have heard about a beautiful wife on another island. This competition for women is the leading force behind the raids and interisland wars. A paradigmatic example in the Ngaputoru political context — an example which still creates hectic disputes wherever Ma'ukeans and 'Atiuans meet — is the case of Akaina. He was Parua Ariki of 'Atiu, and had heard about a beautiful wife of a Ma'ukean chief. So he decided to sail over to Ma'uke to fulfil his desire. The narrative tells us how Akaina arrived on the shore and met there the husband of the woman. In typical 'Atiuan fashion, their version tells how Akaina replied to the inquiry about the purpose of his visit: "I heard about a beautiful woman named Eturere. I have come to sleep with her." To this the husband of Eturere replied: "Welcome, Akaina, we will go to the house". Without opposition he gave his wife to Akaina, who slept the night with her. The men of Ma'uke, however, were not quite satisfied with the situation, and organized a war party to kill Akaina. In this they succeeded, and the killer was the paramount Ma'uke chief Mana's warrior. Mana's younger brother in turn helped the younger brothers of Akaina to escape and return unharmed to 'Atiu. In consequence of this love affair and ensuing fight the 'Atiuans revenged, and transferred the chiefly title on Ma'uke from the *tuakana* to the *teina*, from the elder brother Mana to his younger brother Tava, the helper of Akaina's younger brothers.

In the case of Akaina the result was not birth, but death. Both can have effects on the chiefly succession and the emergence of hierarchy. It is notable that successful genealogical use of the secret deeds of a travelling chief combines path and birth, and gives path its literal meaning, i.e., the way the ancestor has been travelling. In the history of Tangiia, written down by Te Rei Tamuera and

Stephen Savage, we have an example of the way the combination is made. In this narrative Tangiia arrives from the sea to the coast of Huahine. There he is sighted from the land, and an attempt is made to prevent his landing. According to the narrative, Tangiia composes an *aka-enua* song:

> The land is Huahine
> The ariki is Uki-manaka
> Uki-manaka took Rakanui to wife (*ka no'o ki te vaine ...*)
> And they begat Tiraonge ... (*anau tana Tiraonge*)
> The path to Huahine is flat (*paraaraa te ara ki 'Uaine*)
> Now let me land.

(Savage 1907:13)

Travelling Tangiia is really "on the path" of his ancestors. The *aka-enua* is a song composed to demonstrate his kinship ties to the island where he is trying to land. The decisive proof is one's position on the same path, the ability to trace the way the ancestors have travelled — even secretly. The path, the way the ancestor has travelled, and the descendant's attempt to trace that path are actually a Polynesian type tale. The typical tale "tells of a high chief who weds away from home and departs, leaving tokens with the mother for the child about to be born by which the child's paternity may be recognized" (Beckwith 1970:478). So the *ara* is not the descent, but rather the path, of the ancestor. Through their travels the warriors and chiefs create not only genealogical links between different islands, but at the same time a differentiated political space, which is hierarchically organized; and this hierarchy is expressed in genealogical terms. In a dispute about the seniority of rival islands claiming genealogical connections to the same heroic ancestor, the order of his visit to the islands is decisive. The *ara* of the islands is dependent on the route or path of the hero.

The narrative about Akaina is a paradigmatic one because it reveals the constantly recurring pattern, according to which the marriage ties between Ma'uke and 'Atiu affect the chiefly succession. It is not only the hierarchical relationship, but also the gendered values of the different islands which are the determinants of the political power. 'Atiuans as males and lonely warriors of the original genealogical situation reproduce their position by constantly travelling to Ma'uke "to prey for food and women" as Ron Crocombe put it (1967). At the same time the Ma'ukeans proliferate their position as senior and female.

The marriage alliance in this situation is a strange one: it is an alliance without marriage. There is the travelling male and the beautiful woman of the land whom the male visits. He does not stay, but continues his travel, and the paths of these travellers form a web of relationships around the archipelago. The hierarchical position of the island societies in the total polity is determined by the combination of the paths and the births, travels and sexual values of the islands.

Mana enua, mana tangata

In the social situation of the origin genealogies of Ngaputoru, only Ma'uke is complete and able to reproduce itself. 'Atiu, in contrast, is given as a lonely warrior who has to conquer a wife for himself on some other island. This leads to the original marriage between Ma'uke and 'Atiu, and the conceptualization of the island communities continues to give them the values of a husband and a wife, a man and a woman. 'Atiu is claimed to be the island of warriors and Ma'uke the island of *va'ine purotu*, the island of beautiful women, whose beauty is praised in numerous songs.

The conquering of the Ma'ukean women by 'Atiu warriors has not, however, occurred against the will of the Ma'ukeans. In the internal classification of younger and elder lines the connections to the warriorlike 'Atiuans play a decisive role. The internal chiefly rivalry constantly seeks a means of legitimation outside its borders. The interplay of the values of female and wife-giver, male and wife-taker result in the intervening fame of the women's beauty or the event of outside wife-conquering. The alliances created on this basis are unstable ones, and can be understood only as valued by the precedence of a whole set of categorical operators (Fox 1994). When wife-giver is defined as female, it is seen as inferior to the conquering male wife-taker. When the chiefly family is not seen as wife-giver but a senior beautiful woman whose beauty the travelling chiefs can not resist, the external wife-conqueror is utilized to support the claims of the internal chiefly line in question. The set of operators thus includes the distinctions between *elder/younger, female beauty/male conqueror, autochthonous/foreign*. The complementary combination and consequent reversals of the values of social units on the basis of the application of these categories forms the dynamics of chiefly politics.

In the case of Akaina, the killing of the love-hungry visitor led to the transfer of the title from one line to another. Similarly, the giving of daughters as wives to 'Atiu chiefs gives the candidates for a title a decisive advantage: the support of the island of warriors.

The continuation of this situation has not led to a complete and genealogically legitimated 'Atiu dominance in the archipelago, despite the early European impressions and some later interpretations. The path of the Ma'uke chiefs guarantees them their seniority because they can trace their path through the seniors, and the path of the 'Atiuans always passes through the juniors. But this is so only if the path is traced to Uke, the original ancestor of Ma'uke. The place and the ancestor are tightly connected, and the path metaphor highlights this connection. The path is not only the way of counting genealogies, it is also the path of the ancestor and his qualities from beyond to the present island. This ties together the place and the genealogy in a mutual legitimation. A genealogy can be used in one place, but not in another because both are actually expressions of the same process, the extension of the ancestral *tumu* in space and time. Correspondingly the seniority of one place can turn out to be juniority in the context of the polity of the whole archipelago. Precedence is determined in a recursive way, creating an overall social hierarchy.

The place-bound character of precedence is manifest also in the duality of power. *Mana enua*, power over land, can only be possessed by somebody who has a legitimate path to the original ancestor of the place. Conquest did not lead to the alienation of land in the Ngaputoru group. Even if it did, the conqueror had to create genealogical and even legitimate (i.e., through senior lines) connections to the ancestor of the place. *Mana tangata*, power over people, in turn, is able to emerge on the basis of marriage alliances abroad, and is thus able to transcend the horizon of a single island. The duality of power gives rise to a political situation of a relatively stable system of precedence in which a total reorganizing of the power structure in the Hawaiian style is impossible (cf. Valeri 1990).

The 'Atiu chiefs, who held absolute political power in the Ngaputoru group, were *tuakana*, or elder brothers, but they only possessed *mana tangata*, power over people. This power did not enable them to deprive the people of other islands of their land. The Ma'ukeans had *mana enua* on the basis of their path to the ancestor of their own land, and this path reversed the precedence in relation to the place. The overall authorities were said to be juniors, if they came to Ma'uke, because the point of reference — the operator — changed.

References

Beckwith, Martha

1970   *Hawaiian mythology*. Honolulu: University of Hawaii Press.

Biersack, Aletta

1990   Under the Toa tree. The genealogy of the Tongan chiefs. In Jukka Siikala (ed.) *Culture and history in the Pacific*, Vol. 27, 80-106. Helsinki: Transactions of the Finnish Anthropological Society.

Bourdieu, Pierre

1977   *Outline of a theory of practice*. Cambridge Studies in Social Anthropology. Cambridge: Cambridge University Press.

Buck, Peter H. (Te Rangi Hiroa)

1932   *Ethnology of Tongareva*. Honolulu: Bernice Pauahi Bishop Museum Bulletin 92.

Crocombe, Ron

1967   From ascendancy to dependency: the politics of 'Atiu. *The Journal of Pacific History* 2:97-111.

Firth, Raymond

1967   *The work of gods in Tikopia.* London School of Economics Monographs on Social Anthropology Nos 1 and 2. London: The Athlone Press.

Fox, James J.

1994   Reflections on "hierarchy" and "precedence". In M. Jolly and M. Mosko (eds) *Transformations of hierarchy: structure, history and horizon in the Austronesian world. History and Anthropology*, Vol. 7, 87-108. Chur and Reading: Harwood Academic Publishers.

Gill, William Wyatt

1890   The genealogy of the kings of Rarotonga and Mangaia, as illustrating the colonisation of that island and the Hervey Group. *Australasian Association for the Advancement of Science* 2:627-637.

Goldman, Irving

1970   *Ancient Polynesian society.* Chicago: University of Chicago Press.

Hooper, Antony

1981   *Why Tikopia has four clans.* Occasional Paper No. 38. London: Royal Anthropological Institute of Great Britain and Ireland.

Koskinen, Aarne A.

1960   *Ariki the first born: an analysis of a Polynesian chieftain title.* Helsinki: Suomalainen Tiedeakatemia.

1963   *Linking of symbols: Polynesian patterns 1.* Helsinki: The Finnish Society for Missionary Research.

McKinnon, Susan

1990   The matrilateral transference of power in Tikopia. *The Journal of the Polynesian Society* 99(3):227-264.

Sahlins, Marshall

1958   *Social stratification in Polynesia.* Monographs of the American Ethnological Society. Seattle: University of Washington Press.

1981   The stranger-king; or, Dumézil among the Fijians. *Journal of Pacific History* 16:107-132.

Savage, Stephen and Tamuera Te-Rei

1907   An ancient history of Tangiia. MS, The Australian National University Library, Canberra.

Siikala, Jukka

1990 Chiefs, gender and hierarchy in Ngaputoru. In Jukka Siikala (ed.) *Culture and history in the Pacific*, Vol. 27, 107-124. Helsinki: Transactions of the Finnish Anthropological Society.

Sissons, Jeffrey

1989   The seasonality of power: the Rarotongan legend of Tangiia. *The Journal of the Polynesian Society* 98(3):331-347.

Valeri, Valerio

1990   Diarchy and history in Hawaii and Tonga. In Jukka Siikala (ed.) *Culture and history in the Pacific*, Vol. 27, 45-79. Helsinki: Transactions of the Finnish Anthropological Society.

Chapter 4. Rank, Hierarchy and Routes of Migration: Chieftainship in the Central Caroline Islands of Micronesia

Ken-ichi Sudo

Introduction

The traditional political communities of the central Caroline Islands, from Ulithi to Namonuito Atoll, are characteristically small. A politically autonomous community may consist of a single village, a district or a small island, each composed of matrilineal descent groups. The total population of an island or an atoll is, on average, less than 800 persons and its land area is at most five square kilometres in extent. Some scholars have suggested that institutionalized chieftainship in Micronesia, as a form of suprafamilial authority, is directly related to surplus food production (e.g. Mason 1968). Therefore, due to their meagre resource base, the societies of the central Carolines should necessarily be unstratified and egalitarian.

This, however, is not the case. Instead, these polities are characterized by hereditary chieftainship and ranked kin groups. Shimizu (1987) classifies the polities of the Carolines and the Marshalls into two main types:

- chieftainships of a *primus inter pares* type, as in Palau (Belau) and Yap,
- centralized chieftainships, as in the central Carolines, Truk, Pohnpei, Kosrae, and in the Marshalls.

He concludes that political organization in Micronesia shows little correlation with environmental conditions (Shimizu 1987:249).

The matri-clans or matri-lineages of the central Carolines are divided between those of chiefly and non-chiefly rank. Rank is related to the sequence of a clan's or lineage's arrival on an island or in a particular locality (Alkire 1978:117, 1984:6-7). Claims to priority of settlement are generally asserted in terms of oral histories of migration routes and land ownership. In this regard, there exist two "contradictory" narrative traditions concerning the homeland of ancestral migrants to the central Caroline Islands. One is a narrative tradition that links migration to an "eastern route", from "Kachaw". The other link is to a "western route", from the "Yap Empire".

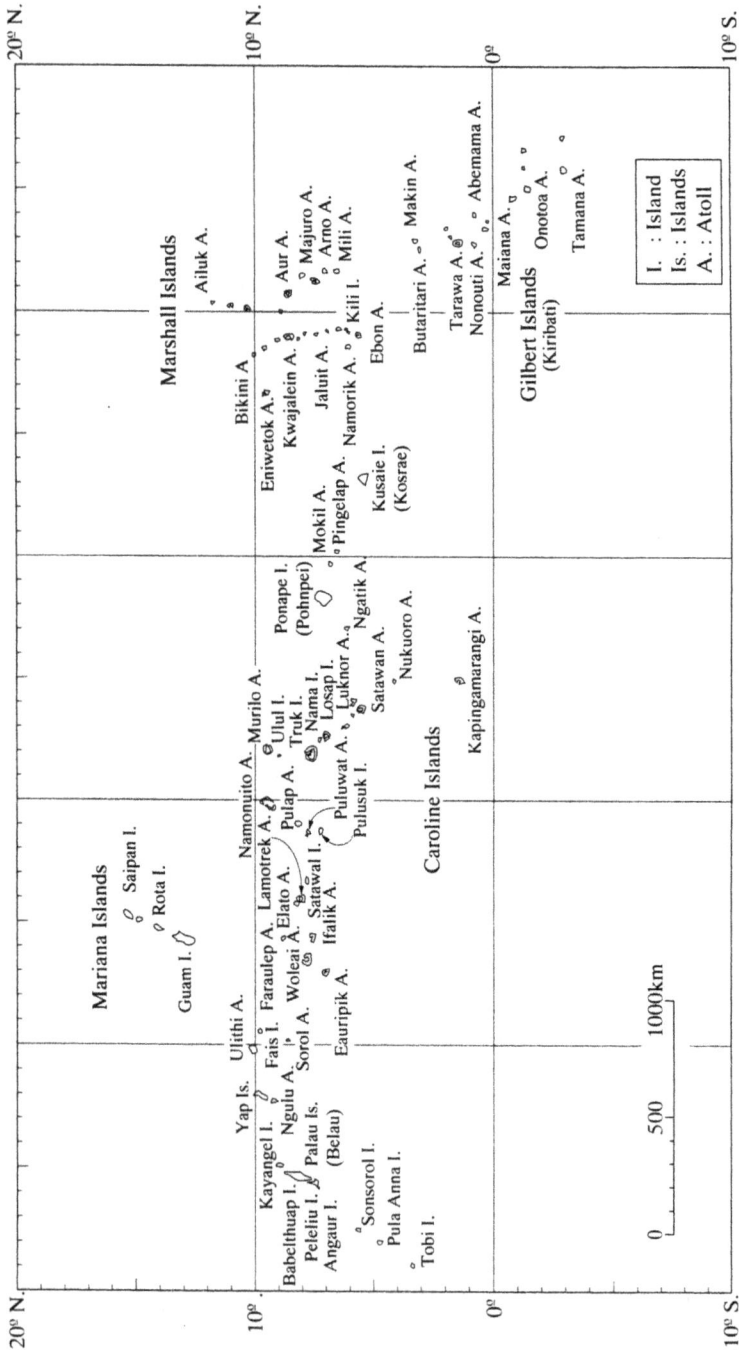

Map 1. The Micronesia Islands.

The aim of this paper is to examine the oral historical traditions that relate to rank among kin groups and islands and to clarify, more specifically, the nature of chieftainship on Satawal Island. I describe mainly the way in which oral traditions of migration help create social rank and legitimize chieftainship according to notions of political precedence among islands and kin groups.

Socio-Political Organization

Satawal is a raised coral island with an area of one square kilometre. It lies 1,000 km east of Yap and 500 km west of Truk (Map 1). The principal kin group and unit of landholding on the island is the matrilineal clan (*yáyinang*) or lineage (*yeew raa*, lit., "one branch of the tree"). The members of a *yáyinang* do not necessarily live only on Satawal; they may also live on other islands. Of those who live on other islands, some are able to trace their genealogical connections to known ancestors, while others simply identify themselves with the name of a particular clan. Clan members are obliged to assist one another and are prohibited from marrying. Residence is matri-uxorilocal and the residential group consists of a matri-extended family. Family members live in adjacent houses built on lineage land and form a corporate, co-residential group called a *pwukos* or homestead. In 1980 there were 15 homesteads on Satawal Island, the largest of which contained 12 households with a total of 71 members (Sudo 1984, 1989).

Satawalese society is comprised of eight matri-clans, each of which is ranked. Clan genealogies can in some instances be traced back eight generations. All clans are conceptually ranked in terms of their arrival on the island. Their rank order is as follows: Neyáár, Yáánatiw, Noosomwar, Sawsát, Kataman, Piik, Sawen, and Maasané. The three highest-ranking clans are known as the "first settlers" and are referred to as "chief clans". The others, except Sawsát, are considered to be later immigrants and are referred to as "commoner clans". Although the Sawsát clan is classified as a commoner clan, its ancestors are said to have come first to the island, before the arrival of the ancestors of the other clans.

The genealogically senior and oldest male of the senior lineage in each clan serves as the clan head. The heads of the three chiefly clans are called "the chiefs of the island" and have authority to initiate and organize island and inter-island activities. The three chiefs and the head of the Sawsát clan make up the chiefs' council. The council discusses important affairs of the island, such as communal fishing, ocean-going expeditions by canoe, sanctions imposed on individuals, and various matters transmitted from the state government. After decisions are reached by consensus, the council calls an island-wide meeting at which these decisions are announced. This meeting is open to all the adult men of the island. At it, members of the chiefly clans and the heads of the commoner clans have the right to speak, while ordinary members of commoner clans are barred from speaking unless asked to by the others.

The three chiefs are also responsible for controlling food resources. For example, in times of scarcity, they may place a taboo on the use of taro patches and coconut palms that are owned by individual lineages, or taboo the use of particular areas of sea. They also have superior authority in maintaining social order and act as mediators or judges, settling conflicts between clans, such as disputes over land boundaries or adultery compensation. Chiefs are therefore expected to be knowledgeable concerning custom, land tenure, genealogies, and command such esoteric knowledge as navigation techniques, divination, and weather forecasting.

The three chiefs are status-ranked; the highest is the chief of Neyáár, the second is the chief of Yáánatiw, and third is the chief of Noosomwar. The chief of the Neyáár clan is entitled to receive tribute of the first breadfruit and the first coconut palm toddy from every household on the island, according to the seasonal calendar. The chief selects his own food and immediately re-distributes the rest to all of the other homesteads. These prestations are considered a token payment of honour to the chief as head of the "first settlers' clan" and as acting agent for controlling the fertility of crops. Before Christianity was adopted in 1953 the chief had power over crops. The chief of the Neyáár clan directed a diviner to foretell the success or failure of the new year's crops and to perform rituals of fertility. Today this tribute is ceremonial rather than substantial. On the other hand, the head of the Sawsát clan has exclusive right to butcher all sea turtles and distribute their meat. As a ceremonial token, the head of the turtle is considered a gift to the Sawsát clan, as the "original immigrants" to the island (Sudo 1985).

The stratified status of chiefly and commoner clans is further supported by oral history and differences in landowning.

Oral History of Satawal: Chiefly and Commoner Clans

The oral history of the central Carolines traces what are claimed to be the indigenous migration routes and the order of settlement of the islands. This history is called *rapito* or *wuruwow*, "original story to come" or "legend", and is preserved as secret knowledge by individual clans. This history is viewed as a central determinant of clan rank. Let me summarize three migration stories from Satawal.

The original settlers of the island are recognized as the ancestors of the Sawsát clan, which means "proprietors of the sea" or "lords of Satawal". The Sawsát clan's oral history is told as follows.

> Long, long ago, warfare on Yarawo (or Kachaw) island, caused by overpopulation and a shortage of food, led the ancestors of the Sawsát clan to leave the island in rafts. They drifted to Truk and then to Puluwat Atoll. Finally four men and seven women arrived at Satawal and settled

on the western coast of the island near the entrance to its lagoon. After a time they decided to invite people from other islands to join them at Satawal, since the island was otherwise uninhabited at the time. Some voyaged to Lamotrek Atoll. There they learned that Lamotrek was a "chiefly island", controlling Satawal and the Elato Atoll.

Accepting the invitation of the Sawsát clan, some Lamotrekan people of the Yatonoyong clan moved to Satawal. The Sawsát people gave them a large parcel of land covering the southern part of the island and directed them to settle there. The chief of the Sawsát clan married a woman of Yatonoyong who bore a son. The chief transferred authority over the island to his son since the latter was obedient and looked after his father and the other members of his father's clan. In return, the Sawsát clan became subordinate to the Yatonoyong clan (Sudo 1985:640-642). After this transfer of authority the Yatonoyong clan changed its name to Neyáár, because its members lived at the time under a *yáár* tree.

According to the traditions of Neyáár, which thereby became the chiefly clan of first rank, its clan ancestors are said to have come to Satawal from Yarawo via Ifalik and Lamotrek. After this, some people of the Mongonufarh clan came to Satawal from Lamotrek. The head of the Neyáár clan directed them to settle the northern part of the island. This group was called "Yáánatiw" and was named for the area they settled. Thirdly, another group from the Mongonufarh clan on Lamotrek migrated to the island and settled in the middle of Satawal island under the direction of the Neyáár clan. This group was called "Noosomwar" (lit., "not moving anywhere").

The oral history of Yáánatiw and Noosomwar, both of which were originally from the same Mongonufarh clan, indicates that their home island was Ifalik Atoll situated to the west of Lamotrek. Their ancestors also left Yarawo and drifted to Yap or Ifalik. On Ifalik three girls were born and placed in cradles hung under a three-pronged branch (*mong*) of a pandanus tree (*farh*). Although one of them stayed on the island, the other two girls were taken respectively to Woleal and Lamotrek by the people of Ifalik. They married and had children on each island. Their matrilineal descendants were called "Mongonufarh". Some members of the Mongonufarh clan of Woleal later came to Lamotrek where they founded a separate "clan" distinct from the other Mongonufarh clan. These two branches of the Mongonufarh clan are called Yáánatiw and Noosomwar on Satawal. They are considered independent "clans" and their members are allowed to inter-marry.

After these four clans had settled on the island, seven clans are said to have come to Satawal from the eastern islands, such as Truk, Tamatam, Puluwat, or Pulusuk. Today representatives of only four of these clans remain on the island.

Each was given plots of land on which to settle by one of the three clans from Lamotrek.

In these oral histories, narratives of all three chiefly clans indicate their original homeland to be Yarawo, and tell of their ancestors coming via the western islands; Yap, Woleai, Ifalik, or Lamotrek. On the other hand, the histories of the five commoner clans, including Sawsát, claim that their ancestors migrated from the eastern islands: Truk, Puluwat, Tamatam, or Pulusuk. According to an oral history of Pulap Atoll the chief of the autochthonous clan of the island passed his authority to his son whose mother came from Yap (Flinn 1982:62; Komatsu 1990:29-30). Thus chieftainship is legitimized by the "fact" that the principal ancestress of the chiefly clan is descended from Yap. Also in Ulul chieftainship was transferred from father (chief) to a son whose mother came from Faraurep Atoll located to the west of Ulul Island (Sudo 1977:212; Thomas 1978:53, 85). In the remainder of the paper I will examine this association of migration routes and rank based on oppositions: first occupant/stranger, western/eastern, chiefly/commoner, in the context of the social and political organization of the central Caroline Islands.

Two Legendary Homelands of the Caroline Islanders

In the oral history of Truk and Pohnpei, an island called Kachaw or Achaw is described as the place from which clan ancestors are said to have come, some as high-ranking immigrants (Goodenough 1986:552-553; Mauricio 1987:63; Sudo 1985:838-844). The Trukese and other central Carolinians identify Kachaw with Kosrae Island, situated between Pohnpei and the Marshall Islands. Some chiefly clans validate their superiority by emphasizing their derivation from ancestral immigrants from Kachaw.

On the other hand, in the oral history of the islands closer to Yap in the central Carolines, Yap is considered to be the ancestral homeland. Thus, the mythical "great ghost" of Ulithi Atoll is said to have come from Yap (Lessa 1976:64-65, 1980:48-53). According to the traditions of Ifalik Atoll, the first settlers are said to have comprised a colony from Yap (Burrows and Spiro 1957:7; Alkire 1984:3-4). A narrative collected by Burrows illustrates this connection (Burrows and Spiro 1957:7):

> Long, long ago, a chief of Garpar (Gatshapar) village, in the Gagil district, Yap, ordered some of his people to go out and colonize the outer islands to the east. He himself remained in Yap.

> In charge of the expedition was a man named Tatar who was accompanied by his sister, Iau. They went first to Mogmog on Ulithi, then to Wetegau (Utagal?) in Woleai, then to Ifalik and the other islands — Faraulep, Elato, Lamotrek, Satawal, and so on to Puluwat and Truk and "all Caroline

place." The chain of command, ever since, is from Yap to Mogmog, from Mogmog to Wetegau, Wetegau to Ifaluk, from Ifaluk to the other islands.

On Ifalik, Tatar left one man and one woman from each of the eight clans. The two from each clan were brother and sister. Their names were

> From Kovalu clan: Maraige and his sister Lemaregara.
> From Sauvelarik clan: Alovar and his sister Eilapikel.
> From Mangaulevar clan: Trigabwa and his sister Ungusaren ...

The descendants of these women, who married the men from other clans, make up the membership of the clans today.

This tradition attributes the first settlement of Ifalik to immigration from Yap and explains the origin of the political order that exists between Yap and the other islands. It indicates also the present-day relationship among the eight clans of Satawal.

In another Ifalik oral history from Burrows (1963:72-77), Ifalik warriors attacked and killed the original inhabitants of the neighbouring islands of Woleai and Lamotrek. They then repopulated the islands and men from Ifalik became the chiefs in Woleai and Lamotrek. The tale of the "Ifalik conquerors" is popular in the oral history of the central Carolines. I collected the same kind of tale on Satawal. The original story of the Mongonufarh clan mentioned above is connected with this tale. These oral histories all assert that the first of the new settlers carried the title of chieftainship to each island and that the ancestors of the chiefly clans migrated from the west, ultimately coming from Yap.

Political Relationship Between Yap and the Outer Islands

The societies of the twenty-four coral islands between Yap and Truk were tied to Yap in a supra-island political system. These islands were obliged to send tribute once a year to the Gagil district of Yap until early in this century. This system of tribute, called *sawei*, defined the "Yap Empire" (Lessa 1950:42). Similar ties existed between the various groupings of outer islands: Woleal, Lamotrek-Satawal-Elato and Puluwat-Pulap-Pulusuk (Alkire 1965:145-149, 1978:119; Flinn 1982:35).

Sawei: Politico-religious tribute system

Yap domination linked the outer islands to one another in a single political system. In general, rank decreased with distance from Yap. Orders for tribute were sent out from Yap through a chain of authority from the highest to the lowest ranking island, beginning with Mogmog on Ulithi and ending with the easternmost of the outer islands. As the lowest in rank, the people of Namonuito Atoll were annually the first to embark on the reverse tribute voyages toward

Yap. Tribute goods moved from lower to higher ranking islands until they reached the Gagil district (Figure 1).

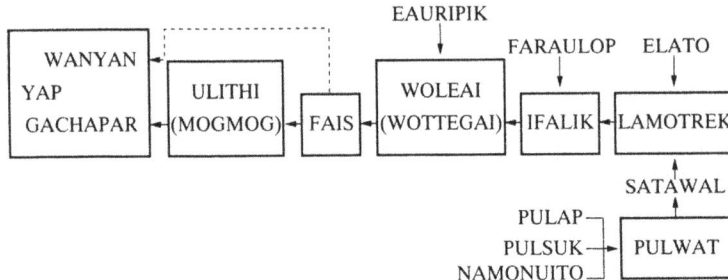

Figure 1. The flow of the tributes (Ushijima 1987).

Representatives of each of the islands carried three categories of gifts, which were "Canoe Tribute", "Religious Tribute", and "Tribute of the Land" (Alkire 1970:5-6). Canoe Tribute and Religious Tribute usually consisted of woven fibre cloth, pandanus mats and coconut oil. They were handed to the chief of Gachapar by the highest ranking island chief, the paramount chief of Ulithi. Canoe Tribute was passed into the hands of the ranking chiefs of Gachapar and Wanyan villages in the Gagil district. Religious Tribute consisted of offerings to the mythical Yapese founder of the *sawei*, Yangolap, who was enshrined on the estate of the chief of Gachapar.

On the other hand, Tribute of the Land was kept by the representatives of the outer islands and given to their respective *sawei* partners on Gagil, whose estates held title to particular plots of land on their islands (Alkire 1970:6; 1980:232; Ushijima 1987:304). This tribute included woven cloth, mats, sennit rope, coconut oil and various kinds of shell. When the outer island people returned to their own islands, their Yapese partners provided them with a number of gifts, including turmeric, yams, bananas, sweet potatoes, bamboo, red soil pigment, pots, and manufactured items which were scarce in the outer islands.

The ideology of *sawei* maintained that the estates of Gachapar and Wanyan villages in the Gagil district held suzerainty over specific outer islands or districts of these islands. Therefore the *sawei* relationship was one of landlord and serf (Lessa 1950:32, 1966:36-39). The superior status of the Yapese over the outer island people was also described in the idiom of a fictive "parent-child" relationship. As "children", the outer island people were obligated to send tribute to the people of Gagil (Lingenfelter 1975:147). In return they were given food and shelter in Gagil whenever they visited Yap. However, they were considered low caste, with the same rank as the lowest ranking members of Yapese society. They were therefore expected to show deference and were prohibited from marrying Yapese (Lessa 1950:144; Ushijima 1987:305).

If tribute was not sent, a Yapese chief or magician might cause storms or epidemics to decimate the offending kin group or to destroy the island which had failed in its obligations. Canoe voyages over long distances were prohibited by the Japanese government in the 1920s so that this system no longer operates. However, on the outer islands, aged men still hold a deferential attitude toward the Yapese and fear Yapese sorcery. The Satawalese people still rely on traditional knowledge of weather-forecasting based on the rising and setting of particular stars and constellations to predict the periodic storms which strike the island each year from the northeast or east (Akimichi 1980:16-29). On the other hand they cannot foretell by such traditional methods the tropical storms and typhoons that strike the island from the west. These, which sometimes cause severe damage, are thought to be caused by Yapese magicians or sorcery.

Although oral traditions of Ifalik suggest that the Yapese invaded the outer islands, there is little archaeological or linguistic evidence to support these narratives. Linguistically the central Carolinian languages belong to Nuclear Micronesian and are grouped with Trukic (Bender 1971:438; Goodenough and Sugita 1980:xii; Tryon 1984:157). The affiliation of Yapese is still unclear. According to archaeological evidence the occupation of Fefan on Truk began by 2000 BP (Shutler, Sinoto and Takayama 1984:60) while Yap was occupied as early as 176 AD (Gifford and Gifford 1959:200). Although archaeological excavations in the central Caroline Islands are still few, they indicate that Lamotrek island was inhabited by 1000 AD and possibly as early as 300 AD (Fujimura and Alkire 1984:125).

In addition Yap is culturally and physically distinct from the central Caroline Islands (Bellwood 1978:285). The central Carolinians from Woleai to Namonuito share some clan names, a similar socio-political organization, traditional belief systems, and many features of material culture with Truk. The people of these islands also made canoe voyages to Truk every two or three years where until the 1960s they exchanged products and turmeric and maintained reciprocal relationships with the Trukese. They were thus able to obtain all their necessities, which were not produced in their island, from Truk, without going all the way to Yap. The central Carolinians were migrants voyaging from Truk, not from Yap (Alkire 1984:3-4). For the outer islanders, *sawei* or tribute and deference paid to Yapese seems to have been based on fear of Yapese sorcery.

Sayiniké: Political ties of Lamotrek and Satawal

A smaller system of tribute and exchange persisted in the Lamotrek-Satawal-Elato Islands until the 1950s. Lamotrek was ranked politically above Satawal and Elato. The relationship between the three islands was called *ké* or "fish hook", because Lamotrek politically controlled the other two islands (Alkire 1965:145-149).

Satawal and Elato Islands were obliged to send semi-annual tribute to Lamotrek. The chiefs of Satawal required each homestead to contribute one basket of preserved breadfruit and hundreds of coconuts. These foods were sent to Lamotrek by sailing canoes. This tribute voyage was called *sayiniké* or the "voyage of the fish hook". The paramount chief of Lamotrek received this tribute and offered some of it to his ancestress. The rest was distributed to all the homesteads on the island. Lamotrek was not required to return anything as a counter-gift because this tribute was recognized as a token payment in return for which Satawal was allowed to exploit the nearby uninhabited islands controlled by Lamotrek. On the other hand, Satawalese people considered these prestations as offerings to their ancestress, from whom the ancestress of the chief of Satawal descended. When Satawal was hit by storms or typhoons and there was a scarcity of food, the chief of Satawal could ask for assistance of taro or coconuts from the chief of Lamotrek.

These tribute systems of *sawei* and *sayiniké* can be interpreted as exchange systems involving "mutual assistance in the form of subsistence" between the high island of Yap and low islands, or between the outer islands and the neighbouring coral islands. On the other hand this system was maintained both politically and religiously by a lineal chain of authority based on a tradition of priority of settlement or resettlement (irrespective of what can be established as the actual historical order of settlement). The important point to emphasize is that the oral history of Satawal, Pulap, Ulul and Ifalik portray the chiefly clans of the outer islands as having migrated from the west; i.e. from Yap, Woleai, Ifalik or Lamotrek, in accordance with the hierarchy as formed by tribute relations.

Clan and Land

Land is another important element in the status system. In Truk and the central Caroline Islands generally it is argued that clan ranking is determined not only by order of settlement but also by the amount of land originally controlled by each clan (Goodenough 1951; Alkire 1970; Nason 1970; Shimizu 1987). This principle of determining clan rank is common in Satawalese society (Sudo 1984, 1987).

On Satawal, however, it is not the first-settlers but the first of the new settlers whose descendants comprise the chiefly clans of the island. According to oral traditions, Sawsát, the original clan, passed its proprietary right to the island's land and to its chieftainship to the Neyáár clan, which was the first of the new settlers to arrive after Sawsát. After this transfer the Neyáár people owned the entire island by the right of being the first settlers from a "high ranking island", Lamotrek, and the Sawsát clan became subordinate to Neyáár. When the other two chiefly groups migrated from Lamotrek, the Neyáár clan gave large amounts of land to them and divided the island into three villages: the south, middle and north. By this division, control of the south village was retained by the Neyáár clan, while the middle and north were granted to the Noosomwar and Yáánatiw clans, respectively.

As the other clans migrated to Satawal, they were, in turn, given several plots of land by one or the other of these three clans, depending on where they settled. Maasané, for instance, is said to have come under the patronage of the Neyáár clan and to have settled near the Neyáár homestead, receiving Neyáár land in the process. The relationship between land-giver and land-receiver is called *yakkune*, which means "to be trustworthy to each other". Land-receivers are linked in a subordinate relationship to land-givers, and are obliged to follow the directives of the latter when requested. The three land-giving clans, Neyáár, Yáánatiw, and Noosomwar, held the highest rank and were known as "chiefly" clans. On the other hand, the four land-receiving clans, Kataman, Piik, Sawen, and Maasané, were subordinate and called "commoner" clans. Though not a land-receiver, the Sawsát clan was, as we have noted, also considered a commoner clan.

The three chiefly clans still own large tracts of land on Satawal. The amount of land that is currently controlled by each of the eight clans is shown in Table 1. The clans of the first settlers from Lamotrek established priority of land control and continue to own the largest amounts of land. Thus arrival sequence of land-ownership is a close reflection of clan rank.

Conclusions

In this paper I have examined the characteristics of chieftainship and the principal elements determining rank and status among kin groups in the central Carolines.

There are two contrasting principles of precedence operating here:

- one based on priority of settlement, referring to migration legends tracing homelands to an eastern island, Kachaw (Kosrae); and
- another based on inter-island tribute and economic relations, connecting to western islands, ultimately to Yap.

Table 1. Lineage, population and landholding in Satawal Island (Sudo 1987)

Clan and Lineage	Households	Population	Lands		Taro Patches		BT[3]	In-marrying 1880-1980	Married-out 1880-1980
			Total	OL[1]	Total	OT[2]			
Neyáár									
Ráápiirakirh	10	32	32	14	18	10	187		
Neyimwenikát	3	13	11	2	6	2	55		
Neyáár	2	15	7	4	7	4	91		
Sub-total	15	60	50	20	31	16	333	74	65
Yáánatiw									
Yáánatiw	5	45	27	17	25	5	130		
Neyán	6	40	28	15	23	14	115		
Wenikeyiya	1	5	11	5	8	2	22		
Sub-total	12	90	66	37	56	21	267	43	60
Noosomwar									
Kaningeirek	7	42	32	16	29	6	113		
Fááyinen	12	71	34	8	46	3	?		
Sub-total	19	113	66	24	75	9	113	56	51
Kataman									
Yóosukunap	8	61	29	16	24	7	138		
Wenikeyiya	2	10	12	7	5	3	?		
Sub-total	10	71	41	23	29	10	138	49	42
Piik									
Nesátikúw	5	20	16	7	11	3	106	22	12
Sawen									
Fááníyór	3	23	27	15	19	10	96	22	26
Sawsát									
Yápééw	5	19	15	7	12	6	151		
Yatiirong	5	39	13	5	17	9	108		
Sub-total	10	58	28	12	29	15	259	32	41
Maasané									
Weyisow	13	57	28	13	28	1	142	32	27
Total	87	492	322	151	278	85	1,454	330	324

Notes:[1] OL: original land; [2] OT: original taro patches; [3] BT: Breadfruit tree.

The first principle is a basic and general element used to legitimize chieftainship. The second principle operates in the acquisition of chieftainship and its maintenance in some island societies — Satawal, Ulul, Pulap — where the chiefly clan became extinct or where chieftainship was usurped by another clan. In this new political order, settlers from western high ranking islands carry the title of chief. Regardless of the actual historical order of settlement, the highest ranking clans articulate their oral history of migration to assert their legitimacy of the chieftainship by claiming as their homeland two centres of influence: Kachaw and Yap.

Another element that validates chieftainship is land-ownership. This is demonstrated not only by the fact that the highest ranking chiefly clan holds the largest amount of land on the island, but also by oral history in which this clan is represented as having originally controlled all of the land of the island. In other words, the first settlers assumed a dominant status as the primary title holders to the entire territory of the island and later settlers were given a subordinate status as secondary title holders. It is a characteristic feature of chieftainship in the Carolines that the most important responsibility of the chief is to manage food resources while maintaining the social order. Thus the superior/inferior relationships are expressed symbolically through gifts of "first crops".

References

Akimichi, Tomoya

1980   Storm star and ethnometeorology on Satawal. *Kikan Zinruigaku* 11:3-15 (in Japanese).

Alkire, William H.

1965   *Lamotrek Atoll inter-island socioeconomic ties.* Illinois Studies in Anthropology No. 5. Urbana: University of Illinois Press.

1970   Systems of measurement on Woleai Atoll, Caroline Islands. *Anthropos* 65:1-73.

1978   *Coral islanders.* Arlington Heights, IL: AHM Publishing Corp.

1980   Technical knowledge and the evolution of political systems in the central Caroline and Western Islands of Micronesia. *Canadian Journal of Anthropology* 1:229-237.

1984   Central Carolinian oral narratives: indigenous migration theories and principles of order and rank. *Pacific Studies* 7:1-14.

Bellwood, Peter

1978   *Man's conquest of the Pacific: the prehistory of Southeast Asia and Oceania.* London: Collins.

Bender, Byron W.

1971   Micronesian languages. In T.A. Sebeok (ed.) *Linguistics in Oceania,* 2 vols. *Current Trends in Linguistics,* vol. 8, pp.426-465. The Hague: Mouton.

Burrows, Edwin G.

1963   *Flower in my ear: arts and ethos of Ifaluk atoll.* Seattle: University of Washington Press.

Burrows, Edwin G. and Melford E. Spiro

1957   *An atoll culture: ethnography of Ifaluk in the Central Carolines.* New Haven: Human Relations Area Files Press.

Flinn, Juliana B.

1982   Migration and inter-island ties: a case study of Pulap, Caroline Islands. PhD dissertation, Stanford University.

Fujimura, Keiko and William H. Alkire

1984   Archaeological test excavations on Farauiep, Woleai, and Lamotrek in the Caroline Islands of Micronesia. In Yosihiko H. Sinoto (ed.) *Caroline Islands archaeology: investigations on Fefan, Faraulep, Woleai, and Lamotrek.* Pacific Anthropological Records No. 5, pp.66-129. Honolulu: B.P. Bishop Museum.

Gifford, Edward W. and Delia S. Gifford

1959   Archaeological excavations in Yap. *Anthropological Records* 18(2):149-224.

Goodenough, Ward H.

1951   *Property, kin, and community on Truk.* Yale University Publications in Anthropology No. 46. New Haven: Yale University Press. [Reprinted 1978, 2nd ed. Hamden, CT: Archon Books.]

1986 Sky world and this world: the place of Kachaw in Micronesian cosmology. *American Anthropologist* 88:551-568.

Goodenough, Ward H. and Hiroshi Sugita

1980 *Trukese-English dictionary.* Philadelphia: American Philosophical Society.

Komatsu, Kazuhiko

1990   A sketch of chieftainship on Pulap: island community and its 'exterior'. In Iwao Ushijima (ed.) *Anthropological research on the atoll cultures of*

Micronesia, 1988, pp.21-34. Tsukuba: Department of Anthropology, University of Tsukuba.

Lessa, William A.

1950   Ulithi and the outer native world. *American Anthropologist* 52:27-52.

1966   *Ulithi: A Micronesian design for living.* New York: Holt, Rinehart, and Winston.

1976   The apotheosis of Marespa. In Adrienne L. Kaeppler and H. Arlo Nimmo (eds) *Directions in Pacific traditional literature: essays in honor of Katharine Luomala*. Bernice P. Bishop Museum Special Publications No. 62, pp.61-81. Honolulu: Bishop Museum Press.

1980   *More tales from Ulithi atoll: a content analysis.* Folklore and Mythology Studies No. 32. Berkeley: University of California Press.

Lingenfelter, Sherwood G.

1975   *Yap: political leadership and culture change in an island society*. Honolulu: University Press of Hawaii.

Mason, Leonard

1968   Suprafamilial authority and economic process in Micronesian atolls. In A.P. Vayda (ed.) *Peoples and cultures of the Pacific: an anthropological reader*, pp.299-329. New York: Natural History Press.

Mauricio, Rufino

1987   Peopling of Pohnpei Island: migration, dispersal and settlement themes in clan narratives. *Man and Culture in Oceania* 3:47-72.

Nason, James D.

1970   Clan and copra: modernization of Etal Island, Eastern Caroline Islands. PhD dissertation, University of Washington.

Shimizu, Akitoshi

1987   Chieftainship in Micronesia. *Man and Culture in Oceania* 3 (special issue):239-252.

Shutler, Richard, Jr, Yosihiko H. Sinoto and Jun Takayama

1984   Preliminary excavations of Fefan Island site, Truk Islands. In Yosihiko H. Sinoto (ed.) *Caroline Islands archaeology: investigations on Fefan, Faraulep, Woleai, and Lamotrek*. Pacific Anthropological Records No. 5, pp.1-64. Honolulu: B.P. Bishop Museum.

Sudo, Ken-ichi

1977   Field notes on an outer island life, Ulul Island of Truk. *Annual Journal of Social Anthropology*, 202-220 (in Japanese).

1984   Systems of land tenure and resource management on Satawal Island, Micronesia. *Bulletin of the National Museum of Ethnology* 10:197-348 (in Japanese).

1985   Structural change in matrilineal descent group in Greater Trukese societies. *Bulletin of the National Museum of Ethnology* 10:827-926 (in Japanese).

1987   Land tenure and social organization in Micronesia. *Man and Culture in Oceania*, 3 (special issue):253-266.

1989   *Matrilineal structure in island societies, Micronesia.* Tokyo: Kinokuniya Shoten (in Japanese).

Thomas, John B.

1978 Adoption, filiation, and matrilineal descent on Namonuito Atoll, Caroline Islands. PhD dissertation, University of Hawaii.

Tryon, D.T.

1984   The peopling of the Pacific. *Journal of Pacific History* 19:147-159.

Ushijima, Iwao

1987   *Society and exchange on Yap.* Tokyo: Kobundo (in Japanese).

Chapter 5. "All Threads Are White": Iban Egalitarianism Reconsidered

Clifford Sather

Ragi ubong samoa dedudok ari burak magang, Tang chura iya digaga' dudi, nya' alai bisi' mansau, Kuning, gadong enggau biru.

All cotton threads start out as white, But after they are dyed, they become red, yellow, green, and blue.

(an Iban saying)

Introduction

The characterization of societies as "egalitarian" — in Borneo as elsewhere in the non-Western world — has come under increasing scrutiny in recent years (Boehm 1993; Flanagan and Rayner 1988; Flanagan 1989; Woodburn 1982). Even so, despite this newfound interest, compared to "hierarchy", notions of equality have been far less explored in the anthropological literature. Part of the reason is almost certainly as Flanagan (1989:261) suggests: that equality tends to be "naturalized" in the social sciences and so regarded as the proto-cultural condition out of which structures of inequality are presumed to have developed by evolutionary differentiation (cf. Fried 1967). Thus it is not equality, but the origin and maintenance of inequality that is viewed as problematic and therefore the primary subject of sociological speculation and theory. Relatedly, inequality is taken by many to be universal (cf. Fallers 1973) — an inherent property of all human social systems; or the term "egalitarian" is applied by default, as a residual category, to those societies that otherwise lack clearly defined hierarchical features.

In discussing "egalitarian" societies, it is useful at the outset to distinguish between "equality", "egality" and "egalitarian". The distinction, I propose, is not unlike the one that some have drawn between the "individual", as an entity arguably constitutive of all societies, and "individualism", an ideology present in some societies, absent in others, that gives accent to the individual, to individual autonomy, and so on. "Egality", like "individualism", is a cultural construct. Following Woodburn (1982:431-432), I would argue that the related term "egalitarian" is therefore best reserved for societies in which relations of equality, to the extent that they exist, are:

not neutral, the mere absence of inequality or hierarchy, but [are] *asserted* [emphasis in the original], ... repeatedly acted out, [and] publicly demonstrated ...

An "egalitarian" society is therefore a cultural configured social system, just as is a "hierarchical" one. These distinctions may be briefly summarized as follows:[1]

egality

1.   Following Woodburn, a cultural construct or set of ideas,
2.   which therefore operates at the level of ideology;
3.   has the potential for creating objective relations of equality; that is, as ideology, of configuring social relationships in its own image; and
4.   has also the mystificatory potential to obscure or conceal relations of inequality.
5.   "Egalitarian" is an appropriate term since in the standard concise Oxford definition, it refers to "the principle of equal rights, etc. for all persons", that is to say, it has to do with the *principle* or *concept* of equality, i.e. with jural rather than *de facto* reality.

equality

1.   refers to the process whereby individuals compare themselves with each other and find themselves the same;
2.   operates at the level of objective conditions of existence.
3.   "Equality", in common standard usage, refers to the notion of equivalence; to "The condition of having equal dignity, rank, or privileges with others; the fact of being on an equal footing" (*The Oxford English Dictionary*, second edition).

Contrasting these terms, in a parallel way:

hierarchy

1.   like egality, is a cultural construct,
2.   which similarly operates as ideology, and
3.   following the numbered points above, has the ability to create and maintain relations of inequality; and
4.   also has a mystificatory potential to conceal relations of equality. [This latter possibility is little discussed by students of hierarchy, although Michael Allen (1987), in pointing up the existence of relations of equality in a Nepalese society, shows how both caste ideology and Dumontian social theory similarly work to mask its presence.]

inequality

1.   refers to the objective conditions of existence in which individuals have different opportunities and achieve different statuses.

The relation between these notions can be depicted by means of a simple four-cell diagram (Figure 1). Here "hierarchy" and "egality" have to do with culture and ideology; "inequality" and "equality" with material conditions and social relationships. Read vertically, "inequality" is opposed to "equality"; "hierarchical" to "egalitarian".

	social relations	ideology
differences between persons	unequal conditions	hierarchical ideology
equivalence between persons	equal conditions	egalitarian ideology

Figure 1. Hierarchy and equality

It follows from these distinctions that conditions of inequality may exist in an "egalitarian society" and those of "equality" in a "hierarchical" one, and, indeed, equality and inequality may coexist as modalities within a single social system (cf. Flanagan 1989:261). Similarly, a point made in this paper, "egalitarian" and "hierarchical" cultural values may be contextually articulated in different domains within the same society. In what follows I use these notions to reexamine a debate concerning the characterization of Iban society as "egalitarianism".

The Iban, Borneo, and the "Egalitarianism" Debate

Most ethnographic observers of the Iban, the most populous ethno-linguistic group of West-Central Borneo, have characterized Iban society as "egalitarian", "democratic" and "classless" (cf. Freeman 1970, 1981; Heppell 1975; Sather 1980; 1978). Thus Freeman (1970:129) asserts:

> Under Iban *adat* all men are equals ... Iban society is classless and egalitarian — its members, individualists, aggressive and proud in demeanour, lacking any taste for obeisance.

Characterized in this way, the Iban are frequently contrasted with neighbouring upland peoples of central Borneo, the majority of whom live in societies formed of ascribed social strata characterized by corvée labour and the monopolization of political authority by an upper stratum of chiefly families (Ave, King and DeWit 1983:16-28; King 1976, 1978:27-32, 1985; Morris 1978, 1980; Rousseau 1978, 1990). Since Edmund Leach's (1950) pioneering account of indigenous structural variation in Borneo, most comparative observers have endorsed, in one form or another, the broad distinction that he drew in this account between "egalitarian" and "stratified societies" (1950:75-78), and, like Leach, have taken the Iban to be the prime paradigmatic example of the former — an "egalitarian society" in which "class stratification ... is absent in a formally instituted sense" (1950:71).[2]

This characterization of Iban society and, indeed, the more general distinction between "egalitarian" and "stratified" social systems has not gone unchallenged. Thus, for example, Alexander (1992:207) notes that Leach's original characterization of Bornean societies "was based neither on wide empirical knowledge nor sophisticated theoretical analysis" and that it, and most subsequent "attempts to rank whole societies and cultures on a continuum from egalitarian to stratified have focused attention on relatively narrow questions of political authority and power". Thus, while ascribed rank may be a salient feature in the political structures of many central Bornean communities (1992:207),

> productive surpluses are small and the means of production are freely available to most households, while ideologies of hierarchy are underdeveloped with expressions of deference limited to specific contexts. In some of these societies ... local communities have considerable economic and political autonomy and the tenor of daily life is more appropriately described as egalitarian rather than hierarchical.

As Alexander (1992:208) goes on to observe, the fact that some political relationships "are grounded in inequality does not entail that equally important economic and gender relationships are similarly constituted", nor should "notions of hierarchy ... be privileged over explicit values of personal and household autonomy", which appear as at least as important in shaping social relationships (see also Nicolaisen 1986). Moreover, as she shows, ascriptive categories — where they exist — are not necessarily ranked lineally, but in many contexts are "constituted by reciprocal rather than subordinate relations", with the result that "hierarchy and equality are not necessarily incompatible", but may and, indeed, regularly co-occur (1992:207). From these observations, Alexander (1992:207-208) suggests that to reify ascribed status as a "system" may constitute "premature conceptualization". The same may be said of "egality" and "egalitarian". In both cases, it is not the presence of a "system", but rather the combination of egalitarian and hierarchical values with structures of equality/inequality that raises the more pertinent questions concerning the processes by which "egality" and "hierarchy" are socially realized and reproduce themselves through time (see Alexander 1992:208).

In an inverse way, others have also questioned the appropriateness of the term "egalitarian" when applied to the Iban. Thus, Rousseau (1980:54) has argued that, in the case of the Iban, "an egalitarian ideology", in actuality, "hid a structure of inequality" and that traditional Iban society was, in fact, composed of three "largely hereditary status levels" (1980:59-60). Freeman (1981), in response, has cogently laid out the distinctively "egalitarian" — and in particular non-ascriptive — features of Iban social and political life. He seriously weakens his argument, however, by downplaying the presence of objective inequalities.

In this regard, Murray (1981), in a less sweeping critique, points up the seemingly contradictory association of an egalitarian ideology with overt social and material inequalities. Unlike Rousseau, she argues, however, for the critical importance of ideology, seeing it as a major factor that prevents these inequalities from assuming a permanently institutionalized form. Later, I will return to these and other arguments, but here, in addressing the larger issues involved, it is important to locate the problematic of the debate where it rightly belongs, within Iban society itself, and so to approach the question of "egalitarianism" by seeing it — not only as a question of analytical concepts — but as an actor's problem as well.

At the level of everyday cultural values, the Iban are an assertively egalitarian people. Thus they guide their daily life by an *adat* order that inscribes equality of condition as a fundamental social premise. According to Iban *adat*, every individual is equal by potential, sharing identical rights and obligations, without inherited distinction or privilege. Like the white cotton threads referred to in the saying by which I preface this paper — and from which Iban women begin the complex process of dyeing and weaving *ikat*-textiles — all persons are thought to begin life equal, equivalent and undifferentiated. But Iban society is also intensely competitive. Through competition individuals gain distinction and earn a place for themselves in the social order. Thus the Iban compete not only to assert their equality — to prove themselves equal to others — but they also seek, if possible, to excel and so exceed others in material wealth, power and reputation.

What is significant to note, however, is that equality of potential is, for the Iban, a precondition for the attainment of achieved inequality. The two, in other words, are not in opposition, but are dialectically related (Sather 1989). Through competition persons are both individuated — gaining for themselves "name" (*nama*) and "reputation" (*berita*) — in short, "making themselves seen" (*mandang ka diri'*) — and, at the same time, they are also socially differentiated, attaining in the process of competition social position and assuming roles and community statuses on the basis of their achieved inequalities of reputation, experience, skills, wealth and power. The resulting outcome is, by intention, unequal. Thus it can be argued that the nature of Iban cultural premises is such that they make cognitive sense of **both** equality **and** inequality — of sameness as well as of difference.

Like the coloured cotton threads which, following dyeing, Iban women weave on their looms to create textile designs, each individual is, at once, differentiated as a result of competition, becoming figurative as the saying says, "red, yellow, green, and blue", and, at the same time, he or she is incorporated into the social fabric by his or her achievements, thereby assuming a unique place within its overall design. The textile metaphor thus maps a cognitive image of society that is by nature both equal and unequal, its members, as social actors, alike in potential, yet differentiated and unequal by outcome.

Beginning with this metaphor, and returning to it once again at the end, I will try in this paper to show how, for the Iban, cultural understandings serve as one of the means by which Iban actors attempt to make sense of the social, political and material inequalities that are present in a society that is otherwise dominated by egalitarian values. Drawing on my fieldwork with the Saribas Iban, I will attempt to show how, in part, inequality of outcome is conceptualized as a kind of "proportional equality" (Lakoff 1964), that is to say, inequality is seen as largely proportional to merit. Thus those who achieve more are expected to win greater honour in relative proportion to their greater achievement. Inequality is also "historicized" and linked to the past achievements of ancestral founders whose accomplishments to some degree "freeze" merit, making its rewards available to successive generations of future descendants.

Finally, while principles of egality structure major areas of Iban social life, they are balanced, particularly in the ritual domain, by principles of precedence and hierarchy. This conjunction of "egality" and "hierarchy", I argue, forms another way in which the Iban come to terms with inequality. The resulting articulation is made possible by the fact that personal success is won largely outside the *adat* community, through actions undertaken in an external world beyond the immediate boundaries of each individual's longhouse. Success, moreover, is valorized by public rituals in which the participants, drawn from a wider regional society, enact a social order modelled, not on the everyday world of immediate experience, but on an unseen, idealized world of the gods, spiritheroes and ancestral dead. Hierarchy is thus constituted within a ritual context, distinct from the largely egalitarian relations of everyday longhouse life, and its constitution projects an image of inequality that is, while non-egalitarian, yet distinctively individuated and non-ascriptive, and so congruent with the essentially egalitarian ethos asserted in other social domains. Each individual, rather than being aggregated into a socially-defined stratum, is expected to gain for himself and to ritually validate a fluid personal ranking, which is fixed and rendered inalterable only by death. At death, a summation is made of each individual's accomplishments. On this basis are determined the details of death and mourning ritual. In Iban belief this final aggregate ranking, together with any other intangible marks of achievement that were won in life, are carried by the soul of the dead on its journey to the Otherworld. Status inequality is thus returned, as we shall see, to the unseen world from which it derives. Paradoxically, while the Otherworld is conceptually hierarchized, achieved inequalities are thereby removed from the living world and so made uninheritable. As a consequence, the members of each new generation must start afresh — like undyed cotton threads — attaining distinction and a place for themselves in the social fabric by their own initiative and effort.

Iban Egalitarianism

The richly detailed ethnographic writings of Derek Freeman (1970, 1981) present the most sustained argument in favour of Iban "egalitarianism". Thus Freeman maintains that Iban social organization, with its pervasive emphasis on "choice rather than prescription", approximates in practice what John Locke (1690) portrayed in the ideal, "a state of perfect freedom and equality" in which all are free:

> to order their actions and dispose of their possessions and persons, as they think fit, ...; without asking leave, or depending upon the will of any other man ... (quoted in Freeman 1981:51).

Freeman's arguments are complex. However, three points stand out as central:

First, under the terms of Iban *adat*, all persons are viewed as "equal" or "alike" (*sama* or *sebaka*) (1981:50). Secondly, while marked differences of wealth, power, and prestige exist, there are no ascribed strata. Thus, in principle, any individual of ability may, by his or her own effort, gain prestige and become a respected leader. In place of ascribed ranking there exists an "elaborate prestige system" in which all are free to compete on a more or less equal footing (1981:38). Unencumbered by hereditary privilege, Iban social organization encourages, Freeman (1981:50) argues, "the emergence of individual talent and creativity", including the rise of "natural leaders" to positions of power.

Thirdly, Iban society was historically acephalous. Until the establishment of the Brooke Raj, beginning in the mid-nineteenth century, there were no permanently constituted positions of formal authority above the longhouse level (cf. Pringle 1970:157). This is not to say that regional leadership was lacking, but that it took a distinctively "egalitarian" character (see Sather 1994:9-17). Thus both regional and longhouse leaders had, and, in the latter case, continue to have, only limited power, exerting authority mainly by persuasion and consensus. In all social undertakings allegiance to leaders is voluntary and the absence of coercive authority — the right of a leader to use force against recalcitrant followers — is pervasive, its absence permeating Iban social life, down even to the level of the *bilik*-family (Freeman 1981:47).

Equality and *Adat*

Although Freeman stresses the significance of *adat*, it figures very little in the Iban "egalitarianism" debate. This is unfortunate as *adat* is seen by the Iban themselves as a normative order that is very largely constitutive of society (Heppel 1975; Sather 1980). Thus every longhouse is thought to comprise an *adat* community, the continued existence of which depends upon its members behaving as the rules of *adat* require. According to *adat*, equality of condition is a fundamental premise. No overt recognition is given to ranking or to hierarchical status in defining interpersonal rights and obligations, with the single, partial exception discussed later in this paper of *adat mati* or death rules. This exception aside, every adult, according to the terms of *adat*, is subject to the same rights and duties, without inherited distinction or regard to his or her achieved status, and, in principle, is equally empowered to act within the longhouse as an autonomous agent in jural matters (Freeman 1981:50). The basic unit of Iban society is the *bilik*-family, and all adult family members, whether they were born into the group, married-in, adopted, or incorporated — male or female — share identical rights of membership (Freeman 1957).[3]

Not only is egality expressed through the normative rules of *adat*, and in adherence to these rules in longhouse relationships, but it is also affirmed in the workings of the *aum* (v.f. *baum*), a deliberative face-to-face meeting of longhouse members convened by the community headman (*tuai rumah*) whenever matters of common interest arise, for deliberations concerned with the administration of *adat*, or with repairing disturbances to the ritual order (cf. Cramb 1989:281; Sather 1980:xxiv-xxvi). Although some families take a more active role in these discussions than others, the tenor of the *aum* is markedly democratic. Every adult has a voice, dissenting views are normally respected, and whenever a decision is reached, discussions are characteristically lengthy and generally strive for unanimity.

By contrast, *adat* in neighbouring "stratified" societies very largely concerns status obligations and entitlements of rank. Thus, coastal Melanau society, to take one example, was historically divided into three rank categories corresponding roughly, Morris (1978:48, 1983) tells us, to "aristocrat" (*menteri*), "freeman" (*bumi*) and "slave" (*dipen*). Not only did elders of the aristocratic stratum monopolize *adat*, its enforcement and oral transmission, but the rules of *adat* themselves functioned mainly in the past to stipulate the ways in which individual Melanau expressed membership in one or the other of these categories in their overt public behaviour. Thus, for example, on the occasions of births, namings and death, *adat* stipulated the details of ritual behaviour and the symbols, insignia and forms of speech appropriate between members of different ascribed strata. It also defined the corvée services and material gifts that commoners and slaves owed chiefly families and the occasions on which these were due (Morris 1983:3).

The Iban situation is profoundly different. While *de facto* inequality is certainly present, the framework of cultural understandings differs with the result that such inequality is perceived as having a different source and is understood and socially expressed in very different ways. Thus, for the Iban, inequality is thought to be a matter of achievement rather than birth-right. Consequently, it is equality, not inequality, that is inscribed in *adat*. While every individual, in principle at least, is thought to begin life more or less equal, it is not "equality" that is the goal in the sense of sameness, but "proportional equality", the ideal that inequality should be relative to merit; that if one person accomplishes more than another, he or she should enjoy greater reputation and esteem in proportion to his or her greater accomplishments. Iban institutions also work, as we shall see, to mitigate the consequences of inequality and so to assure that most persons enjoy some minimum of achieved respect.

Egalitarian Leadership

Of Freeman's three points, the most contentious has proved to be the last: his characterization of Iban leadership as voluntaristic and consensual. Thus Marshall Sahlins (1958:313), in an early review of Freeman's *Iban Agriculture* (1955), noted that while Iban political institutions appear to be "elementary" — "hardly surpassing a family level of integration" — the Iban were historically able to organize large-scale war parties, comprising hundreds, at times thousands, of warriors. Sahlins questioned how this was possible in the absence of chieftainship, ascribed ranking, or corporate descent groups.

In his essay on the kindred, Freeman (1961) gave a partial answer. Thus, he noted that the highly ramifying and preferentially endogamous kindred networks of the Iban extend from longhouse to longhouse, over entire river watersheds, thereby providing the basis for large-scale mobilization, including in the past mobilization of warriors for raiding and predatory expansion, Moreover, as Freeman (1961:214) goes on to observe, in assembling war parties, "institutionalized authority" was not required, that is to say, authority which "allows its holder to discipline unwilling followers". This was because Iban men joined war parties by choice. They come together of their own free will, under the leadership of men of demonstrated ability, who were able to attract and hold their allegiance by virtue of their personal qualities as leaders. Thus Iban war parties took the form of "loosely organized" companies of "free and equal men" (1961:214). Leaders and followers alike shared a common interest in gaining personal renown, were usually kin, and in coming together both, in Freeman's terms, "were doing what they were doing because they wanted to" (1961:214). Each, it may be said, acted in accordance with the Iban notion of *muntis ka diri'*, "choosing for oneself".

Donald Brown (1979) has more recently re-examined the question of Iban leadership. He begins by applauding Freeman's emphasis upon its consensual basis (1979:20) and like Ulla Wagner (1972), he argues that the power of Iban leaders was consistently underestimated in the past because it does not fit well with Western notions of authority. Thus, while the Iban lacked the "hereditary chiefs" and ascribed ranking of some of their neighbours, they nevertheless "did in fact enjoy governmental institutions", including, in the pre-Brooke and early historical period, a permanent pattern of supra-local leadership (Brown 1979:16; see Sather 1994:9-12).

In the Saribas river area of Sarawak, regional leaders were known traditionally as *tuai menoa*. The most powerful of these were drawn from the *raja berani*, literally "the rich and brave", and were typically self-made men with a reputation for military prowess, resourcefulness and wealth. Reputation was gained primarily through farming success, trade in surplus rice, fairness in dealing with others; migrational leadership; and from bravery and personal leadership in warfare and raiding. Greatest renown attached to those who were recognized as major war leaders. Such men were called *tau' serang* or *tau' kayau* [*tau'*, "have the capacity", "be able to"; *serang*, "attack"; *kayau*, "war" or "raid"], and in the past no title carried greater prestige or was more sought after.

In nineteenth-century Sarawak, Iban war leaders, when they were first encountered by European observers, were indisputably powerful figures, capable of entering into military alliances with one another and of mobilizing hundreds of followers under their direction, for territorial expansion, raiding and the defence of their home rivers. In newly-opened regions, *tuai menoa* allocated settlement areas among their followers, arbitrated boundary disputes and set aside forest reserves (*pulau ban*) for communal use as a source of boat- and house-building timber (cf. Sather 1994:11-12). In the past, military status, like many other types of status in Iban society, was finally ranked or *be-rintai*. Thus, a young man who displayed bravery on the battlefield was called a *bujang berani* or "brave bachelor". If he succeeded in killing or taking the head of an enemy (*bedengah*), he was entitled to receive an *ensumbar* or "praise-name". The most successful and experienced warriors serving under a senior war leader's command were called his *manok sabong*, literally his "fighting cocks". In the past *tuai menoa*, including *tau' serang*, generally settled their most trusted *manok sabong* at the *pintu kayau* ("doors of war"), the areas along the frontiers of their domain most vulnerable to attack or invasion. Once a man gained a reputation for bravery and judgment, others might join him, under his leadership, on small raids (*anak kayau*) of his own devising. Only gradually, after having achieved success as an independent leader, was a man likely to begin his ascent to the status of a veteran war leader (*tau' kayau*). Only a man of exceptional abilities, who had managed to gather around him a following of seasoned warriors, and who was able to forge alliances with others and had demonstrated his ability to mobilize and lead large-scale raids and defensive campaigns, was likely to be accorded the highest rank and acknowledged as a *tau' serang* (cf. Sandin 1980:80-81; Sather 1994:12). Such men were extremely rare. They were also believed, in addition, to be supernaturally-inspired.

Brown describes the *tau' serang* as the holder of a political "commission" (cf. Brown 1973a), in this case, what he calls a "charismatic commission". The *tau' serang* obtains his "commission", not by appointment or succession, but by means of a dream experience, or by a series of dreams in which his future success as a war leader is foretold. Such dreams were considered to be a sign of direct spiritual inspiration and were typically accompanied by gifts from the guiding spirit-heroes or gods of magically-potent war charms (*pengaroh*) (Sandin 1966). Success in war served to validate such dreams, giving authenticity to an aspiring leader's commission. It also, as a rule, permitted successful war leaders to attract still larger followings and to enter into warring alliances with other successful leaders.[4] With the establishment of Brooke rule in the second half of the nineteenth century, this pattern of competitive regional leadership was superseded by the creation of formal administrative districts under officially-appointed Penghulu or "native chiefs". Thus the Iban were brought within a centralized governmental structure. Although *tau' kayau* and *tau' serang* were sometimes appointed as Penghulu, this centralized structure was externally imposed and succession was routinized in a way diametrically opposed to traditional Iban political values (Freeman 1981:15-24; Sather 1980:xiv-xxviii).

In referring to Iban war leaders of the past, Brown (1979:18) contrasts a "commission", characterized by what he calls "ad hoc or discontinuous leadership", with an "office", characterized by "a system of perpetual succession". The *tau' serang*'s commission, unlike an "office", attached to his person alone and was not derived from any overarching governmental authority. Instead, it came from what was taken to be a "sign" of direct supernatural authorization. I shall return to the issue of leadership again presently, but the point that Brown makes here is an important one: namely, that the *tau' serang* and other veteran Iban war leaders, though not office-holders or part of a formally constituted hierarchy of authority, represented nevertheless highly effective leaders, who, operating above the level of the longhouse, were a regular feature of traditional Iban society, exercising very real power, even though the positions they occupied were not "regularly constituted" in the sense that each individual leader had to obtain and validate his own personal dream-commission, there being, until the beginnings of colonial rule, "no way to pass one person's commission on to a successor" (Brown 1979:17).

The Concept of *Pun*

In a critical rejoinder to Rousseau (1980), Freeman (1981) presents a more detailed account of Iban leadership than is contained in his earlier work. Here he points up in particular the connection that exists between what he sees as the distinctively egalitarian nature of Iban leadership — its consensual, non-instituted basis — and what he rightly calls "a most fundamental concept of traditional Iban society, that of *pun*" (1981:31).

Literally, *pun* means source, basis, origin, or cause (Richards 1981:290; Sather 1993:75-76). Its root meaning "is that of stem, as of a tree, from which the development of any kind of activity springs" (Freeman 1981:31). In reference to group undertakings, *pun* typically describes the person who initiates or originates an action, who announces its purpose, and enlists others to join him or her in bringing this purpose about. As an example, Freeman (1981:35) describes the *bejalai*, a journey undertaken, primarily by young men to gain wealth and social recognition:

> A *bejalai* group was formed by an experienced individual announcing his intention to undertake such a journey; and as others *chose* [emphasis in the original] to join him, and a group of individuals with common interests formed, so he became its *pun bejalai*, and its leader (*tuai*).

Similarly, with other undertakings — migration, for example, the construction of a new longhouse, or the launching of a raid — each is initiated by a *pun*, who, once the action is under way, became, for the members of the group formed to carry it out, their *tuai* or leader (lit. "elder"). The point that Freeman makes is that anyone who chooses to may assume the role of initiator and provided he proves himself competent, may attract and hold a following as its leader. Those who follow an initiator's lead, and so recognize him as their *tuai*, do so voluntarily, of their own free will. Thus the *tuai*'s position is in no sense ascriptive, or socially prescribed, and, as Freeman (1981:38) aptly puts it, each "individual had [traditionally] to be the source (*pun*) of his own achievements".

But in addition to this, the notion of *pun* has also a range of further meaning that reflects a different and somewhat more complex image of Iban leadership. Not all groups in Iban society are short-lived like those formed for *bejalai* or to carry out a raid. In this respect, the term *pun* may also convey a notion of group continuity. For example, a *pun tusut* refers to a "main-line" genealogy from which branching or collateral lines are said to "break off" (*mechah ari*, v.f.).[5] Each branching line has a new "source" and the potential of becoming a main-line itself in time. This same imagery of "stem" and "breaking off" also applies to the *bilik*-family and is used to describe the processes of family succession and partition. Partition, like genealogical branching, is described as "breaking from the *bilik*" (*mechah ari bilik*). The seceding family is distinguished as the "new family" (*bilik baru*) and, similarly, its founder, with regard to its other members, becomes its new "source" or *pun* (Sather 1990:32-34, 1993:68-70). At the same time, continuity is marked by a succession of *pun*. Thus every *bilik*-family has a *pun bilik*. From its founding onward, it is through the person of its successive *pun bilik* that a family is said "to be continued" (*tampong*) from generation to generation. Thus the *pun bilik* is the acknowledged heir through whom, in each generation, *bilik* rights and possessions are said to devolve (cf. Sather 1993:70). As such, the "family source" represents the living embodiment of *bilik* continuity, the chief link between its present and past generations, and the reference point in terms of whom all other members reckon their *bilik* affiliation. The continuing succession of *pun bilik* thus symbolizes the continuing life of the *bilik*-family, including that of its jointly held assets and sacra, for which the *pun* is the primary custodian. Similarly, every longhouse, too, has a *pun*. At the time of house-construction, the *pun rumah* acts as the original founder by erecting the first house-post, but also, with the passage of time, like the *pun bilik*, the original *pun rumah* is succeeded by a continuing series of successors, each of whom embodies the community's continuing existence and serves as the principal custodian of its sacra, particularly its cooling charms or *ubat penyelap* (Sather 1993:68-74).

Pun in this second sense thus represents a locus of continuity, the "stem" through which the continuing life of any permanently constituted social group is thought to flow. The same principle applies to families, longhouses, and to entire riverine societies, all groups that, for the Iban, endure through time.

Recognition of this double meaning of *pun*, as both initiator and locus of continuity, helps illuminate the historical dynamics of Iban leadership. Thus in times of outward expansion, the Iban were able to throw up an array of effective leaders, who, as initiators of action and organizers of collective projects, led migrations, pioneered new areas of settlement, defeated rivals and competitors in war, felled the jungle, and founded new longhouses and *bilik*-families. Those who were successful in these undertakings were, and continue to be, remembered, and so form the principal founders and connecting links in the main-line genealogies by which the Iban remember and celebrate their ancestral past (Sather 1994:27). Those who can claim direct connection to these leaders stood, and continue to stand the best chance of becoming longhouse *pun* and *tuai* and of making their own genealogies the principal main-line *tusut* of the longhouses and riverine communities in which they live. Later on, in times of social and territorial consolidation, when the flow of migrants slows or ceases, successive generations of leaders, by invoking their genealogical links to these historical founders were able to assert a connection to this formative past, including its initiating "sources" (*pun*), and so were able to link their own claims to leadership to a potent image of societal origins and continuity. Hence, in this way, in long-settled areas such as the Saribas, genealogies and related oral historical narratives assume, in the competition for power and office, major political significance.[6]

Objective Inequality and the Absence of Stratification

In a final critique, Tania Murray (1981) offers what she describes as a "qualification" of Freeman's egalitarianism thesis. She challenges specifically his second point, namely that power, wealth and prestige are equally open to all. Basically Murray (1981:29) argues that "differential access to key means of production", namely to land for swidden cultivation, capital and other resources for investment in cash crops, produce marked inequalities between Iban families and that these inequalities give some *bilik* an enduring advantage over others. Such advantage, however, is never fully institutionalized. This is because of the existence, Murray maintains, of a well-developed "egalitarian ideology" which prevents the crystallization of objective inequalities into a system of formal stratification. In terms of causality, Murray (1981:28) thus argues in her analysis for the relative autonomy of ideology.

In Murray's view a central tenet of Iban ideology is the premise that material success rests chiefly with the individual and is more or less commensurate with effort (1981:29). Here, however, reality, she suggests, is at odds with ideology. Iban *bilik* differ notably in the amount and quality of farmland they possess, with the result that some are much better positioned to succeed than others. Moreover, such advantage is heritable.

In Borneo, in some swidden societies, including, according to Rousseau (1987), the "stratified" Kayan, farmland is said to revert to longhouse management after each cycle of agricultural use.[7] Cultivation rights are thus recongnized for only a single cropping, after which fallow land reverts to the community at large for future reallocation. In contrast, the Iban recognize permanent household rights of cultivation. Once land is cleared of primary forest, rights to its future re-cultivation devolve on the clearer's *bilik*-family and are inherited by successive generations of family members as part of the *bilik*'s estate. Thus, while equal rights prevail within the family, disparities in landholding are not only possible, but are the rule between *bilik*.

As long as stands of primary forest (*kampong*) remain within a longhouse domain (*menoa rumah*), individual families are able to enlarge their estate by annual forest felling (*berimba*). But once all land is felled, they must depend for future cultivation, from this point onward, on inherited plots of farmland cleared originally by previous generations of *bilik* members. It is at this point, when the community moves from a "pioneer" to an "established" system of swidden cultivation, that inherited inequalities in land-holding become permanent. Those who tend to be advantaged are most often core households whose members trace their ancestry back to the original pioneers and house-founders who first settled the longhouse domain and so initiated, and engaged over a greater number of generations, in the process of forest clearing. Such families have generally had a longer time in which to accumulate cultivation plots than those whose founders arrived later in the process. In this regard, economic advantage tends to reinforce the advantage which core families already enjoy in terms of their claims to local political and ritual leadership.

In the Saribas region inherited inequalities in land-holding are well documented. Except for the Rimbas, the principal tributaries of the main Saribas, including its upper reaches in the Layar, were first settled by Iban pioneers some 15 or 16 generations ago (Sandin 1967:16-23). The shift to an established pattern of swidden cultivation was completed, according to local genealogical traditions, some seven to eight generations ago, near the beginning of the nineteenth century, roughly one to two generations before the founding of the

Brooke Raj (cf. Cramb 1987; Sather 1990). Since then, the Saribas Iban have farmed inherited land, recleared each year from earlier cultivation and farmed by means of a long-estalished system of forest-fallow rotation (Cramb 1987; Sather 1985, 1990). Today no primary forest exists in these rivers, except for small ritually-interdicted islets (*pulau mali*), located chiefly along hilltops.[8] In a detailed study of longhouse tenure, Robert Cramb (1989:284-285) has shown that for a representative upper Layar longhouse the most favoured 20 per cent of all *bilik*-families control 33 per cent of the total hill-rice plots within the community; the least favoured 20 per cent, only three per cent; while around a third of all *bilik* have insufficient land to observe an adequate cycle of fallow rotation. While better favoured families may lend or rent land to those who are less favoured, the extent of inequality is pronounced and its consequences are plainly visible.

The felling of primary forest "closes", Murray (1981:32) argues, "channels of social mobility", thereby ensuring the future material advantage of some households over others. The question she poses is why these inequalities have not given rise to institutions of formal ranking such as those that exist among the Kayan, Kenyah, Lahanan and others. Part of the answer, Murray suggests (1981:30-31), lies in migration. "The right of mobility is a key element", representing, she insists, "the crucial political difference" between the Iban and stratified communities like the Kayan, where chiefs strictly proscribe their subjects' movement (Rousseau 1978:86).[9] For the Iban, freedom of movement acted as a check in the past on the authority of longhouse and regional leaders and levelled existing inequalities by allowing those who were disadvantaged to improve their lot by moving to new areas where unfelled land was still abundant. Here new *bilik* estates could be established and ambitious men could gain renown among their contemporaries and prominence among their future descendants as regional pioneers and *bilik*-founders.

The role of mobility, however, is both more limited and more complex than Murray's argument suggests. Although Iban *adat*, in principle, permits families to move "at will" (Freeman 1981:50), it imposes significant jural and ritual constraints on such movement (Sather 1993:73). In addition, migration was, and continues to be organized by groups, and, when it takes place, migration occurs under the guidance of recognized *tuai pindah*. Decisions to migrate are never made on a purely individual basis, but take place as part of a concerted enterprise involving other individuals and families, including, as we have already noted, an initiator (*pun*) and a migration leader (*tuai pindah*). Thus migration, as well as providing a means of social and economic mobility, was also bound up with competition for achieved status, and so was also an arena for future differentiation. Moreover, opportunities for migration were limited, even in the past. High levels of mobility characterized only frontier areas of recent territorial expansion, that in most areas of Iban settlement, disappeared early on in their pioneering history. By contrast, in long-settled areas like the Saribas, migration meant for those who chose to emigrate abandonment of inherited farmland, fruit trees and other assets representing generations of *bilik* investment. Here emigration has occurred chiefly as a counter to the division of *bilik* estates following upon household partition and its effects have been mainly to preserve the agricultural viability of those families that have remained behind. Thus migration has tended, in the Saribas region at least, to reduce land-holding inequalities in the home area, both by removing the most seriously disadvantaged and by the reallocation of land among the remaining *bilik*. But, at the same time, migration also laid the foundations for new inequalities within the areas being settled. Thus migrant families, in pioneering a new area, attempted to lay claim to as large a cultivation reserve as they could by forest felling. In this way they sought to "historicize" their achievement, assuring by this means the future advantage of their descendants over the members of other households.

Finally, it must be noted that by means of the longhouse *aum* temporary cultivation rights may be extended from one *bilik*-family to another, as, for example, through the lending of plots of land for a single farming season (*nasih tanah*), or by gift or rental arrangements (Sather 1980:xix). Such temporary transfers are common and occur primarily as a way of ensuring that all families within a longhouse have access to sufficient land to provide for at least their minimal subsistence needs (Cramb 1989:282). In extreme instances of land shortage this may involve even the pooling of separate *bilik* holdings and their reallocation annually by the community as a whole (cf. Cramb 1987, 1989). An important corollary to Iban notions of egality under *adat* is a strongly developed sense that no family should be shamed or denied the minimal means necessary to assert its self-worth — hence none should be denied the requirements of survival, nor what is minimally required, provided they apply themselves, to compete with others for some modicum of respect. Here clearly egalitarian values play a role in the way in which Iban communities manage their land resources. Thus, in administering cultivation rights, specific *adat* rules, through decisions arrived at by the *aum*, may be modified, set aside, or applied by community consensus in ways that serve the overriding goal of maintaining some minimal degree of equality between longhouse families. These provisions — while not eliminating inequality — work to reduce its consequences, hence assuring, as a matter of community interest, a measure of longhouse equality.

Murray argues, as her final point, that in order to understand why unequal access to land and capital resources have not resulted in institutionalized inequality, we must consider in addition the role of trade and labour relations in the traditional Iban economy.

The Iban have for centuries engaged in inter-regional trade, beginning well before European penetration of western Borneo. For the Iban, rice, the primary food staple, was also traditionally a major item of trade, at least until the introduction of cash crops and more recently labour migration. Thus surplus rice, rather than being redistributed within the community, shared out, or used in feasting or for ceremonial exchange, was externally traded, mainly to coastal Malay enclaves, largely through riverine trading channels. Thus families with surplus rice [and, to a lesser extent, forest products] annually traded these items for durable prestige wealth, principally imported jars and brassware. As an apparent consequence of this trade, intra-community sharing was minimized, and even among kin, rice tended to be traded or sold rather than being shared in the form of gifts or by means of ceremonial exchange. In transactions between kin, other items aside from rice were traditionally given, and indeed still are, notably vegetables, fruit and domestic fowl. Each *bilik*, in terms of its rice production, thus sought to accumulate its own trading surplus, even in the face of uncertain swiddening conditions,[10] thereby reinforcing its relative autonomy *vis-à-vis* others. Owing to these characteristics, Sahlins (1972:224) singles the Iban out, and indeed other Bornean swidden agriculturalists as well, as being atypical of "tribal societies" in the extent to which they limit the sharing of staple food surpluses.

The prestige goods which a household received in return for the sale of its rice, among other functions, served traditionally as a buffer against poor harvests.[11] As Freeman (1970:267) writes:

> In good years when a surplus of *padi* has been gained, it is exchanged for gongs, which are then available in years of shortage. Each season some families succeed in producing a surplus, while others find themselves with a deficit; and so, year by year ..., scores of different families exchange gongs for *padi*, or *padi* for gongs. Jars, though to a much lesser extent, are used in the same way. Again, money — obtained from the marketing of forest produce — is often used to purchase *padi*; and of recent years, cash crops — particularly rubber — have become increasingly important.

Today cash crops and outside wages have very largely taken over the role of rice in trade, but the same principles hold, and the significant point to be made is that each family directs its surplus production to the acquisition of money and durable prestige wealth, and that, while this wealth serves as an insurance against want, it is used, as a rule, neither to increase future household production nor to gain control over the labour of others. In short, it is not institutionally invested to reproduce permanent economic advantage.

This long-standing involvement in trade also shapes, Murray (1981:42) argues, the nature of labour relations, the latter forming, in turn, "a crucial factor in the self-definition of the Iban". The chief norm, largely followed in practice, is that household land is worked by household labour. However, most families also engage, at least two or three times during the annual rice-farming cycle in inter-family labour exchange. This is called *bedurok* and involves primarily close kin, friends and longhouse neighbours, collectively *kaban belayan*. The fundamental characteristic of *bedurok* relations is that they operate on a principle of strict reciprocity. Thus each household gives a day's labour to each of its *bedurok* partners in return for a day's labour from each on its own farm. Labour is thus exchanged for labour on the basis of strict parity and no household gains additional labour from its *bedurok* partners. In this sense, the exchange is a perfect expression of the principle I have labelled "egality". The advantage of *bedurok* is that farm-work is completed more quickly on each *bilik*'s farm and that this work takes place in a sociable atmosphere.[12] Except for the infirm and very young, no one is normally exempt from farmwork, and each household, through its *bedurok* relations, keeps precise control over its labour credits and debts, exchanging labour with others only on the basis of strict equivalence. Thus, again, favoured households can not, as a rule, translate their material advantage into additional labour, nor can they gain through *bedurok* a share of the surplus production of other households. Rice, however, may be traded for labour, giving, as we shall see presently, an edge to those who are economically favoured.[13]

Here Murray (1981:40) argues that these features of Iban society contributed to the formation, and are themselves a reflection, of a distinctive "self-understanding", a collective "definition of self", that constitutes, she maintains, the "generative principle" behind much of Iban social practice, including the absence of ascribed ranking. Thus, in an ideological sense, the Iban define themselves as autonomous, freely-mobile individuals; independent producers, each person separately able to trade his surplus production for a profit, disliking authority, and unhampered by hereditary relations of subordination. This self-definition acts both as a prerequisite to interpersonal competition and, at the same time, makes the Iban "unwilling to work for others and hence curtails the development of [permanent] political and economic inequalities" (1981:35).

While Murray's essay sheds valuable light on the nature of Iban "egalitarianism", pointing up, in particular, the significance of objective inequalities, her distinction between ideology and practice is often obscure and at times circular. Here, I think, rather than arguing for the causal autonomy of ideology, it is more useful to see Iban society, at the level of cultural understandings, as combining, in an internally coherent way, both "hierarchy" and "egality", and it is primarily the implications of this argument that I pursue in the remainder of this paper.

Equality and Hierarchy

Most local communities reside within a single longhouse (*rumah*). The latter consists of a series of laterally-joined family apartments (*bilik*), a passageway (*tempuan*), and open galleries (*ruai*), each section of the structure being owned and maintained by a separate family. The household or *bilik*-family normally contains three generations — parents, a son or daughter, and his or her spouse and their dependent children. The Iban household is ideally a persisting group. It is characteristically perpetuated in each generation by one child, real or adopted, who remains in the natal apartment after marriage and so acts as the principal heir to the household's estate, including its *bilik*. This heir may be equally a son or daughter (cf. Freeman 1957). As we have noted, most longhouses in the Saribas region contain a set of core families whose members are related to one another by close cognatic ties and who claim descent, characteristically by known genealogical ties, through an unbroken line of *pun bilik*, from the settlement's original founders. Such households tend to occupy the central apartments within the longhouse and generally control a larger share of cultivation plots than others. Other households are related more distantly, typically tracing their connections to the community's founders through the genealogies of one or more of its core *bilik*.

A longhouse is typically founded by an accomplished leader, who, once it is established, becomes the community's "house source" (*pun rumah*) and usually also its headman or "house elder" (*tuai rumah*). The positions of "house source" and "house elder" are separable, however, and, subsequent to its founding, they may be held by different individuals. In fact, in the lower Saribas, this is generally preferred, mainly because it is felt that the ritual sacra which the *pun rumah* cares for should not be exposed to the "heat" (*angat*) associated with the trouble cases and litigation which the *tuai rumah* hears at his family's section of the gallery. While the headman typically deals with mundane matters and acts as a local intermediary between the community and the state, the *pun rumah*, as the living embodiment of the community's founding ancestors, performs mainly a ritual office. At its founding, and subsequently each time a longhouse is rebuilt, the *pun rumah* erects the first support pillar (*tiang pemun*). The erection (*ngentak*) of this pillar ritually initiates the main phase of longhouse-construction (cf. Sather 1993:74-75). Ideally this principal source post is erected at the centre of the longhouse structure and as soon as it is raised, the main support posts of each of the other *bilik*-families comprising the house are erected in order, one at a time, moving outward from the *pun rumah*'s central post, first upriver and then downriver (see Sather 1993:76-77). The *pun rumah*'s post can thus be said to centre and establish the principal orientation for the community as an internally structured-whole. The erection of the first source pillar is accompanied by a major sacrifice and invocations which together establish the pillar's status as the principal *tiang pemun* for the community as a whole and its custodian, the *pun rumah*, as the owner of the *adat genselan*, the *adat* by which the longhouse is preserved in a "cool" or ritually benign state (Sather 1993:73). Longhouses are continually threatened with the intrusion of spirits and other malevolent forces, by social disharmony, and the breach of ritual prohibitions (*pemali*), all of which may cause the community to become "hot" (*angat*). When this occurs, the *pun rumah* is normally called upon to perform the rites by which it may be restored to a "cool" or ritually benign state (*penyelap*), including the blood lustration (*genselan*) of the central *tiang pemun* and the application of special cooling charms (*ubat penyelap*) generally kept attached to the top of this post.

What is significant for our purposes here is that the offices of "source" (*pun*) and "elder" (*tuai*) act to hierarchize the chief structural units comprising the longhouse community in the Dumontian sense of "encompassment" (1970). Thus, as we have noted, there are both family and longhouse *pun* and *tuai*. Within the longhouse, each *tuai bilik*, in matters of *adat*, comes under the authority (*kuasa*) of the *tuai rumah*. The incorporation of the *bilik* within the larger *adat* community — and the corresponding relationship between the *bilik* elder and the longhouse headman — are symbolized most explicitly in the rules that regulate the use of the family hearths (*adat dapur*), including their initial installation in the longhouse at the time of house-construction (Sather 1993:73).[14] These rules symbolize the household's jural presence within the community and the bounds that incorporate it in the longhouse as a whole. The rupture of these bounds, as, for example, when a family departs to take up residence in another longhouse, must be preceded by a ritual "throwing away of the hearth" (*muai dapur*) and the payment of ritual reparation to those who remain. Similarly, the relationship between the *pun bilik* and the *pun rumah* is expressed in the ritual priority of the central source post over the secondary source posts belonging to each of the other *bilik*-families in the longhouse. Not only is the central *tiang pemun* the first to be erected (*ngentak ke-dulu*), but it takes ritual precedence over the others in the rites that are believed to safeguard the community's ritual well-being (cf. Sather 1993:75).

Beyond this level of internal encompassment and order represented by the *bilik* and longhouse, their respective "sources" and "elders", and symbolized by the hearths and posts, Iban social organization, as it transcends and knits together these groups, is also "based", as Freeman (1981:50) notes, "on the kindred". Thus, "in the classless society of the pagan Iban, kindred relationships were [and remain] pervasive" (1981:63).

Indeed, for the Iban, these relationships are not only pervasive but they are also highly inclusive. Thus the term *kaban*, which Freeman (1960, 1961) glosses as "kindred", refers, in fact, not only to an individual's cognates, but, in its most inclusive sense, to friends, neighbours, affines and acquaintances — to everyone, in short, who is not a "stranger", that is to say, not an *orang bukai*, literally "other people". Within this highly inclusive social field, the Iban distinguish more narrowly between *kaban mandal*, close personal cognates whose relationships are generally traceable, and *kaban tampil*, affines or, loosely, kin by marriage. At one level, all Iban feel themselves to be *kaban*. But more effectively, interlocking kindred networks, reinforced by endogamous marriage, provide the basis on which a multitude of groupings are typically formed, extending maximally, as we have said, over the entire river region in which each individual lives. In the past such ties were employed by regional leaders and men of ambition to organize war parties, mount *bejalai* expeditions or migrations, and to help keep the peace and arbitrate inter-longhouse conflict. They were also called into play on major ceremonial occasions and when new longhouses were built.

Another feature of Iban *kaban* relations is their strong generational emphasis. This is expressed in both intra-generational unity and inter-generational asymmetry. Thus a strong bond of solidarity characteristically exists between siblings which extends intra-generationally, across each generational level. Thus cousins and close friends, for example, tend to couch their relationship in a sibling idiom, regularly addressing each other as *menyadi*, or siblings. On the other hand, relations between generations are characteristically asymmetrical and generally marked by authority and respect. Consistent with the highly inclusive nature of Iban *kaban* ties, respect relations are generalized outward from the three-generation household and are extended to embrace the entire social field of cognates, affines, friends and longhouse neighbours — to everyone, in other words, who is not considered "other people". This generalization of respect relations is achieved in part by the use of teknonyms. Thus everyone who engages in frequent social relations is addressed, depending on sex and parental status, as "grandfather (*aki'*)", "grandmother (*ini'*)", "father (*apai*)", or "mother (*indai*) of so-and-so", using the name of a particular child or grandchild, or by personal name in the case of individuals who have not yet married and attained parental [or grandparental] status. This pervasive use of teknonyms produces a sociocentric categorization of society into three generational levels. Every person is located according to generation, as a child, parent, or grandparent, ensuring the observance, within the longhouse and among kindred, of appropriate degrees of respect. While inter-generational ties are thus unequal, it is, nonetheless, an inequality that is consistent with the egalitarian premises of Iban *adat*, in that all persons pass through these categories in time, regardless of their birth or achieved status, provided that they marry and bear children.[15] Moreover, while dividing the society into horizontal levels, these levels do not form a lineal order in that political and economic power tend to be concentrated in the parental generation at the middle. Although the young are generally unequal to the old, everyone, it is important to note, has the same opportunity to marry, bear children, and to grow old, hence even for those who otherwise enjoy little success in life, they can usually look forward in time, should they live long enough, to an honoured status in the community as categorical "parents" or "grandparents".

Finally, for the Iban, kindred relations are significantly structured by marriage. Iban marriage is very largely endogamous, both preferentially and in actuality. Iban marriage rules thus act to consolidate kindred ties and, secondly, to incorporate non-cognates and those in danger of becoming non-cognates back into the field of one's close kin. For the Iban, sexual relations (and hence marriage) are prohibited between all cognates of the same household, between siblings (full and half), and all cognates of different generational levels (Freeman 1960:73-74). The first of these prohibitions effectively embeds the household in the wider field of *kaban* relations. Marriage forges bonds of affinity between households, which, with the birth of children and the passage of generations, are converted into cognatic ties. Beyond the prohibited range of siblings, endogamous marriage is strictly intra-generational. Thus,

> The intermarriage of cousins constantly reinforces the network of cognatic ties linking individual Iban, and kin that might otherwise have become dispersed are brought together again (Freeman 1960:76).

The marriage of cousins thus incorporates affines (*kaban tampil*) and prevents the dissolution of existing cognatic networks. Such consolidation is a continuous process, as without intermarriage, cognates are likely eventually to become "strangers".

The emphasis in marital relations is on intra-generational solidarity. Following marriage, affinal ties tend to be reinterpreted as homologous cognatic relations, with the dominant emphasis on the solidarity of affines of the same generation. This is expressed not only at the level of marital alliance — for example, in the absence in most Iban communities of bridewealth and other forms of marriage payment potentially expressive of status differentiation — but it may also be seen in the interpersonal relationships that exist between affines themselves, notably between husbands and wives, their respective parents (*isan*), and co-siblings-in-law (*ipar*). Ideally, and very largely in practice, each of these relationships is complementary and reciprocal. The explicit aim in marriage negotiations is to maintain status equality between marriage partners and their *kaban*, and, following marriage, husbands and wives (*laki-bini*) tend to be treated as a single entity, for example, when they are called upon to perform parallel or complementary ritual functions during public gatherings.[16]

The Political Economy of Traditional Inequality

While relations of inequality are apparent within the longhouse and beyond, the dominant principle of everyday social relationships, as represented, for example, by community *adat* and the deliberations of the *aum*, labour-exchange, and intra-generational relations between kindred and affines, is clearly one of egality. But equally clearly, Iban egalitarianism belongs to the variety that Woodburn (1982:446-447) has called "competitive egalitarianism". Here, in contrast to the "non-competitive egalitarianism" of, for example, the !Kung and Hadza, in which "equality does not have to be earned or displayed ..., but is intrinsically present as an entitlement of all men", equality is, characteristically, "only a starting point, a qualification to compete in a strenuous competition for wealth, power and prestige" (1982:446), the outcome of which may, of course, be highly unequal.

But for the Iban, a further point of significance is that competition, particularly between males, centres largely on activities that are engaged in outside the local community. Hence, as we shall see, it is largely through deeds performed beyond the boundaries of the longhouse that unequal status within it was, and continues to be, measured.

Thomas Gibson (1990:125), in an insightful essay on warfare in insular Southeast Asia, has argued that the interior shifting agriculturalists of Indonesia, Borneo and the Philippines were historically involved in "a loosely integrated regional political economy" dominated, through coastal markets and trading states, by institutions of "raiding and coerced trade". While this economy allowed individual interior groups "a significant degree of autonomy over their internal political and ideological systems", the specific location of each group in terms of regional trade and raiding relations importantly shaped, Gibson (1990:125-126) argues, its members' attitudes not only towards war and aggression, but also, more importantly, with regard to hierarchy and social ranking. While some groups were victims of raiding and expropriative trade, others, like the Iban, dominated these relations at the expense of their regional neighbours.

Historically, down through the beginning of the twentieth century, the Iban flourished as the most expansionistic and successful of all inland shifting agriculturalists in western Borneo (Pringle 1970). Today the Iban number nearly 500,000 and form the largest single indigenous group in Sarawak. Iban longhouses are typically located along the banks of relatively large, navigable rivers and their tributaries, facilitating communication and making possible an often intense involvement in inter-regional trade. At the same time, the existence of rivers has allowed the Iban to mobilize in much larger numbers than other, more remotely located shifting agricultural groups. In the past, their settlement along major rivers also meant that, in order to survive, the Iban had, very early on, "to adopt more aggressive tactics in their own defense" (Gibson 1990:138). Aggression became an integral part of Iban relations with the outside world, and by the beginning of the nineteenth century, the Iban had emerged as a warring, highly expansive population, sweeping, as they moved north and eastward through central Sarawak, virtually all others before them, including a number of stratified communities. Following their pacification, which continued into the first two decades of the twentieth century, the Iban became widely travelled traders and migrant labourers (see Sandin 1994:235ff.; Sather 1994:21-24).

Within this regional setting, the Iban saw themselves, in relation to the external world, largely in predatory terms — as predators on neighbouring tribes, whom they raided for heads, captives and land; on the environment whose forests they felled for farms; and on the regional economy, where they traded rice and forest products and earned wages, or where they gained prestige wealth, as surplus producers, migrant workers and traders (cf. Gibson 1990:140). It was from this predatory engagement with the outside world that prestige, power and wealth were, and, to a large degree continue to be won.

The political economy of the Iban was to a significant degree historically geared to this externally-located quest for achieved status. As we have seen, each household directed its surplus rice production primarily to trade. In addition, traditional methods of swidden cultivation were such that the labour of younger, more able-bodied men was required for less than half of each farming year. Returning to the longhouse for threshing in early April, and staying on through the *gawai* season that follows, men were generally free to leave again after the completion of the felling and clearing of new farms, between late June and August. Most households contain enough women and older men to free them during the rest of the year for such activities as *bejalai*, trading, labour migration, and, in the past, warfare and raiding. Historically, it was primarily through these activities, engaged in outside the longhouse, and also through the partial appropriation of the labour of women and the elderly within it, that Iban males won power, wealth and reputation.

For young men reputation was ordinarily gained initially through *bejalai* — by accomplishing successful journeys abroad (Freeman 1970:223). Later, after a man had married and began a family, prestige and reputation were gained chiefly by successful farming; the acquisition of prestige wealth, mainly through trade and the sale of rice; and, above all, in middle and later life, by success in warfare and headhunting. Greatest honour attached to those who led major migrations, or who, as *tau' kayau* and *tau' serang*, commanded warring expeditions and major raids. Besides taking heads, the Iban also took their enemies captive, chiefly for sale or ransom, although captives were also enslaved in the past. However, as Freeman (1981:43-48) rightly insists, slaves (*ulun*) never formed a permanent, hereditary stratum in Iban society, but, instead, were eventually either ransomed or adopted into an Iban household, usually that of their captor. Manumission by adoption (*betembang*) was marked by a declaration by the head of the adopting *bilik* that its members would kill anyone who persisted in referring to or treating the former captive as a slave (Sandin 1980:81-83). Thus captives were enfranchised and socially incorporated into the community and even *bilik* of their captors.[17] A man who successfully killed in war (*dengah*) was entitled to the use, particularly on public occasions, of an *ensumbar* or "praise-name". In all these competitive undertakings, it was, and continues to be, not only skill, daring and personal prowess that was, and continues to be honoured, but, more importantly, the ability, as a leader and initiator of projects, to inspire and organize collective action, and to attract a following and to lead them, as a *tuai*, in the realization of a collectively shared purpose. Thus achievement was never entirely directed toward individualistic ends (Sather 1994:10).

Although Freeman is right that prestige and reputation are not strictly hereditary, and can be won only by individual effort, the outcome of this quest for honour and prestige was, as we have already noted, markedly unequal. Equality was only an initial precondition, the underlying social state from which individual men and women were expected, in varying degrees, to distinguish themselves. As Gibson (1990:140) observes,

> The over-all ethos is one of achieved ranking. Every individual is expected to prove himself, but there is a finely graded ladder of achievement, with the ranking of individuals according to merit the ultimate goal.

At the bottom of this ladder were families who suffered chronic shortfalls in rice production, who were often unable to feed themselves, and who lacked the prestige wealth needed to fall back on in times of scarcity. Such persons lived in chronic debt to others, and, as a result, were obliged to repay their debts in part, or in whole, with family labour. In relation to their creditors, such families therefore existed in a state of long-term debt-liability (cf. Freeman 1981:49). Such persons were known as *jaum* or *pengurang*.[18] As a rule, only those in extreme need assumed such debts, becoming, in effect, unequal suppliers of labour to their creditors, and although they otherwise enjoyed, unlike captive slaves (*ulun*), the same basic rights as other longhouse members, until they repaid their debts, they lacked the necessary means to compete with others for social position within the community and were generally unable to participate in the major Gawai rituals held in their longhouse and so were precluded from seeking public recognition for their deeds. Hence *pengurang* families were effectively debarred from asserting their equality and from competing with others in the prestige system. At the other end of the achievement ladder were the *raja berani*, the "rich and brave". The *raja berani* were, to begin with, men whose *bilik* produced surplus rice crops year after year; who were successful in amassing prestige wealth, and whose lives gave evidence of supernatural favour and inspiration. Those who received dream authorization and excelled as war leaders were additionally recognized as *tau' serang*. Very often those who attained prominence were said to possess, besides spiritual inspiration, *seregah*, meaning "personal forcefulness", the power to cause others to take notice, to inspire respect or possibly even fear. Thus, it is said that a timid man is "without *seregah*" (*nadai seregah*); a diffident man has only a little (*seregah mit*); while a successful leader characteristically possesses an abundance (*seregah besai*). Significantly, *seregah* is not something that a leader is born with, but is acquired and cultivated in the course of life.

For an ambitious man, acknowledgement as a man of substance was only the beginning of a life-long quest for renown (*benama*). There existed an ascending sequence of ritual festivals, known in the Saribas region as the Gawai Burong, by which if he so chooses, a man might seek to gain public recognition of his achievements, particularly in warfare and other male domains, including today politics and business (Sandin 1977). "Such rituals, the more complex of which (lasting for four or five days)", were arranged in a sequential scale, with the sponsor "taking the invocation a stage further each occasion until, over a span of forty or more years, the sequence was completed" (Freeman 1981:40). Achievement was thus validated through ritual sponsorship and participation in a graded scale of *gawai* rituals, with the pursuit of the full sequence absorbing, for most Iban leaders and men of wealth, their entire adult lifetimes.

Textiles and "Women's Warfare"

For women weaving constituted the chief counterpart to male warfare. Thus, for a woman, the foremost means of acquiring achieved status was through the weaving of textiles, in particular *pua' kumbu'* or ritual *ikat*-cloth. While undyed cotton provides the Iban with a metaphor of equality — finished cloth, by contrast, represents the very embodiment of rank and status distinction. Just as men gained and made public display of their standing through their sponsorship and participation in *gawai* rituals, so too, woven cloth is ranked (*be-rintai*) — its ranking determined by the nature of its designs, the status of its weaver, and the particular ritual or stage of ritual in which it figures as a suitable object. *Pua' kumbu'* are essentially sacred cloth. They differ according to their ritual use and the significance of their designs and are employed in every facet of Iban ritual life, to define ritual space for example, or to create and bridge boundaries between the human and supernatural worlds (see Empiang 1991:81).

Pua' kumbu' designs, in addition to their specific ritual use, are identified by the skill, seniority and expertise of the particular woman who weaves them (cf. Empiang 1991:80). As an embodiment of status, individual cloth designs are graded and each woman weaver is expected, in the course of her career, to progress systematically in her art, stage by stage, being (Empiang 1991:80),

... guided through each stage from the preparation of the cotton ..., the tying of threads, the dyeing process and the selection of a design [by more experienced women, with] ... each stage circumscribed by ritual.

As in warfare, success is believed to require, in addition to diligence and aptitude, spiritual inspiration and gifts of charms (*pengaroh* or *batu*), and through her art a woman is similarly expected, like a successful warleader, to enter into a special relationship with the supernatural. Consequently, like warfare, weaving, too, is also believed to be dangerous. Should a woman breach "the naturally sequenced order sanctioned by the spirits" — attempting a skill or a design beyond her level of attainment — her life is said to be imperilled. Each progressive stage of expertise was marked traditionally by the mastery of distinctive designs and by the increasing width of cloth that a woman was permitted to weave. In addition, in the Saribas, after the introduction of chemical dyes at the end of the nineteenth century, a weaver's status was also denoted by vertical coloured bands added as side borders, the order of colours being indexical of these stages of expertise.[19] Instruction continued until a woman was acknowledged as having attained the stage of *indu nenkebang indu muntang*. At this stage, she was free to weave ritually dangerous patterns, provided she was sufficiently ambitious and daring, and to invent new designs inspired by her dreams. The highest level of attainment is that of *indu nakar indu gar* (or *tau' nakar, tau' ngar*), the phrase meaning, essentially, "women who know how to measure the mordants and perform the rites [with] divine assistance" (cf. Gavin 1991:4).[20] These women are recognized as the most proficient of all weavers and are said to be able to mix the mordant solutions. Completing the *nakar* process successfully is an extremely difficult undertaking and is called, fittingly, *kayau indu*, "women's warfare" (Gavin 1991:5). *Nakar* is performed ceremonially through a ritual called the Gawai Ngar (see Gavin 1991). Here the ritual mixing of mordants is sponsored by a group of women weavers and is led by the *tau' nakar tau' ngar*. In the sense that it valorizes her status, the Gawai Ngar thus functions like the Gawai Burong, except that the *indu tau' nakar* is not the sponsor of the ritual, but its chief officiant.

In the past those women who attained the status of *indu nakar indu gar* received special honours. Thus, traditionally they received from male warriors the newly-taken heads of slain enemies in their *pua' kumbu'* and at major *gawai*, including the Gawai Burong, they were called on to sing praise songs to the trophy heads (*naku antu pala'*) and to receive the pig's liver for divination by the male elders. Expert weavers were also honoured during other male-sponsored rituals, and upon her death, an *indu tau' nakar* could expect to receive the highest *adat mati* that a woman was awarded, higher than that received by all but the most honoured of Iban men. During the Gawai Antu, she alone prepared the special *garong* baskets, dyed brilliant red called *kebur api*, that were used to commemorate the deceased *indu tau' nakar* of previous generations.

Ritual and Hierarchy

Within the wider riverine society, ritual formed the main arena, for both men and women, in which personal accomplishments were traditionally translated into socially acknowledged status. For the Iban, ritual also gives evidence of spiritual favour and provides the chief means by which participants may enlist further spiritual aid in their quest for still greater power and renown. "It was in this testing milieu", as Freeman (1981:40-41) observes,

> that Iban leaders emerged. They were required, initially, to be men of substance and prowess in action; yet, much more important was the securing, in their ritual and spiritual lives, of the approval and support of the gods, for it was from this ... that their special charisma stemmed.

Not only was the status of the Gawai sponsor valorized within this ritual arena, but precedence among its participants was also given overt representation. At the heart of every *gawai* is a complex allegorical invocation (*pengap* [or *timang*] *gawai*) performed by a company of bards (*lemambang*) comprised of a lead bard, answering bard and chorus (Sandin 1977:6-14; Sather 1994:62-63). In this invocation, the gods — at the invitation of the spirit-heroes and their messengers, acting as intermediaries — descend to the earthly world to join the Gawai, bringing with them charms (*pengaroh*) and other spiritual gifts with which to repay the hospitality of their hosts. Here, on the latter's behalf, they are welcomed and entertained by the *Orang Panggau*, the Iban spirit-heroes and heroines. Both gods and spirit-heroes inhabit an unseen world of extraordinary deeds of valour, wealth, fame, spiritual power and honour, characterized by a finely graded hierarchy of achieved precedence and social standing. The chants of the bards both invoke and depict this world. Thus, they follow the journey of the gods as they travel through unseen regions of the cosmos, gaining wealth and spiritual power, clearing farms, or defeating enemies, echoing in these deeds the journeys of Iban men of reputation, on *bejalai*, migration, or as they travel to war or to fell the forest for new farms.

As the gods and goddesses descend to this world, they arrive, one-by-one, in inverse order of status. The last to arrive and be received is the principal god and his wife for whom the *gawai* is being held. Thus, in the case of the Gawai Burong, the principal deities are Singalang Burong, the Iban god of war, and his wife, Endu Sudan Berinjan Bungkong. As the human hosts validate their reputation and seek spiritual favour by feasting their guests, so the spirit-heroes and heroines, acting as hosts in the invisible world, feast the gods and goddesses on behalf of the human celebrants and sponsors. In the Gawai the human participants thus emulate (*nunda'*) the actions of the spirit-heroes, heroines, gods and goddesses, making visible the unseen world invoked in the songs of the bards.

During the performance of a *gawai*, a major task of each household is that of *digir* or *bedigir*, meaning literally, to seat or arrange the celebrants within its section of the longhouse gallery "in order", "to line [them] up", arranging them in a linear ordering in emulation of the gods and heroes, according to their age, sex, generation and achieved ranking. Thus, at major junctures in the proceedings, for example, before feasting and oratory, sacrifice, or ritual processions, the *tuai gawai*, or principal sponsor, waves a cock along the longhouse galleries to signal to the individual *bilik* hosts that it is time to *bedigir*, to arrange the seating of the guests "in a line" according to their age and achievements. Thus, for each *bilik*, someone must be delegated to lead the guests to their seats and to arrange them in their correct order, beginning first with the oldest and most distinguished guests. At times during a *gawai*, guests and hosts are free to move from one gallery to another, mingling with other celebrants, and sitting wherever they please to gossip and joke with their friends and relatives, but at major ritual junctures, this order of precedence must be recreated, especially when food and drink are served (*nyibor*), for oratory, offerings and processions. Thus, for seating, the most honoured male guests are seated along the upper gallery (*dudok diatas*). The most honoured of all visitors are seated at the gallery belonging to the *gawai* sponsor (*tuai gawai*), while others are seated at other family galleries. The highest ranking sit at the middle of the sponsor's upper gallery and are flanked on each side, moving outward in both directions, by guests of descending age and achievement. Men of the host longhouse sit in a line along the middle gallery facing them, with the *gawai* sponsor seated at the centre of his middle gallery facing opposite his highest ranking guests. Women sit behind the men on the lower gallery or are received by their female hosts inside the family *bilik*. In this ordering, an idealized world of precedence is thus given concrete representation, as a finely individuated array of visitors and hosts, as celebrants are ranged along the galleries for feasting, or as they are called upon for oratory, to make offerings, or to circumambulate the longhouse interior in ritual processions.

Each time a *gawai* is held, an individual's achieved status is thus open to reassessment, and, with the passage of years and the birth of children and grandchildren, his or her age and generational status thus also change, and these changes are similarly registered, so that, through repeated participation in *gawai*, a continuous re-ordering of status relations takes place and is publicly acknowledged.

Major *gawai* rituals, although sponsored by a single individual [the *tuai gawai*], and hosted by the separate households that make up the sponsor's longhouse,[21] activate a much wider sphere of relations, bringing together as guests (*pengabang*) and supporters (*kaban*) a far larger group of related longhouses and *bilik*, whose members are allied to one another as *pesamakai* or "co-feasters". In the absence of chieftainship, or of a formal hierarchy of supralocal political offices, *gawai* rituals played in the past, and continue to play, an important role in Iban society, helping to maintain its wider social and cultural cohesion. All major regional groups of Iban share a basically similar *gawai* tradition, although with important differences of detail, and through ritual feasting, inter-longhouse ties are reinforced and personal achievement is given recognition within a larger regional sphere composed of neighbouring longhouses arrayed along the same river or tributary system. In the past this same regional society also formed the primary social field within which the influence of *tuai menoa* and *tau' serang* was acknowledged and from which war parties were recruited and provisioned. Thus traditionally those who feasted together, as well as competing with one another for status, also fought together, intermarried, and settled their differences by arbitration. Unlike the essentially egalitarian longhouse, it was here, within this wider social field, that differentiation was given public expression.

While achieved rank and generational seniority are thus subject to constant ritual reassessment throughout an individual's lifetime, at death a final stock is taken of each person's accomplishments and, on this basis and in terms of the age and generational status he or she has attained, an *adat mati* or death *adat* is awarded by the deceased's kindred and community elders. This *adat* is figuratively reckoned, like a fine, in terms of grades of prestige wealth. *Adat mati* determines the details and duration of mourning observances and the type of *garong* basket that is woven for the deceased during the Gawai Antu, the final memorial rites for the dead held roughly once in every generation (Sather 1993:95ff). In the Paku region of the Saribas, there are eleven major grades (*ripih*) of *adat mati* represented by different *garong* basket designs. Five of these are reserved for children and for young men and women who have not yet married or attained parental status. The remaining six are awarded to adults. Gender is not distinguished, but the four highest grades are awarded on the basis of predominantly masculine achievement. The weaving of the baskets, and the collection of building materials for the construction of tomb huts, together open the first stage of Gawai Antu (Sather 1993:94). Following the main festival rituals, during which the collective dead of the community are recalled to this world, the *garong* baskets are removed from the longhouse and installed in the tomb huts erected during the concluding stage of the Gawai over the graves of the dead in the longhouse cemetery (*pendam*). Thus, for the Saribas Iban, achieved rank is not only fixed at the time of death but, on this occasion alone, and during the mourning and memorial rites that follow, it is specifically registered in *adat* distinctions which differ according to achieved rank.

In death, however, an individual's accrued status is also removed from the living world and transposed to the Otherworld of the dead (*menoa Sebayan*), a transposition symbolized by the transfer of the *garong* baskets from the longhouse to the cemetery, where they are placed in the tomb huts, together with furnishings such as miniature sunhats, carrying baskets and fish traps, meant to serve the spirits of the deceased in the Otherworld. This transposition also applies to any marks of precedence, such as praise-names and honorifics (*julok*). These, too, are believed to be taken by the deceased on his or her journey to the Otherworld, where they remain attached to his person and therefore unavailable for inheritance by his descendants. In a sense, the relationship between the living and the Otherworld reverses, for the Iban, that of their Malay neighbours. Unlike the Iban, the latter live, in life, in a highly stratified society, but in death, they are stripped of all marks of status and buried in a plain white shroud, so that they enter the Otherworld, without distinction, as equals, much in the same way, conversely, as the Iban believe that the newborn enter the living world as undifferentiated equals, to begin, like undyed cotton thread, their social careers. For both, death may be said to transform the relationship that exists between egality and hierarchy, but in opposite ways.

This removal of the deceased's achieved ranking from the social world of the living — and its transposition to the Otherworld of the dead — is of utmost social significance. Here the ritual transformation effected by the Gawai Antu reverses, in a critical sense, that of the Gawai Burong and other major *gawai* celebrations, including the Gawai Ngar. For the Saribas Iban it completes a symbolic economy by which inequality and ritual are inter-related. Rather than replicating an unseen spiritual hierarchy in the human world, human hierarchy, in death, is given a final transposition to the Otherworld of the dead. Removed from this world, the deceased's rank, his praise-names, fame and other intangible marks of his or her status are thus rendered uninheritable. They remain attached to the individual who achieved them and therefore cease to have any living presence in "this world". As a consequence, the deceased's sons, daughters and other descendants, must begin life anew, like all others, equal and undifferentiated, and must win a place for themselves in the visible society of the living by their own efforts and through projects of their own devising.

Conclusion

The representation of Iban society as "egalitarian" has stirred considerable contention. For most anthropologists who have worked with the Iban, the debate is a source of no little misgiving. On the one hand, competition and achieved inequality occupy a central place in Iban society. On the other, Rousseau's (1980) view that an "egalitarian rhetoric" masks hereditary leadership and a tripartite system of stratification (1980:57) is based upon a profound misreading of the Iban ethnography (cf. Freeman 1981).

My purpose in this paper is essentially to move the debate from its present impasse by introducing two additional dimensions. First, I have sought to relocate

103

the analysis of relations of egality and hierarchy within a wider field of action, stressing the significance of external relations in generating inequality within Iban society. I have also tried to show how cultural understandings shape and give cognitive meaning to the existence of **both** equality and inequality. Secondly, I have sought to highlight the role of ritual, particularly in giving social expression to hierarchy. Not only does ritual sponsorship provide the chief means by which personal achievement is translated into social ranking, but ritual practice also gives concrete shape to Iban constructions of hierarchy, representing them, as we have seen, as a recreation of the unseen world of the gods, spirit-heroes and the dead.

My main argument here is that Iban society is most usefully seen — not as unequivocally "egalitarian" — but as structured around an articulation of principles of both "egality" and "hierarchy", with relations of equality predominating internally — especially within the local longhouse community — in *adat* and relations within the family and between kindred and affines — while hierarchy is externally derived and, as a rule, valorized within a larger regional society through major ritual gatherings or *gawai*.

While it tends to be assumed that the stratified societies of Borneo evolved from more egalitarian ones, an assumption linked in some instances to the tendency, noted at the beginning of the paper, to "naturalize" equality, seeing it as socially anterior to hierarchy, it is quite possible that Iban "egalitarianism" represents a recent and highly specialized development, evolving historically as a successful adaptation to a regional system of inter-tribal raiding and trade. Along these lines, Gibson (1990:141) has suggested, more generally, that the frequent absence of formal hierarchy among inland shifting agriculturalists in insular Southeast Asia represents a defensive response to lowland and coastal states.

> All these societies represented specialized adaptations to the regional political economy. All lack instituted hierarchy. The extreme emphasis on individual autonomy and rejection of super-household authority evident among them must be seen as a rejection of the political values of their predatory lowland neighbors. Far from constituting primordial classless societies, they must be seen as political groups which have been able to maintain significant degrees of autonomy only by developing special social mechanisms for evading control by the lowlands.

The situation among inland shifting agriculturalists in Borneo is far more complex than represented by the examples that Gibson uses for these generalizations. Here many inland groups did in fact develop instituted stratification, with the role of the upper stratum closely linked to leadership in war and control over external trade (cf. Morris 1980). In contrast, the Iban social system, combining initial equality with achieved, ritually valorized ranking, is closely bound up, as I have tried to show in this paper, with a markedly successful adaptation, as vigorous predators, within a wider inter-regional economy of trade, conflict and migration. In this regard, there is some merit, I think, in Rousseau's (1980:60) suggestion that a major difference between the "stratified" Kayan and the "egalitarian" Iban was historically that Kayan "structures of exploitation" were internal, existing between the strata comprising Kayan society, while among the Iban "exploitation" was directed externally, at outsiders.

In this connection, we might speculate, I think, that relations of internal equality contributed to the major advantage that the Iban enjoyed in their competition with other "tribal" groups in western Borneo, namely their ability to maintain a high degree of cultural homogeneity in the face of territorial expansion and the extensive incorporation of captives and other outsiders through marriage and adoption. Hierarchy, at least in pre-state societies, tends to foster cultural differentiation and, in Borneo, as Brown (1973b) has shown, it often leads to the genesis of ethnic and subethnic divisions, while egalitarianism tends, by contrast, to be assimilative, breaking down such divisions. In this respect, egality very likely contributed to the powerfully assimilative nature of traditional Iban society. At the same time, Iban society, existing as it did historically in a social context of warfare and trade, also incorporated ritual elements of hierarchy, rewarding, within this context, those who excelled at gaining mastery over the external world. Thus personal achievement was linked through ritual to the common interests of society at large, ensuring that those who succeeded did so in ways that perpetuated the Ibans' predatory advantage over their neighbours.

References

Alexander, Jennifer

1992   Must ascribed status entail inequality? Reproduction of rank in Lahanan society. *Oceania* 62(3):207-226.

Allen, Michael

1987   Hierarchy and complementarity in Newar caste, marriage and labour relations. *Mankind* 17(2):92-103.

Appell, G.N.

1978   The status of social anthropological research in Borneo. In George N. Appell and Leigh R. Wright (eds) *The status of social science research in Borneo*. Southeast Asia Program, Data Paper No. 109. Ithaca: Cornell University.

1986   Kayan land tenure and the distribution of devolvable usufruct in Borneo. *Borneo Research Bulletin* 18:119-130.

Ave, Jan, Victor King and Joke deWit

1983   Introduction. In *West Kalimantan: a bibliography*. Dordrecht: Foris Publications.

Béguet, Véronique

1993   *Sama bilik*, le pot, le feu, les nattes. Les relations sociales au sein des maisonnées Iban de Bornéo. MA thesis, Université Laval.

Boehm, Christopher

1993   Egalitarian behavior and reverse dominance hierarchy. *Current Anthropology* 34(3):227-240.

Brown, Donald E.

1973a   Inter-hierarchical commissions in a Bornean plural society. *Southeast Asian Journal of Social Science* 1(1):97-116.

1973b   Hereditary rank and ethnic history: an analysis of Brunei historiography. *Journal of Anthropological Research* 29:113-122.

1979   Iban leadership. *Sarawak Museum Journal* 27:15-23.

Chan Chok Khuang, Henry

1991 Historical development of the Belaga Kayans and their land tenure system: a case study of a Kayan community in Sarawak. M.Phil. dissertation, Institute for Advanced Studies, Universiti Malaya, Kuala Lumpur.

Cramb, Robert

1987   The evolution of Iban land tenure: a study in institutional economics. PhD dissertation, Monash University.

1989   Explaining variation in Bornean land tenure: the Iban case. *Ethnology* 28(4):277-300.

Dumont, Louis

1970   *Homo hierarchicus*. Chicago: University of Chicago Press.

Empiang Jabu (Datin Paduka)

1991   *Pua kumbu* — the pride of the Iban cultural heritage. In Lucas Chin and Valerie Mashman (eds) *Sarawak, cultural legacy*, pp.75-89. Kuching: Society Atelier Sarawak.

Fallers, Lloyd

1973   *Inequality: social stratification reconsidered*. Chicago: University of Chicago Press.

Flanagan, James

1989   Hierarchy in simple societies. *Annual Review of Anthropology* 18:245-266.

Flanagan, James and Steve Rayner

1988   Introduction. In James Flanagan and Steve Rayner (eds) *Rules, decisions, and inequality in egalitarian societies*, pp.1-19. Aldershot: Gower Publishing Company.

Freeman, J.D.

1955   *Iban agriculture: a report on the shifting cultivation of hill rice by the Iban of Sarawak*. London: H.M. Stationery Office.

1957   The family system of the Iban of Borneo. In Jack Goody (ed.) *The developmental cycle in domestic groups*, pp.15-52. Cambridge Papers in Social Anthropology, No. 1. Cambridge: Cambridge University Press.

1960   The Iban of Western Borneo. In G.P. Murdock (ed.) *Social structure in Southeast Asia*, pp.65-87. Chicago: Quadrangle Books.

1961   On the concept of the kindred. *Journal of the Royal Anthropological Institute* 91(2):192-220.

1970   *Report on the Iban*. LSE Monograph, No. 41. London: Athlone Press.

1981 *Some reflections on the nature of Iban society*. Occasional Paper, Department of Anthropology, Research School of Pacific Studies. Canberra: The Australian National University.

Fried, Morton

1967   *The evolution of political society: an essay in political anthropology*. New York: Random House.

Gavin, Trude

1991   *Kayau Indu*, the warpath of women (a *ngar* ritual at Entawau, Baleh, 1988). *Sarawak Museum Journal* 42:1-41.

Gibson, Thomas

1990   Raiding, trading and tribal autonomy in insular Southeast Asia. In Jonathan Haas (ed.) *The anthropology of war*. Cambridge: Cambridge University Press.

Heppell, Michael

1975   Iban social control: the infant and the adult. PhD thesis, The Australian National University.

King, Victor T.

1976 Some aspects of Iban-Maloh contact in West Kalimantan. *Indonesia* 21:85-114.

1978   Introduction. In Victor King (ed.) *Essays on Borneo societies*, pp.1-36. Hull Monographs on South-East Asia, 7. Oxford: Oxford University Press.

1985   *The Maloh of West Kalimantan*. Dordrecht: Foris Publications.

1990 Cognation and rank in Borneo. In F. Husken and J. Kemp (eds), *Cognation and social organization in Southeast Asia*. Leiden: Koninklijk Instituut voor Taal-, Land- en Volkenkunde Press, pp.15-31.

Lakoff, Sanford

1964   *Equality in political philosophy*. Cambridge: Harvard University Press.

Leach, E.R.

1950   *Social science research in Sarawak*. London: HMSO.

Mashman, Valerie

1991   Warriors and weavers: a study of gender relations among the Iban of Sarawak. In Vinson Sutlive (ed.) *Female and male in Borneo*, vol. 1, pp.231-270. Williamsburg: Borneo Research Council Monograph.

Morris, H.S.

1978   The coastal Melanau. In Victor King (ed.) *Essays on Borneo societies*, pp.37-58. Oxford: Oxford University Press.

1980   Slaves, aristocrats and export of sago in Sarawak. In James L. Watson (ed.) *Asian and African systems of slavery*, pp.293-309. Oxford: Blackwell.

1983   Kinship and rank among the coastal Melanau of Sarawak. Amsterdam: University of Amsterdam, Seminar on Cognatic Forms of Social Organization in Southeast Asia, January 6-8th.

Murray, Tania

1981   People on top (*orang ka-atas*): the question of Iban egalitarianism. *Cambridge Anthropology* 7(1):28-46.

Ngo, T.H.G. Mering

1991   Ambiguity in property rights: lesson from the Kayan of Kalimantan. Paper presented at Interdisciplinary Conference on the Interactions of People and Forests in Kalimantan. New York Botanical Garden, June, 1991.

Nicolaisen, Ida

1986   Pride and progress: Kajang response to economic change. *Sarawak Museum Journal* 36:75-116.

Pringle, Robert

1970   *Rajahs and rebels: the Iban of Sarawak under Brooke rule, 1841-1941.* New York: Macmillan.

Richards, Anthony

1981   *An Iban-English dictionary.* Oxford: Clarendon Press.

Rousseau, Jerome

1978 The Kayan. In Victor King (ed.) *Essays on Borneo societies.* Oxford: Oxford University Press, pp.78-91.

1979   Kayan stratification. *Man* 14:215-236.

1980   Iban inequality. *Bijdragen Tot de Taal-, Land en Volkenkunde* 136:52-63.

1987   Kayan land tenure. *Borneo Research Bulletin* 19:47-56.

1990 *Central Borneo: Ethnic identity and social life in a stratified society.* Oxford: Clarendon Press.

Sahlins, Marshall D.

1958   Review of J.D. Freeman's Iban agriculture. *Journal of the Polynesian Society* 67:311-313.

1972   On the sociology of primitive exchange. In *Stone age economics,* pp.185-275. Chicago: Aldine Publishing Company.

Sandin, Benedict

1966   Iban hero dreams and apparitions. *Sarawak Museum Journal* 14:91-123.

1967   *The Sea Dayaks of Borneo before white Rajah rule.* London: Macmillan.

1977 *Gawai Burong: the chants and celebrations of the Iban bird festival.* Penang: Penerbit Universiti Sains Malaysia.

1980   *Iban adat and augury.* Penang: Penerbit Universiti Sains Malaysia.

1994 *Sources of Iban traditional history.* Clifford Sather (ed.) Special Monograph, No. 7, *Sarawak Museum Journal.*

Sather, Clifford

1980   Introduction. In Benedict Sandin, *Iban adat and augury,* pp.xi-xlv. Penang: Penerbit Universiti Sains Malaysia.

1985   Iban agricultural augury. *Sarawak Museum Journal* 34:1-35.

1989 Traditional Iban society: reflections on some dialectical themes. *Sarawak Museum Journal* 40:51-57.

1990 Trees and tree tenure in Paku Iban society: the management of secondary forest resources in a long-established Iban community. *Borneo Review* 1:16-40.

1993   Posts, hearths, and thresholds: the Iban longhouse as a ritual structure. In James J. Fox (ed.) *Inside Austronesian houses*, pp.64-115. Department of Anthropology, Research School of Pacific and Asian Studies, Canberra: Australian National University.

1994   Introduction. In Benedict Sandin, *Sources of Iban traditional history*, pp.1-78, 268-271.

Sellato, Bernard

1987   Note preliminaire sur les societes "a maison" a Borneo. In Charles Mcdonald (ed.) *De la Hutte au Palais: Societes a Maison en Asie du Sud-Est insulaire*, pp.15-44. Paris: CNRS.

Sutlive, Vinson

1978   *The Iban of Sarawak*. Arlington Heights: A HM Publishing Corporation.

Wagner, Ulla

1972   *Colonialism and Iban warfare*. Stockholm: Obe-Tryck Sthlm.

Woodburn, James

1982   Egalitarian societies. *Man* 17:431-451.

Notes

[1] Here, in formulating these distinctions, I have benefited greatly from the comments of Robert Barrett. I also wish to thank George Appell, Aletta Biersack, James J. Fox, Trude Gavin and Vinson Sutlive for their valuable comments.

[2] See, for example, Appell (1978:61-62), Ave, King and DeWit (1983:16-28), King (1978:27-32, 1985:205-209, 1990), Morris (1978:37) and Sellato (1987).

[3] Béguet (1993) contests this, noting that in a strict sense in-marrying spouses are not granted these rights automatically but must win them through prolonged residence and by gaining the confidence of members born into the *bilik*.

[4] Spiritual guidance was believed to be essential to military success. No matter how skilful a man might be as a warrior or tactician, without dream authorization, he could never lay claim to the status of *tau' serang*. The best known historical example of this is Penghulu Bantin, the brilliant, turn-of-the-century Ulu Ai rebel warrior who, though he led the largest uprising again Brooke rule in Sarawak history, was never acknowledged as a *tau' serang*, but fought throughout his career under the leadership of Ngumbang, who, unlike Bantin, possessed the requisite dream "commission" (Sandin 1966:113-115; Pringle 1970:220).

[5] Literally, *tusut* means "tangled" or "knotted" (Richards 1981:405). Iban society is bilateral and oral genealogies are commonly compared to a cast-net (*tusut sigi' baka jala*). Thus when strangers meet they may *betusut*, "recite their *tusut*", in order to establish — i.e. "disentangle" (*nusut*) — a common ancestor from whom they "are jointly descended" (*saturun*). On this basis, they establish themselves as "kin" and determine the generational distance (*serak ke dulu'*) that separates them (see Sather 1994:47-55).

[6] In contrast, *tusut* traditions understandably appear to be much less developed in recently settled Iban areas such as the Baleh studied by Freeman. Although they are best documented for the Saribas, extended *tusut* are also known from the Batang Ai and other long-settled areas of the Sri Aman Division. For a discussion of the connection between migration, political leadership and the *tusut*, see Sather 1994:47-57, 268-271).

[7] This aspect of Kayan land-tenure, as reported by Rousseau, is highly problematic, however, and has been disputed by others (cf. Appell 1986, Chan 1991, Ngo 1991). Unfortunately, patterns of land control remain poorly documented among most "stratified" communities in Sarawak, making it difficult to compare them with the Iban and to speculate on the possible connections between stratification and

control over agricultural resources. In some instances, for example with the Maloh of Kalimantan Barat, these patterns are said to have broken down to such an extent that their "traditional" forms are no longer recoverable (cf. King 1985). According to Rousseau, Kayan aristocrats did not have redistributive powers over land traditionally nor did they, he claims, control larger areas of land than commoners (1979:223; 1990:200-201). This latter claim would also seem problematic, given their presumed greater command of labour (see, for example, Alexander 1992:213).

[8] Even these are often in mature secondary forest.

[9] There is some evidence, however, that these powers, if not entirely the product of colonial intervention, were greatly strengthened during the early years of colonial rule. Thus, Nicolaisen (1986:83) argues that nineteenth century Brooke rule, rather than undermining stratification, promoted the differentiation of ranked strata in Punan Bah society and formalized and extended "aristocratic" privileges. Whereas previously aristocratic authority had depended on public support, aristocrats were given the right to prohibit the movement of commoners between longhouses and to impose fines on those who attempted such moves (see also Alexander 1992:209).

[10] Some indication of the extent of this uncertainty can be gained by the fact that during the 1949-50 farming year, when Freeman carried out his now classic study of swidden cultivation among the Baleh Iban, two-thirds of the households in the longhouse he studied failed to obtain enough rice to meet their subsistence needs (1970:266). The harvest was one of the poorest in memory, but even so, the important point to be made is that families with sufficient rice continued to sell their surplus, despite the prevailing scarcity (1970:272-273).

[11] Thus still further reducing the need for sharing between households as a means of making up subsistence deficiencies in times of need.

[12] In the past, when raiding and inter-regional warfare were endemic, *bedurok* relations also provided security to those working outside the longhouse.

[13] The outcome was traditionally a form of debt relationship, discussed presently, in which the creditor expects repayment in the form of *bilik* labour. Hence, it is not entirely accurate to say, as Murray does, that there were no traditional means by which one family might gain command over the labour of another.

[14] Thus, for example, the hearths should be installed in the same order as the erection of source posts and the first fire to be lit, after they are installed, is at the *tuai rumah*'s hearth, with each of the other households lighting their first fire from the headman's *dapor*, thereby signifying, through these rules, the latter's precedence within the house (Sather 1993:73).

[15] In contrast, among "stratified" groups in Borneo generational terms may be applied to mark rank distinctions. Thus, for example, among the Maloh, King (1990:18) reports that aristocrats address commoners by "child" or "grandchild" terms, while they in turn are addressed by the latter as "parents" or "grandparents". This does not seem to be the case among the Lahanan, however, who appear to practice a teknonymic system much like that of the Iban (Alexander 1992:217).

[16] These structural features point up several important aspects of Iban "gender equality" — itself a significant aspect of the egalitarianism debate — but one which I can only touch on here, as it clearly calls for fuller treatment in its own right (see Mashman 1991). The tendency to treat husbands and wives as a single entity is also reflected in Iban genealogies. Thus, *tusut*, when they are recited, generally consist of personal names (*nama*) connected by *bebini* ("took a wife") or *belaki* ("took a husband") and *beranak ka* ("bore a child"). Thus, for example, *Sawai belaki diambi' Kaya, beranak ka Jantan, bebini ngambi' Jemat ...* ("Sawai took a husband Kaya [and they] bore Jantan, [who] took a wife Jemat ..."). Thus the name of the descendant through whom the *tusut* is traced does not normally occur alone but is usually paired with that of his or her spouse, as in the examples just cited (e.g. Sawai and Kaya; and Jantan and Jemat). Thus, in each generation, genealogies are typically traced through sets of married couples. This pairing of husbands and wives makes it possible to connect branch-lines with main-line genealogies, reflecting the bilaterality and highly ramifying nature of Iban kinship. It also reflects *bilik* composition and the importance of marriage generally in maintaining kindred relations (see Sather 1994:47-55).

[17] However, it must be added that former slaves and their descendants were, and in some instances continue to be, socially and economically disadvantaged. With limited ancestry, such persons generally have less access to land and other resources than others. In addition, other families, particularly core households whose members are especially conscious of ancestry, are normally reluctant to marry their children into families founded by former slaves, or those connected by marriage with former slaves or their descendants. Public reference to slave ancestry is a fineable offence, making it a difficult topic of inquiry. However, in the Saribas, it is widely believed that the descendants of former slaves were

disproportionately represented among those who migrated during the nineteenth and early twentieth century to the former Third, Fourth and Fifth Divisions. If so, this would suggest that the practice of enfranchisement may have contributed to the further expansion of the Iban.

[18] *Pengurang*, from the root, *kurang*, "want", "deficiency". Although Sandin (1980:80) lumps together what he calls "debt-slaves" or "serfs" (*jaum*) and "captive slaves" (*ulun*), the two statuses, as Freeman (1981:49) rightly stresses were, in fact, very different historically. Thus it is a serious error to describe the *pengurang* as "slaves". Those to whom a *pengurang* owes labour, *padi*, or other debts, did not, in fact, "own" his person in the sense of being able to transfer rights over his labour, etc. to other persons through sale or exchange, nor did the *pengurang*'s creditors have command over the debtor and his family outside of the debt relationship. Thus once the individual repaid his debts, he ceased to be a *pengurang*. However, the existence of a status of long-term debt-liability poses a serious challenge to Freeman's view of Iban society. As indicated here, *pengurang* suffered serious disabilities. He and his household were in effect excluded from competing in the prestige system; and they lacked the means to take part in Gawai rituals, and to compete for positions of longhouse leadership.

[19] The Saribas saying cited at the beginning of this paper refers specifically to these bands, which were a distinctive innovation of Saribas weavers (Trude Gavin, pers. comm.). "Yellow", "green" and "blue" were not colours used in traditional *pua' kumba'* cloth. Rather, the dominant dye was, and remains, red. In Iban the principal term for red is *mansau*, which has also a double, deep-language meaning of "cooked" or "ripe". Hence the principal distinction in ranking cloth is between contrasting degrees of "ripeness" (*mansau*) and "rawness" (*mata'*), with the status of the most proficient weavers measured chiefly by the depths and intensity of "redness" that they are able to achieve through their knowledge of mordants and dyes.

[20] *Indu tau' nakar tau' ngar* were, Datin Empiang (1991:81) claims, often of "an ancestral line of weavers and dyers" who acquired their knowledge of dyes and inherited charms from their families. The status, however, like others in Iban society, was essentially achieved and required the acknowledgement of other women weavers. While many women had a knowledge of mordants, very few were willing to assert this knowledge publicly, and to gain the status of *indu tau' nakar*, a woman had to be engaged by others as their leader in the process of mixing and applying mordants (*nakar*).

[21] Given the voluntaristic nature of all group undertakings in Iban society, when a *gawai* is being held, the individual families residing in a longhouse are always free to opt out, if they choose to, or should they lack the economic means or kindred support to participate in the ritual as hosts.

Chapter 6. Origin, Hierarchy and Egalitarianism Among the Mandaya of Southeast Mindanao, Philippines

Aram A. Yengoyan

This paper develops two major themes of Mandaya social structure which operate at different levels of social and political activity. One of these principles or themes is the structure of hierarchy or precedence which operates primarily at the political level of leadership and warfare as it articulates the domination of the centre or points of origin to the periphery of social life. In this context the dominant expression of precedence is based on the political role of the *bagani* (the warrior class) and the various sub-units of political authority which traditionally inhabited the lands of the Mandaya. The second theme is the expression of egalitarianism which dominates throughout the domestic domain of social life and how domestic domains relate to one another as a means of establishing and cementing bonds within and between hamlets. Egalitarianism is expressed through gambling of rice harvests, through cockfighting and through mutual activity of sharing in activities which cross-cut different hamlets and communities.

These different forms of hierarchy and structure are the basis of internal contradictions which at times erupt into actual overt conflict. Although these two different domains of hierarchy are critical for assessing the importance of genealogical depth and genealogical domination within various segments of Mandaya society, in actuality, kinship groups and marriage alliances moderate potential conflict as expressed through intra-tribal economic interactions. Furthermore, Mandaya interactions with their neighbours (Bisayan, Mangguangan, Mansaka) also express this dualistic aspect of hierarchy and mythic domination towards those societies considered inferior (based in part on slavery and/or asymmetrical economic exchange) and those who control capital allocation and marketing networks.

Based on Dumont's conception of hierarchy, in part this paper develops horizontal modes of hierarchy which appear to have received less attention in the literature on upland peoples in Mindanao. Although mythic and genealogical depth translate into various aspects of hierarchy and eventually domination between the Mandaya and the Mangguangan, this expression of vertical hierarchy creates contradictions and conflicts with the internal expression of egalitarianism which pervades each society.

Culture as Value and as Precedence

The idea of culture in Dumont's (1975, 1979, 1980, 1982) framework enters his interpretation through the concept of value. A hierarchical framework divorced from value reverts toward a structural analysis in which culture and value do not underwrite the analysis. As noted by Dumont (1979, 1980, 1982) and Fox (1990), the animation and understanding of the hierarchical structure into a local context revolves on the recognition of value which is not only at the heart of a particular social life, but also dominates various spheres of social rank. As Fox (1990:7) notes, hierarchy without value is a categorical phenomena which has implications within the realm of social relationships. Dumont's India has a single all-encompassing value, that being the contrast between purity/impurity which is the basis of all hierarchy. However, Dumont goes further by arguing that hierarchy as the dominant ideology is almost always linked to purity/impurity. Fox (1990:7) notes that this coupling, which might work for India, virtually excludes all other possible alternate value(s).

Hierarchy *per se* cannot be limited to an analysis and understanding of the form and expression of opposition, contrariness, complementarity and encompassment. In Dumont's language (1980), the principles of exclusion and inclusion establish different landscapes through which hierarchical principles occur in a variety of combinations which on the surface might appear as radically different. One has only to look at Dumont's (1975, 1980) reading and comparison of vertical structuration in Indian caste structure in which the whole subsumes the parts to his rethinking of the Nuer where horizontal structuration establishes a whole, yet each segment relates to the whole in ways which are quite different from caste in India. This structural side of Dumont's analysis always focuses on the various structural permutations which exist as theoretical possibilities regardless of culture and/or value.

If value is a culturally specific feature, we must assume that the range of differences in the construction of value is greater than the specific hierarchical features (i.e., the notion of opposition and its various permutations) which are the basis of the structural scaffolding which articulates value(s) throughout a social system. In his rethinking of the Dumontian framework, Fox (1990) correctly notes that the issue of purity does not exist as value in Indonesian society, and from this observation Fox appears to dissolve hierarchy, as established in Indian caste-like structures, into a category of limited utility in the context of Indonesian societies. By creating a theory of precedence based on a broad range of asymmetrical pairings of categorical oppositions which are linguistically labelled and linked with one another, Fox argues that precedence exists in terms of age (elder-younger, first born-last born), gender (male-female) directions, space and colour. In a number of Rotinese examples, Fox notes that most contrasts are based on one side as being greater, prior, or superior to the other. Greater or superior is basic to a theory of precedence in which "all of these categories are complementary but also asymmetric" (Fox 1990:9).

Yet, a question still remains. What is value in the Indonesian context? Precedence, in which one side of a binary contrast is given primacy over the other, could be understood as value though in many features it still possesses marked similarities with hierarchy except that most of the contrasts are asymmetrical whereas for Dumont, encompassment is based primarily, but not always, on symmetry. Throughout Indonesia and the Philippines, many cultures have different types of precedence, some of which deal with kinship and rank, others also extend the rule of precedence to categorical divisions based on the natural world as well as the social world. Fox's (1990) work illuminates these differences in three specific ethnographic cases. From these cases one finds parallels with the Mandaya where precedence is the dominant rule in kinship relations (consanguineal and affinal) as well as how the body becomes a metaphor for precedence within and between generations.

Precedence, as a structural concept, is basic to cases like the Mandaya as a means of understanding questions of rank, status and origin. This is best exemplified when we look at the *bagani* (warrior) complex, how genealogical depth is an expression of origin and rank, and, in turn, how centres become the over-arching key to understanding how Mandaya relate place to history and myth.

What then is the constitution of value in southeast Asian society if a theory of precedence is primarily a structural canopy? In terms of my analysis of the Mandaya, I will argue that precedence as structure has a firm foundation in categorical imperatives as well as in how origin, centres and place are connected through genealogical depth from which the role of the *bagani* is the political manifestation. However, value is expressed in terms of an egalitarian ethos which pervades the structure and action of exchange within and between households and hamlets. Egalitarianism is best expressed in how gambling is constituted as a means of levelling and curtailing social differentiation between individuals and groups.

What transpires is a social and cultural disjunction with precedence acting as the basis of a political structure which invokes history and genealogical depth to support its position in opposition to an egalitarian ethos which dominates exchange and social differentiation. Value as egalitarianism is partially muted in the political structure where rank and status are the markers of political activity.

Dumont (1979) makes the assumption that equality is only expressed as a modern ideology and that only occurred once, that being our Western ideologies of equality which are maintained as our dominant philosophical and political foundations since the eighteenth century. This assumption is partially valid, yet at the same time, we can note that there are many southeast Asian societies which veer towards an egalitarian ethos as cultural value which might or might not have an ideological component. In such cases, the egalitarianism is expressed as cultural axioms or as tacit agreement which is not created through wilful or rational action based on group interest or even self interest.

The Context of Mandaya Precedence and Egalitarianism

Traditionally, the Mandaya inhabited the coastal and interior areas of the eastern cordillera mountain chain in southeast Mindanao, Philippines. Mandaya ethnography has been reported by Cole (1913), Garvan (1931), and Yengoyan (1964, 1965, 1966a, 1966b, 1966c, 1970a, 1970b, 1971, 1973, 1975a, 1975b, 1977, 1983, 1985, 1988); thus, only those aspects of the ethnography that relate to the issue of precedence and egalitarianism will be discussed. On the eastern Davao cordillera, the Mandaya are shifting cultivators who occupy both the foothills up to 1000 feet where they are involved in hemp production, and the interior uplands to an elevation of 3,200 feet in which a mixed system of dry rice cultivation and the planting of tubers is their basic mode of subsistence.

Just as the subsistence base varies, the settlement pattern also covaries with economic demands. With dry rice cultivation, the settlement pattern consists primarily of a single household adjacent to cultivated fields. Households are moved as often as swiddens are relocated, virtually every year, and are synonymous with the nuclear family; thus, each family unit is also the unit of production. Distances between swiddens vary from 0.5 to 2 miles. However, in the relocation and creation of new swiddens, households are situated in visual contact with at least one other household, either across the valley or on top of a range of hills. With the sedentary system based on hemp production, one finds the beginnings of settlement nucleation in which hamlets of five to eight households form a cluster and, in some cases, hamlets are also semi-nucleated in small villages.

The coastal areas are occupied by either Bisayans, who migrated from Cebu, Leyte, and Bohol, or by **conquistas**, who are the descendants of Christianized Mandaya. In general **conquistas** have relatively few kinship ties with the interior Mandaya and at the same time they do not claim to have Bisayan ancestry. The **conquistas** do not consider themselves as Mandaya descendants, but as Bisayan since they have been baptized. In fact, the Christian act of baptism is primarily a means by which one's identity changes from Mandaya to Bisayan; thus, spiritual rebirth has almost no bearing on the volitional act (Yengoyan 1966a). Other influences are critical to understanding the means by which group identity comes about, but baptism among the Mandaya in the late nineteenth century is the key to understanding the emergence of the **conquistas**.

Although either wet rice or coconut cultivation has traditionally dominated most lowland populations, over the past twenty years Bisayans and **conquistas** have moved into the foothills and started hemp cultivation. This penetration into the foothills and the usurping of lands from the upland Mandaya have brought forth considerable conflict, since Mandaya hold land by usufruct and their land is never surveyed and titled, while the Bisayans claim that title to land, and not actual possession, is the sole basis of ownership. Since the 1950s, the foothill Mandaya, who have lost their land to Bisayan encroachments, have either reverted to dry rice cultivation by moving into the forested interiors or have become part of a rural proletariat, working for minimal wages from Bisayan landlords on land they once possessed.

Coastal Bisayans and **conquistas** not only maintain their hegemony through land control, but most of the political and commercial power is in their hands as well. Although some of the larger shops in towns such as Manay, Cateel and Baganga are owned by Chinese, the local Bisayans have either set up their own shops or have worked out financial arrangements with Chinese in which the Chinese are "up front" with their activities, while the Bisayans have invested in them and/or have offered them protection. Most local political positions are held by Bisayans and a few **conquista** families, and in a number of cases two or three intermarrying families have developed a web of mutual interest and have virtually sealed off a town from outside intrusion. Because the coastal highway beyond Mati has never been completed and an air service is unavailable, shipping is the only means by which outside contact is maintained.

The Mangguangan are located in the densely-forested interiors where a semi-nomadic life-style is maintained through collecting, hunting and trading for forest products with the Mandaya. As of ten years ago, almost no territorial conflict occurred between the Mandaya and the Mangguangan, since Mandaya swiddens were seldom located at an elevation of more than 3,200 feet and did not impinge on the Mangguangan.

However, the Mandaya have historically raided the interior for "slaves", especially for young Mangguangan females, who were then raised as domestic servants and later married among the Mandaya. The Mandaya claim that this is an old practice and remark that the Mangguangan are a weak people since they do not cultivate rice though they know its value. Although the Mandaya refer to their slaves as **posaka,** and in some cases set them apart from normal domestic and religious relations, this seldom extends beyond one generation. The cultural and social hiatus that we attribute to slavery is practically absent, since most young Mangguangan slaves maintain contact with their natal family.

Within this context of competing economic and cultural practices, the Mandaya are in the middle since there is seldom any direct contact between the Mangguangan and the coastal Bisayans and **conquistas**. The Mandaya perceive

117

the Bisayans as either land-grabbers or potential land-grabbers who have used the political and administrative structure for their own benefit. Thus, the question of tax collection, in which the Bisayans irregularly request that land taxes be paid, simply increases the tension on both sides. The conflict is provoked to higher degrees of tension when Mandaya who have lost their land have decided to remain as labourers. Violence and homicide occur sporadically; the most common cause is usually the Mandaya's inability to maintain their landholdings against Bisayan encroachment.

Mandaya who think and act like Bisayans (i.e., by converting to the Catholic Church, wearing Western-type apparel, cutting their hair, and taking Christian surnames) attempt to maintain their commercial transactions by selling hemp and acquiring credit with the Chinese merchants in the coastal towns. The Chinese usually deal in straight commercial transactions without nefarious perceptions that characterize Bisayan-Mandaya relations.

Conceptions of Precedence

Mandaya hierarchy and rules of precedence takes a number of forms, some of which are embedded and expressed in social structural features which give rise to social activity, while others occur primarily at the conceptual level of cultural categories which embrace the idea of origin and the contrast between the centre and the periphery. Within the kinship system, terminological contrasts are made between the first born child and the last born, also elder siblings are contrasted to those who are younger. Relative age, by contrastive position, dominates within each generation as well as among kinsmen of preceding generations though it does not occur in generations younger than ego. Furthermore, relative age is the critical measure of precedence which is given social recognition through terms of address and reference as well as behavioural features such as respect and honour. Just as age is the dominant feature which establishes the critical contrastive categories in social life, gender differences are seldom if ever utilized as contrastive markers within each generation. Like other cases within the Austronesian cultural world as expressed in many insular southeast Asian societies, gender is seldom a primary differentiating feature in establishing contrasts between groups and individuals.

Mandaya principles of precedence as cultural categories are primarily linked to the idea of place which has a number of implications based on conceptions of origin, place, encompassment as well as political action. A sense of place means that certain particular locales, which are primary with regard to the origin of myths, are the focus and have precedence over other places and events. Traditionally, the Mandaya have also viewed their neighbours in this scheme of things.

Before the final breakdown of the warrior/chief complex (*bagani*) in the 1930s, Mandaya lands occupied most of what is now eastern Davao as well as the southern parts of Surigao. In the widest sense of place, this broad geographic region embraced all coastal lands westward to the cordillera and into the Maragosan valley. Some of the Mandaya in the Maragosan area called themselves Mansaka, but again this term implies a particular place. The land was divided by riverine valleys which emptied into the Pacific Ocean on the east and by interior valleys encompassed by high mountains which divided one valley from another. It is difficult to assess just how much knowledge individuals possessed regarding the whole of Mandayaland; however, it does appear that groups had a strong sense of place as it related to the domains which were the ancestral lands of particular *bagani* as a warrior class. These domains embraced individual households, small hamlets and nondiscrete communities composed of hamlets which had spatial proximity to one another. Each domain was circumscribed by a mountain ridge or rivers which were natural barriers setting one domain off from another. Furthermore, most of these domains were primarily endogamous in that individuals would marry within the domains. Endogamy was not simply an expression of geographic confines, for in most cases the domains as named localities were genealogically and ancestrally linked to a famous *bagani* from past generations.

Garvan (1931:203) describes the Manobo *bagani* as a priest of war and blood, whose main role is the sacrifice of captives in war. The Mandaya *bagani* appears not to have religious or supernatural functions and can not be described as a warrior priest. Although captives taken during the head-hunting raids were sacrificed by the *bagani*, such behaviour did not deal with any supernatural phenomena or interpretation since the sacrifice was made to avenge the death of a cohort or to obtain powers, courage and ability of a brave opponent warrior whose heart was removed and eaten by the *bagani* and his warriors (*maniklad*). Although a *bagani* might be assisted by certain spirits, the primary aim in taking captives was not to fulfil the dictums of his supernatural guides.

The requirements in becoming a *bagani* consisted of personal valour, fortitude, physical strength, and being the son of a former *bagani*, but above all a certain amount of *charisma*, the ability to gain the respect of your following in terms of leadership and the possessing of personal qualities which one's constituency values in personality behaviour. Each *bagani*, before assuming the title and role, had to kill seven to nine men in battle or through surprise raids upon neighbouring areas. The number of required killings varied from locality to locality since Garvan (1931:142) notes that five lives were the necessary amount among the Manobo while Cole (1913:180-181) state, that the Mayo Bay Mandaya *bagani* took ten or twelve lives while among the Mansaka near Piso, King-king one needed thirty killings before being acclaimed a *bagani*. Furthermore, in upper Manay only adult males were accredited to the *bagani* killing record while the Mayo Bay Mandaya and the Mansaka attributed no attention to sex and age. Each *bagani* had his domain of political authority where his rule was law; however, the exact dimensions of one's domain were not always the same during his lifetime or that of his successor. The acquiring and possessing of suitable primary forest for a *bagani* following was important, thus borders gradually shifted; however, the territory which a *bagani* extended his authority over was usually recognized as the collective historical area of its inhabitants.

The *bagani* were distinguished from other warriors and commoners by their clothing which was a tight-fitting two-piece abaca-woven suit of dark red, maroon and black colours with embroidered designs. A turban-like headpiece was also worn. Although each *bagani* had autonomous rule, his behaviour and actions were occasionally curtailed by the sanctions of public opinion as manifested through his advisory council. The advisory council (in some localities in upper Manay this council was referred to as the *angtutukay*; however, this term was not familiar in all areas) was composed of a few old men of the *bagani* domain whose judgment and integrity were respected by the commoners and the people.

If the claims which one demanded were justifiable or if a *bagani* desired to lead a raid, the warriors (*maniklad*) were called together to initiate preparations for the raid. A commoner of extraordinary valour and strength could become a *maniklad* by taking three lives. *Maniklad* uniforms were similar to a *bagani* though only one-half of the body was covered by the red maroon and black suit. The average size of an attacking force was composed of forty to forty-five men, with **the range** extending from twenty-five to sixty. However, in all cases, size of a potential warrior group varied with the number of people under the *bagani* jurisdiction. The raiding party was not always composed of *bagani* and *maniklad* since able-bodied commoners were temporarily enlisted if the object of the raid required a large force of men. Warriors were only armed with spears, shields (*kasag*) and daggers; however, in special cases and in limited areas slat armour of iron or highly polished hardwood such as *Narra* or *Kamagong* were used. If the individual sought lived within the *bagani* domain, he was taken alive, charged with his crime and if judged guilty was killed and beheaded. The *bagani* would take the victim's wife or wives' children, concubines and slaves for himself along with *agongs* and any piece of *pinggan* (Chinese trade ware), while the warriors and the accuser would divide the remainder of the belongings which in most cases were quite limited and provided little for each warrior. Raids were conducted at dawn when the warrior group surrounded the house of the one sought as part of the vendetta. If the dwelling was not accessible by ladder, the *nipa* or *anahaw* roof was set afire thus driving the inhabitants out of the burning dwelling. Children and women were taken captive while the men were beheaded. If the person sought was captured alive, he was taken to the *bagani* settlement and ritually sacrificed.

Unlike the longhouses of Borneo or the elaborate *datu* dwellings found in the eastern Bisayan Islands during the seventeenth century, the *bagani* quarters were not much larger than any other ordinary dwelling. The only diagnostic mark of a *bagani* settlement was the number of compartments in each house which were divided by split bamboo walls. Each apartment was the living quarters of a wife or concubine of the *bagani*, which usually ranged from nine to twelve women per warrior chief. *Bagani* settlements were usually in the centre of the domain or in a location in which followers and warriors could easily gather for raiding preparation.

Each *bagani* had his lands cultivated by slaves or labour-service from his followers who furnished the subsistence needs for the *bagani* and his families. In turn the *bagani* protected his followers from inter- and extra-territorial raids as well as administering law, justice and order within his domain. When harvests failed or labour-service was not adequate to cultivate all *bagani* lands, tribute in the form of food staples was collected from each household head in accordance with the amount of land one had cultivated and the number of dependents each cultivator had.

The inheritance of the *bagani* title was not automatic in the sense that a successor gained the position solely by his genealogical relationship, nor is it possible to describe the succession as "no heredity chieftainship" which Garvan (1931:140) denotes for the Manobo. *Bagani* succession among the Mandaya was semi-structured on a genealogical basis, though one was required to fulfil the conditions before acquiring the title. If a *bagani* died of natural causes or was killed in battle, his council of advisers selected the cleverest of his sons from his first wife. After selection, the *bagani* "protem" had to kill the required number of men as well as learn the use of authority and leadership among his followers. If the requirements were not fulfilled or if the advisers recognized that the one selected was unable to wield authority and/or lacked personality, features which were a necessity for effective leadership, another son of the first wife was chosen. Upon selection of the new *bagani* candidate, the *angtutukay* pressured the first nominee to withdraw by renouncing his claim to the title; however, cases have occurred where two brothers claiming the title would gather their supporters and fight for the position or for the creation of two domains within the original one. If warfare came about between competing siblings and the one who was forced to vacate his earlier claim by the *angtutukay* won the battle, the victor imprisoned the *angtutukay* until order was again restored within the domain. Upon selection of a new council, the *bagani* and his advisers held a "mock" trial in which the former *angtutukay* were killed or severely tortured for their disloyalty.

Upon the death of a *bagani*, the successor inherited all secondary wives and concubines while the deceased *bagani*'s first wife took all other possessions. If the transformation from the deceased *bagani* to his successor was smooth and without sibling rivalry, the succeeding son usually retained his father's *angtutukay*. When an adviser died the *bagani* chose his successor from the sons of the deceased or another person who possessed the necessary qualifications.

The *angtutukay* was composed of two to five men depending on the size of the *bagani* domain and the number of inhabitants; however, three advisers per *bagani* was the average. Advisers could not request tribute to labour-service nor did they partake in the partitioning of material gains acquired through interterritorial raids. Within an area, each *angtutukay* was highly respected for his wisdom and sense of reason, but above all for their age since advisory councils usually consisted of older men within the *bagani* jurisdiction. The *angtutukay* functioned as middle men who transmitted grievances of the commoners to the *bagani*, thus they also provided the only effective internal means of checking the authority and actions of the warrior chief since decision-making and political power were vested in the *bagani*. The most effective check on *bagani* authority came from external sources such as the power, size and mobility of the neighbouring *bagani* forces since seldom would a *bagani* risk an attack on a stronger neighbour if his motives had no justification.

Although the roles and functions of the *bagani* may appear quite structured, in actuality the acquiring of the position required strong personal qualities and *charisma*. All *bagani* were claimed to be immune to death by killing due to the powerful *anting-anting* (charm) they possessed to escape death in battle. Informants have noted cases where a *bagani* was stabbed in the back, but returned to his settlement without a trace of blood. It is claimed that anyone who became *bagani* had strong *anting-anting*, but if a *bagani* was killed in battle his *anting-anting* was weak and he deserved to die.

The *bagani* complex was not only a framework of warfare and political entourage, it also represented a statement of mythic existence. Throughout the various domains in upper Manay and Cateel, cosmological centres coexisted with the political structure as an expression in which mythic origin legends (which have their genesis in the sky) are established as part of a sacred and revered landscape (Yengoyan 1985). These centres of sacred power exist in the form of particular environmental features which possess darkness as a common feature. Thus, centres exist in deep dark standing pools of water or in *bud-bud* (banyan) trees which are known for their dark, almost mysterious properties.

Each of these various mythic and cosmological centres provide the essential linkages with the sky on one side and the underworld on the other. Although the Mandaya do not possess full-time spiritual custodians, the *bagani* and his entourage was responsible for maintaining the sacredness of these spiritual localities by performing necessary rituals at these sites, by protecting banyans from being destroyed, and by curtailing all sites from outsiders who were not part of their domain.

Thus the domains provided the widest discrete unit in which all political and ritual activities occurred within specified calendrical time sequences. In earlier times, the *bagani* would lead raids on neighbouring Mandaya populations from adjacent and extra-adjacent units. When the Spanish arrived on the coast in the 1850s, missions were established in small settlements such as Baganga, Cateel and Manay. From the Jesuit *cartas* after 1860, we are provided vivid accounts of raids by *bagani* warriors which appear to be larger in terms of what can be established as the normal pattern of raiding. The size and scope of the raiding parties indicates that a number of *bagani* joined together as a means of mobilizing powerful forces against the Spanish forts and churches. However, the raiding size of these parties (which in some cases are noted as over 400 warriors) might have been exaggerations, consciously created, by Spanish administrators and clergy as a means of securing more resources for their local endeavours which were always limited by logistical factors.

Besides the hamlet-community, pattern and the *bagani* domains, the broadest scope of encompassment embraced the interior Mangguangan who, as noted earlier, the Mandaya raided for "slaves". Young female slaves eventually married within the Mandaya and within a generation the roots of one's slave background virtually evaporated. The Mangguangan represented the third and last tier of encompassment from the various *bagani* domains. In the Mandaya sense of place, the Mangguangan had an existence and after the 1850s, the coastal Spanish were encompassed as a threat although the Spanish themselves seldom penetrated into the upper foothills or interiors. After 1900, the American colonial system established seats of local government in these towns and the Catholic missions no longer had a political structure to render assistance. Furthermore, the colonial administration through forcible means attempted to curtail the warring complex and by the 1930s, the days of the *bagani* were past.

However, the historical basis of the adventures of the *bagani* starts anew through the veneration of ancient activities of war, conflict and strength through a re-metaphorization of these deeds in oral tradition which becomes the major vehicle of the mythic past. The myth of each individual *bagani* is different, for each deed and venturesome behaviour of the *bagani* is codified in the landscape as markers and testimony to a glorious past in which history becomes living myth. Origins based on deeds of past warriors and nobles are always perpetuated through ritual, but the rituals can only take place in the exact location where the *bagani* maintained themselves as the centre of their activities. There are many different centres throughout time, but each of the centres can be characterized by a sense of scale in which external forces impinge on the traditional domain. Distinctions like interior/exterior are only meaningful when understood through a historical perspective which has permitted domains to expand and curtail their scope of influence.

Hierarchy as a cultural logic is premised on the idea of precedence which provides primacy to mythic places as expressed in local territories, *bagani* domains, and eventually extensions to other cultural groups such as the Mangguangan, coastal Spanish in the nineteenth century, and an insipid colonial administration after 1900. Precedence based on heroic and mythic centres establishes the broadest confines for signifying the role of place and locality within a scheme of social, political and economic forces. In the past two decades, the centrality of place(s) which are the foundations of origin, myth and the *bagani* complex, are now considered as the interior, the heartland which provides the emotional sustenance to what the Mandaya consider as their past in its present expression. As one moves from the centre(s) a sense of borderlands emerge, as areas and places which are divorced from cultural symbols and historical meaning, these are the areas which are now contested with the encroaching Bisayans from the coastal areas. The periphery is fuzzy and undefined, but the contestation means that Bisayans armed with legal documents and a political semi-state apparatus have little or no respect for traditional Mandaya lands and culture. The conflict situation peaked in the middle 1970s, but by the late 1970s, most areas in the foothills were controlled by the NPA (National People's Army) who gradually forced the Philippine army to retreat which in turn forced out the commercial loggers and hemp interests who no longer had a military infrastructure to support their activities.

In summary, Mandaya hierarchy based on a scheme of places which have different roles in terms of myth, origin and centrality emerges both in the kinship structure in contrasting between first born/last born and through generational terms which are metaphorically linked to the body where the grandparental generation is combined with the sole of the foot while the parental generation is the heart. As a cultural logic, precedence provides the historical existence, but within the social/kinship framework hierarchical principles are always juxtaposed to a strong egalitarianism which pervades the interaction between individuals, households and hamlets.

Egalitarianism as Culture Value

Throughout the domestic domain as expressed in households, hamlets and non-discrete communities, the basis of social activity and interaction is characterized by systems of exchange and reciprocity based on a strong conviction of egalitarianism. The idea of sharing food, commodities and activity is closely linked with a strong sense of equality which individuals recognize as the key to all human interactions. Hierarchy as expressed through precedence, rank and status which pervades the political structure as well as religious symbolism rests above the structure of equality which dominates the social and economic sphere of society. In most cases, structural conflicts and contradictions do not occur, for both spheres of culture address themselves to different tasks. Furthermore, with the decline of the *bagani* in the 1930s, political process and warfare are no longer a matter which the domestic structure must relate to in terms of food giving or services.

Reciprocity is the basis of most labour involved in the maintenance of upland rice cultivation. Nearly all aspects of the production cycle require the exchange of labour. In some phases such as the felling and clearing of forest growth the demand on labour exchange is greater, in other phases, such as planting, the basic extended family usually takes care of its own needs. However, exchange is not only labour, but also the sharing of food and other commodities between families living in the same hamlet as well as those who reside within nondiscrete communities. Reciprocity and a sense of giving is seldom based on the idea of a created debt which will be compensated at a later time. One gives to another in many ways. In some cases, there is a perceived need, in other cases, the giver has an abundance of goods and/or time which he/she might share with another individual. However, the foundation of the egalitarian ethos goes beyond the realm of giving and exchange. The marked conviction is that all individuals (except children and infants) are equal, thus the system of exchange is fundamentally an expression of the equality of individuals from which all social relationships flow. In many ways, this sense of equality is similar to what Gibson (1985, 1986) has described for the Buid of Mindoro. However, the comparison of the Mandaya with the Buid also reflects one major difference. From my reading of Gibson (1985, 1986) it appears that egalitarianism among the Buid is a means of maintaining community integrity which is essential to evading domination by economically and politically powerful lowland neighbours who are engaged in some form of commercial agriculture on the Mindoro coast. One can also note the same kinds of economic changes and demands with the Mandaya, but I am convinced that the dominant egalitarian ethos is not solely a response to external pressure. The ethos of equality also exists among upland Mandaya communities which have had minimum contact and impact with coastal economic domination. The ethos might be fortified, but it is difficult to accept a position that the ethos was initially created as a response for maintaining community solidarity.

If the egalitarian ethos is socially framed in the context of reciprocity and giving among individuals who are equals, the institution of gambling as a cultural focus best exemplifies the importance of how equalness operates through a system of redistribution. Since gambling is always connected to rice production, the importance of rice must be discussed. All Mandaya are upland rice cultivators and all suffer from a shortage of rice. The range of variation in rice consumption indicates that those families with higher rice yields consume tubers about ten per cent of their yearly food intake, while those at the lower end of the scale consume root crops within a range of 40 to 50 per cent of the total food intake.

Although this differential exists and the Mandaya are aware of such a contrast, the egalitarian nature of the social structure is not disrupted or verbally denied. The preservation of this structure is made possible by the Mandaya attitude toward land use and their conception of the rice and its presence in the community. Because land is a free good and open lands for cultivation still exist, each person has access to land as a resource. Similarly, rice is seen, not as a commodity but as food. Everyone grows rice and the entire annual community yield is always consumed, yet all families revert to the consumption of root crops when rice is no longer available. Each family continuously plants tubers for pig food; yet, they all realize that a certain time after the harvest, they will be forced to consume root crops until the next rice harvest is available. The Mandaya have no concept of the market value of surplus rice because a surplus never exists. Thus, a class structure based on differential land availability or differential rice stores does not occur.

Although cockfighting is the most interesting form of gambling among the Mandaya, most gambling activities in which rice harvests are redistributed involve playing cards which the Mandaya obtain through trade from the coastal settlements. Various card games exist but the one which is commonly played at the post-harvest gatherings is one which resembles a form of poker with certain similarities to what is called Greek rummy in the United States. Where they learned this is difficult to determine and I personally could not follow all the rules of the game. Each game might have three to four individuals and possibly up to a dozen. Also, only one game is played at any one time and the game is repeated depending on who still survives.

Gambling occurs on a small scale throughout the year, but the major gambling feasts occur during the immediate post-harvest period. Virtually all households are involved in the gambling of rice. Furthermore, the post-harvest rituals and gambling are probably the only time when all families within a particular domain come together for rituals, cockfighting and gambling. Gambling and the eventual redistribution of rice involves individuals and families who are related to one another, but in some cases, this will be the only time they see one another. Occasionally, an individual from a neighbouring domain can partake in rice gambling but he/she has no guarantee that losses in rice during gambling will be compensated later. Theoretically, the ideal culmination of these gambling feasts, which might last three or four days and nights amid heavy bouts of eating roasted pork, rice and drinking, is to gamble what rice one possesses until virtually the total community-produced rice is controlled by six to eight individuals. In some cases, the centralization of rice might be controlled by two or three individuals, especially if gambling feasts are extended to six or seven days. When the feasts end and virtually all locally-produced rice is controlled by a few individuals, either male or female, a long process of redistribution ensues in which individuals who have lost their yearly crop are replenished with rice. The key to understanding the redistribution process is to establish what one has gambled and what one obtains in return. Those families who were at the lower ranges of production are normally supplied with more returned rice than they produced and, in turn, those families who had a good harvest may lose in the process of redistribution. No family has any say about what they and other families obtain on the return, since only individuals who now control rice through gambling will establish how the return is to be made and in what quantities. The authority invested in those who control the rice redistribution is never extended beyond the domain and derives from the conception of gambling as a respected skill. What gambling does is to equalize marked differences in production, thus allowing poorer families to consume rice over a number of months before reverting to root crops and vegetables. Gambling is a structured mechanism that minimizes possible class divisions; consequently, self-esteem is never lost. Since gambling is conducted without a profit motive, what does it mean? Basically, gambling with the ability to win or at least come up near the top of the finalists is a representation of the skills one possesses. A smart and shrewd gambler is respected for being able to make a bold and creative move and for being capable of long-range planning.

The effect of gambling rice is to enhance social differentiation temporarily by centralizing virtually all rice yields in the hands of a few individuals. In this sense, inequality is heightened and differences are asserted in the act of gambling, but through redistribution actual crop yield differences between households are partially reduced. Yet, production and crop yields are never equalized through gambling. As one old and wizened woman said, "getting ahead in the rice gambling means eating less tubers." It goes without saying that the fear of eating tubers throughout most of the year would be enough incentive to enhance one's ability to consume rice if the opportunity occurs.

Cockfighting also involves a certain amount of betting, especially money which is acquired through trade and selling of certain commodities to traders who come up from the coast. Betting on cockfights is minimal and the nature of bets seldom involves rice, though food items like parcels of pork are exchanged. All Mandaya cocks are locally grown, thus breeds which are better competitors seldom enter the arena of the fight. However, individuals know that cocks from the coast are stronger and more fierce, thus in some cases individuals will acquire them through trade. It is also the case that imported cocks win more often, but again the gains through gambling does not offset the cost.

The egalitarian ethos is premised on the fact that adult companions are equal and the creation of social relationships is built on and through a set of equals who share activity and commodities in common. Local level social structure which embeds families, households and hamlets into overlapping units of interaction and exchange is based on an ethos in which individuals are one and a social organization and cultural institution which minimizes differences.

Conclusion

Precedence as an expression of hierarchy occurs as cultural categories based on kinship, taxonomic structures of fauna and flora, and in certain aspects of religious and political structures and symbols which deal with the idea of origin and place. In analyzing the structure of the *bagani* complex; the link to the past as manifest in deeds, locality and origin is established in and through genealogical depth and the meaning of genealogy through history and myth. The basis of hierarchy is where the origin of events and places are established through a sense of time.

This system of structured inequality, which is the basis of political process, is contrasted with various local level activities and organizations of networks which emerge as egalitarian frameworks based on the sharing of food, commodities and activities. The articulation of local and regional activities is highly visible when one calculates how human resources are moved over the landscape as a means of economic exploitation. Domestic units such as household, family and hamlet require mobility which is paramount and vital for economic activities. Under the *bagani* system, most movements were within the domain boundaries, but since the 1940s movements have been more far-reaching.

The articulation of egalitarianism on the local level and precedence on the political level is achieved through a common concern for the validation of origins as they relate to the past. These centres and places of origin are not only spatially delimited, they are also expressed in primary events and actions in which the deeds of past heroes and *bagani* are understood as an ongoing historicity which confirms and ratifies status and rank.

Although the *bagani* political structure is no longer a system of action, it still remains the central key linkage with the past and with religious symbolism which sanctifies the past as mythic threads linking the sky and the underworld. Again, the natural landscape encodes origins and events as semi-sacred based on the deeds of a heroic past which is now entering a period of endangerment.

Origins as the expression of precedence and egalitarianism as value present an interpretation of society and a cultural logic which moves away from a unified coherence, one in which all the strands of society work in a collective and harmonious manner. This kind of dual structure is based on the imperative quality that origin cannot be reduced to egalitarianism and, in turn, a system of local level equality is established and maintained by limiting rank and status differentiation to those realms of cultural institution which will not impinge on daily life.

References

Cole, F.C.

1913   *The wild tribes of Davao district, Mindanao*. Chicago: Field Museum of Natural History.

Dumont, Louis

1975   Preface by Louis Dumont to the French edition of *The Nuer*. Translated by Mary and James Douglas. In J.H.M. Beattie and R.G. Lienhardt (eds) *Studies in social anthropology*, pp. 328-342. Oxford: Clarendon Press.

1979   The anthropological community and ideology. *Social Science Information* 18:785-817.

1980   *Homo hierarchicus: an essay on the caste system*. Revised edition. Chicago: University of Chicago Press.

1982   On value. In *Proceedings of the British Academy*, Vol. 66, pp.207-241. Oxford: Oxford University Press..

Fox, James J.

1990   Hierarchy and precedence. Working Paper No. 3. Canberra: Comparative Austronesian Project, Department of Anthropology, Research School of Pacific Studies, The Australian National University.

Garvan, J.M.

1931   *The Manobos of Mindanao*. Memoirs of the National Academy of Sciences, Vol. 23. Washington, DC: Government Printing Office.

Gibson, Thomas

1985   The sharing of substance versus the sharing of activity among the Buid. *Man (N.S.)* 20:391-411.

1986   *Sacrifice and sharing in the Philippine Highlands: religion and society among the Buid of Mindoro*. London School of Economics, Monographs on Social Anthropology No. 57. London: The Athlone Press.

Yengoyan, Aram A.

1964   Environment, shifting cultivation, and social organization among the Mandaya of eastern Mindanao, Philippines. PhD dissertation, University of Chicago.

1965   Aspects of ecological succession among Mandaya populations in eastern Davao Province, Philippines. *Papers of the Michigan Academy of Science, Arts and Letters* 50:437-443.

1966a   Baptism and "Bisayanization" among the Mandaya of eastern Mindanao Philippines. *Asian Studies* 4:324-327.

1966b   Marketing networks and economic processes among the abaca cultiv-
        ating Mandaya of Eastern Mindanao, Philippines. Report to the Agricul-
        tural Development Council, New York.

1966c   Marketing networks and economic processes among the abaca cultivat-
        ing Mandaya of Eastern Mindanao, Philippines. Reprinted from report
        and abstracted in R.E. Borton (ed.) *Selected readings to accompany getting
        agriculture moving*, Vol. 2, pp.689-701. New York: Agricultural Develop-
        ment Council.

1970a   Man and environment in the rural Philippines. *Philippine Sociological
        Review* 18:199-202.

1970b   Open networks and native formalism: the Mandaya and Pitjantjatjara
        cases. In M. Freilich (ed.) *Marginal natives: anthropologists at work*,
        pp.403-439. New York: Harper and Row.

1971   The Philippines: the effects of cash cropping on Mandaya land tenure.
        In R. Crocombe (ed.) *Land tenure in the Pacific*, pp.362-376. Melbourne:
        Oxford University Press.

1973   Kindreds and task groups in Mandaya social organization. *Ethnology*
        12:163-177.

1975a   Introductory statement: Davao Gulf. In F.M. LeBar (ed.) *Ethnic groups
        of insular Southeast Asia: Philippines and Formosa*, Vol. 2, pp.50-51. New
        Haven, CT: Human Relations Area Files Press.

1975b   Mandaya. In F.M. LeBar (ed.) *Ethnic groups of insular Southeast Asia:
        Philippines and Formosa*, Vol. 2, pp.51-55. New Haven, CT: Human Re-
        lations Area Files Press.

1977   Southeast Mindanao. In F.M. LeBar (ed.) *Insular Southeast Asia: ethno-
        graphic studies*, Section 4; *Philippines*, Vol. 1, pp.79-116. New Haven,
        CT: Human Relations Area Files Press.

1983   Transvestitism and the ideology of gender: Southeast Asia and beyond.
        In Vivian Patraka and Louise A. Tilly (eds) *Feminist re-visions: what has
        been and might be*, pp.135-148. Ann Arbor: University of Michigan,
        Women's Studies Program.

1985   Memory, myth and history: traditional agriculture and structure in
        Mandaya society. In Karl L. Hutterer, A. Terry Rambo and George
        Lovelace (eds) *Cultural values and human ecology in Southeast Asia*,
        pp.157-176. Ann Arbor: University of Michigan, Center for South and
        Southeast Asian Studies Paper No. 27.

1988   Hierarchy and the social order: Mandaya ethnic relations in Southeast
        Mindanao, Philippines. In A. Terry Rambo, Kathleen Gillogly and Karl
        L. Hutterer (eds) *Ethnic diversity and the control of natural resources in*

Southeast Asia, pp.173-195. Michigan Papers on South and Southeast Asia Number 32, Center for South and Southeast Asian Studies. Ann Arbor: The University of Michigan.

Chapter 7. The Transformation of Progenitor Lines of Origin: Patterns of Precedence in Eastern Indonesia

James J. Fox

Introduction

This paper forms part of an extended argument that is concerned with ideas of origin and precedence among Austronesian-speaking populations (Fox 1988a, 1989, 1990, 1994, 1995). It examines the way in which culturally specific ideas of origin give rise to different forms of social precedence in a number of societies in eastern Indonesia. As such, the paper is also concerned with comparison. It explores, within a particular region, the possibilities of comparison among societies that share a common heritage of ideas — in this case, expressed in terms of related concepts of origin.

The context for this argument was set forth in the paper, "Models and Metaphors: Comparative Research in Eastern Indonesia", which constituted my concluding comments to *The Flow of Life*. In that paper, I argued for a wider Austronesian framework for the comparative consideration of the societies of eastern Indonesia. Although eastern Indonesia may contribute a great deal toward the reconstruction of a model of a proto-Austronesian social world, nevertheless the region represents only one area of a vast Austronesian world. On methodological grounds, sound lexical construction must be based on a whole range of evidence from the entire Austronesian language area (Fox 1980:328-329). Thus F.A.E. van Wouden's inspired attempt (1935, 1968) to give a privileged position to the evidence from the societies of eastern Indonesia for the construction of a model of ancient Indonesian society was inevitably suspect because of the regional limits he himself set for his particular attention. Moreover, by concentrating on a particular "model" based on a structural core of formal constructs, van Wouden focused attention on certain characteristics of marriage alliance that have since become an emblem for distinguishing eastern Indonesia from the rest of the Austronesian world. As a result, eastern Indonesia may appear to stand apart from the rest of the Austronesian world.

In the paper on "Models and Metaphors", I went on to argue that the tendency of recent ethnographic research in eastern Indonesia was to study each society from within and in terms of its own social categories:

Research on the social categories of particular societies has not tended to dispel the notion of a structural core but rather to reinterpret it. Instead of relying on a formal model consisting of predefined elements, researchers have begun gradually to redefine a structural core in terms of a common set of shared social categories (1980:330-331).

This shift from a study of models to a study of social metaphors provides a better linguistic basis for comparative analysis. Without diminishing the distinctiveness of the region it may also allow the means of interpreting the evidence of the region within a wider framework. The task is to reinterpret this regional evidence systematically but in such a way as to permit comparison with other Austronesian societies.

Finally, in the same paper, I argued specifically that adopting an analysis of the distinctive social categories that constitute the "idiom of alliance" in eastern Indonesia would "eventually alter the conceptual status and relevance of van Wouden's most important analytic categories — those of wife-giver and wife-taker" (1980:332). To this end, I provided several examples of the distinct social categories from different societies in eastern Indonesia that were glossed by different ethnographers as "wife-giver" or "wife-taker". I also pointed to the recurrent use of a botanic idiom and of particular cognates of the Austronesian term for "trunk", "root", "base" or "origin" in the metaphoric conceptualization of alliance relations.

It is to these issues that I wish to return in this present paper. However, I want to attempt to do more than offer a linguistic exegesis of a set of related social categories. Rather I would like to advance a corresponding sociological analysis based on the concept of precedence.

Precedence in Eastern Indonesia

Precedence is an oppositional notion based on the assertion of a relational asymmetry. It is thus a socially-asserted claim to difference that generally involves an affirmation of some form of "superiority" and/or "priority". As a relational assertion, it is invariably applied recursively to create a concatenation of relationships. Recognizable concatenations of such relationships may be distinguished as "lines" or "orders" of precedence (Fox 1994). The study of precedence requires that attention be focused on: 1) the categorical bases for the assertion of precedence; 2) alternative, competing claims to precedence among groups and individuals; and 3) the consequence of the social competition for precedence.

In eastern Indonesia, precedence is linguistically constructed by recourse to any of a variety of complementary categories (such as male/female, elder/younger, first-born/last-born, inside/outside, prior/later, or trunk/tip). These categories serve as linguistic "operators" that are asymmetrically marked and recursively applied (Fox 1989). Unlike the Dumontian notion of hierarchy based as it is on a single-valued all-encompassing relationship, precedence is structurally relative, temporally contingent, and often disputed. Different operators may be invoked to create alternative forms of precedence. Precedence may serve as the means for establishing rank; but it is not the equivalent of hierarchy. Based on differentiation, precedence may be used to create or to undermine what are generally regarded as "hierarchical structures" (Fox 1990, 1994).

Using this concept of precedence, I would like to reexamine the formal categories designated as "wife-giver" and "wife-taker" in eastern Indonesia. As formal categories, they correspond to no single set of identifiable native categories in these different societies. One of my intentions in this paper is therefore to survey those categories that are in fact "translated" as "wife-giver" and "wife-taker". I want to consider these categories as they are used within each society and to consider the relationships that they define.

The Concept of Origin Group: Genitor and Progenitor

An analysis based on the concept of precedence must be linguistically grounded in terms of the categories used to create that precedence. Discussion of the categories glossed as "wife-giver" and "wife-taker" in eastern Indonesia opens up an elaborate metaphoric epistemology of origins, itself a reflection of a distinctive Austronesian view of life. In accord with this view of life, various social groups in eastern Indonesia (and elsewhere among Austronesian-speaking populations) may appropriately be regarded as "origin groups" since what they claim to share and to celebrate is some form of common derivation. This derivation is socially constructed and may be variously based on the acknowledgement of a common ancestor, a common cult, a common name or set of names, a common place of derivation, and/or a share in a common collection of sacred artefacts. In eastern Indonesia, comparative sociology begins with a study of these "origin groups" and their relationships to one another.

There is a comparative linguistic aspect to this comparative sociology in that both notions "origin" and "relationship", are expressed in similar sets of idioms, frequently (but by no means exclusively) based on botanic metaphors. Understanding these idioms and their use as discourse provides an initial basis for understanding relations among groups.

For the purposes of this paper, as an initial approach in keeping with the idioms that I am attempting to explore, I would like to distinguish between "genitor" and "progenitor". All "origin groups" in eastern Indonesia perpetuate themselves by reference to either "genitor" or "genetrix" lines of derivation.[1] Internal relations among these lines, which share a common origin, are based on various forms of precedence, such as elder/younger, male/female, inside/outside, first-born/last-born. Relationships between different origin groups, however, are structured on other criteria of precedence. Origin groups generally acknowledge and give precedence to a "progenitor" line (or lines). By this, I mean a line (or lines) that stand in relation to a genitor/genetrix line as "life-giving" pro(to)-genitor. This relationship is critical — particularly in an epistemology of origins — since this line is the "origin of life" for another origin group.

Exploration of these notions is a complex task and this paper provides only a bare sketch of aspects of these notions. One of the most interesting features of this exploration is that societies with origin groups based on genetrix lines are not simply a mirror image of societies with origin groups based on genitor lines. It is this feature that I wish to examine after sketching the outlines of a number of societies based on genitor-progenitor relations.

My initial task is to identify such lines in a number of different societies so as to make clear what it is that I mean by the relationship genitor/progenitor. My second task is to examine how such lines function in these different societies, thus setting the stage for consideration of how these relationships may be transformations of one another.

In this paper, I want to consider progenitor relations of origin in six separate societies of the Timor and Flores area. These societies are: 1) the Mambai, 2) the Ema, 3) the Rotinese, 4) the Timorese or Atoni (Pah) Meto, 5) the Tetun of Wehali, and 6) the Ata Tana 'Ai. The languages of these societies are relatively closely related and all are classified as belonging to the putative "Timorese subgroup" of Central Malayo-Polynesian. Linguistic similarities among these languages facilitate examination of the epistemology of social practice.

I begin therefore with the mustering of the basic evidence for my argument.

1. The Mambai

The Mambai of East Timor provide an appropriate starting point for this analysis since the notions I wish to examine have already been brilliantly highlighted by Elizabeth Traube in her monograph, *Cosmology and Social Life* (1986) and particularly in her paper, "Obligations to the Source" (1989).

The Mambai constitute a population of approximately 80,000 living in dispersed hamlets in the mountainous area of east central Timor. The Mambai, who rely mainly on the swidden cultivation of maize, rice and root crops, do not have centralized villages. Hamlets consist of small groups of houses (*fada*) which function as minimal lineages. Houses are divided into a large number of cult groups (*lisa*) each of which shares a common cult house (*fad lisa*) and serves as the locus for ceremonial activity. These cult groups are in turn organized into a "great cult" (*lis tu*) whose house constitutes the "stem house" or "house of origin" (*fada ni fun*). Several great houses may share a single hilltop site with each huge house arranged in a circle around a round stone altar at the centre of which stands a three-pronged ritual post.

Various idioms are used to describe cult relations. Members of a great cult are elder/younger (*kak-alin*) to one another. The great cult house is "mother and father" (*inan nor aman*) and the lesser houses are its children (*anan*). Alternatively, these lesser cult houses are the "twigs" (*snikin*) established by a younger sibling who "plucks a leaf//breaks a branch", selects a rock and a sacred object and sets out to found his own separate house. The scattered children of a great house are supposed to unite periodically at their "source" or "origin" (*fun*). The organization of this kind of origin group is traced through males and is supposed to be exogamous. These houses that recognize a common "house of origin" form a single "origin group" based on "genitor" lines.

Among the Mambai, each origin group recognizes two progenitor houses (or lines). Collectively, these primordial progenitors are referred to as *umaen fun* (lit., "male houses of trunk or origin") or *nai fun* (lit., "mothers' brothers of origin"). Alternately, these lines are distinguished as "mother water buffalo and father water buffalo" (*arabau inan nor arabau aman*). The "father water buffalo" designates the earliest progenitors; the "mother water buffalo" the subsequent progenitors. Together these progenitor lines are described as "those who support the rock//those who steady the tree". As Traube makes clear, this botanic idiom is pervasive:

> Symbolically, the original "trunk" givers of women are the source of all persons engendered in the wife-taking house, and they are linked through the daughters of their daughters to still other wife-taking houses. As the Mambai say of marital alliance: "Its trunk sits there. The bits of its tip go out again and again" (1986:86).

From the perspective of the progenitor lines, the lines they engender are referred to in various ways. In contrast to their own *umaen fun* (the "male houses of origin"), they are *maen heua*: lit., "new males", a term which is the kin category for daughter's husband (DH) and sister's child (ZC). In opposition to their *nai fun*, "mother's brothers of origin" they are the *kai akin*, "father's sisters (FZ) of long ago".

This primordial relationship between progeny and progenitor is described by the Mambai as "sisters since the base of heaven//brothers since the rim of earth" (*tbo hoir lelo fun//nara hoir rai ehan*). Here, too, there is the recurrent emphasis on category of *fun*: "base", "origin", "trunk", "source". Traube adds the important qualification for an understanding of nature of this primordial relationship:

> If a man wants to marry a woman from an unrelated house, he must first ask ritual permission of his *umaen-fun* ("wife-givers of origin" or "trunk wife-givers"). He must pay his *umaena* for the *seita nor aifa* ("the torch

and the fire") to "light the dark path" as he searches for a wife among strangers (1980:353, n.10).

In this way, the primordial relationship of progenitor of origin is retained through the vicissitudes of changing alliances.

2. The Ema

The Ema are a population of over 50,000 living in the mountains to the west of the Mambai. Their main subsistence crop is maize but they cultivate both wet and dry rice and maintain terraced fields built on rocky slopes. The Ema speak a language that is closely related to that of the Mambai, though this language does not have the metathesis common in Mambai. They have been described in general and in detail by Brigitte Renard-Clamagirand in an important paper, "The Social Organization of the Ema of Timor" (1980) and in the monograph, *Marobo: Une société ema de Timor* (1982). Despite a slightly different theoretical terminology, the description of the Ema points to considerable similarities with the Mambai.

The Ema recognize two types of settlement. *Ilat* land located on the upper slopes of Mount Marobo which is subject to ritual prohibitions and *rae mdon* which is open land, available as new farm land and free of ritual prohibition. "Core houses" (*uma lulin*: "sacred house" or *umar no apir*: "house and hearth") are built on *ilat* land and oriented to the west. These core houses play a central role in the ceremonial life of various lines of elder/younger (*ka'ar-alir*) brothers who inhabit dependent houses, designated by different terms depending on their relation to their core. As among the Mambai, elder/younger categories can also be used to designate a relationship between independent core houses that claim a common origin, which is often marked by a shared name (1980:136-139).

These variously named core houses can be regarded as origin groups structured on the basis of genitor lines. There is, however, an aspect to these origin groups that is elaborated much more among the Ema than among the Mambai. Although Traube mentions that there is some relative ranking among great cult houses, this dimension does not appear to be highly developed among the Ema. By contrast, among the Ema, precedence exists not only within core houses but also among core houses. All core houses are divided into two categories: autochthonous core houses and immigrant core houses. The immigrant core houses are derived from three ancestral founders who assumed different functions within the society as a whole. One of these founders established a political dimension to Ema society by giving rise to the three chieftains who rule Marobo.

Like the Mambai, the Ema recognize two progenitor lines that are referred to as *uma mane*: "masculine houses" or "male houses". (The equivalent Mambai term is elided and metathesized as *umaen*.) The term, *uma mane pun*, literally "male house(s) of origin" is also used in this connection. The multiple senses of the cognate term, *fun/pun*, allow a variety of translations for expressions that are clearly related. Thus Traube translates *umaen fun* as "wife-givers of origin" or "trunk wife-givers" whereas Renard-Clamagirand translates *uma mane pun* as "base house of the wife-givers". In this paper, I refer to both as "progenitors of origin". These progenitors are also identified as *na'ir no tatar*, "mother's brothers and ancestors" or sometimes as *inar no amar*, "mothers and fathers". As among the Mambai, Ema progenitors refer to their engendered lines as *mane heu*, "new males", who may also be spoken of either as *kir no bagir*, "father's sisters (FZ) and their husbands (FZH)" or as *mtor no anar*, "sisters and their children".

The established relationship between progenitor and progeny is described by the expression, *ai mea*. Although Renard-Clamagirand does not provide a translation for *ai mea*, a literal rendering of this expression would be the "red tree" or more appropriately, the "dry tree". A careful reading of the ethnography suggests that the Ema oppose the categories *mea/mdon*, "red/green" or "dry/fresh", implying that what is red or dry is old and set with ritual prohibitions; whereas what is green and fresh, and thus still sprouting, is new and as yet free of ritual injunctions — as, for example, the *rae mdon*. An appropriate translation of this Ema expression would be "old tree". Certainly the botanic metaphor of a tree is consistent with other Ema expressions for this relationship. Thus the progenitors refer to those engendered by their progeny as their "new male leaves and tree tops" (*mane heu tahan no laun*).

Although the *ai mea* relationship is regarded as primordial, Renard-Clamagirand remarks that in fact "the '*ai mea*' title does not always correspond to the most ancient ties because when a previously allied group disappears or ties with an allied group are severed, the title is bestowed on another core house" (1980:142).

At this point following a geographical progression, it would be appropriate to consider the case of the Tetun and then that of the Atoni Meto who form the dominant population of West Timor. However, for purposes that will become clear as I present my argument, it is more appropriate to consider next the case of the Rotinese.

3. The Rotinese

The Rotinese, who number over 120,000, occupy both the island of Roti, off the west tip of Timor, as well as stretches of West Timor. Since the seventeenth century, Roti has been divided into various separate domains known as *nusak* that have consistently endeavoured to distinguish themselves from one another. There were seventeen such domains with considerable variation — linguistic, social and political — among them. I confine myself here to common cultural features of all the domains.

Each Rotinese domain is composed of a number of named *leo* which are internally segmented to the level of individual *uma*. These are the Rotinese origin groups. Residence is scattered and members of different *leo* live interspersed with one another. All *leo* acknowledge a shared origin (*hu*) and formerly, this common heritage was celebrated at an annual Feast of Origin (*Hus*) performed around a large living tree ringed by rocks. The idea that the *leo* was once represented by a single cult house persists, especially in parts of West Roti, but in fact, after several centuries of Christianity, *leo* no longer possess a common ceremonial focus.

The different lines within a *leo* are described as its branches (*ndanak*) and precedence among these branches is structured according to relations of elder/younger (*ka'a/fadi*). Elder generally takes precedence over younger, although in some instances of succession, ultimogeniture overrides precedence by relative age. Thus the "last-born" (*mulik*) may take precedence over the "firstborn" (*uluk*). The last-born son, for example, inherits the parental house and the ancestral cult that it houses.

Some *leo* are divided into named "stomachs" or "insides" (*teik*); in such cases, the *teik* rather than the *leo* is the exogamous group. *Teik*, in turn, are described as consisting of *uma*, "houses". Links between *uma* or between *teik* within each *leo* are traced by reference to a succession of patronyms. This reckoning distinguishes the genitor lines of each origin group. They are the structural equivalent of the *fada/lisa* lines among the Mambai and of the various *uma* segments among the Ema.

Rotinese society shows greater similarities to the Ema than to the Mambai and indeed Rotinese society has developed and elaborated tendencies that Renard-Clamagirand identifies in Marobo. All *leo* are either autochthonous *leo* or immigrant *leo*, with immigrant *leo* overwhelmingly predominant — both numerically and socially. In all domains, however, autochthonous *leo* retain precedence in matters of ritual, particularly rituals of the earth.

In each Rotinese domain — as is the case in Marobo — one immigrant line is the source of political authority and claims precedence over all other *leo*. This line is the "source" of nobility which is defined by an equation between "rule" and "maleness" (*mane* = male, lord). This lordly line sets the point in relationship to which status is determined according to a complex system of precedence. The status of all *leo* — and their segments — is thus politically defined. To exist within the domain, a *leo* must be recognized by the royal court. This pervasive political dimension to Rotinese society is not a recent phenomenon but can be traced back to the seventeenth and early eighteenth centuries (see Fox 1979a,b).

The prior "cult" foundation of *leo/teik/uma* has been transformed within a court framework.

Like the Mambai and Ema, most Rotinese acknowledge two progenitor lines.[2] They are referred to collectively as the *to'o-bai-kala*, "mother's brothers and mother's mother's brothers". Specifically, the representative of each of these progenitor lines is identified as the *to'o-huk*, "mother's brother of origin", and the *bai-huk*, the "mother's mother's brother of origin". The recognition of progenitors is not acknowledged at the level of the *leo* nor — except in the case of a few royal lines — at the level of the *teik*, but only at the level of the *uma*. This means that progenitors are not regarded as primordial but differ for each sibling group derived from the same mother.

For purposes of comparison, it is worth noting here that the Rotinese have a term for son-in-law or daughter's husband, *mane feuk*, which literally means "new male". This term is cognate with the Mambai term *maen heua* and Ema *mane heu*. However, among the Rotinese, "new male" is not used in a wider sociological sense to define a line of engendered progeny. The female equivalent is "new female", *feto feuk*, which refers to a daughter-in-law or son's wife.

Among the Rotinese, a progenitor relationship is recreated for each generation. Instead of focusing on the *mane feuk*, this relationship focuses specifically on the sister's child who is referred to as "plant" (*selek*) or as the "planted sprout" (*sele-dadik*). In Rotinese, there is no other "kin term" for sister's child except this designation as "plant" (see Fox 1971).

In this situation, the payment of bridewealth is fundamental to the establishment of a progenitor relationship. Bridewealth (*belis*) serves as a critical marker of the relationship and the amount of bridewealth paid is an index of the "status" of the progenitor line. However, equally crucial to this relationship is temporality. It is not an enduring relationship. Severance of this relationship is essential to it. Mortuary payments do not simply acknowledge this relationship. At the appropriate point, they formally sever it. Thus the progenitor relationship is explicitly one of short duration. It always exists but it changes in each generation.

The situation can — and does — occur where genitor and progenitor relationships are confounded. This occurs whenever bridewealth is not paid and a woman's child is incorporated in his or her mother's origin group. Rotinese prefer to cast a shroud over occurrences of this kind but they are always made evident when mortuary payments must be made. When a house has no sons and only a daughter, the daughter may be allowed lovers in the hope of giving birth to a son who will continue the male line. This is described as "retaining a sister [for her] to give birth for her father and brother".

Alternatively a stranger — someone from outside the domain or preferably from another island — may "marry" a daughter of the house and have children who are regarded as children of their mother's origin group. After two generations, the tracing of origins by the recitation of a succession of genealogical names obscures this situation and the names of children of women are assimilated to the male line. The adoption of children, except of children of the closest members of one's own origin group, is rare and is not given social approval.

4. The Atoni Meto

The Atoni (Pah) Meto are the dominant population of west Timor. For more than two hundred years, they have steadily expanded westward and northward from the eastern uplands of west-central Timor. Their population now numbers over 750,000 and their social organization shows two modalities that are each the expression of similar organizing principles under different conditions. In one modality, older political centres endeavour to maintain formal relationships established in the past while in another modality, newer settlements establish new relationships as expansion continues.

This sketch derives from various sources: 1) my own intermittent fieldwork in southern Amanuban; 2) the excellent thesis, *Narrating the Gate and the Path*, by Andrew McWilliam (1989) on the basis of extensive fieldwork throughout Amanuban; 3) the University of Indonesia thesis, *Ekologi, persebaran penduduk dan pengelompokan orang Meto di Timor Barat*, by Hendrik Ataupah (1992) on the Sonbai area to the north of the Noil Mina; and 4) the "classic" studies of the Atoni by Clark Cunningham (1966, 1967), P. Middelkoop (1931) and H.G. Schulte Nordholt (1971).[3]

Like the Rotinese, the Atoni Meto recognize origin structures of long and of short duration. The Atoni Meto are divided into as many as 400 separate origin groups, each of which is distinguished and identified by the sharing of a common name, *kanaf* (or in ritual language, *kanaf ma bonif*). Implied in the possession of this common name is a common origin from an ancestor identified by the term, *u(f)*, which is the metathesized cognate of the terms, *fu/pu/hu*. The place of origin of the first ancestor is generally associated with an unusual rock outcrop, *fatu* (or in ritual language, *fatu ma hau*, "rock and tree"). Andrew McWilliam describes this botanic metaphor brilliantly but succinctly:

> The Atoni Meto "conceive of the name group in a botanical idiom whereby the founding ancestor is considered the trunk (*uf*) and his descendants are the small branches (*tlaef*), the tips (*tunaf*), or the flowers (*sufan*). The name group is therefore considered as a tree (*hau uf mese* — one tree trunk) in which there is an unbroken and organic link to the ancestral 'trunk' father" (1989:142).

Despite their emphasis on a common trunk, individual segments of a *kanaf* or "name group" exist as fragments scattered over all of west Timor, clustering in greater concentrations in certain areas but still scattered. Certain name groups hold political dominance over particular territories and have gathered other name groups around them in specific ritual relationships. Knowledge of past genealogies is limited. Instead of tracing social origins by means of a succession of genealogical names — as among the Rotinese — Atoni Meto trace their origins spatially as a journey of the *kanaf* name through a landscape of place names.

The scattering of segments of the *kanaf* has given rise to the spectacular expansion of the Atoni Meto but it does not of itself provide a basis for the structure of the society. The real genius of the system is the way in which these fragments are structured by means of precedence based on progenitor lines of origin.

Like the Rotinese, the Atoni Meto use the same metaphor of "trunk" to describe origin structures of relatively short duration. Every Atoni settlement must have a *kua tuaf* who, as lord of the settlement, is referred to as its *uf*, "trunk" or "origin". In theory, this "trunk" (*uf*) represents the name group (*kanaf*) whose original ancestor founded the settlement, the right to do so having either been delegated from a political centre or from a name group with higher authority in the area. To gain admission to the settlement and to rights to land around it, each incoming member of another name group has to secure a relationship to the settlement's "trunk". Those who join a settlement are "those who come wandering" (*atoin anao amnemat*) or the "strange-eyed [hawk-eyed] people" (*atoin mata teme*).

A "settlement lord" (*kua tuaf*) becomes the *atoin amaf*, "mother's brother", a term which in this context designates the ultimate progenitor of the settlement. Generally a settlement lord establishes his position as progenitor by giving a woman to the first, and possibly the second, in-coming member of a different wandering name-group fragment. These groups, in turn over time, give women to other in-coming name groups so that — in theory — a well-ordered settlement is based on a clear line of precedence emanating from a single *uf-* progenitor. In contrast to the group of the settlement lord, the rest of the settlement are "in-marrying people" (*atoin asaot*) (see McWilliam 1989:143).

To understand the complexities of this system it is necessary to indicate the complementary categories or operators by which this system is structured. One set of categories is, as might be expected, "earlier"/"later" (*nahun/namuni* — *na-hun* being based, I believe, on an earlier form of the term, "trunk"). As the settlement lord's group develops, it segments along "elder/younger" (*tataf/olif*) lines, with the *tataf* or elder line retaining the institutional position of "mother's brother" (*atoin amaf*). This means in effect that members of an *olif* or younger line may marry in ways that do not maintain precedence but do not necessarily jeopardize the overall order of precedence in the settlement that is maintained by the elder line. Relations of precedence based on a uni-directional flow of women from the *atoin amaf* are phrased in terms of the categories of "male/female" (*mone/feto*). These categories are used as relational terms to define precedence. Progenitors are "male people" (*atoin amonet*) as opposed to the "female people" (*atoin amafet*), whom they engender. The term, "new male" (*mone fe'u*) is also used for sons-in-law and more generally all junior males who have received a woman from a particular group. The *atoin amaf* as ultimate progenitor of the settlement can be described figuratively as the "male or bull" (*mone/keso*) of the settlement.

Although there are established areas on Timor where bridewealth is important, in the expanding domain of Amanuban and especially at its southern and western periphery, bridewealth was previously not recognized and now is still only of minor significance. Formerly, a child was returned for the gift of a woman. As a result, any name group but particularly the name group of the settlement lord may include its own returned progeny. By the logic of the system, these returned progeny and their offspring are categorized as "female". Thus a settlement lord's group may have not only "elder/younger" lines but also an internal "female" line. This creates a certain ambiguity. The "male" line of a name group may marry with its internal "female" line. The group as a whole, however, also marries with its initial in-marrying "female" group from which its internal "female" line is often derived. Thus the name group of the settlement lord, in particular, engenders "female" -classified progeny both in the name group to whom it gives women and within itself. In established settlements, these two "female" groups/lines may merge so that it may be difficult to distinguish members of the "female" line of the settlement lord's group from members of the initial in-marrying group who — as is customary in Timorese tradition — act on behalf of their progenitor.

Only the directionality of the flow of women determines who is classified as "male" or "female" in this situation. Thus a line of precedence is never permanent. By reversing the direction of marriage, which is possible in the Atoni Meto symmetric marriage system, a name group or a line within such a group can alter its relative position of precedence. "Female" can become "male". This can occur at any position within the progenitor line. Any settlement lord who takes a wife from a female line or from another group in his settlement ceases to be the trunk of the settlement since he must acknowledge his progenitor as the new "trunk" or "origin" of the settlement.

5. The Tetun of the Southern Plain of Wehali

To this point, I have considered only societies with origin groups based on genitor lines. The Tetun of Wehali present the exceptionally interesting case of a society based on genetrix lines. With its genetrix lines, Wehali is distinguished from the majority of Tetun-speaking peoples who recognize genitor lines.

Wehali is a ritual centre on the south coast of central Timor whose population numbers approximately 40,000. The alluvial plain (*fehan*) on which Wehali is located stands in contrast to the mountains (*foho*) where most Tetun live. Wehali is considered *rai feto*, "female land", as opposed to *rai mane*, "male land", and is the traditional site of the Maromak Oan who is also described as the *Nai Bot*, "The Great Lord", or *Nai Kukun*, "The Dark Lord". To this Lord, tribute was paid by other Tetun for performance of the rituals of life. Two PhD dissertations have been written in the Department of Anthropology at The Australian National University on Wehali: G. Francillon's *Some Matriarchic Aspects of the Social Structure of the Southern Tetun of Middle Timor* (1967) and G.T. Therik's *Wehali, The Four Corner Land: The Cosmology and Traditions of a Timorese Ritual Centre* (1995). I have drawn this analysis from these two important studies.

Wehali is regarded by its population as the first dry land to have emerged from a primordial sea. This dry land first emerged in the form of an enormous banyan tree. Thus, as in other Timorese societies, "trunk" (*hun*) is conceived of, both literally and figuratively, as "origin". Ideas of origin are critical and pervasive in all narratives of the past. The origin narratives of the "earth" (*rai lian*), as indeed other "true narratives" (*lia tebes*), are all recited in a form of parallel language which is in fact known as "trunk" or "origin" language (*lia hun*).

In the first narrative of the earth, the "Only Woman on Earth" gave birth to a daughter whose umbilical cord was intertwined in the roots of the banyan. As she grew, so did the banyan to become dry land. As "trunk", she produced both sons ("fruit": *klaut*) and daughters ("flowers": *funan*) shaded by an evergrowing banyan. In local conceptions, Wehali is thus the first-born centre of the earth, its navel and "trunk land" (*rai hun*) (see Therik 1995:73-76). Settlement is localized and hamlets are classified ritually as either "male" or "female" depending on their ritual functions in relation to the central "female" settlement of the Maromak Oan. By recourse to folk etymology, the shade of the banyan (*leon*) and the male and female hamlets of Wehali (*leo*) are symbolically equated.

Conceived of as a female centre, Wehali is regarded as having sent forth its male progeny and to have shed all that is associated with male attributes, including wealth and power. According to a local saying, having given away the "sword", Wehali retains only its "sheath" (Fox 1983:25). This image provides the model for Wehali social life: men are sent forth while women remain to continue the flow of life from the first woman. All order in Wehali is therefore based on genetrix relations.

Wehali's origin groups resemble those of the other societies we have so far considered. Such groups are based on *uma*, "houses". An *"uma* group" consists of a "group formed by one house and its offshoots" (Francillon 1967: 331).

These named *"uma* groups" are the matrilineages that comprise matriclans known as *fukun*. *Fukun* may refer to the group as well as the head of this group, but it also designates "the knot, joint or node" of a stalk of bamboo. Relations within *uma*-groups (and within *fukun*) are considered as relations between "elder/younger" sisters (*bin/alin*), even when, as is often the case, exact genealogical relations between members of the group are unclear. A house or house group can be referred to as *inan feton*, "mother/sister" and a larger group as *ina bin alin*, "mother/elder-younger sister". The youngest sister (*feto ikun*) generally retains occupancy of her mother's house which continues to be the focus of ritual performance. In a large origin group, ritual functions may be divided and coordinated among constituent houses. In relative terms, one's natal house (or "birth place house": *uma moris fatik*) is regarded as one's origin house (*uma hun*), and this house serves as the point of reference in the arrangement of marriages.

Houses are exogamous and exchange males among each other. Residence is strictly uxorilocal. From this one might expect that houses would have progenitor relations with one another similar to the other societies that we have so far considered. However, this is not the case. The *mane foun*, the "new male", simply takes up residence with his wife. The gift of a male is not significant. What is significant is that for every male given to another house, a child, invariably a woman, must be returned. Thus every house receives a share of its own female progeny and engenders differentiation within itself. Every house is also its own progenitor via an intermediate genetrix-house.

The exchange of wealth at the time of marriage is not significant. What is important are subsequent exchanges that begin with the return of "source seed" (*mata musan*) following immediately on the death of the "new male". A person, either man or woman, can be designated as "source seed" to be returned to the husband-giving house. If the "source seed" is male, he is expected to marry his FZD (*talain feto*); if female, she is expected to marry her FZS (*talain mane*).

In practice, "source seed" is invariably a woman. The husband-giving group can delay mortuary ceremonies until their demands for a woman are granted and if no woman is available, then the return of "source seed" may be delayed a generation. The woman eventually given as "source seed" may in fact marry some other in-marrying male rather than her cross-cousin but in whatever way she marries, she and her daughters initiate a new line within the house (Therik 1995:127-130).

This exchange obligation between the two houses continues for a further generation. One of the daughters of the "source seed", preferably the eldest daughter, must be given back to the house from which her mother came.[4] This daughter is referred to as "banana head" (*hudi ulun*).

Thus each in-marrying male initiates an exchange that entwines two female-centred houses for at least two generations: "like storage baskets tied together or like wax candles that have melted into one" (see Therik 1995:124).

One implication is that progenitor lines in each generation replant new genetrix lines. The exchange of wealth to mark a distinction between genitor and progenitor, as among the Rotinese, does not occur nor is it considered necessary. However, as in Roti, a progenitor line is recognized for three generations back to an initiating "origin house" (*uma hun*). This line comes to the fore during mortuary ceremonies, particularly in negotiations over "source seed" before burial can take place, and this progenitor line continues for yet another generation to "entwine" the two exchanging houses.

To consider further the implication of this system, it is useful to consider another society like the southern Tetun with origin groups exclusively organized in terms of genetrix lines. This society is that of the Ata Tana 'Ai.

6. The Ata Tana 'Ai

Like the Tetun of Wehali, the Ata Tana 'Ai of central east Flores form a "female" enclave centred on the ritual domain of Tana Wai Brama. Within this enclave, a population of approximately 4,500 persons acknowledges a single source and unlike the surrounding population, recognizes genetrix — rather than genitor — lines of origin. E. Douglas Lewis in his recent book, *People of the Source* (1988), has provided a brilliant and thorough-going analysis of this remarkable society. My purpose here is merely to attempt to sketch elements of this ethnography in order to make comparisons with the other societies — particularly the Tetun — that I have so far considered.

In extending this analysis to this sixth case, we move a further "linguistic distance" from the other societies in this comparison. The Mambai, Ema, Rotinese, Atoni Meto and Wehali Tetun all speak languages that are more closely related to each other than any of these languages is to that of the Ata Tana 'Ai. Similar sociological structures are evident as are the general idioms that describe these structures but specific linguistic cognates, although they exist, are less immediately apparent.

Among the Tana 'Ai origin groups are known as *sukun*. These groups are appropriately described as "clans". Tana Wai Brama consists of four such *sukun* plus a central founding *sukun*, the *sukun pu'an*. This "source clan" presides over an order of precedence among the constituent clans that is believed to have been maintained since the founding of the domain.

Sukun are, in turn, divided into houses (*lepo*) consisting of consanguineally-related women (and their brothers). The inheritance of land, possessions and ritual rights passes from mother to daughter. *Lepo*, too, are ordered by precedence based on the categories of "elder/younger" (*wue/wari*) sister. There is a *lepo pu'an*, "source house", in each *sukun*. This is the highest ranking house in order of precedence within the *sukun*.

Men pass between *lepo*. As among the southern Tetun, an exchange of wealth at marriage does not occur. In a certain sense, marriage itself is not significant. It is not marked as a special event. There is no exchange or formal ceremony. What is marked, however, as among the southern Tetun, is the return of a child of a man who has served as progenitor in another *lepo*. This is referred to as the return of the "father's forelock" (*ama 'lo'en*) and is described as the return of the "father's blood". This exchange is marked by the payment of wealth in the form of a fixed quantity of elephant tusks and gongs (*to'o-balik*). This is, in some ways, the equivalent to "bridewealth" in societies such as Roti. Those who make the payment are called "the mother and father who buy and pay" (*ina ama baha boter*). Instead of creating a progenitor relationship of the sort that bridewealth establishes, this payment plants a new genitrix within the order of precedence of the *sukun*. A woman who is returned in this fashion is called an "ancestral mother" (*ina puda*) and she is seen as the founder of a new house in the clan. Again, as among the southern Tetun, such a woman may marry her FZS who is referred to as "elder" (*wue*) in a *wue/wari* relationship.[5]

Initially, the woman given as "father's forelock" and her descendants are *tudi manu*, "knife chicken" to the house that paid the wealth for her. This status is altered only when they in their turn pay *to'o-balik* to obtain the return of a "father's forelock" and thus become *ina ama baha boter* in their own right.

Exchanges do not end at this point. An *ina puda* line continues to acknowledge as *sukun pu'an*, "source clan", the clan from which their "ancestral mother" originated. Four generations later this line is supposed to return a woman (DDDD) "to replant the ancestral mother in the source clan". This woman as *mula puda* founds a new house in close relationship to the house from which the *ina puda* originated. She is expected to marry a son of the house of the "source clan" and this group returns half of the *to'o-balik* they received when the original *ina puda* was given. This then ends the cycle in which two *lepo* or their immediate replacement *lepo* have in the course of four generations each "planted" a woman as genitrix in the other. The botanic markers of relationships of origin are as clearly articulated among the Ata Tana 'Ai as in the other societies of the region.

Perhaps, however, the most significant evidence of the difference in the conception of progenitor lines between a society like Roti (or Sikka) and that of the Ata Tana 'Ai is in the performance of the mortuary ceremonies. On Roti, for example, these ceremonies are the occasion for payments to the progenitor line for its essential ritual services. Mortuary rituals can not be performed without the progenitors. In contrast, among the Ata Tana 'Ai, the *lepo* of the deceased makes all of the arrangements, provides all the goods necessary for burial, and feeds all of the guests — a majority of whom are members of the *lepo* itself (Lewis 1988:120). Performances, however, require an opposed mutuality and for this purpose, each clan is paired with a clan from another domain. The opposite paired clan comes from outside the domain to perform specific ritual services at the time of burial. The emphasis in these ceremonies is on the integration of the spirit of the deceased into the *lepo*. On Roti, such ceremonies can not be initiated by an origin group until the last payments for the deceased have been made to the progenitors.

Comment and Conclusion

This paper has presented a complex comparative argument. Its first purpose was to develop a form of comparative analysis that does not rely on the formal categories such as "wife-giver" and "wife-taker" (or their converse, "husband-giver" and "husband-taker"). The southern Tetun and the Ata Tana 'Ai provide ample evidence of the need to develop a different comparative framework. The use of the notions of progenitor and origin are intended to approximate conceptions that societies which I have considered, hold of themselves. The clues to these conceptions are indicated by the recurrent use of common botanic ideas of origin.

The first step in a comparative analysis of these societies is to note that all of them rely on "elder/younger" categories to distinguish genitor or genetrix lines and to order precedence among such lines. This is a common feature of societies of eastern Indonesia where such relative age categories are applied between same sex siblings and marks an important contrast with other Austronesian societies where such categories are applied both among same sex and opposite sex siblings.

Relative Age Categories: Genitor and Genitrix Lines

Mambai	*Kak - Ali*	Genitor lines
Ema	*Ka'ar - Alir*	Genitor lines
Rotinese	*Ka'a - Fadi*	Genitor lines
Atoni Meto	*Tataf - Olif*	Genitor lines
Wehali Tetun	*Bin - Alin*	Genitrix lines
Ata Tana 'Ai	*Wa'e - Waro*	Genitrix lines

There is more to this use of relative age categories among same sex siblings. As is evident among the Ata Tana 'Ai, "elder/younger" categories may also be applied to cross-cousins to designate potential spouses. Relative age categories can thus occur both in a marked and in an unmarked form, a feature which is widespread in Austronesian-speaking societies. In various eastern Indonesian societies where relative age terms are used to refer to same sex siblings, when these terms are applied between members of the opposite sex, they mark out the "marriageable category" of cross-cousins for purposes of directed marriages. Similarly, where the use of relative age terms is not confined exclusively to same sex siblings, as is the case among Javanese or Malay-speakers, these marked forms are used as intimate terms of endearment between a husband and wife or between lovers.

Proceeding further in a comparative analysis of these six societies, we may consider the various cases as relevant pairs as a means to identify commonalities and differences among them.

All of the societies with genitor lines recognize clearly defined progenitors. The Mambai and the Ema recognize two progenitor lines that are ritually fixed. They are conceived of as primordial and the establishment of relationships with other progenitors is mediated through these lines. These primordial progenitors provide the ritual services for those whom they have engendered. In contrast, the Rotinese, who acknowledge a two-generation line of progenitors, establish new lines for each generation of siblings. Bridewealth is essential to the creation of these lines and mortuary payments affirm and eventually serve progenitor relationships. On Roti, these progenitors of short duration perform the necessary rituals for those whom they have "planted". Among the Atoni Meto of Amanuban, progenitor lines are used as the primary mechanism for structuring new settlements. The progenitor line established by the head of a settlement provides a system of order for the settlement as a whole. A progenitor line of this sort is as precarious as the stability of a settlement.

Idioms of Origin: Progenitor Lines and their Progeny

	Progenitor	Progeny
Mambai	*Umaen Fun*	*Maen Heua*:
	"Male Houses of Origin"	"New Males"
	Nai Fun	*Kai Akin*:
	"Mother's Brothers of Origin"	"Father's Sisters of Long Ago"
Ema	*Uma Mane Pun*	*Mane Heu*:
	"Male House(s) of Origin"	"New Males"
	Na'ir No Tatar	*Kir No Bagir*:
	"Mother's Brothers and Ancestors"	"Father's Sisters and Their Husbands"
	Ai Mea	*Tahan No Laun*:
	"Dry Tree"	"Leaves and Treetops"
Rotinese	*To'o-Huk/Bai-Huk*	*Sele Dadi*:
	"Mother's Brother/Mother's Mother's Brother of Origin"	"Planted Sprout, Sister's Child"

Atoni Meto	*Uf* "Trunk, Origin"	*Tlaef, Tunaf, Sufan*: "Small Branches, Tips, Flowers"
	Atoni Amaf "Mother's Brother"	*Mone Fe'u*: "New Males"
	Atoni Amonet "Male People"	*Atoni Amafet*: "Female People"
Wehali Tetun	*Uma Hun* "Origin House"	*Mane Foun*: "New Male"

The relation of progenitor and progeny is expressed as a relative dyadic relationship rather than, as is commonplace in formal analysis, a tri-partite relationship involving the inclusion of a hypothetical ego-line. The various terms that describe and define this relationship have a similar metaphoric cast among all of the related Timorese language populations. They are phrased in a botanic idiom, often contrast male to female, the mother's brother to the father's sister, or brother to sister, and invariably trace origins from "trunk" to tip. Similar idioms occur among the Wehali Tetun and among the Ata Tana 'Ai, where progenitor-progeny relations are transformed and internalized. Males marry out requiring progeny to be returned to form new origins with the genetrix group.

Marriage sets the pattern of progenitor-progeny relations.[6] Among the Mambai and Ema, these relations are conceived of as continuing. They are regarded as ancestral and it is essential that they be renewed through further marriages. As such, the directionality of these marriages is maintained. For the Rotinese, new progenitor-progeny lines are created with each marriage. They continue for two generations as "the path of life" from progenitor to progeny but they need not be renewed. Hence the directionality of marriage can shift from generation to generation. Among the Atoni Meto, marriage relations, unless they are institutionalized in ritual forms, are only as stable as particular settlements. Reversing the directionality of marriage changes political relations within settlements.

The payment of bridewealth and the return of progeny are critical to these relations. Among the Rotinese, bridewealth is considered essential for the establishment of a progenitor-progeny relationship. In cases when a woman becomes pregnant but bridewealth is not paid, progenitor and genitor are confounded and various devices are used to obscure the fact that a progeny has been incorporated as part of the genitor group. Among the Atoni Meto, the incorporation of progeny is a common practice. Traditionally, in Amanuban, a child was returned from each marriage as the appropriate payment for the gift of a woman. This returned progeny established a "female" line in relation to the "male" line of the original genitor group. Theoretically over several generations, this "female" line had three possibilities: 1) to continue as a "female line" with special ritual authority in the origin group; 2) to replace the "male" by reversing the directionality of marriage — the same mechanism utilized by any subordinate group to replace its superordinate in an order of precedence; or, 3) to sever dependent relations to the "male" line by establishing itself as a new "male" line in another settlement, a mechanism also open to any subordinate group in a settlement.

The Atoni Meto with their practice of returning one child from a marriage provide suggestive comparison with both the Wehali Tetun and the Ata Tana 'Ai where the return of progeny is of critical importance. In both of these societies, the return of a woman in place of her father eliminates any need for the payment of bridewealth. Progenitors thus engender themselves via an engendered group. Among both the Wehali Tetun and the Ata Tana 'Ai, it is evident that whereas a group engenders itself by means of an engendered group, this initial engendered group, at a further generation removed, receives a returned progeny and thus also engenders itself. Following the metaphors of the Ata Tana 'Ai, there occurs a reciprocal "planting" of new genetrix-founders.

This paper offers an initial analysis of progenitor lines of origin and their transformations in several related eastern Indonesian societies. In my sketches of each society, I have endeavoured to attend closely to metaphors of relationship and to follow the implications of what they imply. It is thus possible to see how each of these societies is an expression of a set of common concerns about the nature and continuation of life.[7]

These concerns are not exclusive to eastern Indonesia. They are, rather, a particular expression of ideas found throughout the Austronesian-speaking world. Hence this short paper suggests a form of comparative analysis that might be extended to focus on the transformation of Austronesian ideas of origin and derivation.[8]

References

Ataupah, Hendrik

1992 Ekologi, persebaran penduduk dan pengelompokan orang Meto di Timor Barat. Unpublished PhD thesis, Universitas Indonesia.

Cunningham, Clark E.

1966   Categories of descent groups in a Timor village. *Oceania* 37:13-21.

1967   Recruitment to Atoni descent groups. *Anthropological Quarterly* 40:1-12.

Fox, J.J.

1971   Sister's child as plant: metaphors in an idiom of consanguinity. In R. Needham (ed.) *Rethinking kinship and marriage,* pp.219-252. London: Tavistock.

1979a   A tale of two states: ecology and the political economy of inequality on the island of Roti. In P. Burnham and R.F. Ellen (eds) *Social and ecological systems*, pp.19-42. London: Academic Press.

1979b   Standing in time and place: the structure of Rotinese historical narratives. In A. Reid and D. Marr (eds) *Perceptions of the past in Southeast Asia*, no. 4, pp.10-25. Kuala Lumpur: Heinemann Educational Books (Asia) Ltd.

1980   Models and metaphors: comparative research in Eastern Indonesia. In J.J. Fox (ed.) *The flow of life: essays on Eastern Indonesia*, pp.327-333. Cambridge, MA: Harvard University Press.

1983   The great Lord rests at the centre: the paradox of powerlessness in European-Timorese relations. *Canberra Anthropology* 5(2):22-33.

1988a   Origin, descent and precedence in the study of Austronesian societies. Public Lecture in connection with De Wisselleerstoel Indonesische Studien, given on 17th March 1988. Published, Leiden University.

1988b   Foreword to E.D. Lewis, "People of the source: the social and ceremonial order of Tana Wai Brama on Flores", pp.xi-xiv. *Verhandelingen van het Koninklijk Instituut voor Taal-, Land- en Volkenkunde* No. 135.

1989   Category and complement: binary ideologies and the organization of dualism in Eastern Indonesia. In D. Maybury-Lewis and U. Almagor (eds) *The attraction of opposites: thought and society in a dualistic mode*, pp.33-56. Ann Arbor: University of Michigan Press.

1990   Hierarchy and precedence. Working Paper No. 3. Comparative Austronesian Project. Department of Anthropology, Research School of Pacific Studies, The Australian National University.

1994   Reflections on "hierarchy" and "precedence". In M. Jolly and M. Mosko (eds) *Special Issue of History and Anthropology. Transformations of hierarchy: structure, history and horizon in the Austronesian world*, 7(1-4): 87-108. Chur and Reading: Harwood Academic Publishers.

1995   Origin structures and systems of precedence in the comparative study of Austronesian societies. In P.J.K. Li, Cheng-hwa Tsang, Ying-kuei Huang, Dah-an Ho and Chiu-yu Tseng (eds) *Austronesian studies relating to Taiwan*, pp.27 57. Symposium Series of the Institute of History & Philology: Academia Sinica 3. Taipei.

Francillon, G.

1967   Some matriarchic aspects of the social structure of the Southern Tetun of Middle Timor. Unpublished PhD thesis, The Australian National University.

Graham, Penelope

1994   Alliance against hierarchy: affinal distinctions and sovereign rights in Eastern Flores, Indonesia. In M. Jolly and M. Mosko (eds) *Transformations of hierarchy: structure, history and horizon in the Austronesian world. Special Issue of History and Anthropology*, 7(1-4):339-362. Chur and Reading: Harwood Academic Publishers.

Lewis, E. Douglas

1988   People of the source: the social and ceremonial order of Tana Wai Brama on Flores. *Verhandelingen van het Koninklijk Instituut voor Taal-, Land- en Volkenkunde* No 135. Dordrecht: Foris Publications.

McWilliam, Andrew

1989   Narrating the gate and the path: place and precedence in South West Timor. Unpublished PhD thesis, The Australian National University.

Middelkoop, Peter

1931   Gegevens over het Timoreesche Adat-huwelijk. *Bijdragen Koninklijk Instituut voor Taal-, Land- en Volkenkunde* 88:239-286.

Renard-Clamagirand, Brigitte

1980   The social organization of the Ema of Timor. In J.J. Fox (ed.) *The flow of life: essays on Eastern Indonesia*, pp.134-151. Cambridge, MA: Harvard University Press.

1982   *Marobo: Une société ema de Timor*. Langues et Civilizations de L'Asie du Sud-Est du Monde Insulindien No. 12. Paris: SELAF/CNRS.

Reuter, Thomas

1992 Precedence in Sumatra: an analysis of the construction of status in affinal relations and origin groups. *Bijdragen tot de Taal-, Land- en Volkenkunde* 148:489-520.

Schulte Nordholt, H.G.

1971   The political system of the Atoni of Timor. *Verhandelingen van het Koninklijk Instituut voor Taal-, Land- en Volkenkunde* No. 60. The Hague: Martinus Nijhoff.

Therik, Gerzon Tom

1995 Wehali: the four corner land: the cosmology and traditions of a Timorese ritual centre. Unpublished PhD thesis, The Australian National University.

Traube, Elizabeth

1980   Mambai rituals of black and white. In J.J. Fox (ed.) *The flow of life: essays on Eastern Indonesia*, pp.290-314. Cambridge, MA: Harvard University Press.

1986   *Cosmology and social life: ritual exchange among the Mambai of East Timor*. Chicago: University of Chicago Press.

1989   Obligations to the source. In D. Maybury-Lewis and U. Almagor (eds) *The attraction of opposites: thought and society in a dualistic mode*, pp.321-344. Ann Arbor: University of Michigan Press.

van Wouden, F.A.E.

1935   *Sociale Structuurtypen in de Groote Oost*. Leiden: Ginsberg.

1968   *Types of social structure in Eastern Indonesia*. The Hague: Martinus Nijhoff. [English translation by Rodney Needham.]

Notes

[1] Here I intentionally wish to avoid the use of the term "descent" which in eastern Indonesia is often misleading and metaphorically inapt; I also want to avoid special reliance on criteria of genealogical reckoning. Only a few societies — or rather, certain segments within a few societies — in eastern Indonesia insist upon the maintenance of strict genealogical reckoning and it is, in fact, a sociological and historical question why this genealogical reckoning should be so prominent in these particular societies.

[2] On Roti there is differential recognition accorded progenitor lines as one moves from east to west. In the east three lines or three generations are recognized; in central Roti, two lines and as one moves to the further western end of the island, only one generation is said to be given full recognition.

[3] Part of this sketch has already been presented in Fox (1994, 1995).

[4] If there is only one daughter from a marriage and therefore no extra woman available to be returned to her father's house, the obligation is, by agreement, continued to the next generation. This is referred to by the expression "to raise the earth, to dam the water" (*tate rai halu we*). According to Francillon, "these are gardening terms and acts, the significance of which is to invigorate a plant" (1967:363). If ever a *mata musan* is not returned, it is said that the name of the man who was exchanged is "lost" (1967:364).

[5] Quite clearly the Ata Tana 'Ai recognize the implications of their system in comparison with that of the majority Sikkanese population who have a system of bridewealth payments like that of the Rotinese. As an Ata Tana 'Ai explained to Lewis, the Sikkanese "buy wives"; they "buy children" (Lewis 1988:211).

[6] In this paper, I have avoided discussing the formal marriage rules of these different societies. If one were to rely on marriage rules as formal criteria for the typological classification of these societies, these societies would be considered differently and the similarities that exist among them might be obscured. Of the six societies I have considered, one or possibly two would be classified as having asymmetric prescriptive alliance; one, symmetric prescriptive alliance while three have no marriage prescriptions but only formally expressed preferences that favour the directionality of marriage.

[7] I have already enumerated what I consider to be some of these common concerns in my Foreword to E.D. Lewis' *People of the Source* (1988:xii). A critical aspect of this concern for the continuation of life involves the aspiration to reunite that which was separated in a previous generation, namely, the sibling pair of brother and sister. The Mambai express this aspiration by conflating space and time and thereby describing the primordial relationship between progeny and progenitor as "Sisters since the Trunk of Heaven//Brothers since the Rim of the Earth".

[8] Analysis of these ideas of origin and derivation have already been undertaken by a number of students and colleagues from the Department of Anthropology. In addition to studies already cited and those

by B. Grimes, E.D. Lewis and M. Vischer in this volume, I would also point to papers by T. Reuter (1992) and P. Graham (1994).

Chapter 8. Origin Structures and Precedence in the Social Orders of Tana 'Ai and Sikka

E. D. Lewis

Both the people (*ata*) of Tana 'Ai and of Sikka, who inhabit the Regency of Sikka in east central Flores, refer to the past and, specifically, to myths of origin to explain the "sources" of the various groups which constitute their societies. The mapping of contemporary social organization onto events of the past and the invocation of mythic histories to explain the contemporary relations of social groups is significant in attempting to explain the apparent rank ordering of the social groups. Thus, in east central Flores, the legitimation of contemporary forms of social order is founded in contingent sequences of past events and it is with these representations of events, in history, that an analysis of hierarchy in Tana 'Ai and Sikka must begin. The result of such analyses is the specification of what Fox (1988:10-14) has termed "origin structures".

Origin structures are the representations of history by which contemporary social organization is legitimated and explained. Both the Ata Tana 'Ai and the Ata Sikka possess myths in which these origin structures are encoded. In both representations, a principle by which society is ordered is precedence, the sequence in time in which the constituent groups of society were founded or in which they became members of society. However, because origin structures are dependent upon contingent events, they differ from one society to another. What is consistent in both Tana 'Ai and Sikka is the centrality of precedence, the interplay of dual divisions of authority, and the role of alliance and exchange in the representation of society. In this paper, I will be concerned with the different ways in which these features of origin structures have operated to produce different social organizations in Tana 'Ai and Sikka, two societies which are closely related culturally.

Clans, Houses and History: The Origin Structure of Tana Wai Brama

The mythic histories which recount the foundation of the Tana 'Ai domain of Tana Wai Brama are essentially the story of one clan, Sukun Ipir Wai Brama, whose ancestors, Hading Dai Dor and Uher La'i Atan, were the first people to find and settle the land of the domain. The stories of the subsequent arrivals of the ancestors of clans Tapo, Mau, Magé and Liwu, the lesser clans of Tana Wai Brama, are cast in relation to the temporal priority and social and ceremonial precedence of Sukun Ipir. The *ngeng ngerang*, "history", of each subordinate clan establishes the legitimacy of the clan by tracing its obligations and prerogatives in the ceremonial system of the domain, its rights to land and its *hadat* ("customs", "rituals") to prestations by the ancestors of Ipir. The relations of the five clans to one another are thus founded, not on the reckoning of common origin or descent from a common ancestral line, but are represented as deriving from ceremonial alliances formed among people who were, originally, quite alien to one another. In this respect, it is proper to conceive of the domain of Wai Brama as consisting of peoples of five different nations joined in a confederation held together by a single ceremonial regime, what the people of Tana Wai Brama refer to as *hadat*. This regime is essentially that of clan Ipir, the founding, and hence *pu'an* ("source", "trunk") clan. The precedence of the clans of the domain is, as a consequence, strictly that whereby Ipir holds ultimate rights to the land, rights which over time were delegated variously to clans Tapo, Mau, Magé and Liwu. In all matters pertaining to *hadat*, Ipir is source and arbiter and, in ritual practice, is acknowledged as holding *oda*, "precedence", over all others, even those to whom the right to perform a rite may have been delegated.

Each clan consists of a number of "houses", the relations among which, in parallel to the order of clans in the domain, are ordered in terms of their precedence. The *oda* of houses within a clan is determined by the sequence of events in time by which the various houses were founded. Older houses are temporally closer to the source and thus take social and ceremonial precedence over more recently founded houses.

Protogenitrix Lines and the Precedence of Houses Within Tana 'Ai Clans

Every brother-sister pair in Tana Wai Brama is potentially the source of a new house. The socially reproductive potentialities of cross-sex siblingship are realized only when one of the pair, or both, marry someone of a different clan. A consequence of interclan marriage is the alienation of the brother's "blood" from his own maternal descent group, since "blood" and descent group affiliation are transmitted from mothers to daughters only. When a man who was father to children in a clan other than his own dies, one of his daughters, who is a member of her mother's clan, is returned to the father's clan, wherein she becomes the founder of a new house. Intraclan marriages entail no such exchanges since the father's blood remains within his clan, if not within his natal house. Thus each house in Tana Wai Brama traces its origin to a genitor (a father) of its own clan and a genitrix (a mother) of another clan. However, the genitrix, or *ina puda*, "ancestral mother" or "founding, original mother", is the ancestor of greater importance whose name identifies the house. Thus all of her descendants through women are her *pun* and it might be said, for example: "Ami lepo é'i Dala pun", "We of this house are Dala's people (Dala's descendants)". While people who are descended from a named *ina puda* constitute a group, these groups themselves recognize common origins in a prior protogenitrix line which locates its ancestry and source in the line of the *ina ama pu'an*, the founding ancestors of the clan. For reasons I have outlined elsewhere (Lewis 1988:231-232, 309-310), the source houses and older protogenitrix lines of a clan tend to die out, but the proliferation in time of new houses allied to protogenitrix lines insures the continuation of the clan.

The people of each house also recognize, in addition to a genitrix, a protogenitrix, either by name or, more commonly, by reference to the living descendants of the protogenitrix. Protogenitrix lines are those which were generated directly from the origin line of the clan, that is, the direct descendants through women of the clan's founding ancestors. It is through the links of genitor/genitrix and genitrix/protogenitrix that an Ata Tana 'Ai calculates a house's origin and its relation to the founding ancestors. A clan in Tana Wai Brama is thus a good example of what Fox has called an "origin group", that is, a group of people who:

> claim to share and to celebrate in some form of common derivation. This derivation is socially constructed and may be variously based on the acknowledgment of a common ancestor, a common cult, a common name or set of names, a common place of derivation, and/or a share in a common collection of sacred artefacts (Fox this volume:132).

This point is important for the analysis of the society of Tana Wai Brama because it indicates that at the heart of the domain's constitution is the idea that the domain's clans are fundamentally social entities of independent and diverse origins, even though in contemporary times they are closely bound together by both ritual and affinal relations. It is nevertheless the case, however, that the principles which govern the generation and organization of houses within the domain's clans are the same.

The Generation of Houses Within Tana 'Ai Clans

New houses are generated within a clan by the exchange of a man's daughter as *ama 'lo'en*, "father's forelock", for gongs and elephant tusks, the exchange occurring between two houses of different clans. While the dynamics and mechanism of these exchanges and their consequences can be demonstrated in genealogical terms (see Lewis 1988), the people of Tana Wai Brama do not themselves conceive of them primarily in this way. Rather, the idiom and metaphors they employ are those of the distinction between the trunk and leafy tips of a tree and the generation of offshoots from the nodes of a bamboo's culm. The mode of representation is thus, in terms of the Ata Tana Wai Brama themselves, a cladistic one in which a contemporary set of relationships among houses is the result of historical bifurcations from an original line of women.

While the genealogical relationships between house founders and their descendants may be remembered, it is not necessary to know them in detail in order to calculate the status of a house or individual in a clan. In effect, the contemporary rank ordering of houses preserves and collapses into the present relations of temporal precedence which result from dynamic processes of generation and reproduction. These relationships are represented as much, if not more, in established patterns of ceremonial and ritual obligation than in genealogy.

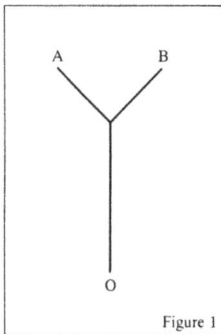

Figure 1

The first principle of the generation of a new house is that the protogenitrix line abides and survives the generation of the new house to coexist with it. This is a crucial point in the logic of precedence by which clans are organized. The bifurcation of a trunk can take place in two ways (Figure 1).

In this case, A and B both have their origins in O (origin), but neither is O. As a consequence, O, having given rise to two branches, that is, to two new lines simultaneously, disappears. The Ata Tana 'Ai liken this pattern of bifurcation to that of a tree's trunk at its first branching.

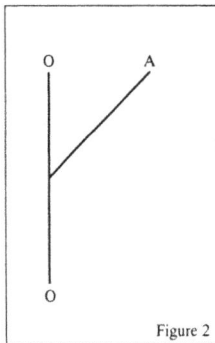

Figure 2

The second way a trunk can bifurcate is one which preserves the trunk while still generating new growth (Figure 2).

As the Ata Tana 'Ai pointed out to me, a tree's trunk can give rise to only two branches, but a bamboo's culm can give rise to many branches, one or more at each of its *matan*, "nodes". Indeed, in order for this to happen the trunk, or origin, must be preserved throughout the chain of branchings. Thus, sequential bifurcations from the trunk can give rise to the pattern shown in Figure 3.

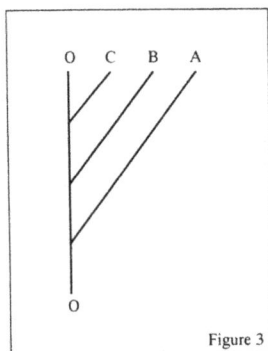

Figure 3

In this representation, a single, surviving trunk has given rise to many branches, one after another in sequence. This is the pattern of generation of houses within a clan and it is perhaps for this reason that the morphology of the bamboo is the most frequent source of metaphors for processes of social generation and reproduction in ritual language (cf. Lewis 1988:73-76).

Both patterns can, logically, provide the basis for the generation and differentiation of social groups from a single source. In the first case, however, two features of generation which may be exploited ideologically and in the ordering of the relations of social groups are lost. First is the temporality of the bifurcation. Both offspring groups are generated at the same time and, as a consequence, priority (or sequence) of generation cannot be invoked as a basis for subsequent differentiation of the groups without the imposition of another, externally derived principle. Second, neither group can be related in any material way to the origin line after the bifurcation because the origin line has ceased to exist of itself. Thus, the second pattern is perhaps better suited for the calculation of precedence, upon which the relationships of houses in Tana Wai Brama are articulated; first, because the origin group is always present and can more easily serve as the point of reference in the system and, second, because the generation of new groups occurs as a sequence of discrete events, each of which gives rise to one new group rather than to two. Thus, the new group can be juxtaposed to and differentiated from the original line without the invocation of additional principles, but merely by the application of a single value which accords superiority to the elder and relative inferiority to the younger. This single rule, applied sequentially as new lines are generated from a line of origin, is sufficient to order a limitless number of new lines in terms of precedence.

Not all houses in a clan of Tana Wai Brama arise directly from the line of ancestral founders. Houses, once generated, can themselves generate new houses, thus giving rise to the pattern implicit in Figure 4.

Two major conclusions may be drawn from this rather formalistic consideration of Tana 'Ai clanship.

First, if the order of society is considered atemporally at a particular moment in its history, then we might be led to conclude that Tana Wai Brama is a good example of a society consisting of rank-ordered groups — that is, that it consists of hierarchically ordered social groups. This conclusion would, of course, be in error. As time passes, old groups die out and new groups are created. As these events unfold, the statuses of individual persons change, sometimes radically, as when a high ranking group becomes *pu'an*, "source", within its clan.

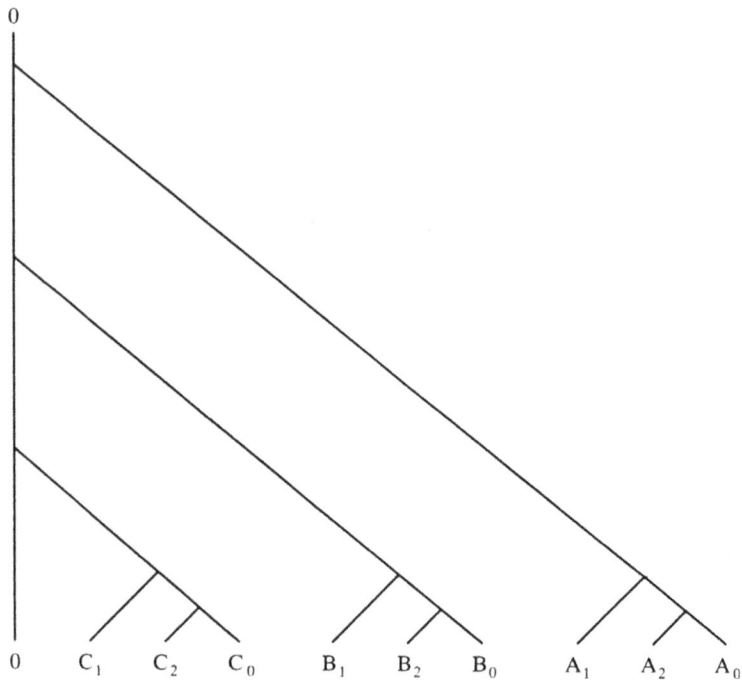

Figure 4

Second, in such a dynamic system, there is considerable scope for the negotiation of relationships in particular circumstances. For example, a particular exchange might occur which appears to violate rules governing the relations between groups of different status, but which does not threaten the whole system. Thus, this is a social order which is not only dynamic, but also extremely flexible and resilient to individual action contrary to accepted norms.

To this point I have dealt with what might be thought of as the fundamental order of the constituent groups of society, an order sanctioned in the mythic histories of the domain and articulated in its most important exchanges — i.e., in marriage. My argument has been that precedence, rather than hierarchy, is the fundamental operator which gives Tana 'Ai society its particular form.

There is, however, another aspect of hierarchy which must be considered in relation to the Tana 'Ai case, and that has to do with authority and power in Tana 'Ai society.

Precedence and the Delegation of Authority in Tana Wai Brama

In Tana Wai Brama, all rituals are celebrations of origins and the authority to conduct ritual is vested ultimately in the *tana pu'an*, the "Source of the Domain", who is always a man of clan Ipir and who, as a living descendant of the founding ancestors of the domain, is responsible for the maintenance of *hadat*, especially in matters pertaining to the relations of people to the land. However, the *tana pu'an* rarely performs ritual himself. Rather, he delegates to others the performance of particular rituals, just as the ancestors of clan Ipir delegated land and rights in the ceremonial system to the lesser clans of the domain. Thus, each clan of Tana Wai Brama includes a number of ritual specialists, each of whom is a chanter who knows the *ngeng ngerang*, the mythic histories, of his clan and who is skilled in the conduct of ritual. As these leaders derive their authority in ritual from the *tana pu'an*, so too do they further delegate the actual performance of ritual to other men who, in turn, may delegate further, even to young boys. Such delegations of the performance of ritual are represented in terms of *oda*, "precedence", such that whoever might actually sacrifice an animal in a ritual will say that he has been told to do so by someone else closer to the "source" of authority in the community.

Thus, with respect to the pragmatics of ritual performance in Tana Wai Brama, the Source of the Domain, the ritual leader of the community, delegates his authority to a hierarchy of ritual specialists who are thereby empowered to act, according to *hadat* on behalf of the Source. While the people of Tana Wai Brama locate the origin of the Source's authority in the mythic origins of the domain, they also say that his authority to act in particular situations derives from his sisters. A good example of how this works out in practice is the sacrifice of animals in ritual. An animal is usually killed by a person who lacks authority in the ritual. This actor is empowered through delegation to kill the animal by a ritual specialist who, in turn, has received his power by delegation from a higher ranking ritual specialist, and so on. The concatenation of delegation originates with the Source of the Domain. What this means is that the person one sees doing something is the least likely person to claim the primary authority to be doing that thing.

In daily life, in the cycle of annual rituals and in the larger ceremonial cycles which are completed over a number of years, the delegation of ritual performance recapitulates and is modelled on the precedence ordering of social groups in the community, which itself derives from the precedence, the origin structure, of society as a whole. Similar conceptions of order and of the nature of authority and power are found in Sikka, which, despite possessing a culture closely related to that of the Ata Tana 'Ai, has had quite a different history.

Precedence, Delegation and the Origin Structure of Sikka

The people of Sikka Natar, the village of Sikka, occupy an inhospitable sliver of sandy reef which faces the tempestuous waters of the Savu Sea and backs onto the degraded hills of the southern escarpment of the island of Flores. Despite the poverty of the site of the village or, as some Ata Sikka (People of Sikka) argue, because of it, the people of the village have traditionally made their living neither by agriculture nor by fishing, as have other villages to the west and east; rather, the village was, until 1954, the seat of Kerajaan Sikka, the Rajadom of Sikka, a petty state, a confederation of villages and domains, which at one time encompassed much of east central Flores and, the Sikkanese claim, regions beyond. The people of this unprepossessing little village secured their livelihood, first, as rulers and, later, as educators, government officials, traders and proprietors of land in other parts of the island. Today, the Ata Sikka still live to some extent off economic, political and social capital amassed during more than three centuries of rule and their identity as former rulers informs their contemporary relations with other peoples of Flores. Even though the Rajadom of Sikka was wholly dissolved by the end of the 1950s, other peoples of Flores still regard Sikka Natar as one of the important centres of high culture on the island of Flores. For the Ata Sikka themselves, the unique past of their village as the centre of a *negeri*, a "nation", is the most potent of many features of their history and culture which define them as distinctive from — and, indeed, superior to — their neighbours.[1]

As in Tana Wai Brama, the history of Sikka is the history of the coming together of different peoples to create a single society which nevertheless remains a confederation of groups, each of which has its own unique history. In Sikka, the histories of these origin groups are recounted both in oral narratives and in a body of written works. One of the written histories is a history of the Rajadom of Sikka written by Mo'ang D.D.P. Kondi, a minister in the government of the last Raja of Sikka, Raja Don Thomas Ximenes da Silva, some time after the Second World War and in the closing years of the Rajadom.[2]

Just as the *ngeng ngerang* of Tana Wai Brama is primarily the history of the founding clan of the domain, so too is Kondi's account of the history of Sikka that of the founders of Sikka, the descendants of a protogenitor line whose members brought into a confederation people of diverse origins. The history thus reveals, in textual form, the origin structure of the Sikkanese royal house and provides a detailed foundation for the legitimacy of the power and authority of the Rajas of Sikka over their domain. Furthermore, the historical narrative provides information sufficient to legitimate the social and political positions of all those persons and groups other than the royal lineage who claim authority in the contemporary community. Thus, there are many detailed accounts of the conclusion of alliances between the Rajas of Sikka and the heads and *tana pu'ang* ("sources of the earth") of various villages and minor domains on Flores (see Figure 5).

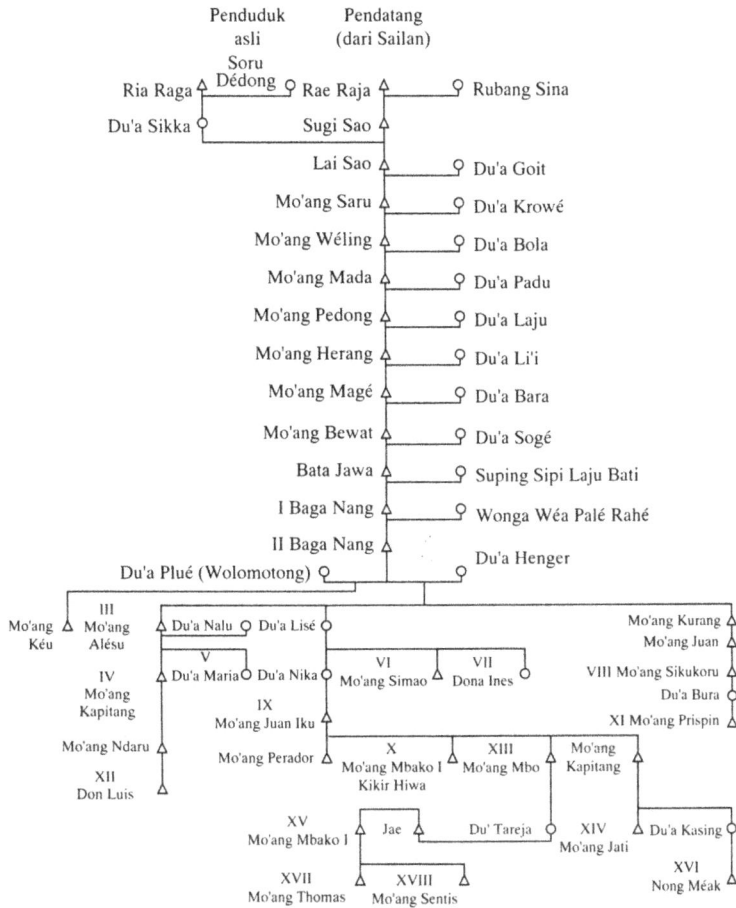

Figure 5. A version of the genealogy of the Ratu of Sikka. [Source: Mo'ang Mandalangi Pareira, Sikka Genealogy Book, pp.112ff.]

Among the Ata Sikka, claims to title, power, authority and precedence are not made alone by reference to the events by which the ancestors of the rajas established the community, but also by reference to a dynastic genealogy of the rajas. This dynastic genealogy establishes at once the origins and succession of power in the rajadom and, insofar as a person or group can demonstrate relatedness to the royal lineage, the legitimacy of power and precedence which devolved from the royal house of Sikka to the *mo'ang pulu*, "the ten lords" (the noble houses of Sikka which are closely allied politically and historically to the rajas' house) and, through them, to all the residents of the domain.

In their oral traditions, the Ata Sikka trace the origin of Sikka Natar to the man Ria Raga and his wife, Soru Dédong, who were "penduduk asli" (Malay: "native inhabitants") of Sikka. Their daughter, Du'a Sikka, married Sugi Sao, the son of the man Rae Raja and his wife, Rubang Sina, who were "pendatang dari Sailan" (Malay: "immigrants from Ceylon"). Du'a Sikka gave birth to Lai Sao, whose male descendants are traced through eleven generations of men to Don Alésu, the first *ratu* of the Rajadom of Sikka. The names of the ancestors who appear in the genealogy of the Sikkanese royal house are significant. Among the wives of the descendants of Lai Sao are Du'a Krowé, Du'a Bola and Du'a Sogé. Krowé is the region of the central hills of Sikka, from which the rulers of Sikka originated, and Bola is a village on the south coast of Flores to the east of Sikka Natar. Both Krowé and Bola are areas later incorporated into the Rajadom of Sikka. Sogé is the Sikkanese word for Ende, from where a large number of immigrants to Sikka fled after a war between Endenese Catholics and Muslims, which the Catholics lost.

Du'a Sikka's husband, a foreigner, was named "Raja", which means "ruler". Du'a Sikka herself bears the name of the future Rajadom and it is significant that she, who was of autochthonous origin, was female. She was, by implication, *tana pu'ang*, the "source of the earth". In terms of precedence, Du'a Sikka was thus prior to her husband, just as the Sources of the Earth of Sikka were of greater precedence than the rajas who, while they were rulers, were descendants of a male outsider. As elsewhere in eastern Indonesia, these representations take on special significance because Sikka had a diarchic division of authority between the lord or source of the earth who held ritual authority over the land and who was classified as feminine and the *ratu*, the secular ruler who was classified as masculine in terms of an encompassing system of dual symbolic classification. The genealogy of the rajas of Sikka is thus traced through an unbroken line of males to a male immigrant who married an indigenous woman. In ritual language it is said, "ina Sikka ama jawa", "the mother (from) Sikka, the father from far away" and "ina ratu ama raja", "the mother (was) the ruler, the father (was) the raja", a reference to the government of the rajadom and to the encompassing polity of Sikka in which one is reminded that the rajas gained their powers from the *tana pu'ang*.

The histories of Sikka credit Bata Jawa, a descendant of the eighth generation after Lai Sao, and his son, Igor, with establishing the major customs governing religious practice, marriage and the settlement of disputes in Sikka. His son, Baga Nang, a descendant in the tenth generation after Lai Sao, was the first Sikkanese to settle at the site of Sikka Natar. The history recounts how Baga Nang acquired the site from its aboriginal inhabitants, the people of Hokor, by an act of subterfuge and usurpation, a theme common in the origin myths of eastern Indonesia, by which he caused the Hokor people to flee the site. Only one of the aboriginal Hokor people remained behind, and that was the *tana pu'ang*, the "source of the earth" who held authority in matters pertaining to the rituals of the land and agriculture.

In the narratives of the Sikkanese history, Bata Jawa's and Igor's creation of *hadat* and Baga Nang's acquisition of the site of Sikka Natar are prelude to the main story, which is that of the foundation of the rajadom by Don Alésu in the eleventh generation after Lai Sao.

Alésu was the third raja of Sikka according to the royal genealogies, the first raja having been Mo'ang Igor, the son of Mo'ang Bata Jawa, and the second Mo'ang Baga Nang, the son of Mo'ang Igor. In the Kondi text and in the mythic histories which I recorded from informants in the late 1970s, Alésu is a culture hero of considerable stature. The Ata Sikka take considerable pride in their Catholicism and in the time they have been Catholics, which by their account has been almost four and a half centuries. More than any other element of Sikkanese life and dominion over their rajadom, Catholicism is at the root of Sikka's claim to legitimate rule in eastern Flores. Alésu is the figure who brought Catholicism to Sikka, who converted the people, and who thereby secured Sikkanese hegemony over the whole of east central Flores. Thus, the origin and foundation of the rajadom is linked inseparably to the coming of Catholicism to the Sikkanese.

In the narrative, the heads of the clans and domains of Sikka chose Alésu to replace Baga Nang after his death. After becoming raja, Alésu travelled to Malacca, where, under the patronage of Raja Worilla, he converted to Christianity and was educated in theology and law. After three years, Alésu asked Raja Worilla to allow him to return to Flores and to provide a teacher of religion for his people. The Raja sent his son, Augustinu da Gama, to Flores as a teacher. Alésu then returned to Flores with the great wealth which Worilla had given to him when he departed from Malacca. Upon reaching Flores, he resumed his position as ruler of the Sikkanese with the assistance of Augustinu da Gama. The wealth with which he returned he distributed among the *mo'ang pulu*, the "ten nobles" of Sikka, the clan headmen, *tana pu'ang* and minor rulers of Sikka, thereby cementing the alliances upon which the rajadom was founded.

In the era of the rajadom, Sikka Natar was a stratified society consisting of four classes: the *ratu* and his kin, noblemen, commoners and slaves. The royal house of Sikka is Lepo Geté, the "Great House", and the people who made up the Great House bore the Portuguese name da Silva. Their name in *hadat* is Lésupung. Lésu is an elision of Alésu, who is recognized as the founder of the house,[3] and *pung*, a polysemous word meaning: (1) to possess, possession (Bahasa Indonesia: *punya*) and (2) grandchildren, descendants. It is a reflex of the word *pu*, which means, among other things, "ancestors" or "forebears". *Pung* is semantically linked to the word *pu'ang*, which means "source", "origin", "trunk (of a tree)". People who are "Lésupung" are thus "the descendants of Alésu" and the people whose protogenitor was Alésu.

Next to the *ratu* in rank were people of the nobility, who made up the *kuat wungung*, "houses", into which Sikka Natar was divided. Each noble house occupied a *wisung*, "territory" or "ward", in the village. All of the people of the *kuat wungung* have both *hadat* names and Portuguese names. In addition to da Silva, the name carried by members of Lepo Geté, the nobility of Sikka carried such names as Fernandez, Pareira, da Cunha, da Gomez, da Lopez, and so on. It was from the nobility that the *mo'ang pulu*, the "Ten Lords" came. In the reign of the last raja, the *mo'ang pulu* made up an advisory council to the raja and each *mo'ang* ruled his ward in Sikka Natar and lands and villages attached to it outside of the village of Sikka. In the 1930s, the Dutch reorganized the government of the rajadom and appointed *kapitan* to serve as resident administrators in the various administrative divisions of the rajadom. These administrators were largely drawn from the *mo'ang pulu*, the nobility of Sikka Natar, and were known as the *kapitan lima*, the "five captains", although in later years there came to be seven.

Each of the *kuat wungung* of Sikka Natar is said to have originated outside of Sikka and to be made up of the descendants of immigrants who joined the *ratu* at different times. Kondi (n.d.:11) identifies thirty-six places of origin, including east Flores, Lio to the west, Solor, Adonara, the Kei islands, Bima, Bali, Savu, Ambon, Kisar, Wetar and Sumba.

In the compilation of origins, the rajadom, which defined Sikka as a society, consisted of no indigenous people since the aboriginal inhabitants who occupied the site of the village, the people of Hokor, were forced to flee. Thus, the ruling village of Sikka is represented both in oral and textual sources as consisting of peoples of diverse origins. Among these various groups, the house of the raja is temporally prior to all of the others and thus claims social and political precedence in the community.

Authority, Precedence and Delegation in Tana 'Ai and Sikka

In both Tana 'Ai and Sikka, the dynamics of social organization, whereby new social groups are created within society and alien groups are incorporated, produce a social order which is represented in terms of its origins.[4] The tracing of contemporary social relations is structured just as the processes of generation are orderly and origins themselves are structured. By reference to their origin structures, the members of a community maintain the continuity of society as it changes. Indeed, it is upon change that origin structures are predicated. In all cases and at every level of social life, from the ideological to the immediately pragmatic, the origin structures of Tana 'Ai and Sikka allow for the transaction of authority. Thus origin structures can be mapped by tracing the authority structure in a community at a given time.

In both societies, just as no group claims an autochthonous origin, no group or person claims innate authority to act. Rather, all authority is traced to a source and, except in the cases of the *tana pu'an* of a Tana 'Ai domain and the *tana pu'ang* of Sikka, a person acts or exercises power legitimately, i.e., in accord with *hadat*, only if the authority inherent in the act has been delegated by another person closer to the source in a chain of precedence.

Precedence systems are multiplexly asymmetric and open ended, which is to say that new groups can be generated and power delegated endlessly. It is only at the source that problems of a conceptual or logical nature arise. In Tana Wai Brama, for example, the *tana pu'an* holds his authority by virtue of his membership in a group whose members are descendants of the first of the ancestors to settle in the domain. Even so, the power and authority of those ancestors was not simply a consequence of their priority of immigration and primacy of precedence, but derives from an act of usurpation — of land, power over animals and ritual potency — of the aboriginal spirits of the domain (cf. Lewis 1988:270-274). Similarly, the authority of the *ratu* of Sikka derives from the usurpation of Sikka Natar's aboriginal inhabitants, whose descendants are, even today, recognized as the *tana pu'ang*. That authority is represented as having been delegated by the *tana pu'ang*, who retains ritual authority over the land and it is upon this delegated authority that the *ratu*'s legitimacy is founded.

In both societies, authority and power are linked in such a way that authority is prior to power. So, too, the person who holds authority is prior to and holds precedence over the person empowered to act. Thus, in both Tana 'Ai and Sikka, there is a principle of delegation by which those who hold authority delegate to others the power to act.

Such delegation can be seen in the relation of the *tana pu'ang* of Sikka and the *ratu*. The Source of the Domain had ritual or religious authority over all the land of Sikka and its people. In the myths of the foundation of the domain, it is told that the Source of the Earth delegated to another person the power to act. That second person became the raja. Even in Sikka today, one finds a division of authority and power, the Source of the Domain, the *hadat* leader, exercising spiritual authority in the community which, over the years, has been delegated to the raja. In the process of this delegation, the Source's spiritual authority is transformed into secular, political power. This pattern, by the way, is so common in eastern Indonesia, that anthropologists use the term *diarchy* (rule of pairs) to describe the organization of sacred power and secular authority in all eastern Indonesian societies.

The Sikkanese rajadom was abolished in 1954 and by the 1960s the secular power of the raja was transferred to the local Bupati and the officials of his government. But to the people of Sikka, the basic division between authority and power has been maintained continuously in an unbroken sequence from the past.

Similarly, in Tana 'Ai, the Source of the Domain, the ritual leader of the community, delegates his authority to a hierarchy of ritual specialists who are thereby empowered to act, according to *hadat* on behalf of the Source. The Source himself, it is interesting to note, derives his authority in turn from his sisters.

To an English speaker, *authority* is (1) the power to influence or command thought, opinion or behaviour and (2) an individual cited or appealed to as an expert. Both of these definitions hold well enough for persons who have *kuasa, newang* and *hak* (Sara Sikka and Sara Tana 'Ai; note that *kuasa* and *hak* are cognates of words in Bahasa Indonesia), "power", "authority", "obligation", "right". People in both societies recognize authority both as influence to command thought, opinion or behaviour and as something characterizing an individual who is cited or appealed to as an expert of some sort. Such authority and authorities as persons command and influence only locally and on the basis of *hadat*. This means that authority is an aspect of *hadat*. And *hadat* is the "source" or "origin" of the community itself. One finds this relationship between origins and authority expressed in local mythic traditions, the myths handed down from the ancestors which serve as charters for the way things are and ought to be and which recount the creation, not only of the world, but of the social order. These are foundation myths which are cited as the authority for the way things are today. Thus things are the way they are today because that was the way they were in the past.

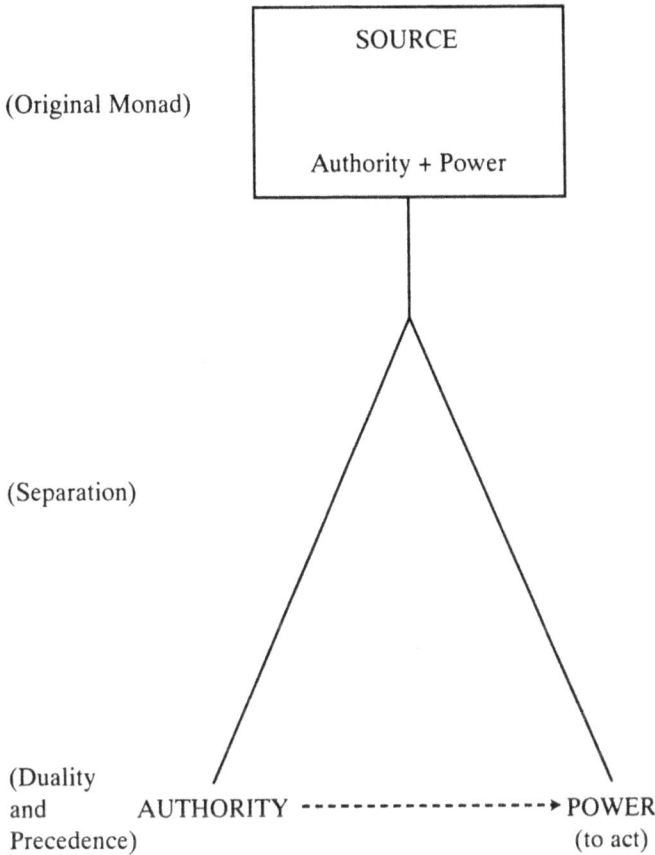

```
                         ┌─────────────────────┐
                         │       SOURCE        │
  (Original Monad)       │                     │
                         │  Authority + Power  │
                         └──────────┬──────────┘
                                    │
                                   ╱ ╲
                                  ╱   ╲
  (Separation)                   ╱     ╲
                                ╱       ╲
                               ╱         ╲
                              ╱           ╲
                             ╱             ╲
  (Duality                  ╱               ╲
  and          AUTHORITY ------------------▶ POWER
  Precedence)                                (to act)
```

Figure 6

One of the practical corollaries of this division between authority and power and one of the practical results of the principle of delegation is that, in societies such as those of Timor and Flores, the person seen to do something, the person apparently empowered to perform an act, is not the person who has the authority to get the thing done.[5]

In the time of origins (or before the time of origins), authority and power are not separate but are monadically combined. In the creation of the social order, the two were separated, resulting in a dual division (Figure 6). In some societies, such as Sikka, the *tana pu'ang*, "Source of the Earth", once held all power. In Sikkanese myth, Don Alésu went to Malacca and there acquired *agama* (Christianity) which he carried back to Sikka. *Agama* (a foreign religion) enabled the establishment of the Sikkanese rajadom, but only after the delegation of power from the *tana pu'ang* to the *ratu*. Through this delegation and division of authority, the *ratu* acquired power and a diarchy was created. The *tana pu'ang*, who still held (and holds) authority, retired to the background: as source, he holds authority, but not power. The *ratu*, in turn, further delegated power to the *mo'ang pulu*, the "ten lords" or nobles of Sikkanese society who are themselves ranked in terms of their precedence with respect to the acquisition of power from the raja. Thus, with respect to Sikka, the general separation of authority and power must be rewritten to take into account the specificities of Sikkanese history and culture as in Figure 7.

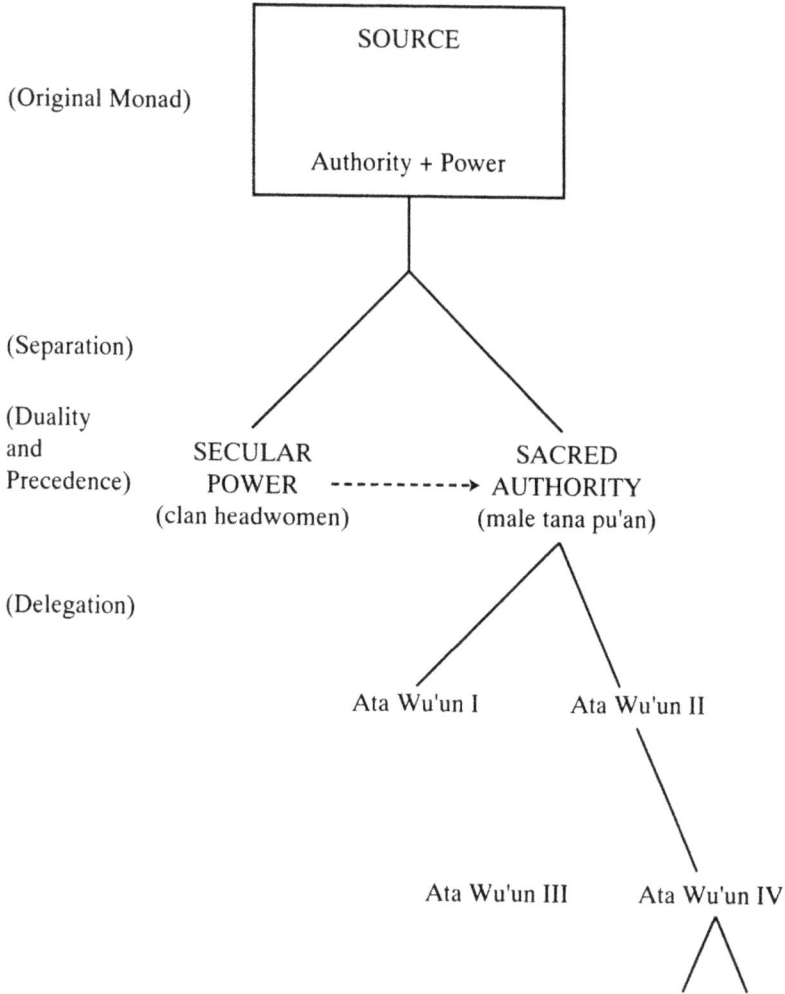

Figure 7

Two important points must be noted. First, the relations of the *mo'ang pulu* and the *ratu* appear hierarchical, as, with respect to power, they indeed are. However, this apparent hierarchy masks as essential heteroarchical diarchy between sacred authority and secular power, the relationship of which is as much complementary as hierarchical. Second, the principle which governs the apparent hierarchy is not one of gradations of an absolute power. Rather, in delegating power to the *mo'ang*, the *ratu* holds relative authority over them.

The same relationship of authority to delegated power holds for the relationship of each pair of *mo'ang* as well. Thus at every level of the apparent hierarchy, what Fox (1989:52) has called *recursive complementarity* governs the structure of relationships. Thus, the relationship of the *tana pu'ang* to the *ratu* is one of authority to power; the relationship of the *ratu* to the highest ranking *mo'ang* is one of authority to power; and the relationship of each higher *mo'ang* to the next lower ranking *mo'ang* is one of authority to power.

In Tana 'Ai, the same basic principle works out in a different way. Tana 'Ai never had a raja and there is not the division of the sacred and the secular as we find in Sikka. The system is not, in other words, *diarchical* in the sense that the term describes the case of Sikka. Yet Tana 'Ai manifests a similar pattern. In the myths of origin of the Ata Tana 'Ai, the time before the creation of the social order was a time in which the major categories of later creation were monadically whole. But the idiom is one of life and death and male and female. In the precreation epoch, there was no death and there was no sex; human beings neither died nor were created through sexual congress and the firmament and the earth were connected. When the earth and sky were separated, male and female came into being as did the living and the dead. As humans came to be divided as male and female, so too did society come to be divided into clans, one of which, the founding clan, is temporally prior to the others. That is the clan of the *tana pu'an*, the "Source of the Domain". The Source of the Domain is the ultimate authority in social life and combines in his being both authority and power. However, as in Sikka, the creation of the social order required the delegation of authority as power. The Source of the Domain thus empowered the lesser clans which are themselves ranked according to the principle of *precedence* (Figure 8).

Once again, the *tana pu'an* delegates authority which becomes, through delegation, power and each *ata wu'un* is related to every other *ata wu'un* as either the delegator of prior authority or recipient of delegated power. The classificatory system at work is governed by complementary recursivity and not by absolute hierarchy. The pattern is set in the mythic histories of the domain, in which each clan received rights to land and the performance of ritual from the *tana pu'an*. The sequential order in which the *tana pu'an* delegated specific rights establishes the precedence of the clans. Today, those original relationships are refracted in the order of rights manifested in the performance of particular rituals. The power to perform is a function of those at the end of the chain of precedence; the earlier the precedence, the less active ritual practitioners are.

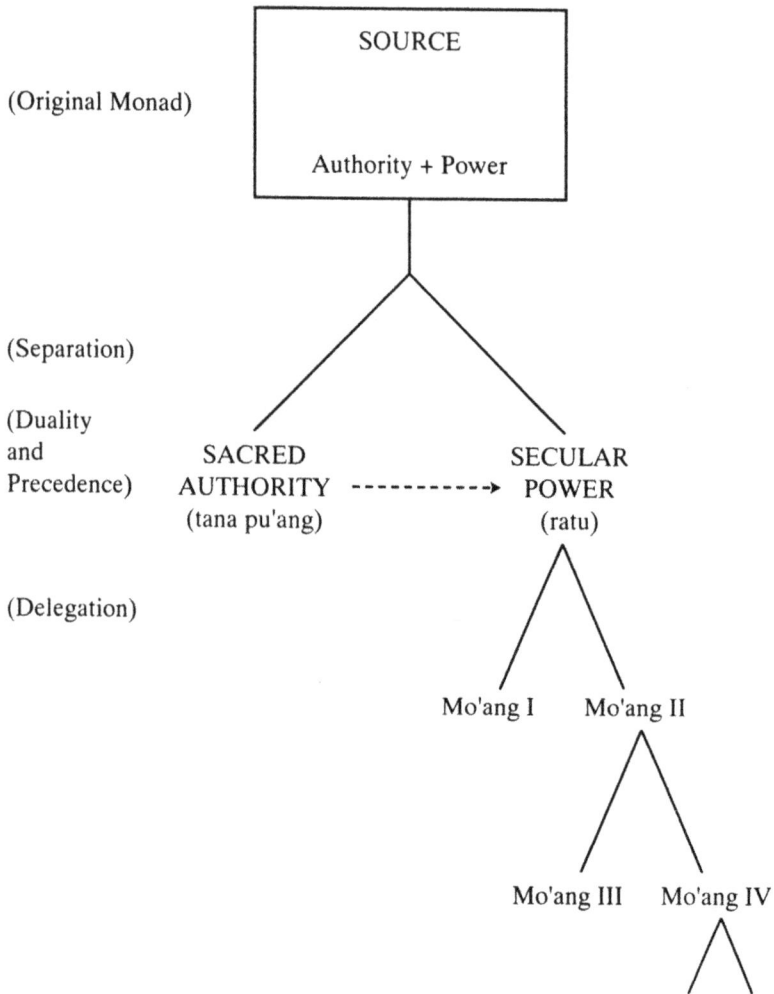

Figure 8

A single model can be extracted from the Sikkanese and Tana 'Ai cases (Figure 9).

Conclusion

Throughout eastern Indonesia, the people of local communities trace their origins from diverse sources. Typically, the people of a community may be divided into a number of what can be called origin groups, each of which claims a unique origin from another place (often another island). In some communities, such as Sikka Natar and the Domain of Wai Brama on the island of Flores, these groups are ordered in rankings that appear to be social hierarchies, but which actually reflect the sequence in time in which each group's ancestors arrived and joined the community. In Sikka Natar, major social groups called *kuat wungung* are so ranked with the first group claiming status as Source of the Earth, the group from which the ruling rajas of the old Sikkanese rajadom came claiming second position, and the remaining constituent groups of the village ranked in order of their ancestors' arrival in Sikka. In Tana 'Ai, the five *sukun* (clans) of the Domain of Wai Brama each trace an independent origin from ancestors who came from other regions of Flores and from other islands in eastern Indonesia. As in Sikka, the *sukun* are rank ordered in the ceremonial system of the community in terms of their temporal precedence. In addition, the *lepo* (houses) of which a clan is composed are also rank ordered in terms of the order in time in which they were created through affinal exchanges between two clans. On Flores, as elsewhere in eastern Indonesia, the precedence of origin groups is the principle underlying and generating what is manifested as hierarchy within a contemporary society.

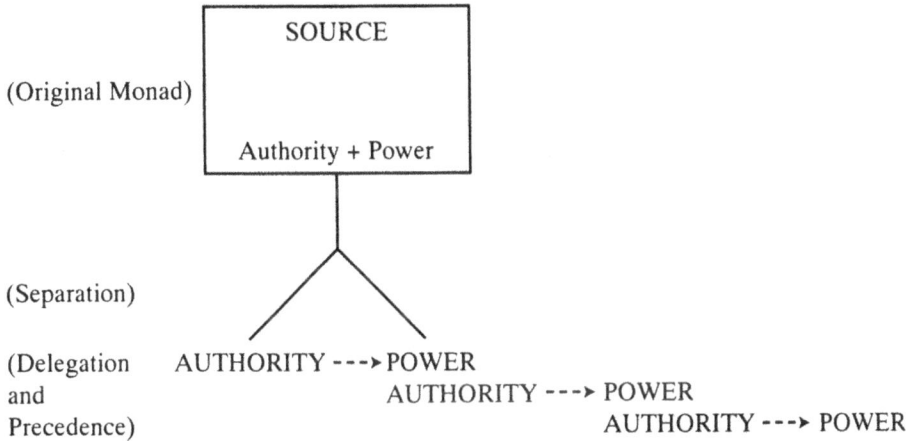

Figure 9 (cf. Fox 1989:52)

In the case of Flores, the royal house of Sikka Natar was linked over time by affinal alliance to other rajadoms on the island and on Sumbawa and Sulawesi. These links were essentially political and social, and not ceremonial, in nature. The ranking of the Sikkanese royal house in relation to others was established on the principle that wife-givers are superior to wife-takers and that the older an alliance, the greater its value. Thus, in contracting marriages with the ruling houses of other areas of Flores, the rajas of Sikka aimed to provide daughters in marriage to the sons of the rajas of Larantuka, Paga and Wolowaru while celebrating the antiquity of alliances in which they were wife-takers. Elsewhere on Flores (as in Tana 'Ai) analogous links between communities were (and still are) ceremonial in nature and not political. As ritual life reflects social precedence *in* these societies, it is likely that relations *between* such communities are also ordered in terms of precedence.[6]

Two points of theoretical import arising from the analysis of the social orders of Tana 'Ai and Sikka are worth reiteration. First, the order of relationships which obtain among the constituent groups of society are extremely fluid and dynamic and operate in such a fashion that relationships of statuses of persons within these communities are also flexible and change to a significant degree through time. Second, the dynamism of Tana 'Ai society is paralleled by a conception of history, authority and power by which the perquisites of status are easily transferable between groups, except that one group is, in terms of the mythic origins of society, immutably the "origin". In Tana 'Ai, that origin is represented by the Source of the Domain. Standing in a relation of priority to the Source of the Domain, however, is another veiled source which is represented variously as the women of the original clan (and the sisters of a Source of the Domain) and as the aboriginal spirits of the land. The same is true of the Rajadom of Sikka, in which the *ratu* was immutably the point of origin and reference for the reckoning of the social position of other groups in society. As in Tana 'Ai, prior to the *ratu* is a source of spiritual authority, the aboriginal Hokor people, who were usurped but whose spiritual authority over the land is recognized in the person of the *tana pu'ang*, the Source of the Earth. In both Sikka and Tana 'Ai, social order rests upon a conception of precedence by which power and authority are transacted among the constituent groups of society.

References

Echols, John M. and Hassan Shadily

1989 *An Indonesian-English dictionary*. Third edition. Ithaca: Cornell University Press.

Fox, James J.

1988 Origin, descent and precedence in the study of Austronesian societies. Public lecture in connection with De Wisselleerstoel Indonesische Studien given on 17th of March 1988, Rijksuniversiteit te Leiden, The Netherlands.

1989 Category and complement: binary ideologies and the organization of dualism in Eastern Indonesia. In David Maybury-Lewis and Uri Almagor (eds) *The attraction of opposites: thought and society in the dualistic mode*. Ann Arbor: University of Michigan Press.

Fox, James J. and E.D. Lewis

1993 'Ata Sikka of Flores, Eastern Indonesia. In P. Hocking (ed.) *The encyclopedia of world cultures*, vol. V: *East and South East Asia*, pp.19-22. Boston: G.K. Hall & Co.

Lewis, E.D.

1988 *People of the source. The social and ceremonial order of Tana Wai Brama on Flores*. Verhandelingen van het Koninklijk Instituut voor Taal-, Landen Volkenkunde 135. Dordrecht, Holland: Foris.

Notes

[1] For a brief description of Sikkanese society and culture see Fox and Lewis (1993) and Lewis (1988:9-19). The word *negeri* in Bahasa Indonesia means "land" and "country" and, in eastern Indonesia, "village" (Echols and Shadily 1989:387). Sikkanese writers before the 1950s and 1960s used literary Malay in which the word means "land" and "country". From the contexts in which the word is used in Kondi's history, *negeri* should be translated as "country" rather than as "village". It is thus the Malay equivalent of the Sara Sikka word *tana*, "land", "territory", "domain" and bears the connotation of "polity" of that word.

[2] Kondi's history has not been published. It is an untitled work of some 76,430 words in typescript. In 1961, Kondi gave his history to Professor Clark E. Cunningham, who made a photocopy of the manuscript in Surabaya. The manuscript was then typed at the University of Illinois. In 1977, as I was preparing for my first fieldwork in Sikka, Professor Cunningham supplied me with a photocopy of the typescript. The manuscript has since been lost.

[3] It is worth noting that in Sara Sikka, *lésu* is also the word for a species of eagle.

[4] Thus the puzzle of why, in Tana 'Ai and Sikka, origin myths are essentially the narratives of a single group (clan Ipir and Lepo Geté, respectively) rather than of all groups can be understood: myths of origin are not histories for the sake of history; they are not intended to chart the unique histories of the various groups which make up society, but the way in which those groups came to form society. That formation is in both cases the result of actions by the central founding group alone. Hence, the mythic histories of Tana Wai Brama are the history of clan Ipir and, despite the multifarious origins of its people, the history of Sikka is the history of the royal house. The histories of individual groups may be (they are usually not) remembered, but they are not pertinent to the origin structure of society.

[5] For an anthropologist, it does no good to ask the young boy who is killing a pig in ritual *why* he is killing the pig; one must locate and seek out the person in authority from whom his power to kill the pig has been delegated. The problem is that sometimes that other person is bound by *hadat* to remain mute when faced with outsiders. Here the problem is that, being the *authority*, such a central person does not take orders or suggestions from others but is rather the *source* of orders and suggestions.

[6] It is possible that precedence may order not only relations of groups within societies and relations between petty states, but also the larger relationships of other communities and societies of the region.

Chapter 9. Precedence Among the Domains of the Three Hearth Stones:

Contestation of an order of precedence in the Ko'a ceremonial cycle (Palu'é Island, Eastern Indonesia)

Michael P. Vischer

Introduction[1]

The island of Palu'é,[2] located off the north coast of Flores, covers seventy square kilometres and consists of a population of approximately 10,000. It is divided into fourteen separate territorial, political and ceremonial domains known as *tana*. One of the remarkable features of the island is the absence of accessible drinking water. During the long dry season its inhabitants rely mainly on the juice of the lontar palm (*Borassus flabellifer* or *Sundaicus*) for their daily intake of fluid. Water for cooking is tapped from banana trunks, bamboo and from a number of trees, and in some places volcanic steam is trapped in earth catchments and condensed in bamboo poles.[3] The circular island consists of an almost nine hundred metre high mountain and of a number of active volcanic vents which are slightly to one side of the mountain top. Everyday life on Palu'é is overshadowed by the constant threat of eruptions which can shower fields and settlements with rocks and hot ashes.[4]

Equally remarkable from a cultural standpoint are the ceremonial cycles of the island's domains. Of the fourteen domains, seven maintain ceremonial cycles culminating in the sacrifice of water buffalo[5] whereas the other seven domains conduct cycles involving the sacrifice of pigs. At the opening of a new cycle water buffalo are purchased on the neighbouring island of Flores and brought back to Palu'é. There the animals are raised over a period of five years at the end of which they are sacrificed in a large-scale ceremony. Considering the lack of water on the island raising these animals represents a considerable achievement. More often than not water buffalo fail to adjust to the dry environment and die before the prescribed five-year period is up. In such a case another ceremonial purchase must be carried out in order to open up the cycle as soon as new resources are available.[6]

The individual ceremonial cycles of each domain provide an arena for the contestation of an order of precedence.[7] By employing specific strategies aimed at enhancing its prestige a given domain can emerge from a cycle in a new position of precedence among its allied domains. After the cycle has been completed this new position is often consolidated through warfare. In the following such a process will be illustrated by means of a case study of one complete ceremonial cycle. Precedence is invariably subject to contestation and understanding the dynamics of contestation is essential for understanding the social life of these societies. Some aspects of the process of contestation of an order of precedence at the level of traditional domains will be analysed here by applying a set of analytic tools[8] to a number of key events surrounding the cyclical ceremonies of the domain of Ko'a. In societies with a "hierarchical" use of dual categories, such as those found throughout eastern Indonesia, an order of precedence involves the conjunction of several analytical features, the most important of which are recursive complementarity, categorical asymmetry and categorical inversion.[9] These features are exemplified in this paper.

Before proceeding to the description and analysis of a number of key events that occurred during the last ceremonial cycle of the domain of Ko'a some general information on Palu'é categories of social order will be given as well as an outline of the ceremonial cycle and an overview of political and ceremonial alliance.

Some Categories of the Social Order

Society on Palu'é is House-based.[10] In each domain two separate groups of Houses trace their origins through a succession of men and place names to two different sets of primordial ancestors. Members of these two groups of first settling Houses are referred to as "father people" (*hata hama*) whereas members of subsequently settled groups of Houses are referred to as "child people" (*hata hana*). Within each group of Houses, one House assumes a position of seniority. Such a House is called "elder sibling" (*hata ka'é*), whereas all the other Houses are referred to as "younger siblings" (*hata hari*). The most senior male member of a House of "elder brother" status is himself classified as "elder brother" (*ka'é*) and the most senior male members of Houses of "younger brother" status as "younger brothers" (*hari*). The two priest leaders of a domain are recruited from the two Houses of "elder sibling" status of the domain's two first settling groups of "father people". Although all male members of Houses of "father people" status can be referred to as "strong men" (*lakimosa*) in practice only the most senior male member of the senior House of each of the two groups of "father people" is addressed as such. They are the two political and ceremonial leaders of the domain. These two priest leaders maintain separate spheres of ritual influence within the domain and separate ceremonial centres, whereby the priest leader of one group of "father people" always takes precedence over the priest leader of the other. The position of this lesser priest leader varies. In some domains he functions primarily as a ceremonial leader and much of his political authority has been transferred to the main priest leader and in other domains he no longer exercises his ceremonial office and only nominally maintains "strong man" status.[11]

The Ceremonial Cycles of the Domains of Water Buffalo Blood

The fourteen domains of Palu'é are distinguished by their adherence to one of two ceremonial systems. The seven domains employing pigs as their main sacrificial animals are referred to as "domains of pig blood" (*tana laja wawi*) whereas the seven domains practicing the sacrifice of water buffalo are referred to as "domains of water buffalo blood" (*tana laja karapau*) (Table 1). The domains of Palu'é are listed here according to their adherence to a ceremonial system (for their respective locations refer to Map 1). The present investigation is mainly concerned with relations among the first three of the "domains of water buffalo blood" — Tana Ko'a, Tana Cawalo and Tana Tomu.

Table 1. Domains of water buffalo and pig blood

Domains of water buffalo blood	Domains of pig blood
1. Tana Ko'a	1. Tana Malurivu
2. Tana Cawalo	2. Tana Édo
3. Tana Tomu	3. Tana Woto
4. Tana Kéli	4. Tana Awa (formerly water buffalo blood)
5. Tana Nitu	5. Tana Téo (formerly water buffalo blood)
6. Tana Cua	6. Tana Ngalu
7. Tana Ndéo	7. Tana Mudé

Blood offerings that accompany every major ceremonial event are ranked according to the ritual potency of the blood employed. In such a ranking only the blood of the water buffalo is considered to be "big blood" (*laja ca*), that is, of the highest ritual potency. The blood of pigs and chicken and in some cases the blood of dogs is also considered to have ritual potency, but only to a lesser extent. On the basis of this ranking all of the "domains of water buffalo blood" consider themselves to be superior to the domains practicing the sacrifice of the pig.

The killing of the main sacrificial animals takes place at the two central ceremonial courtyards (*tupu*) of the domain, each of which usually consists of a number of named monoliths set on top of a circular mound at the centre of each of the two main villages. In terms of cosmology the central ceremonial courtyard is the place of connection with the multilayered universe. From here access can be gained to both the terrestrial layers and to those of the firmament. By sacrificing the "big blood" of the water buffalo at the central ceremonial courtyard the Supreme Being can be reached. In ritual speech the Palu'é Supreme Being is referred to by the couplet sun-moon, stone-earth (*era-wula, watu-tana*). The sacrifice of water buffalo ensures the support of the Supreme Being for the well-being of the people, the proper sequence of the seasons, a plentiful harvest and good fortune in warfare. Establishing contact with the Supreme Being by sacrificing "big blood" thus results in prosperity for the domain. This in turn ultimately reflects upon its status among the other "domains of water buffalo blood".

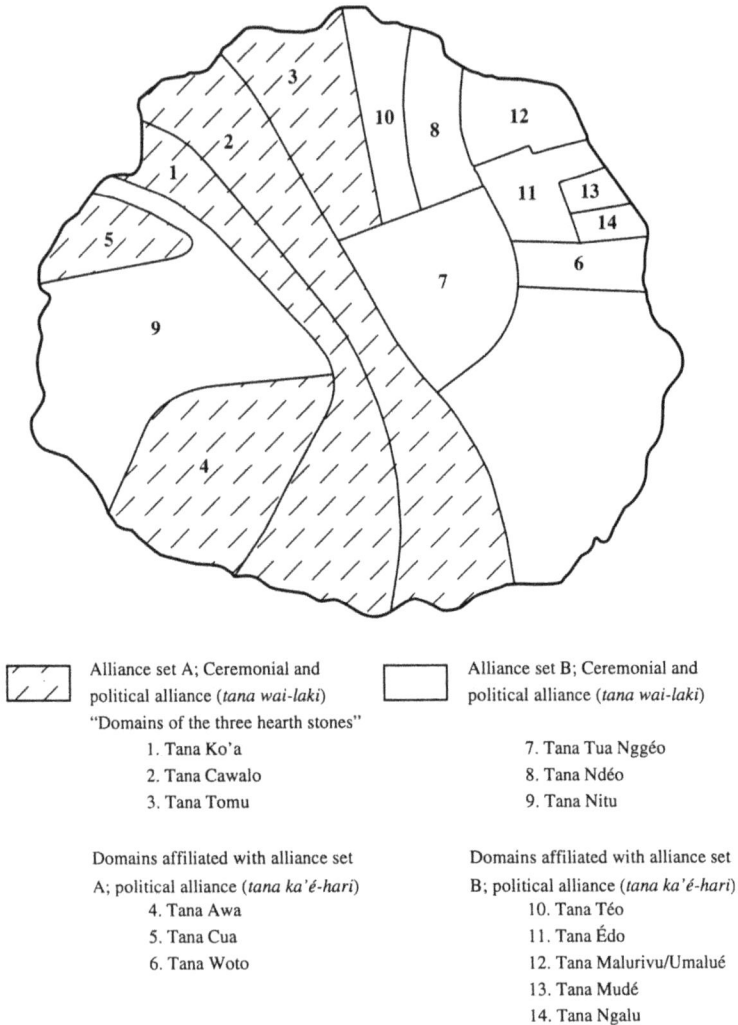

Alliance set A; Ceremonial and political alliance (*tana wai-laki*)
"Domains of the three hearth stones"
1. Tana Ko'a
2. Tana Cawalo
3. Tana Tomu

Alliance set B; Ceremonial and political alliance (*tana wai-laki*)

7. Tana Tua Nggéo
8. Tana Ndéo
9. Tana Nitu

Domains affiliated with alliance set A; political alliance (*tana ka'é-hari*)
4. Tana Awa
5. Tana Cua
6. Tana Woto

Domains affiliated with alliance set B; political alliance (*tana ka'é-hari*)
10. Tana Téo
11. Tana Édo
12. Tana Malurivu/Umalué
13. Tana Mudé
14. Tana Ngalu

Map 1: Political and ceremonial alliance among the "domains of water buffalo blood".

The ceremonial cycles of both groups of "father people" of a domain run parallel to each other. Each group purchases its own sacrificial animal, raises it in the domain and stages the sacrifice on its respective ceremonial courtyard. However, every stage of the cycle is always initiated by the group of the main priest leader. Different ceremonial offices are assigned to individual Houses of each group. The location of the dwellings of their holders surrounding the ceremonial courtyard reflects the order of these offices. A number of Houses located at the upper half of the circle are referred to as "uphill people" (*hata réta*) as opposed to those of the lower half who are called "downhill people" (*hata lau*). The latter are in charge of the purchase of the animals and in that context they are also referred to as the "purchasing people" (*hata puané*), whereas the former who carry out the final sacrifice are called "sacrificing people" (*hata patiné*).

A complete cycle ideally extends over a period of five years. The "purchasing people" initiate the cycle by the exchange of yearling animals against golden ear-pendants, ivory tusks and harvest goods with allies of the sacrificing domain on the neighbouring island of Flores.[12] The purchasing voyage is highly structured and begins with the construction of the "large sitting platform" (*woga ca*) next to the ceremonial courtyard. For the duration of the cycle ceremonial gongs and drums are hung from the ridgepole of its roof. At night the water buffalo is usually tied up in the space beneath the raised platform. This structure is also referred to as "the House of the water buffalo" (*nua kerapau*).

During the voyage all members of the fleet of the purchasing party are subject to strict rules of conduct. Participants are not allowed to sit in the shade, no food or drink is consumed on the boats, and smoking and chewing of betelpepper and areca-nut is only permitted at brief moments between chants. The voyage across the straits to Flores follows a prescribed route, each stage of which is marked by the chanting of a fixed set of ritual chants. Most of these chants contain sexual allusions that refer to a man coming to Flores for the purpose of finding a spouse. At the end of the fifth chant the purchasing party lands on Flores where it is received by its allies. A stall for the buffalo is built on one of the boats of the purchasing fleet. After the exchange with the allies has taken place the animals are taken aboard and penned up. On the return trip another set of five chants is recited.[13] Some of these are addressed to the sacrificial animal which, in order to keep it calm, is told (lied to, as it is put) about the life of abundance it will be leading back on Palu'é. The landing is marked by a metaphorical inversion. As soon as the animal lands at the shores of the domain the metaphor of its being a bride which is brought back to the island to be wed changes to one whereby the animal becomes the groom who will be married to one of the daughters of the priest leader of the purchasing party. During the five-year period preceding the sacrifice she is responsible for his welfare. At the end of this period the animal is handed over to the "sacrificing" people. There again an unmarried woman takes charge of the buffalo. After the sacrifice both ceremonial virgins are subject to restrictions similar to those applied in mourning for a spouse.

The sequence in the handing over of the tether of the sacrificial animals serves to illustrate the precedence the main priest leader takes over the lesser priest leader. Upon disembarking the holder of a ceremonial office whose group of Houses is said to "stand in the middle" (*téi rora*), i.e. in a position serving both ceremonial courtyards, takes the ropes from both priest leaders. He leads the animals along a specific path up the mountain to the boundaries of the village of the main priest leader. There he hands over both animals to the main priest leader who then enters the main village. After his animal has been installed in the "house of the water buffalo" he leads the second animal up to the boundary of the village of the lesser priest leader where he hands it over to him. At every stage at which the rope changes hands the recipient reciprocates with a prestation of gold or ivory.[14] Throughout the entire cycle this precedence of the main priest leader is expressed by his "going first" (nolo). Any ceremonial activities are first carried out by him or by officiants associated with his ceremonial centre. Although these activities are paralleled at both centres, there is always a brief delay between the two.

The arrival of the animals on the island and their naming is honoured by all the allies of the purchasing domain by their attendance at the circular dances at the ceremonial centres. These dances extend over a period of several weeks and during this time of celebration everyday rules governing sexual relations are considerably loosened. At both ends of the cycle, at the purchase and at the final sacrifice, the whole network of social relations of every House in a domain is fully activated and relations are acknowledged and reinforced by the exchange of pig meat and harvest goods.

The passage of each year after the purchase of the water buffalo is marked by a ceremonial dance which is again attended by the allies of the sacrificing domain. During a five-year period the economic activities of the Houses of a domain are directed towards accumulating the large number of pigs and harvest goods required for the ceremonial exchanges that accompany the final sacrifice and for the feeding of the numerous guests. Because undertakings within the domain that involve large-scale ceremonies and ceremonial exchange, such as the construction of houses and boats or the setting of mortuary monoliths, must be completed before the sacrifice, a concerted effort must be directed towards finalizing these matters. Following the sacrifice the skull of the buffalo is tied to a wooden pole which is then erected on the ceremonial mound. Until this pole has decomposed and fallen over no new sacrificial animal can be purchased and no large-scale undertaking can be commenced. Thus the five years devoted to raising the buffalo are characterized by a great economic effort by every House of the domain to meet the demands entailed by the final sacrifice. After the sacrifice the domain is virtually stripped of resources.

Five years after the purchase of the buffalo, at the beginning of the rainy season, the preliminary ceremonies for the sacrifice begin. Once again the allies come and dance. A fixed set of traditional chants are recited, an important one of which is referred to as the "carrying and dragging (of) the black patola stone" (titi céi watu mité patola). In this chant the voyage of the mythical ancestors of the domain is recounted. The chant consists of a chain of hundreds of paired place names marking stages of the ancestral voyage through symbolic space from a mythical place of origin in the far west. It tells of how the ancestors carried with them on their boat "the stone and the soil" (*tana watu*), a metaphor which stands for the island. Once they had reached their destination this primordial "stone and soil" grew to become the island as we know it now. In the last section of the origin chant actual place names of the domain (*tana ngarané*; lit. the names of the domain) are evoked, beginning at the four corners of the domain and leading to its centres, towards the two ceremonial courtyards (Map 2). Then in a ceremony called "erecting the ceremonial courtyard" (*kota tupu*) a large stone is set on each of the two ceremonial mounds and soil is taken from the lower and the upper part of the domain and placed around it. This "stone and soil" is then believed to grow in size just as the mythical "stone and soil" from which the island originated.

Following the fixed set of ceremonial chants both allies and hosts create new chants in poetic language which allude to any unsolved conflicts or outstanding debts between the participants. Those targeted then attempt to settle the issue by chanting a response. The chanting and counterchanting goes on until a satisfactory solution has been found. In every cycle a different allied domain is chosen as the guest of honour of this final stage. All members of the sacrificing domain travel together to the domain of the chosen guest and in a mock battle they conquer their ceremonial centres. On the day before the sacrifice the guest domain in turn attacks the sacrificing domain and in turn conquers its two centres. The actual day of the sacrifice is referred to in ritual speech by the couplet "to make the trunk fall, to cut off the tip" (*poka bu'u, supo ngalu*). Here the botanic metaphor describes the life of the buffalo which is to be sacrificed to the Supreme Being. Most of the population of the allied domains as well as numerous individual groups from all over the island come to attend the sacrifice. A sacrifice is said to have been good if the cuts of meat offered to the guests are large and the palm gin flows copiously. Another criterion is that of how long the cutting down of the buffalo is drawn out by skilful slashing before the animal finally collapses.[15] This is referred to as "the dancing of the water buffalo" (*coka kerapau*).

Finally, an important criterion of the success of the sacrifice is that of reciprocity in exchange. At a number of stages of the ritual cycle ceremonial exchange takes place. Prestations and counterprestations of raw pig-meat against rice and harvest goods (mung-bean, cow-pea, tuber, maize) reach their grandest scale during the days preceding the sacrifice. This is a time in which the total social network of each House is activated. Not only do the various groups of Houses of wife-givers and wife-takers engage in exchange but individual Houses of quasi-consanguineal kin status from all over the island also participate. The specifics regarding the amount and kind of exchange are based on exchanges effected on similar occasions in the past and great care is taken to reciprocate accordingly. Finally, on the last day before the sacrifice, members of the allied domains and large numbers of individuals visiting from all other domains make prestations of harvest goods that must be reciprocated with pig-meat. At that stage the reputation (*ngara ca*, lit. the big name) of each House of the sacrificing domain hinges on whether or not it was capable of reciprocating to all of these prestations. The larger the cuts the more the recipients will praise the individual Houses and the sacrificing domain as a whole upon returning to their villages.[16]

Before the animal is entirely disposed of[17] there is a final night of chanting attended only by the sacrificing domain. In these chants the history of the animal is recounted from the initial purchase through the years during which it was raised on the island to its final sacrifice. In the early morning the ceremonial objects, gongs and drums are put back into storage until the next cycle can be opened. The closing of the cycle is marked by the setting of offerings along the boundary lines of the domain. This is said to be the most auspicious moment to make war on a non-allied domain.

Any one of the "domains of water buffalo blood" can lose its ability to sacrifice the "big blood" of water buffalo. When it does, a general decline in its prosperity is believed to follow. According to one myth the first water buffaloes were brought to the island by a domain called Awa located near the volcano. Awa had purchased eight animals from its allies in the Lio region on the island of Flores. These yearlings were to be raised in Awa and then sacrificed. However, shortly after their arrival, the animals fled Palu'é and swam back to Lio. Since that time Awa has never again attempted to reinitiate a water buffalo sacrificing cycle but has resigned itself to the sacrifice of pigs. By supplying pigs and rice it now actively supports the water buffalo sacrifice of Ko'a, a domain to whom it stands in a relationship of younger to elder sibling *(ka'é-hari)*. This classification by Ko'a is a metaphor for Awa's subordinate position within the political and ceremonial alliance between the two domains. Its population has remained small and its territory has continuously been encroached upon by its neighbours so that now Awa virtually perches at the edge of the volcano. Unlike Awa the domain of Téo actually used to sacrifice water buffalo, but when several animals died during the prescribed period preceding the sacrifice Téo renounced its claim to be a "domain of water buffalo blood" and has since only sacrificed pigs. Like Awa, Téo has become small and insignificant and now supports in a subordinate position the sacrifice of the neighbouring domain of Ndéo. However, Awa and Téo are the only two of the five "domains of pig blood" that stand in a relation of ceremonial alliance to any "domain of water buffalo blood".

Political and Ceremonial Alliance

It lies beyond the scope of this paper to provide an overall view of ceremonial and political alliance on Palu'é.[18] Here I shall restrict my focus to three domains:

Ko'a, Cawalo and Tomu. Within the system of ceremonial and political alliance that encompasses all fourteen domains of the island these three make up the core of one alliance bloc (Map 1). This core is set against a nonallied grouping made up of three other "domains of water buffalo blood": Kéli, Ndéo and Nitu.[19] Ko'a, Cawalo and Tomu are referred to as "the domains of the three hearth stones" (*tana liga telu*). Their alliance is both political and ceremonial. It is political in that every appointment of a new priest leader is subject to confirmation by the priest leaders of the two allied domains and in inter-domain warfare, which until very recently was endemic on Palu'é, these three domains are ideally expected to lend each other their unconditional support. Open warfare against each other is prohibited by a mutual non-aggression pact (*tura caji*). The alliance between these domains is ceremonial in that at all stages of the water buffalo sacrificing cycle the allies are the guests of the sacrificing domain. By their presence they enhance its prestige and contribute to the success of the sacrifice. According to popular interpretation, the designation of the three domains as "three hearth stones" implies a notion of equality. It is said that "no stone may be higher than the other lest the pot breaks".

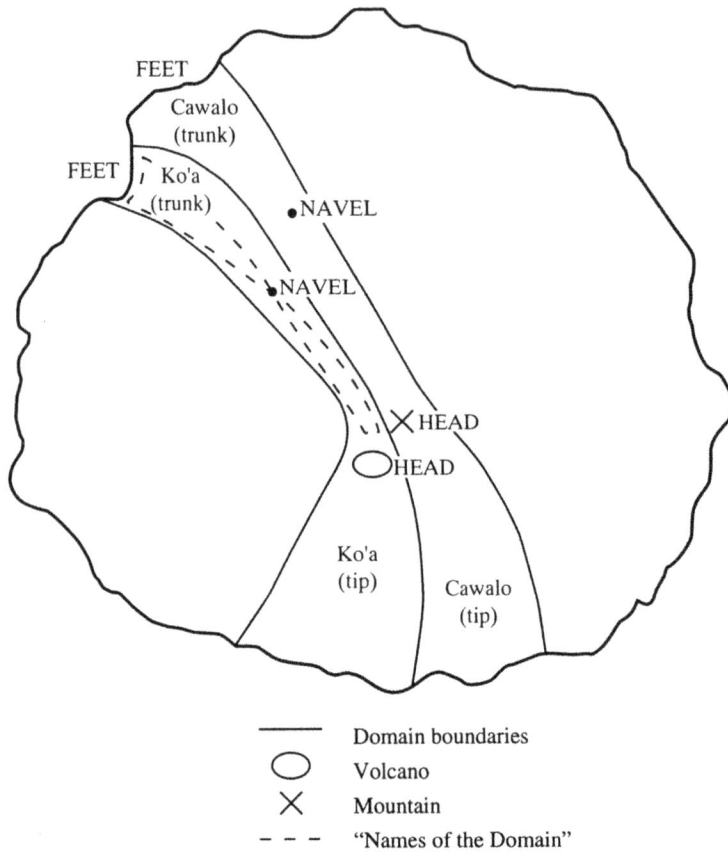

Map 2. Tana Ko'a and Tana Cawalo: the "domains of the coconut palm tree".

At another level, this notion of equality is overridden by a system of dual classification. In a recursive and complementary mode each domain classifies the other as either conceptually male (*laki*) or conceptually female (*vai*). Categorical asymmetry is achieved by defining male as being superior to female. This form of male-female classification is a relative one and it is crucial to note that the category to which a domain is assigned varies according to the standpoint of the classifier.

An important criterion of maleness is the size of the population. Another one is the notion of the "head" (*taba*) and "feet" (*va'i*) of a domain. Thus, if a territory reaches from the sea up to the mountain top, its "feet" are at the sea and the "head" at the top of the mountain. Only if a domain has both "head" and "feet" is it ritually complete and can exploit the whole range of ritual manipulations that are based on the concept of the domain as a living body (Map 2).

Finally, the actual size of the territory claimed by a domain may also be an important factor in its classification. In the chanting of "the names of the domain" preceding the sacrifice, place-names are evoked that trace lines from the four corners of the domain towards its ceremonial centre. In terms of the body metaphor applied to the domain this chain of names corresponds to lines reaching downhill from the "head", or rather from both its "shoulders" (*baja*), to its "navel" (*busé*) and from its "feet" uphill again to the "navel" (Map 2). This movement towards the "navel" is referred to as "taking in the names of the domain" (*nala tana ngarané*). In structural terms the domain contracts during the ceremonial cycle towards its two centres, the ceremonial courtyards. After the cycle is completed the centres are believed to have the potential to increase in size. In an expansive movement its "sides" (*ka*) can grow outward. It is these expanding "sides" that constitute the boundary lines towards the neighbouring domains. By setting offerings to the Supreme Being at intervals along the "sides" of the domain claim is laid over the space delineated by them. When these lines conflict with those of the neighbouring domain then, unless there is a pact prohibiting armed conflict the boundaries are redefined by means of warfare.[20]

The "Domains of the Three Hearth Stones": Pre-Sacrifice

I now turn to the situation among the "domains of the three hearth stones" as it presented itself before 1985, when Ko'a initiated its last ceremonial cycle.

With respect to the criteria of population and size of territory Cawalo is clearly the first among these three domains. It has a population of approximately 1,200 people and claims a territory of more than ten square kilometres. Ko'a, its southern neighbour, has a population of only 380 people and at present its territory is less than eight square kilometres. Finally, the population of Tomu to the north of Cawalo numbers approximately 600 people. Its population is larger than Ko'a but Tomu claims a territory of only two and a half square kilometres. Only the domains of Cawalo and Ko'a are ritually complete in that they have both "feet" and "head", their territories reaching from the sea up to the mountain top. The domain of Tomu only has "feet", the "head" section being occupied by the domain of Kéli.

Cawalo and Ko'a are also known as the "domains of the coconut tree" (*tana nio bu'uné*) (Map 2). At one level this designation is an allusion to the shape they make up together. Both territories run alongside each other from the sea up to the mountain, whereby the actual mountain top is part of Cawalo and the neighbouring volcano part of Ko'a. Together these sections of their territory make up what is referred to as "the trunk" (*bu'u*) of the coconut tree. Past the mountain top and the volcano their territories stretch in two long strips again all the way down to the sea. The two strips represent the fronds or "the tip" (*ngalu*) of the coconut tree. Because of the proximity of the volcano "the tip" is at present not habitable. Implicit in this botanic metaphor is the same notion of equality we have encountered in the image of the "three hearth stones". At this level both domains are considered to be of the same size, or as they put it, "like the two halves of a coconut tree".

On the basis of these main criteria, Cawalo, in the years preceding 1985, regarded itself as conceptually male with respect to both of its allies, Ko'a and Tomu. This view was not challenged by either of their main priest leaders and they largely accepted their conceptually female status with regard to Cawalo. In past times, however, the population of Ko'a was proportionally larger. Due to warfare, bad harvests and disease, numbers have declined, hence its smaller population in relation to Cawalo. Furthermore, Ko'a territory was almost identical in size to Cawalo until 1972 when Ko'a lost about a third of its "trunk" in a war against the domain of Nitu, its neighbour to the north. In that unfortunate war all of its villages were burned to the ground and its ancestral treasures and most of its livestock were lost. This was the last of a series of wars which Ko'a had lost and only recently had the domain begun to recover. From the point of view of Ko'a, Cawalo was regarded as its conceptually male counterpart. However, at least some of the Ko'a elders who had seen better times maintained that this need not always remain so. Ko'a still had enough "maleness" to maintain this position with respect to Tomu and might one day even be able to challenge Cawalo.

The priest leaders of Tomu, the third ally, were never very explicit about their domain's position with regard to Ko'a. Relations between the priest leaders of the two domains were cordial and visits between them frequent. At such occasional meetings the rhetoric displayed by the priest leaders in ritual speech never touched upon their respective maleness and femaleness. However, if questioned separately both would consider themselves to be conceptually male with respect to the other. A recurrent topic of discussion at such meetings was the deteriorating relations of the priest leaders of both domains to the main priest leader of Cawalo. Tomu could come up with a number of misgivings directed against Cawalo and so could Ko'a. At the bottom of these misgivings lay the fact that the main Cawalo priest leader was an ambitious younger man and a Christian who showed little respect for the two considerably older main priest leaders of Ko'a and Tomu. The Cawalo priest leader's father, the former priest leader, whom those of Ko'a and Cawalo may not have been fond of but whom they respected, had failed to teach his son all the intricacies of ritual speech and, therefore, communication with him was always felt to be unsatisfactory and prone to misunderstandings. Such was the situation before the Ko'a ceremonial cycle was opened in 1985. Table 2 brings together the relative positions of the "Domains of the Three Hearth Stones" at that point in time.

Table 2. Categorical asymmetry and recursive complementarity: pre-sacrifice (m = male, f = female; male > female)

Ko'a perspective:	Ko'a :	Cawalo	= f : m
	Ko'a :	Tomu	= m : f
Cawalo perspective:	Cawalo :	Ko'a	= m : f
	Cawalo :	Tomu	= m : f
Tomu perspective:	Tomu :	Ko'a	= m : f
	Tomu :	Cawalo	= f : m

One event that created misgivings between the three allied domains deserves mentioning because it sheds light on the strategies employed by the Cawalo main priest leader to manipulate internal tensions between the two groups of "father people" of Ko'a. A number of years earlier the Cawalo priest leader had offered an ivory tusk to the two Ko'a priest leaders in order to get them to accompany his purchasing party to Flores to obtain water buffalo. At the time the main Ko'a priest leader had refused this traditional prestation that secures the following of the allied domain because of some unresolved conflict between him and the main Cawalo priest leader. The lesser Ko'a priest leader, however, had accepted the tusk and instead of the main Ko'a priest leader one of his "younger brothers" had accepted the prestation on behalf of the main ceremonial courtyard. In doing so he had assumed the position of a House of "elder sibling" status. Also, because the Cawalo priest leader had given the tusk to a person of "younger brother" status the position of seniority of the main Ko'a priest leader had come to be questioned. Rumours were spread that he was not really the rightful main priest leader and that his grandfather, the father of the former main Ko'a priest leader, had originally been adopted from outside the domain into a Ko'a family. Furthermore, the fathers of the "elder" and of the "younger brother" had in the past exchanged their infant sons for a period of time. Eventually, however, both sons had returned to their natal Houses. Because of this interrupted process of child transfer the status of these sons with respect to inheritance was somewhat unclear. After the death of both of their fathers they engaged in a series of litigations over a contested piece of land. The end of these litigations had not yet been reached at the time when the "younger brother" was offered the ceremonial prestation of an ivory tusk by the Cawalo priest leader.

The Ko'a Ceremonial Cycle, 1985-1988: Categorical Inversion

By the very fact that Ko'a during its ceremonial cycle of 1985-1988 was acting as a host to its allies, these were placed, at least for the duration of the final sacrifice, in a subordinate position.[21] In terms of categorical asymmetry this signified that Ko'a temporarily became male with respect to all of its guests. However, the crucial question was whether Ko'a could maintain precedence beyond the day of sacrifice. If Ko'a indeed remained male with respect to both of its allies, it would be in the position to rally their support against Nitu and reclaim the lost territory. A victory against Nitu then would doubtlessly reconfirm the precedence of Ko'a. Table 3 indicates the instances of temporary categorical inversion in the relative positions among the "Domains of the Three Hearth Stones" brought into effect by the sacrifice.

Table 3. Categorical inversion: duration of sacrifice

Ko'a perspective:	Ko'a :	Cawalo	= m : f	(inverted)
	Ko'a :	Tomu	= m : f	(unchanged)
Cawalo perspective:	Cawalo :	Ko'a	= m : f	(threatened by inversion)
	Cawalo :	Tomu	= m : f	(unchanged)
Tomu perspective:	Tomu:	Cawalo	= f : m	(unchanged)
	Tomu :	Ko'a	= f : m	(inverted)

Events such as the "conquering" of the ceremonial courtyards by the guest of honour indicate, however, that the relation between guest and host is not one of unconditional temporary submission but that strong tendencies to maintain a position of superordination are involved.[22] In the course of this mock battle between guests and hosts men on both sides act out a display of aggression by scaling and defending the fortifications of the village, shouting loudly and shooting peas and seeds at each other by means of blowpipes or carved wooden toy guns. According to accounts of Ko'a elders, this "conquest" was not always playful. Until the district government prohibited it, weapons were used to kill the ally's livestock and physical fights resulting in bodily harm were frequent. In order to curtail physical violence agreements were reached between the priest leaders of the "domains of water buffalo blood" that in case of an injury the conquering domain would immediately return home without consuming any of the food prepared by the host.

In December 1985 Ko'a decided to initiate a water buffalo sacrificing cycle. On two occasions in previous years water buffalo had been purchased and both times the animals had died shortly after their arrival in Ko'a. For the upcoming purchase resources were scarce and there was great concern in the domain as to whether this time everything would go well. The death of a third purchased buffalo might entail such a loss of prestige for Ko'a that it might have to resign itself in the future to the sacrifice of pigs.

Initially the purchase was very successful even though some of the Houses of the "younger brothers" of the main Ko'a priest leader had not contributed the amount traditionally expected of them. Representatives of the priest leaders of Cawalo and Tomu, as well as a large number of followers from those domains had accompanied the purchasing party and the animals had been safely brought back to Ko'a. Things began to go wrong when one of the "younger brothers" of the main priest leader died just as the ceremonial dances were about to begin. As is customary in such cases the dances were not interrupted. There was general relief about the fact that this "younger brother" who had not contributed to the purchase and who had not accompanied the party had died instead of the new buffalo. This reasoning is based on the notion that the sacrificial animal is closely in touch with the ancestors as well as with the Supreme Being. At the opening and at the end of the ceremonial cycle any conflicts between the Houses of the "father people" of a domain must be solved lest the sacrifice be negatively affected. If solutions are not sought, offenders are either directly punished by the ancestors, as was seen to be the case here, or punishment is indirectly inflicted through the water buffalo who can maim or even kill a culprit.[23] However, in some cases the animal can die in place of an offender, thereby bringing the ceremonial cycle to a halt and effectively forcing the "father people" to seek a solution to the conflict.

On the second day of the dances following the death of the "younger brother" the water buffalo of the main ceremonial courtyard broke loose and in a desperate search for water ran all the way up to the volcano where it eventually collapsed. That night, the main Ko'a priest leader called a meeting of all the domain in which he voiced his discontent about the lack of support given to the opening of the sacrificial cycle. The following morning the animal was found dead beneath the "large sitting platform". Divination was conducted to determine the reason for this death and it became apparent that the same "younger brother" of the main priest leader who had once accepted the ivory tusk from Cawalo, had in the past committed incest with his classificatory sister. According to customary law he and his sister were to be put to death.[24] However, in order to stay within the confines of modern Indonesian law his sentence was converted into an obligation to purchase a water buffalo that was to be put to death in their place at a ceremonial courtyard located at the top of the mountain.

Even though at this point there were few resources left to stage another purchase the party travelled back to Flores to purchase two more animals. The second purchase was carried out according to the prescribed ways and Ko'a finally managed to open its cycle in the presence of all of its allies.

Because of previous unsuccessful attempts by Ko'a, it was decided to shorten the period of raising the buffalo to two years and so, in December 1987, preparations began for the sacrifice to take place in the following January. The two preceding harvests had been plentiful and the amount of goods brought back by seasonal migrants of the domain had exceeded all expectations. Even sons who had been working in Malaysia for many years for the first time had sent money back home and a group of about ten of them had returned to the island to witness the sacrifice. The prospects were judged to be favourable and some of the elders thought that this time, even though the population of Ko'a was smaller than that of Cawalo, Ko'a might maintain precedence beyond the sacrifice and become conceptually male in respect to both of its allies.[25]

About a week before the Ko'a sacrifice, there were indications that some of the "father people" of Cawalo were feeling threatened. Quite out of keeping with the ceremonial schedule, the Cawalo main priest leader purchased a young water buffalo from Flores. This was declared to be a preliminary sacrifice. At the sacrifice a letter in Indonesian was read out at the main Cawalo ceremonial courtyard. During the previous year this Cawalo priest leader had been chosen by the regency's Department of Education and Culture to represent the "domains of water buffalo blood" at a cultural meeting in Jakarta. As a reward for having provided information on the ceremonial cycle, the government had endowed him with a letter stating that Cawalo was to be the centre of the new "Organization of the Sun and Moon" ("Organisasi Era-Wula"). The ceremonial cycles of all of the "domains of water buffalo blood" were to be united into this one cultural organization under the leadership of Cawalo. In the future, the central government would pay for the costs of the ceremonies through its Cawalo chairman. Of course the allied priest leaders thought little of this proposal which went against the very nature of their system of alliance. Nevertheless, Cawalo had made its point and had reasserted its "maleness".

As the day approached when Cawalo was expected to be coming to Ko'a to attend the ceremonial dances rumours were heard that its main priest leader refused to come if Ko'a also invited Tomu. Upon hearing this, the main priest leader of Ko'a stated publicly that he did not care if Cawalo did not come and reconfirmed that Tomu had been chosen as the guest of honour of this cycle. When his position became known, the people of Ko'a pleaded with the same "younger brother" of the main priest leader who had earlier been found guilty of incest to negotiate with the Cawalo priest leader. This choice had doubtlessly been influenced by the fact that he had been the person who in the past had received the ivory tusk from the main Cawalo priest leader.

Against the will of his "elder brother", the "younger brother" together with the lesser priest leader went to Cawalo to talk. The outcome of the talk was that the priest leaders of the "Domains of the Three Hearth Stones", Ko'a, Cawalo and Tomu, were to hold a meeting in Ko'a in order to clear the air. The meeting took place the next day. At it very little of relevance was said. However, one point the Cawalo priest leader kept making to the large audience was that they should all stop following the orders of the two old priest leaders and that this was a new age and a time for the young. Since these statements were not made in ritual speech, the priest leaders from Ko'a and Tomu simply ignored them. But the very fact that the meeting had taken place in Ko'a strongly supported Ko'a's attempt to gain precedence over its allies. In the evening the dances were attended by the people of Cawalo, although its main priest leader did not come. The next day Ko'a was to go to Tomu to invite its main guest. Tomu was expecting large numbers of people from Ko'a and had been preparing food since the early morning. As the Ko'a mock war party was about to traverse the territory of Cawalo, they were met by envoys of the Cawalo priest leader who warned that any Ko'a trespassers would be harmed. Once again the main Ko'a priest leader refused to negotiate. However, his "younger brother", who by now had not only redeemed himself in the eyes of the people of Ko'a but had gained a reputation as a mediator, went to negotiate with the Cawalo priest leader. After a few hours he returned and announced that Cawalo had granted passage, but only after he had agreed to pay a specific amount of goods to Cawalo. Apparently the Cawalo priest leader had demanded these goods as a collective fine for all the real and imaginary transgressions Ko'a had committed against Cawalo in the past. By giving in Ko'a had clearly lost its claim to precedence over Cawalo.

Two days later the actual sacrifice proceeded without any further complications. Everyone hailed it as an outstanding success. Tomu had been invited and had in turn come to Ko'a and conquered its ceremonial courtyards. Even the Cawalo priest leader and his people had attended. The water buffalo had "danced" well, large crowds had been amply fed, the palm-gin had flowed freely and prestations had been reciprocated in a satisfactory way. It is significant, however, that at the closure of the cycle no offerings were set along the controversial boundary between Ko'a and its longstanding enemy Nitu. Because Ko'a had not been able to assume precedence over both its allies, a war with Nitu, which might have been triggered by such offerings, would probably have had to be fought without the support of Cawalo. The main priest leader of Ko'a must have recognized that such a confrontation could not be risked and so he had cancelled the offerings. Finally, now that his "younger brother" had gained so much popularity with the people of Ko'a at the expense of his own authority it would have been doubtful if at this point his "child people" would have supported him in such a venture.

Table 4 summarizes the order of precedence between the domains of the three hearth stones after the closing of the Ko'a ceremonial cycle. The individual positions are indicated with reference to the situation preceding the sacrifice. As it turned out, the Ko'a sacrifice of 1988 changed very little in the order of precedence among the "Domains of the Three Hearth Stones". The only lasting change in position was that Tomu recognized its femaleness with respect to Ko'a.

Table 4. Categorical asymmetry and recursive complementarity: post-sacrifice

Ko'a perspective:	Ko'a:	Cawalo	= f : m	(position unchanged)
	Ko'a:	Tomu	= m : f	(position unchanged)
Cawalo perspective:	Cawalo:	Ko'a	= m : f	(position unchanged)
	Cawalo:	Tomu	– m : f	(position unchanged)
Tomu perspective:	Tomu:	Cawalo	= f : m	(position unchanged)
	Tomu:	Ko'a	= f : m	(position changed)

Conclusion

In the description of the categories which structure political and ceremonial alliance we have twice encountered Dumont's "scandale logique": at the highest organizational level the unity and equality of allied domains are expressed by the metaphor of the "three hearth stones". At that same level inequality is expressed by means of asymmetric recursive complementarity in the idiom of a male-female classification. In different contexts either one or the other metaphor is applied to the relations between the three allied domains. In our account of the events surrounding the Ko'a ceremonial cycle the metaphor of unity was evoked only at one instance, when the three domains came together in Ko'a in an effort to solve conflicts existing between all three of them. During most of the cycle, however, the dominant metaphor was either explicitly or implicitly that of inequality. The unity between Ko'a and Cawalo expressed in the metaphor of the "domains of the coconut tree" was repeatedly called upon by the Ko'a negotiators at their meetings with the Cawalo priest leader. However, for the main priest leaders of both domains, the male-female classification remained in the foreground throughout the cycle.

It is in the tension created between the two seemingly contradictory notions of equality and inequality that the potential of a categorical inversion is located which lasts beyond the period of the sacrifice. In this investigation of the Ko'a sacrificial cycle the potential was only realized in the relationship between Tomu and Ko'a in that Tomu came to recognize the precedence of Ko'a. The relationship between Ko'a and Cawalo was subject to influences originating at other organizational levels.

In contrast to Dumont's characterization of Indian society, in which one set of oppositions, pure and impure, is portrayed as hierarchically structuring and pervading society at all levels, the example of Ko'a has shown that in this case there is no such all-pervasive opposition but that several classificatory oppositions at various levels are involved in the process of contestation of an order of precedence. The male-female opposition has been shown to be the idiom of relations between domains that stand in a relationship of ceremonial and political alliance, whereas their relationships to other allied domains who participate in the cycle but do not practice the water buffalo sacrifice are marked by an opposition based on a distinction of relative age, i.e. elder and younger sibling.

At the intra-domain level the relationship between the groups of Houses of priest leaders and those of subsequently settling groups of Houses is marked by an opposition based on a generational distinction, i.e. "father people" and "child people". Here the possibility for categorical inversion is not given and the space for contestation is minimal. The asymmetric aspect of the "father-child" relationship between priest leader and population of a domain is stressed by a ritual speech couplet which states that "the *lakimosa* carries (his people) in the folds of his loin-cloth, he cradles (them) in his lap" (*lakimosa tongo lae rongo, kai lae ka'i*). However, a contrasting couplet which is often evoked by both sides in decision-making processes at formal meetings of the whole of the domain modifies this asymmetry and emphasizes interdependence and complementarity by stating that "a father needs children (as much as) children need a father" (*hama tau no'o' hanané, hana tau no'o hamanê*). It is this aspect of their relationship that permitted the "child people" of Ko'a to plead with the "younger brother" to mediate between Ko'a and Cawalo.

Interestingly the relationship between the two groups of "father people" of the same domain is not marked by a metaphorical opposition. As this case has shown both their priest leaders were considered to be equal by the Cawalo priest leader. In the account of the Ko'a ceremonial cycle a distinction was made between a main priest leader as opposed to a lesser priest leader (*lakimosa ca, lakimosa lo'o*, lit. the big *lakimosa*, the small *lakimosa*). However, these attributes are only employed in an informal context and do not constitute formal designations. The asymmetry of the relationship is most evident in the sequencing of ceremonial events. Once again we are confronted with an apparent logical contradiction in which the status of the priest leaders is both equal as well as unequal. Although the ethnographic record is not conclusive on this point there are indications that in the past the two positions have undergone inversions. Cawalo countered the Ko'a claim to precedence in part by exploiting the tension created by the two opposed notions for its own ends.

Relations within groups of Houses are marked by an elder-younger sibling distinction. Here complementarity is no longer recursive in that the marked categories consist of one single House that assumes a position of seniority which is opposed to all other Houses of the same group. Relative age with respect to original descent establishes the seniority of this House. Even though the opposition is not recursive, the intricacies and ambiguities of child transfer and succession can provide an opportunity for the playing out of claims to elder sibling status both within the same House as well as between Houses, as was the case with the main Ko'a priest leader and his "younger brother". Here again Cawalo managed to manipulate the situation and gain advantage.

The various sets of oppositions at all of these levels are involved in the contestation of an order of precedence between allied domains. This Ko'a case study does not presume to represent an exhaustive treatment of this process. It has confined itself to demonstrate by way of example and by focusing on a sequence of key events how the analytical features of recursive complementarity, categorical asymmetry and categorical inversion operate in such a process.

References

Dumont, L.

1966 *Homo hierarchicus: le systeme des castes et ses implications*. Paris: Gallimard.

Eibl-Eibesfeldt, I.

1989 *Human ethology* [Translation of *Die Biologie des menschlichen Verhaltens*]. New York: Aldine de Gruyter.

Forth, G.

1981 *Rindi: an ethnographic study of a traditional eastern Indonesian domain* (Verhandelingen van het Instituut voor Taal-, Land- en Volkenkunde 93). The Hague: Martinus Nijhoff.

Fox, J.J.

1989 Category and complement: binary ideologies and the organization of dualism in Eastern Indonesia. In D. Maybury-Lewis and U. Almagor (eds) *The attraction of opposites: thought and society in a dualistic mode*, pp.33-65. Ann Arbor: University of Michigan Press.

1990 Hierarchy and precedence. Working Paper No.3. Canberra: Comparative Austronesian Project. Department of Anthropology, Research School of Pacific Studies, The Australian National University.

Jansonius, H.

1971 *Niew Groot Nederlands-Engels Wordenboek voor Studie en Praktijk*. 3 vols. Leiden: Nederlandsche Uitgeversmaatschappij N.V.

Lewis, E.D.

1988 *People of the source: the social and ceremonial order of Tana Wai Brama on Flores* (Verhandelingen van het Koninklijk Instituut voor Taal-, Landen Volkenkunde 135). Dordrecht: Foris.

McWilliam, A.R.

1989 Narrating the gate and the path: place and precedence in southwest Timor. PhD thesis, The Australian National University, Canberra.

Schulte-Nordholt, H.G.

1966 Het politieke systeem van de Atoni van Timor. PhD thesis, Free University of Amsterdam, Driebergen, Offsetdruk van Manen & Co.

1971 *The political system of the Atoni of Timor* (Verhandelingen van het Koninklijk Instituut voor Taal-, Land- en Volkenkunde 60). The Hague, Martinus Nijhoff.

Vischer, M.P.

1992 Children of the black patola stone: origin structures in an Eastern Indonesian domain. PhD thesis, The Australian National University, Canberra.

1993   Hata Lu'a. In E. Levinson (ed.) *Encyclopedia of world cultures*. Vol. 5.
         New Haven: Human Relations Area Files Press.

1994   Black and red, white and yellow: Palu'é textiles as representations of
         socio-cosmic ideas. In: Roy W. Hamilton (ed.) *The gift of the cotton
         maiden: textiles of Flores and the Solor Islands*, pp.246-268. Los Angeles:
         Fowler Museum of Cultural History, University of California.

Notes

[1] This paper represents a revised version of a paper presented at the conference on "Hierarchy" of the Comparative Austronesian Project held in Canberra in 1989. As such it reflects the state of research at that point in time. Versions of this paper were presented at seminars in Melbourne and Leiden and a German translation of it in Göttingen and Mainz. I would like to thank the participants at these seminars as well as the editors of this volume for their useful comments. Of course the usual disclaimers apply.

The research upon which this paper is based was conducted during two field trips, from December 1984 to February 1987 and from December 1987 to March 1988. The projects were conducted under the auspices of the Indonesian Science Council LIPI and with the sponsorship of Universitas Nusa Cendana of Kupang/Timor and The Australian National University, Research School of Pacific Studies.

[2] The endonym is Nua Lu'a. The official Indonesian designation is "Perwakilan Pulau Palue", "Subdistrict of Palue Island".

[3] Recently a number rainwater tanks provided by the government, the Catholic church and by an Indonesian NGO allow for water storage during the rainy season. This water is mainly used at feasts and ceremonial occasions.

[4] A major eruption of the volcano Mutu (or Rokatenda as the volcano is referred to outside Palu'é) occurred in 1927. This has been followed by a series of relatively minor eruptions and gas explosions at almost regular intervals, the last of which took place in January and June 1985.

[5] There are some indications that these domains represent the oldest population of the island.

[6] Until recently the animals were left to roam about on their own every morning in order to lap up dew from leaves and grasses. Nowadays a limited amount of water from rainwater tanks is made available to them.

[7] Recently the usage of the term order of precedence has been traced back to Louis Dumont (Fox 1990:1) who in "Homo Hierarchicus" alludes to such a concept: "... *la hiérarchie, ou plutôt l'existence d'un ordre de préceance* ..." (1966:104). I would like to add here another author to share this claim to anthropological ancestry, the Dutch scholar H.G. Schulte-Nordholt, in whose thesis on the political systems of the Atoni of Timor the term is used to characterize relations among Atoni lineages based on the categorical distinction between elder and younger sibling. The thesis was published in the same year as "Homo Hierarchicus". In his original version Schulte-Nordholt employed the term "sociale rangorde" (1966:47). According to Jansonius (1971) the primary meaning is order of rank, the secondary meaning order of precedence. The English translation of his thesis (1971:104) actually employs the term order of precedence. Since Dumont and Schulte-Nordholt a number of authors working on eastern Indonesian material have employed the term in various ways in the analytical description of specific processes of social differentiation in the societies in which they had conducted fieldwork (Forth 1981; Lewis 1988; McWilliam 1989; Vischer 1992). However, none of these authors has found it appropriate to define the concept at a more abstract level. It is not the aim of this paper to do so either, mainly because I feel that an abstract definition at this stage may well have an adverse effect on the further experimental development of the concept.

[8] My analysis here is informed by the ongoing discussion of the concept of precedence in the "Eastern Indonesia Seminar" chaired by James J. Fox at the Australian National University of which I have been a long-term member.

[9] For a more general assessment see Fox (1989).

[10] In order to distinguish the house as a physical structure from the house as a social category I employ for the latter a capital H.

[11] For a more extensive overview of Palu'é society see Vischer (1993).

[12] These alliances (*tura caji*) go back several centuries and are founded on mutual assistance in warfare against the Portuguese and later the Dutch.

[13] In Palu'é thought the number five represents the notion of completeness.

[14] This prestation has recently been reduced to a nominal sum of money.

[15] The actual cutting is always carried out by members of two different Houses of the "sacrificing people". One House traditionally provides officiants who cut the animal at its shins (*pati witéné*) and another those who cut it at its throat (*pati pokéné*). Ideally the slashings alternate between throat and shins.

[16] During the Ko'a sacrifice of 1988 the thirty-eight Ko'a Houses of "child people" status effected an average of sixty individual exchanges. Fifteen of these were exchanges between groups of Houses of wife-givers and wife-takers and Houses of quasi-consanguineal status. Exchanges effected by each of the sixteen Houses of "father" people status averaged approximately twice that amount.

[17] Because the "purchasing people" are prohibited to eat their own sacrificial buffalo the two ceremonial courtyards each exchange a hind leg of their respective sacrificed animal. The head and neck of their own animal go to the "sacrificing people". Specific cuts of this animal are then divided between the Houses holding ceremonial offices and other parts are distributed to "child people" Houses.

[18] For a more extensive treatment of Palu'é alliance including alliances with outside groups see Vischer (1992).

[19] The position of Cua, the seventh of the "domains of water buffalo blood", is ambiguous. From the Ko'a point of view Cua used to be a traditional ally. However, during the last war between Nitu and Ko'a, Cua did not support Ko'a but appears to have sided with Nitu. It may well be that in this system of two times three allies the seventh domain maintains shifting loyalties.

[20] In recent years inter-domain warfare has been restrained by the establishment of a semi-permanently staffed police station on the east coast of Palu'é and by the installation of radio communications with the district capital on the mainland by means of which military support can be called in and deployed within two days. Following military intervention boundary disputes are usually referred to district courts.

[21] The subordinate position of a guest is a widespread phenomenon in eastern Indonesia and can be linked to the presence of the host's ancestors inside of his dwelling. In order to counteract this relation of inequality between host and guest and make him feel at ease the head of a Ko'a household will often be apologetic about his house and about the meal served and call his dwelling unworthy of the visitor and claim that his food is insufficient and of bad quality.

[22] The human ethologist Eibl-Eibesfeldt refers to such behaviour as "rituals of friendly greeting" and observes that these always contain the combination of two antithetical elements, one of display and one of appeasement (1989:493-496). In Palu'é mock battles this element of appeasement is represented by women who partake in the conquest by throwing ceremonial rice kernels generally employed as ritual offerings. However, in the case of Ko'a this element is only on the surface an appeasing one. Some of these rice kernels are customarily mixed with a magical substance that is aimed at leading those who come into contact with it to commit acts of sexual transgression.

[23] Evidence of this can be found in nearly every domain that sacrifices water buffalo. Persons who have survived attacks as a consequence are often disabled and serve as living examples of the veracity of these admonitions.

[24] Of people who commit incest it is said that "their blood will rise and make their head swell up" (*laja tuka soko*) and this swelling will eventually lead to death. Incest among "father people", however, presents a special case because of their strong identification with the domain. A rising of their blood will also cause the "blood" running beneath the surface of the ground to rise and create a "swelling" at the "head" of the domain. The consequence of this "swelling" of the domain is that the "sea rises upwards and the mountain falls down into the sea" (*tai tuka reta ili pere lau*), i.e. a volcanic eruption, a landslide or an earthquake will ensue. In order to prevent this from happening ancestral law requires the incestuous couple to be buried alive head first in the ground at the top of the mountain and stabbed to death by means of digging sticks. By drenching the ground with their blood the "swelling" at the mountain top is released and disaster is averted.

[25] Only a few months previously I had the opportunity to implement a project for the construction of rainwater tanks in cooperation with the people of Ko'a. By the time of the sacrifice every second house in Ko'a had its own tank containing the water of the first rains. At the time Ko'a derived considerable prestige from having these tanks. Such a large amount of water had never been seen on Palu'é and in the past water for large ceremonies had had to be brought over from Flores and carried up the mountain

in bamboo containers. Rainwater tanks had also been built in the domain of Awa that customarily supports Ko'a during a sacrifice and Awa was expected to express its gratitude by contributing substantially to the coming ceremonial events.

Chapter 10. The Founding of the House and the Source of Life: Two Complementary Origin Structures in Buru Society

Barbara Dix Grimes

On the eastern Indonesian island of Buru people express ideas about origin and cause with metaphors based on the imagery of a living plant or tree. The roots and trunk of a tree (*lahin*) and the young leaves which appear at the tips of the branches (*luken*) are the culturally significant points of reference for these metaphors. Many events, including sickness, litigations and warfare as well as simple narrations and tape recordings, are conceptually structured in terms of beginning at a "root" (*lahin*) and having "young leaf tips" (*luken*) as their end result or consequence. As they say on Buru, things progress "from the root until emerging at the tips" (*fi di lahin eta suba luken*).[1]

These epistomological metaphors are applied to many things in Buru. This paper focuses specifically on how these metaphors and ideas about origin are applied to people in the context of social groups in Buru society. Two types of conceptual structures of origin are discussed. The first concerns *noro*, the primary Buru social groups, which are defined by the unique ways in which they were founded, and by males who remain in them throughout their lives. The second concerns life which has a separate origin structure and is transmitted through females, giving individuals unique sources of life. In complementing each other, these two origin structures are the foundation for the construction of social relations on Buru.

An Overview of Buru

The island of Buru is approximately 140 kilometres east to west and 90 kilometres north to south. It is the third largest island in the Indonesian province of Maluku, second in size only to Seram and Halmahera. Just 110 kilometres of Banda Sea separate Buru from the provincial capital on the island of Ambon, but despite its geographical proximity Buru has historically been on the periphery of much that has occurred in the regional context. Having no native clove or nutmeg trees, Buru was of little importance to the spice trade which brought Asians and Europeans to other islands in Maluku as early as the fifteenth and sixteenth centuries. Not only did the boats of the spice trade by-pass Buru, much of the foreign contact that came to the region did as well (Map 1).

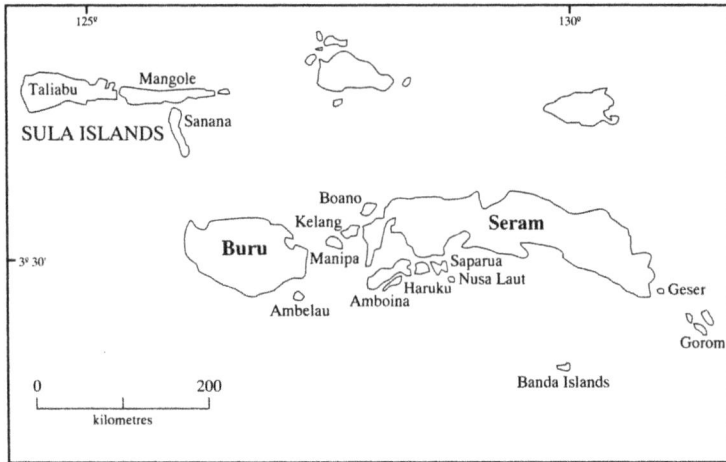

Map 1. Central Maluku.

Approximately 43,000 people consider themselves "people of Buru island" (*geb fuku Bururo*) and although they freely acknowledge some dialectal differences, they insist on being considered a cohesive linguistic and ethnic group belonging to this relatively large island by virtue of their origins. It is significant that the *geb fuku Bururo* comprise less than half the total population of 102,000 inhabitants on the island. Thousands of immigrants, particularly from the islands of Buton and Sula, have colonized the north and west coasts of Buru. Many of these colonies have been on Buru for several centuries and still regard themselves as ethnically distinct from Buru people and often continue speaking the languages of the islands from which they originated. Recently around 23,000 more people have come to the island, some brought initially as political prisoners after the 1965 political upheaval in Indonesia and others later as transmigrants. This predominantly Javanese influx has been localized on the island and almost without exception, all the immigrants on the island — longterm residents as well as recent arrivals — reside along the coast or on a few flat plains areas near the coast.

The interior of Buru is very mountainous, covered with dense jungle. *Geb fuk Bururo* often prefer to live in the mountainous jungle of the interior, rather than on the coast. The island of Buru can thus be characterized as having an indigenous minority population which is traditionally-oriented to the vast interior of the island while numerous colonies of immigrants from other parts of the archipelago fringe the coastal regions. The majority of immigrants on Buru are Moslem as well as a portion of the *geb fuk Bururo* now living on the coast. In the interior of the island *geb fuk Bururo* practice both Christianity and their traditional religious beliefs.[2]

The daily activities of *geb fuk Bururo* living in the interior of the island centre around gardening and hunting. Extensive hunting is done by men for wild pig, deer, cuscus and other small animals. Gardens are made, often on steep mountainsides, and shifting cultivation focuses around yams, cassava, and taro with smaller amounts of millet, dry rice and corn also grown. Where the terrain is suitable, sago is planted and cultivated. Considerable labour is necessary for gardening, particularly for opening new gardens in the jungle and for harvesting. During these long labour-intensive periods, people often live in their isolated garden huts scattered across the mountains. They may also have a house in a village but as it may be many hours' walk away from their gardens they return to live in the village only when the garden work temporarily permits them to do so. When fully inhabited, interior villages consist of 50 to 200 people living in 10 to 30 households.

Hunting and gardening is the responsibility of each household which typically includes a man, his wife or wives and their unmarried children. The individuals in each household are incorporated into higher level social groups called *hum lolin* and *noro*. A *hum lolin*, which literally means "house-circle", consists typically of agnatic kin related over four or five generations. In this paper I refer to *hum lolin* both by the Buru term and by "House", as it is a social group conceptualized in terms of a house metaphor. The genealogical connections between all the members of a *hum lolin* are known, and kin terms are used to refer to everyone within an ego's *hum lolin*. Leadership of a House is invested in *geb emtuato* meaning "old people", a term used to refer to parents and what approximates the English term "elders". In a political sense, *geb emtuato* are men who function in decision-making and negotiations as representatives of their House, particularly in matters concerning land and marriage.

Several *hum lolin* together comprise a *noro*. The relationship between a *noro* and its separate Houses is expressed as a whole which has broken into sections, using the term *ekfakak* meaning "to be broken into pieces". Each House has a "founding father" (*tama*) and "founding mother" (*tina*) who were the first to establish the House as separate from other Houses in the *noro*. Same sex sibling terms of relative age (*kai* "elder"/*wai* "younger") are used to describe the relationship between the various Houses within a *noro*.

A *noro* is the highest level social or political structure in Buru society and the total *geb fuk Bururo* population is divided into over 35 *noro*. No centralized political hierarchy unifies the different *noro* on the island and the situation, as they say, is one where "each noro governs its own noro" (*noro saa printa tu nake noro*). Marriages must be transacted between Houses of different *noro*. What defines Buru society as a whole is not any overarching political order, but networks of inter-*noro* relationships which can be characterized as much by alliance and marriage as by hostility and warfare. Although there may be less inter-*noro* warfare today than in the past, marriage alliances do not preclude warfare between *noro* and the threat of hostility from people of other *noro* is always considered present.

Before considering how the identity of Buru Houses and *noro* are articulated in terms of their origin structure, it is necessary to first discuss how individuals become affiliated with these social groups. Marriage and bridewealth are very important aspects of affiliation on Buru. Upon marriage, men "stay in the house to guard the sharpening stone" while women "exit" (*suba*) their natal House to "return" (*oli*) to the House and *noro* of their husband. Marriage thus transfers a woman to another House and *noro*, and hopefully results, through her fecundity, in the increase of her husband's House. Because of this, marriage is very much the concern of the *hum lolin*. When a "son" of a *hum lolin* is to marry, it is the responsibility of the entire *hum lolin* to contribute to the bridewealth, part of which goes to the actual parents of the bride and part to her *hum lolin* elders.

After a woman marries, children born to her belong to the House and *noro* of her husband. While it may in effect appear as if the father-child link is the important criterion, affiliation to Buru social groups is not constructed in terms of such links.[3] People on Buru formulate their ideas about the affiliation of children in terms of "child rights" (*hak anat*) which are transferred in the marriage process from a woman's natal *hum lolin* to the *hum lolin* of her husband in a different *noro*. The affiliation of children is thus intricately tied to the marriage process. It is only *after* the bride's House has received some form of "compensation" (*filin*) for their loss of the bride and the final stages of the marriage process have occurred, that *hak anat* is transferred to the House and *noro* of a woman's husband. *Before* marriage negotiations for a particular woman have been initiated, *hak anat* belongs to her natal *hum lolin*. Any children born to her before she is married belong to her natal *hum lolin* and *noro*, the *noro* of her brother, who is under those circumstances called her child's "father" (*ama*).

In many cases bridewealth is given to replace the bride and bridewealth becomes an important indicator that *hak anat* has been transferred. Then, as they say on Buru, bridewealth should "bear fruit". That is, bridewealth should result in the increase of members in the House. This idea is expressed in a number of different ways. When a woman is barren, her bridewealth is said to have borne no fruit and the collection of it by her husband's House is considered to have been wasted effort. If a young bride dies before she has given birth to a child, her natal House is obligated to replace her with another bride, because the bridewealth has not yet borne fruit. However, if a bride dies after giving birth to a child, it is not necessary for her natal *hum lolin* to replace her. If the child she has borne is a son, the bridewealth has borne fruit and her husband's House has increased. If she has borne a daughter, the daughter will eventually "return her mother's bridewealth" to the *hum lolin* when she marries. Beside bridewealth, there are other ways to replace a bride. A child can be given to the bride's House or sister-exchange can take place. Whether it is by bridewealth, a child, or another bride, when the bride has been replaced, the affiliation of her future children belong to the House and *noro* of her husband.

The Founding of the House

Fox has noted there are various social groups in societies throughout eastern Indonesia which can be characterized by what he calls *origin groups* in that:

> ... what they claim to share and to celebrate is some form of common derivation. This derivation is socially constructed and may be variously based on the acknowledgement of a common ancestor, a common cult, a common name or set of names, a common place of derivation, and/or a share in a common collection of sacred artefacts (this volume:132).

The Buru *noro*, composed of Houses, is such a social group, sharing and celebrating a common origin. In this section I describe the configuration of ideas which make up the "origin structure" of a Buru *noro*.[4]

Most important in the origin structure of each *noro* is a *moyang*. For convenience I gloss this Buru term as "founding ancestor" but it is important to understand how Buru people use the term as there are some significant semantic differences between the Buru meaning of *moyang* and the English meaning of "ancestor", as well as between the Buru meaning and the standard Malay or Indonesian meaning of the same form which is in more ways like that of the English term "ancestor". The English term is based on genealogical criteria and denotes a person at the apex of a genealogical relationship (Keesing 1975:21). On Buru, genealogical links to individuals in the past are recognized (*enohon enatin*), and can be important at times, but genealogical links are not the basis for an individual's relationship with his *moyang*. It is an individual's affiliation to a particular *noro* that determines his or her particular *moyang*.

Moyang are culturally significant for many reasons, one of which is that they are potentially involved in the everyday affairs of living *noro* members. There are numerous cases on Buru where people change their *noro* affiliation and "enter" (*rogo*) a new *noro*. This occurs most frequently with women through marriage, but there are also various kinds of adoption (cf. B.D. Grimes 1990). When people change their *noro* affiliation for whatever reason, they acquire the *moyang* of their new *noro* who can be pleased or displeased with the conduct of their newly affiliated offspring.

As spirits who have the potential for both blessing and punishing their living *noro* offspring, *moyang* are in some ways similar to the spirits of dead *noro* members (*nitu*) who can also bless or curse their living kin. And yet *moyang* and *nitu* are very different. *Nitu* are the spirits of very normal humans who have died relatively recently, while *moyang* were physically present on earth in the remote past, in the founding time of society.

In attempting to grapple with Lao categories of spirits in Fiji, Hocart noted that a class of spirits called *vu* (which he also referred to as "gods") had as their chief characteristic "originating". He also noted "the Fijians are very careful to distinguish between the spirits of the dead and these [*vu*] gods" (1952:9). While admitting the difficulty of finding an adequate gloss for *vu*, Hocart referred to them as "founder-gods". The Buru concept of *moyang* has many similar features. The chief characteristic of *moyang* is that they each founded a *noro* which later divided into various Houses. There are no *moyang* who are not originators. At the same time, *moyang* have semi-divine characteristics in that they were not ordinary humans. As founders of society they are known to have performed supernatural deeds having more power than is associated with normal humans.

So while all *moyang* are founders of *noro*, each *moyang* is considered to be unique and to have founded a unique *noro*. Differentiation is constructed among *moyang* in several ways, including gender, how they came to be on Buru, and where they became established on Buru. The first of these criteria establishes a *moyang* as either male or female which may be specified as "father founding ancestor" (*ama moyang*) or "mother founding ancestor" (*ina moyang*). While the gender of a specific founding ancestor is always known, there is no social differentiation made between *noro* on the basis of the gender of their founding ancestor, nor is there any difference in the affiliation rules between *noro* with male or female founding ancestors.

The second way in which *moyang* are differentiated is in the manner associated with their appearance on Buru. The founding ancestors of some *noro* are autochthons who "appeared" (*newa*) at the headwaters of streams on the island, while the founding ancestors of other *noro* came to Buru by boat from other islands. This is the case for example with the founding ancestress of the Mual *noro*, Bokis Raja, who came from the Hoamoal peninsula on Seram to Buru.

Thirdly, each *moyang* is associated with a unique place on Buru, giving each *noro* a place of origin. The place where the *moyang* was first established on the island is called the *tean elen* which literally means the "place of the planted house pole". The *tean elen* of autochthonous *moyang* is at the specific spring or stream in the mountains where the *moyang* appeared. The *tean elen* of a *noro* with non-autochthonous *moyang* is the place where the *moyang* first went after arriving on the island by boat: the stream or river they came to and subsequently planted a house pole. The name of the stream at which a *moyang* established itself is often given to the *noro* and referred to as the "ancestral water/stream" (*wae moyang*) of that particular *noro*. There is an additional place on the coast associated with non-autochthonous *moyang*: the place of the "boat disembarkation" (*waga enohon*).

There are ties to this place as well as to the "place of the planted house pole" and the "ancestral stream", associations of the journey and power of the *moyang*.

There is a well defined and often large territorial area surrounding the place of origin which belongs to the *noro* and is divided into portions belonging to each *hum lolin*. Land rights and hunting rights to the territory are inherited by Houses, and people of other groups must request permission to make gardens or to hunt there. Today there is a far from perfect correlation between the places where people currently reside and their places and territories of origin because of frequent migrations to other parts of the island. Mass sickness and death are the most frequent reasons given for such migrations, some of which have brought people to live at places on the island far from their original *tean elen*. The important point is that even if people no longer live in their original territory, they still inherit this land and they still control rights to its use because it is part of the origin structure of the House and *noro* to which they belong.

Near or at the *tean elen* is a *hum sikit* or house in which its various heirlooms are stored. Heirlooms typically include ruling cloths, staffs and other objects of *noro* history. Because migrations have been so frequent and people do not live near their *tean elen*, these houses have been difficult to keep up. In actual fact, many *noro* have not had a *hum sikit* for many years. *Hum sikit* are never the focus of much activity and many people are rarely at their *tean elen*, but the idea that each *noro* should have a *hum sikit* in which to store the objects of its history is still present on Buru.

Around 1990 one *noro* rebuilt their *hum sikit* near their *tean elen* far in the interior of the island. This involved carrying metal roofing up the mountain several days' walk to use in the construction. This innovation was not missed by other *noro* in the area and they also began discussing how to collect money to buy roofing and then construct a "modern" *hum sikit* for their own *noro*. The value of metal roofing is in very practical terms the fact that it will outlast thatch roofing for many years and make the *hum sikit* last many more years before repairs are needed.

The origin structure of a Buru *noro* also includes names for the *noro* as well as its Houses. A *hum lolin* is frequently named after a prominent geographical feature such as a river, stream, tree or rock near the garden house of the "founding father of the House" (*tama*). Names for *noro* come from a variety of sources. Sometimes the name of the founding ancestor is reflected in the name. Another naming strategy already mentioned is to make use of the origin place name. The "ancestral stream" (*wae moyang*) of the Wae Temun *noro* is a small stream called *Wae Temun*. The Wa Kolo *noro* has its origin place at Wa Kolo, an alternate name for the lake (*Rana*) in the centre of the island.

Each *noro* has two names: an "inside" name and an "outside" name. The inside name is referred to as the *noro* name and the outside name is called the *fam* [5] name or the "Indonesian name". The outside name is used much like a surname when people interact with the Indonesian state, such as when enrolling their children in school, signing legal documents and so on. Non-Buru immigrants and other outsiders are said to only have an outside (*fam*) name. Because the origin structure of a Buru *noro* includes both inside and outside names, the lack of an inside name is seen as evidence that these people lack a Buru origin structure and therefore cannot be "people of Buru island" (*geb fuk Bururo*).

The origin structure of a *noro* thus includes a founding ancestor, a place of origin called the *tean elen* where ideally a *hum sikit* is maintained for storing heirlooms, a traditional territory belonging to each House, and inside and outside names. These origins are not just seen as facts of history, but are relevant to everyday life. People may seek the help and blessing of their *moyang* in any place, but it is always much more efficacious to ask for blessing at the *tean elen*. This ideology results in one of the many ways in which people on Buru strive to return to their origins for blessing. If it is deemed necessary, people who have moved away will spend much time, money and effort to return to their *tean elen* to seek the blessing of their *moyang*.

The uniqueness of each *noro* and House is constructed in terms of differences in the salient features of their origin structures. Equally significant, Buru ideas about social hierarchy and equality are also articulated in terms of these origins. In discussing hierarchy in eastern Indonesia, Fox has noted hierarchy is both structured and countered through the use of dual categories. When dual categories structure hierarchy he states:

> The hierarchical use of dual categories depends upon the conjunction of two analytic features: recursive complementarity and categorical asymmetry (1989:59).

These two analytic features can be illustrated at precisely the place where hierarchy occurs in Buru society: at the ranking of Houses within a *noro* and the ranking of same sex siblings within a House. In these cases hierarchy is constructed through the use of the complementary dual categories of elder-younger same-sex sibling terms. These categories are asymmetrical in that the superiority of the elder is always stressed on Buru and reflected in statements such as "an elder [same-sex sibling] (*kai*) will always be an elder [same-sex sibling] (*kai*) and must always be treated as such". These asymmetrical categories are then applied recursively to produce precedence within the *noro* and House.

elder	younger			
	elder	younger		
		elder	younger	
			elder	younger

Precedence within a House and *noro*.

This ranking or precedence is fixed. Within a House, it is fixed among same-sex individuals according to the timing of their relative births. Within a *noro*, it is fixed among Houses according to the timing of their relative establishments. This is often geographically objectified in that a *noro* is associated with a particular river or stream and the origin place of each House along the river system is known. Elder Houses were always established first, closer to the source of the river and therefore upstream to younger Houses. Precedence thus flows from elder to younger, from upstream to downstream, from the headwaters in the mountains at the centre of the island to the periphery of the island at the coast.

Turning from internal relationships within a *noro* where precedence is established between Houses and individuals, to external relationships between *noro*, categorical asymmetry is no longer found. Dual categories exist in the classification of *noro*, just as they exist in the classification of Houses and individuals, but this time no asymmetrical value is assigned. People in every *noro* express profound respect for and stress the uniqueness and power associated with their particular founding ancestor, but none of the differences among founding ancestors — their maleness or femaleness, their autochthonous or non-autochthonous origins, their order of appearance — translates into categorical asymmetry. Reflecting the classification of their *moyang*, people can be called "original people" (*geba dengen*) or "people who arrived" (*geba enadut*), but again superior value is assigned to neither category. Difference is constructed, but it does not produce precedence or rank.

This construction of difference and the assignment and non-assignment of superior value to the resulting categories formulates the nature of social relationships on Buru. Within the *noro*, House relationships are both inalterable and hierarchical. Similarly, within a House every individual knows his or her place in the ranking of generations and the ranking of elder and younger samesex siblings. Of only one person and one House can it be said "There is no one elder."

Between *noro*, however, where there is no established precedence, it is possible to avoid relationships of asymmetry. The ideology of "a person replaces a person" (*geba gati geba*) is the primary operating principle in inter-*noro* relations and applies equally to the loss of women in marriage as it does to the loss of men in warfare. In warfare "revenge killing" (*kalungan*) demands that there be an equal number of deaths between two *noro*. In marriage, the cultural option of "reciprocally exchanged maidens" (*emhuka eptukar*) allows for the simultaneous exchange of women between two groups. This makes the two *noro* and Houses simultaneously both "wife-givers" (*kori*) and "wife-takers" (*sanat*) to each other and makes two men simultaneously both WB and ZH to each other.

Symmetrical marriage exchanges can occur between two groups at a single point in time through *emhuka eptukar*, but they also occur over time through the accumulation of bi-directional single marriages. Arrangements involving the marriage of only one bride always necessitates the asymmetry of *kori* over *sanat* and of the WB over his ZH in the context of that particular marriage. However, the cumulative effect of bi-directional marriages between *noro* — both single marriages and *emhuka eptukar* marriages — allows two *noro* to see their overall relationship as one of symmetry. Positive relationship between two *noro* is equated with the symmetry that occurs when "they are WB and ZH to each other" (*du wali-dawen*). The relationship between men who are "reciprocally both WB and ZH to each other" (*wali-tal-dawet*) exemplifies Buru ideals of the intimate friendship and equality that can exist between men and social groups in symmetrical relationships.

It is thus the assignment and non-assignment of value to features in the origin structure of *noro* and Houses that formulates the context for social relations on Buru. There is a perpetual deference to the hierarchy of elders within a House and *noro* and at the same time a continual striving for equality in relationships with other *noro*. Hierarchy within the House and *noro* is fixed and permanent, while equality between *noro* must continually be achieved and maintained.

The Source of Life

The way in which people on Buru conceptualize their ideas about the source or origin of life is reflected in certain kin terms which are listed in the following table.

yoi	FZ
wate	FZH
mem(e)-lahin [a]	MB
wate-lahin	MBW
emdaa	MBD (m.s. and f.s.)/FZC (f.s.)
wali lahin	MBS (m.s.)
naha lahin	MBS (f.s.)
wali ennewet	FZS (m.s.)
feta ennewet	FZD (m.s.)
ana ennewet	ZC (m.s.)
wate	WBC/HZC

Selected Buru terms for kin in other *noro*.

^a Throughout this paper I gloss *mem-lahin* as MB for the sake of convenience, but on Buru the genealogical relationship is not the only criterion. While a *mem-lahin* is genealogically MB, he *must* belong to another *noro*. In other words, ego's mother must be married. If ego's mother is not married, his or her genealogical MB is called *ama* (father) as they belong to the same House. *Mem-lahin*, as I was told, is a term which has to have "two *noro*". I similarly gloss the other terms here with genealogical relationships, but they all include the obligatory social fact of being relationships between individuals in different *noro*.

Many of these terms are based on the epistomological metaphors of the living tree mentioned at the beginning of this paper. In these cases, the terms are compounds, composed of a kin term plus a metaphor as a modifier. The kin terms upon which the compounds are based include:

wate — "reciprocal relationship between ego and his or her spouse's cross sex sibling's child" (WBC/HZC/MBW/FZH)
meme — "parent's male sibling"
wali — "brother-in-law" (m.s.)
naha — "brother" (f.s.)
feta — "sister" (m.s.)
ana — "child"

The two modifiers are *lahin* ("root/trunk") and *ennewet* ("life"). The compound terms can thus be given more specific glosses as follows:

mem-lahin (MB) — "root/source uncle"
wate-lahin (MBW) — "root/source aunt"
wali-lahin (MBS — m.s.) — "root/source brother-in-law"
naha-lahin (MBS — f.s.) "root/source brother"
wali ennewet (FZS — m.s.) "life brother-in-law"
feta ennewet (FZD — m.s.) "life sister"
ana ennewet (ZC — m.s.) "life child"

A girl and boy who are reciprocally *emdaa* (MBD/FZS) are in an avoidance relationship as they are both potential and ideal marriage partners. Children are told "Play with your elder and younger siblings; don't play with your *emdaa*." People have told me that a boy could call his MBD *feta lahin* ("root/source sister") and a girl could equally call her FZS *naha ennewet* ("life brother") but this is not necessary, as they are *emdaa* and that term is preferred. While these additional terms are seldom used, as equivalents they point out the consistency in the structure of the kin terminology for the descendants of a brother and sister. Relatives traced through a mother's brother are described as *lahin* kin while those traced through a man's sister are *ennewet* kin.

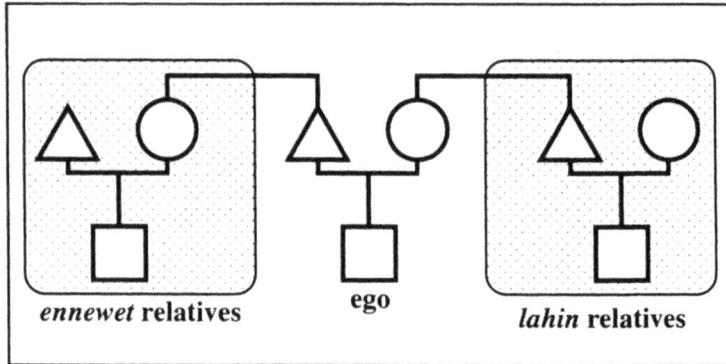

Figure 1. Life (-*ennewet*) and source (-*lahin*) relatives.

Concepts of source and life are thus used to express the relationship between the offspring of a brother and sister, and even more significantly, between a man and his sister children, a "source uncle" (*mem-lahin*) and his "life children" (*ana ennewet*). While these metaphors were mentioned earlier, it is helpful to consider them in more detail here. If someone on Buru were asked to point out a *lahin*, it would be a "wood-*lahin*" (*kau lahin*) which would include the main trunk of a tree, the base of the tree and its major roots. A typical *kau lahin* would be a tree with a tall single trunk such as a "coconut tree" (*niwe lahin*), "sago tree" (*bia lahin*), or "canarium tree" (*ipa lahin*). Based on the imagery of the life-producing roots and trunk of tall trees, *lahin* is an ideal metaphor to express a cultural concept of causality which sees subsequent events as stemming from an origin, cause, foundation, beginning or source.

The counterpart to *lahin* is *luken* which refers to the tiny new leaves that grow off the tips of branches, as in *mangkau luken*, the young new leaves picked to eat from the top of the cassava plant. As a continuation of the botanical imagery, *luken* is metaphorically used to refer to the tip, the end, the results, or the ramifications of someone's deeds, and not surprisingly, to someone's "descendants". Anyone who reckons his genealogical connections to an important person in the past will proudly tell you "I am a tip from him" (*Ya puna luken fi di rine*). Buru ideas about personal origins are thus turned upside down to European ideas about "descent", a point which Fox (1988) has noted as occurring in many eastern Indonesian societies. While Europeans talk about "descendants" in reference to someone's CCC, on Buru people talk about CCC as *luken* — "ascendants" or "tips". The social unit of the *hum lolin*, as another example, can be described as the "tips" of the "founding father" (*tama*).

The Buru idea being expressed in the kinship terminology is that life has a source. Life comes from females giving birth to children. Because a woman changes her affiliation and "enters" (*rogo*) her husband's *noro* and House when she marries, her brother represents the source or origin of her children's life.

He is thus their "source uncle" and they his "life children". Botanically life in the young leaf tips comes from the root. Metaphorically this is true of humans as well and is reflected in the statement of one old man who proudly told me he had "young leaf tips of life children" (*ana newe luken*) all over the mountains of south Buru.

The relationship between source and life is also reflected in the cultural responsibilities assigned to a "source uncle" in regard to his "life children". A man is responsible for the life of his sister's children. He is ritually responsible to ensure the fertility of his sister, that her children do not die at birth, and that appropriate marriages are arranged for them. A child is taught to respect his *mem-lahin* and the curse of sickness and bad fate hangs over anyone who does not obey their *mem-lahin*. A *mem-lahin* is not responsible for the sustenance of his *ana ennewet*, however. That is the responsibility of his sister's husband, *hum lolin, noro,* and ancestors.

So while a man's "life children" do not belong to his House or *noro*, he is responsible both for the transmission of life to them and through them. Because of this he plays an important role not only when they are infants, but also in selecting marriage partners for his "life children". The best way to ensure numerous and healthy children as the result of a marriage is for a man to return to the group which represents his own source of life and seek as a wife either his actual *emdaa* (MBD) or someone from another House in his mother's natal *noro*. If the *mem-lahin* has a marriageable daughter he has the prerogative to say to his sister and her husband "cause your child to become [my] son-in-law" (*pemsawan nim anat*) and so a boy's *mem-lahin* (MB) becomes his *ama kete* (WF). If his sister's son does not marry his daughter, the *mem-lahin* must be the one to "give the machete to cut open the path for marrying someone else" (*duwe todo la sasa tohon la ketik geba meget*). The *mem-lahin* then acts as one of the spokesmen in the marriage negotiations of his ZS as well as his ZD. Marriage is thus another case where Buru ideas about returning to one's source are enacted.

Sources of life are kept track of for two generations on Buru. Two terms, *mara* and *halan*, are used specifically to define relationships of individuals to other *noro* through which they trace their source of life. *Mara* refers to the *noro* of an ego's *mem-lahin* and *halan* is the *noro* of an ego's *mem-lahin's mem-lahin* (MBMB). These connections are illustrated below:

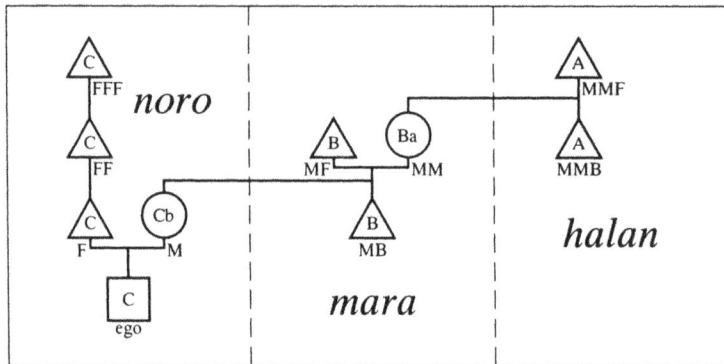

Figure 2. *Mara* and *halan*: reckoning maternal *noro* as the source of life.

At birth, individuals are affiliated with their natal *noro* but trace their origin of life through female connections to their *mara* and *halan*. The ties to these two other *noro* do not diminish an individual's membership in his own *noro*, but are the recognition of his source of life. On the basis of these ties he can request hunting rights or permission to build gardens in the land of his *mara* or *halan*. And most importantly, it is to his *mara* or *halan* that he should return when seeking to marry and propagate new life.

Conclusion

In this paper I have discussed two cultural concepts constructed around ideas of origin and source in Buru society. The *noro* is a social group composed of Houses defined by males who stay in them. These groups celebrate a unique founding and have an origin structure which includes a founding ancestor, a "place where the house pole was planted", heirlooms, a house in which to store them, an inherited territory and inside and outside names. Hierarchy and equality in Buru society is formulated based on value assigned to features of origin structures. Where asymmetrical value has been culturally assigned, precedence is given to elder Houses within a *noro*, for they were established prior and upstream to younger Houses, and to elders within a House, for they were born before juniors. Between *noro*, however, there is no asymmetrical value assigned to origin structures. Consequently, there is no established precedence and the possibility of equality exists in relationships with other *noro*.

There is also an origin structure associated with life, based on the metaphor of tall standing trees where life in the young leaf tips comes from the root and trunk. Women produce life and the source of a child's life is in his mother's natal *noro* and House. Because women marry and change their affiliation as they "exit" and "enter" Houses of different *noro*, the source of their children's life is represented by their brothers. "Source uncles" (MB) and "life children" (ZC) are thus in a well defined relationship of life.

These two origin structures complement each other and are the basis for Buru social life. Their significance can be seen again in a case where the two concepts are conflated: the social position of an *an tunin*. This phrase literally means "original child" and refers to children born to women before they are married. Because *an tunin* are born before the *hak anat* of a woman has been transferred to another House and *noro* through marriage, these children belong to the natal *hum lolin* and *noro* of their mother and their mother's brother is their *ama* (F). They are "original children" because their source of life originates from the House to which they belong; their source of life and House are one and the same. In these cases the *noro* perpetuates itself internally rather than externally through the children of married women who have their source of life in another *noro* and House.

References

Fox, J.J.

1971   Sister's child as plant: metaphors in an idiom of consanguinity. In R. Needham (ed.) *Rethinking kinship and marriage*, pp.219-252. London: Tavistock.

1980a Introduction. In J.J. Fox (ed.) *The flow of life: essays on Eastern Indonesia*, pp.1-18. Cambridge, MA: Harvard University Press.

1980b   Models and metaphors: comparative research in Eastern Indonesia. In J.J. Fox (ed.) *The flow of life: essays on Eastern Indonesia*, pp.327-333. Cambridge, MA: Harvard University Press.

1988   Origin, descent and precedence in the study of Austronesian societies. Public lecture in connection with De Wisselleerstoel Indonesische Studien, 17 March 1988, Leiden University.

1994   Reflections on "hierarchy" and "precedence". In M. Jolly and M. Mosko (eds) *History and Anthropology. Transformations of hierarchy: structure, history and horizon in the Austronesian world*, 7(1-4):87-108. Chur and Reading: Harwood Academic Publishers.

Fox, J.J. (ed.)

1980   *The flow of life: essays on Eastern Indonesia*. Cambridge, MA: Harvard University Press.

Grimes, B.D.

1990   The return of the bride: affiliation and alliance on Buru. MA thesis, The Australian National University.

Grimes, C.E.

1991 The Buru language of Eastern Indonesia. PhD dissertation, The Australian National University.

Grimes, C.E. and Kenneth R. Maryott

1994   Named speech registers in Austronesian languages. In Tom Dutton and Darrell Tryon (eds) *Language contact and change in the Austronesian world*, pp.275-320. Berlin: Mouton de Gruyter.

Hocart, A.M.

1952   *The northern states of Fiji*. London: The Royal Anthropological Institute of Great Britain and Ireland Occasional Publication No. 11.

Keesing, R.M.

1975   *Kin groups and social structure*. New York: Holt, Rinehart, and Winston.

Traube, E.

1987   Obligations to the source: complementarity and hierarchy in an eastern Indonesian society. In D. Maybury-Lewis and U. Almagor (eds) *The attraction of opposites: thought and society in a dualistic mode*. Ann Arbor: University of Michigan Press.

Notes

[1] See Fox (1971, 1980, 1988) and Traube (1987) for discussions of concepts similar to Buru *lahin* in other eastern Indonesian languages. In many of these languages this "origin" concept is expressed by a word cognate with Proto-Austronesian * *puqun* ("tree") (cf. also Fox 1988:14). Following regular historical sound changes this protoform appears in Buru as *puun*, but with a slight semantic shift, referring to plants which are more along the lines of what would be called a bush or shrub in English, rather than tree. The Buru word *lahin* is thus not cognate with * *puqun*, but is very similar semantically to both botanical and metaphorical meanings associated with regional cognates of * *puqun*.

[2] This segment of Buru society, the indigenous people living in the interior of the island, was the main focus of the research upon which this paper is based. The research was carried out under a cooperative agreement between Pattimura University in Ambon and the Summer Institute of Linguistics under the auspices of the Indonesian Department of Education and Culture during 1985-1991.

[3] Buru ideas regarding affiliation are discussed more fully in B.D. Grimes (1990).

[4] The phrase "origin structure" comes from Fox (1988) where he used it to refer to similar Rotinese epistomological ideas about origin and cause.

[5] *Fam* is an Ambonese Malay word of Dutch origin and is used throughout parts of Maluku to refer to various types of kin groups.

Chapter 11. Histories of Diversity, Hierarchies of Unity: The Politics of Origins in a South-West Moluccan Village[1]

Sandra Pannell

> Narratives are not only structures of meaning but structures of power as well.
>
> Edward Bruner (1986:152)

Introduction

Writing of local origin "myths" from the "Timorese Archipelago" and the "Moluccas", F.A.E. van Wouden observes that "one is struck by the remarkable points of resemblance ... [between] ... the system delineated in these myths ... [and] ... the structure of society" (1968:195). The legitimating potential of local origin narratives alluded to by van Wouden has also been discussed in a number of more recent studies[2] of cultural groups in "Eastern Indonesia" although few of these works extend the analysis of "myth" beyond the charter paradigm originally proposed by Malinowski (1926) and adopted by van Wouden.

In conceptualizing myth narratives as epiphenomenal charters for the organization of local social and political orders van Wouden and others generally ignore the historical context in which such narratives are constructed, expressed and rendered meaningful.[3] As Sahlins (1981, 1985) suggests, cultural narratives cannot, in fact, be isolated from the wider social and political context in which they are located. Such narratives are shaped by and gather force from their dialectical engagement of other historically-specific stories (see also Bruner 1986 and Kapferer 1988). In this respect, narratives and the particular cultures in which they are articulated are not as isolated or as pristine as many anthropologists would have us believe. Indeed, as James Clifford points out with reference to the Trobriand Islanders, individuals "invent their culture within and against the contexts of recent colonial history" (1988:12). Clifford's remarks also apply to the cultures of the so-called "Eastern Indonesia" field of study, among which the people of the village of *Amaya*, Maluku Tenggara may be counted by some.[4]

Although positioned on the geographic margins of the archipelago, the people of *Amaya* are directly incorporated within the framework of the Indonesian

Nation-State and have long experienced the effects of European colonial encapsulation and Christian proselytization. As a result, local origin narratives are but one of several discursive elements which inform social and political life in *Amaya*. In this respect, the ideologies and ontologies of Protestantism, Indonesian Nationalism and modern capitalism create "new spaces in discourse" (Bruner 1986:152) within which the politics of identity and authority are given expression. These inter-connected "spaces" are interwoven with existing cultural forms and meanings to produce new symbols of opposition, new relations of asymmetry and new orders of hierarchy (cf. Lattas n.d.).

It is precisely through their engagement and coalescence with the discursive structures which inform daily life that the stories contained within local narratives resonate with the same configurations of logic which mediate social action and notions of identity. Consequently, these narratives are held to express stories of ontological and cosmological significance and it is in the circumstances of quotidian life that the themes, relations, and hierarchical possibilities folded into the narratives are realized (cf. Kapferer 1988).

In this paper, I focus primarily upon the conjunction of local origin narratives with the logic and practices of the Indonesian State. In so doing, I "emplot" (Ricoeur 1988:4) some of the hierarchical relations and disjunctions which are empowered by this nexus. I begin by considering some of the themes contained in an abbreviated version of the central *Mayawo* origin narrative. Of specific concern here is the process by which social narratives are naturalized and, at the same time, represented as historical truth. I then locate the narrative themes of origins, precedence and hierarchy within the context of everyday life in *Amaya* and examine particular aspects of their engagement with the locally articulated ideology of the Indonesian State. In conclusion, I discuss some of the wider social implications of the dialectics of politics and culture at *Amaya*.

The Setting

The village of *Amaya* is situated on the NNW coast of the volcanic island of Damer (*Asomo*) in the Maluku Tenggara region of the Province of Maluku, Indonesia. At the most inclusive level, the approximately 600 Austronesian-speaking inhabitants of this village refer to themselves in the vernacular as *Mayawo* which, literally translated, means the "people of Amaya".[5] The appellation *Mayawo*, however, can also be used in a more restrictive sense to distinguish descendants of autochthonous ancestors (*upho mamso*) from those individuals broadly classified as "immigrants" (*deyo dachmodini* "people afterwards they came"). Commonly referred to as **pendatang** in Ambonese-Malay, "immigrants" are those people who arrived at *Amaya* in the present century, the majority of whom came in the period after the Second World War, and the descendants of such individuals. These people are further identified on the basis of their place of origin. "Immigrants" from other villages on the island of Damer are called *larso* while those individuals who originate from other islands in the region are referred to as *awvno*.

The indigenous village residents are variously affiliated with one or more of the local descent-based groups referred to as *Uma*. The term *Uma* is not used to denote groups of **pendatang** individuals. Groups of related "immigrants" (both *larso* and *awvno*) are alternatively referred to as **marga** (a term which, although commonly used throughout Maluku, actually derives from Sumatra, where it can mean either "district" or "clan"), **pamili** (derived from the Dutch word for "family") or **fam** (< Dutch: "familie").

The term *Uma* has two basic levels of signification. On the one hand, *Uma* signifies a physical structure or dwelling. On the other hand, it denotes a group of related individuals who recognize a common ancestor, or group of ancestors, and share a common ancestral name.[6] Prior to the early 1900s, *Uma* was used in the latter context to describe each of the 13 indigenous matri-lines which occupied separate "houses". However, as a result of early twentieth century Christian influences (notably, the patriarchal emphasis of the Dutch Reformed Church and the Ambonese evangelists who were instrumental in disseminating Protestantism throughout Maluku Tenggara) and the influx of numerous family groups from nearby islands which followed the Dutch pacification of the war-like *Mayawo*, *Uma* is now generally used to describe indigenous groups of differentially related cognatic kin living in several dwellings. Notwithstanding these on-going transformations, *Uma* are locally regarded as unique configurations of people (both past and present) and places. For indigenous *Mayawo*, the identification of *Uma* with place and their relationships to other "houses" is narrativized in local "histories" of origin.

"Histories" of Diversity

Mayawo regard their accounts of the origins of each of the seven founding *Uma* in *Amaya* as historical fact. In the vernacular, these narratives are called *hnyero*, a term which is interchangeably used with the Indonesian word *sejarah*, and like its Indonesian synonym, *hnyero* is locally translated as "history". These narratives are specifically distinguished from the genre of stories known as *tintincha* which are considered to be fantastic "tales" or "myths".[7]

The corpus of *Mayawo* "historical" narratives does not explicitly constitute esoteric or restricted knowledge in *Amaya*. Most people have some knowledge, albeit fragmentary, of the events spoken of in these "histories". There are, however, a handful of elderly men who are considered by the community as the most knowledgeable with regard to the details of these narratives. These men are, for the most part, the "leaders" (*ryesro*) of the several village *Uma* and are knowledgeable not only about the origin "history" for their own *Uma* but also know something of the stories of other *Uma*. In addition to the *ryesro*, there is one person, in particular, who is locally considered to be the repository for this body of knowledge (cf. Fox 1979). This person is accorded the title of "the one who speaks" (*orliro*) and is locally regarded as the "mouth" (*nungcho*) for the "house" of the "village head" (***Kepala Desa/Bapak Rajah***) and other indigenous *Uma*.

While local origin narratives primarily recall the origins and arrival of the seven founding *Uma* in *Amaya* they also disseminate details of the origins of a number of other *Uma*, which are in some way linked to or derive from one of the seven original "houses". The incorporation of these secondary "histories" within this wider narrative structure reflects, to some extent, the nature of the relationship which exists between these connected groups.

On the occasion of public rituals, the "histories" of the seven founding *Uma* are narrated in sequence, beginning with the first *Uma* to arrive at *Amaya* and concluding with the last arrival (*Surlialy, Soplero, Helweldery, Awyeti/Tronanawowoy, Halono, Newnuny* and *Umpenwany*). Generally speaking, only cursory references are made to the origins of the associated "houses" and no reference is made at all to the more recent arrivals in *Amaya*.

Before I present a version of the narrative which recounts the origins of *Amaya*, there are a number of points I wish to emphasize here with respect to *Mayawo* "histories". The first is that historical knowledge does not constitute an immutable field of meaning but is subject to cultural variation and innovation. As Bruner (1986) rightly points outs, the telling of these origin narratives is informed by the context, the audience and previous "tellings". Given these considerations, the reproduction of the narrative becomes also a dimension of its transformation (cf. Sahlins 1985). In this connection, it is interesting to note the incorporation of other narrative structures within these local accounts.

Secondly, these "histories" make powerful political statements about both cultural unity and diversity as well as providing social and historical comment on the authentication of local practices, beliefs and positions of authority. In this respect, these "histories" can be viewed as representing important discursive forms for the expression and validation of identity.

Thirdly, following Foucault's (1978) thesis that knowledge and power directly imply each other, the negotiability of these "histories" is not so surprising especially in light of the tensions that exist between certain individuals and groups within the village and the political significance attached to these accounts.

In the following extensively abridged version of the central *Mayawo* origin narrative, the ***Kepala Desa*** or ***Bapak Rajah*** of *Amaya* relates the "history" of his own *Uma* called *Surlialy*. Significantly, this recitation also includes references to the other *Uma* which founded *Amaya* for, as the *Kepala Desa* pointed out, and I began to realize during my stay in the village, the "history" of each local "house" cannot be disengaged from the origin "histories" of other village "houses". Indeed, it is precisely through this cross-referencing that the "history" of each *Uma* gains its significance. The narrative begins at *Mt Lumtuni*, the ancestral "home" of many of the indigenous "houses" in *Amaya*:

> The ancestors of the "house" of *Surlialy* originated from the peak of the mountain *Lumtuni*.[8] From the mountain they descended to the sea and walked in an easterly direction until they eventually arrived at a cape, where they met with the people of Melu [Melu is a neighbouring village]. They called this place *Lulsunloyeni*. Then they returned to the mountain *Lumtuni*.[9]

> Once again the *Surlialy* people left the mountain and descended towards the sea. On the way they stopped at a place which they named *Kokomani* after the *Koko* tree which grows there. They then continued on until they arrived at *Amaya*. Here they built a village and enclosed it with a stone wall. Then they set off again and stopped at the beach *Avwara*. At this place they met with the two *Soplero* ancestors. These two people were siblings who originated from the volcano on the eastern side of the island called *Vworlale*. The *Surlialy* ancestors invited the two siblings to come and join them in *Amaya*. However, one of the siblings did not want to go. This person took one half of the cooking pot they carried with them and set out alone towards the east. The other sibling, gathered up the remaining half of the earthen vessel and followed the *Surlialy* ancestors to *Amaya*.

> Later there arrived at *Amaya* the ancestors of the group *Helweljeri*, who originated from the southern side of the mountain *Lumtuni*. The three groups came together to form one village, *Amaya*. The ancestors of *Surlialy*, because they were the first to arrive at *Amaya*, divided the village land between all the groups. Those people settled the village which started from that day until the present.

> The ancestors of the three groups then formed a decision making body in *Amaya*. Previously people did not follow government like the government there is today. The government of those people was still carried by tradition and they made a government where one person was leader. Previously, the ancestors of *Surlialy* were two people, younger brother and older brother. They did not know who of the two should become leader and carry the people of *Amaya*. Then the older brother said to his younger brother, "I will stay below and I will follow you". From that moment on, they became *Uhro* and *Mahno*. The *Uhro* person who was the oldest was named *Uhrulu Uhrulyai* and his younger brother who became *Mahno* was called *Marnulu Lokelyawo*. From that moment

on there existed in *Amaya Uhro* and *Mahno*. The *Surlialy* people became both *Uhro* and *Mahno*, they own that history until now. Those people were related and I don't know now why one is below the other, why they made it like that, *Uhro Mahno*.[10] When the village was finished and had become one, the people of *Surlialy, Soplero* and *Helweljeri* assembled and named three leaders, one for each "house".

Not long afterwards, the war began and the people ran everywhere.[11] Then the people who originated from the island of *Dai*, the people of *Awyeti* and *Ttasuni* [who amalgamated to form the *Tronanawowoy Uma*] as well as the people of *Newnuny* came to *Amaya*. After the war had finished the people from Luang came, the *Halono* people. Not long afterwards the last to arrive in *Amaya* came, the people of *Wenowani*. After they had all arrived there were then seven leaders (*Ryesro*) who controlled *Amaya*. Each brought their own beliefs and practices [**adat**] and little by little these were amalgamated to form the traditions and customs [**adat**] of *Amaya*. *Surlialy* invited those people and one by one they came to *Amaya*. *Surlialy* then carried those people like an older brother carries his younger brother and so it has been that way until this day.

The "houses" of *Helweljeri, Soplero* and *Surlialy* together they owned land around the village. When *Awyeti, Newnuny* and *Ttasuni* came they brought with them land and gardens and gave their gardens and land to all the people of *Amaya* so that everyone in the village could use this land. Thus, from the day they came to *Amaya* until now, this has been the case.

As the foregoing version indicates, the central *Mayawo* origin narrative represents, to borrow Ricoeur's phrase, "a temporal synthesis of the heterogeneous" (Ricoeur 1985:157). The unification of diverse elements, represented in the form of the different ancestral *Uma*, provides the dominant and mediating theme of this narrative. The narrative variously "emplots" this theme through a triadic sequence consisting of disorder, a journey and the restoration of order.

The first part of the narrative establishes the existence of a number of different ancestral groups which originate from various places, both on Damer and on the nearby islands of Luang and Dai. These groups, for various reasons, leave their sites of origin.

The second phase of the narrative recalls the journeys of the different groups and details their passage over the landscape. The places where the ancestors of each group stopped and performed certain activities are, in the narrative, transformed into durable "traces" (Ricoeur 1988:120) and significant places through the act of naming. In this way, history is incorporated as a dimension of the physical landscape through the process of identifying the events and identities inscribed in the narratives with the topographic features of the environment. The landscape, therefore, constitutes an historical text which can be read and interpreted by members of *Mayawo* society. Reference to these marks in the landscape represents the means by which the present can be engaged to account for the veracity of the past.

The third phase delineated in the narrative refers to the restoration of order through the amalgamation of the different *Uma* to form the *"negri"* (cf. Geertz 1980) or localized "state" of *Amaya* and the subsequent social classification of this difference.

The logic for this classification is expressed in the narrative in terms of the intra-generational difference and opposition between younger and elder siblings. The division within the "house" of *Surlialy*, based on the relative age distinctions between the two primal male siblings, does not result in the fragmentation of this "house". Instead, this diversity becomes the model or scheme for a new social and political order. The "house" of *Surlialy* is, in this instance, depicted as the generative source for a series of relations largely represented in terms of the oppositions and asymmetries of younger and elder, ruler and ruled, encompassed and encompassing.

The theme of siblingship suggests difference and opposition, with respect to age, and unity and complementarity, in the form of common origins. In a Dumontian sense, therefore, the "houses" are differentiated in their relation to the founding "house" and unified in their identification with place. Diversity, as depicted in the narrative, is thus legitimated through unity and the integrity of the group (as well as that of the individual) is constructed as dependant upon the encompassing unity and hierarchical proclivity of the wider configuration (cf. Kapferer 1988).

In addition to the notion of siblingship discussed above, the relationship between the "houses" is also expressed in terms of temporal and spatial precedence (cf. Lewis 1988). In this connection, the "house" of *Surlialy* precedes all other groups mentioned in the narratives and thus broadly defines the social and spatial placement of all subsequent "houses" within *Amaya*.

A number of other oppositions and asymmetrical relations are expressed within the context of the *Mayawo* origin narrative. Briefly, these include the distinctions between inland and coast, highland and lowland, rulers and ruled, male and female, autochthencs and immigrants. This latter opposition remains a point of contention among members of the two "houses" which stand in a sibling relationship to each other.

A significant dimension of these "histories" is the portrayal of the role of the founding "house" in the establishment of *Amaya*. According to these "histories", the reconstitution of order and the construction of a new sociopolitical organization is brought about by the benevolent actions of the founding "house" of *Surlialy*. In the narrative, violence and force are not the devices employed to create this unified body. Rather, it is the conformity and assent of the differentiated parts which legitimates and empowers the encompassing system. It is interesting to note in this connection that the origin narrative for the founding "house" of *Surlialy* encompasses the origins of all the "houses" in *Amaya* and, in so doing, reflects both the themes of local histories and the structures of contemporary *Mayawo* society.

Unlike Dumont's characterization of Hindu society, in which hierarchy is exclusively linked to the "opposition between the pure and the impure" (1970:66), the relationship between social groups, as articulated in the above narrative, is not informed by a singular, dominant oppositional principle. Instead, a plurality of oppositions, asymmetries and disjunctures which, either singularly and/or in various combinatory relationships, inform, reproduce and refract multiple hierarchical potentialities, are expressed within the framework of this narrative (see Foucault 1978; also Fox 1989). I stress here that local narratives do not explicitly define a specific hierarchical structure — they signify the ideological, tropic and ontological[12] configurations inhering to a number of hierarchical expressions which may be given realization within the context of social action.

For the immigrant residents of *Amaya*, however, local "histories" of origin do not hold the same value and meaning as they do for the indigenous members of the village. Immigrants can be viewed as displaced persons; dislocated from the culturally constituted source of their own identity and not able to locate themselves in relation to the social ontology idealized in local narratives. For these people, the Indonesian Nation-State (as well as the Protestant Church of Maluku) is perceived as offering alternative modes of being, corporate groups of affiliation and origin narratives.

Hierarchies of Unity

In *Amaya*, "metaphors of history" (cf. Sahlins 1981) have, in many instances, become idioms of practice. In this section, I examine how the oppositions, asymmetries and disjunctions disseminated in local narratives are ideologically reproduced as hierarchical relations.

The seven founding "houses" of *Amaya*, together with six other "houses" which are considered to originate from, or be closely linked to them, are all classified as *mahno* — a derivation of the name of the younger of the two primal male *Surlialy* siblings who figure prominently in local origin narratives. Of the two non-*mahno* "houses", one is classified as *uhro*, after the eldest ancestral *Surlialy* sibling, and the other as *ota*. Members of this last "house" are locally regarded as descendants of slaves brought from East Timor hundreds of years ago who were adopted by a *mahno* "house".[13]

In accordance with the themes disseminated in local origin narratives, the "house" locally classified as *uhro* is considered to be "lower" (*lo arè*) in status and rank than those "houses" which stand as "younger siblings" (*mahno*) to this "house". Both *mahno* and *uhro* "houses", however, are locally regarded as standing "above" (*ahuli*) the only "slave" (*ota*) "house" in the village.

The classification of all but two of the indigenous *Uma* in *Amaya* as *mahno* does not mean, however, that each of the respective "houses" shares the same social and political status. In this connection, the "house" of *Surlialy*, which is portrayed in the narrative as the first founding "house", is widely accorded socio-political authority in relation to the other "houses" and groups in the village. On the basis of their historically verified temporal and spatial precedence, this "house" claims, among other things, the title of *lelehro* ("ruler" [of the village]) or **Bapak Rajah** ("king father")/**Orang Kaya** ("powerful person") in Ambonese-Malay. In accordance with the logic of precedence, the title and office of "ritual leader" (*ryesro kpawo*) is associated with the second "house" to arrive at *Amaya* while the position of "Lord of the land" (*dochnuda dorraso*) or **Tuan Tanah** in Ambonese-Malay is claimed by the third "house".

The large number of local residents classified as "immigrants" or *pendatang* are not directly incorporated into this system of social classification. However, their very exclusion from this framework effectively structures their social placement on the margins of *Mayawo* society.[14]

The differential classification of local "houses" and their constituent members as *mahno, uhro, ota* or **pendatang** is culturally expressed and validated in terms of the dialectical interplay of the logic and continuities of local origin "histories" with present social practices. It is important to note here that, in the contemporary situation, the social expression of these classifications is fundamentally contextual and relational. The classification of certain individuals as **pendatang**, for instance, is suspended on those occasions when notions of a unified community are ideologically stressed and politically enacted (e.g. "National Independence Day"). Similarly, while local people acknowledge the broad social category of *mahno* they also, however, construct and recognize an infinite number of classificatory permutations arising from, they say, "marrying inside" (*mehlim arolmo*).

Marriage constitutes one context in which these social classifications are accorded significance (see Pannell 1989). In *Amaya*, marital alliances between "houses" are primarily negotiated on the basis of the culturally disseminated belief that "*mahno* must marry *mahno*" (*Mahnoni mehlimo mahnoni*). According to this principle of group endogamy, *uhro* should marry *uhro* and *ota* marry *ota*. However, whether people of these two *Uma* conform to this prescript or not is not generally considered to be as important as maintaining the integrity of those "houses" classified as *mahno*.

The culturally-recognized body of men empowered to act on the occasion of marriage is known as *ryesro viti mahnoni po viya*, literally, "seven *Uma* heads plus *lelehro* makes eight". These men are also locally regarded as responsible for the "proper" observation of *hnulcho* (or **adat** in Ambonese-Malay) defined practices.[15] As the name suggests, not all of the "houses" in the village are represented by this council of elderly men. Only the heads or *ryesro* of the seven original *Uma* and the **Bapak Rajah** comprise this group. The other village *Uma* classified as *mahno* are considered to be represented by their source "house". Members of immigrant families, *uhro* and *ota* "houses" are prohibited from holding office on this council.

According to local perceptions, the organization of this body of men is structured in accordance with the events and themes delineated in local "historical" narratives. The men who make up this council are regarded as the most knowledgeable concerning these "histories". The position of these men engenders the degree of knowledge they possess which, in turn, substantiates their standing in the political order. Thus, claims of authority made by this body are legitimated by an ideology empowered by local origin narratives rendered as "history". The political justification of this system of authority gains further weight when linked to the administrative practices of the Republic of Indonesia.

For many of the immigrant residents of the village, and those people affiliated with the "houses" classified as *uhro* and *ota*, the State is seen as offering the means by which the disenfranchised can become franchised members of the national community and subsequently, the local political community. I suggest here that the structures and principles upon which the State operates represent for these people utopian alternatives to what are regarded as restrictive modes of being and strategies of integration. To the historically-generated hierarchies of power and ontology, the State offers the egalitarian alternatives of democracy and equality.[16] However, as I discuss in this section, in practice the myths of nationalism and those of local culture are politically folded upon each other so as to appear to delineate similar strategies, oppositions and themes — themes which coalesce around the notions of unity and diversity.

Within the administrative hierarchy of the Indonesian State, the village or *desa* is the smallest unit. The organization of local government in each village or *desa* in Indonesia is theoretically quite similar and consists of a pyramid-type structure of authority. The highest authority in the village is the **Kepala Desa** or "village head" who is responsible for, among other things, the welfare of residents, the maintenance of law and order, the collection and payment of local taxes, the registration of births and deaths, upholding the principles of **Panca Sila** (the five tenets which inform the practices of the Nation-State) and representing the interests of the Indonesian Government. Generally, the appointment of the **Kepala Desa** is made by the district administrator (**Camat**) based upon recommendations received from village residents. The office of **Bapak Rajah** ("king father"), the "cultural head" of the village, on the other hand, is one inherited according to local **adat** practices. In recent times, with the movement towards total State hegemony, there has been a trend in the more developed and less remote areas of the Province of Maluku for the position of **Kepala Desa** to be filled by a different individual from that of the **Bapak Rajah**. In *Amaya*, however, the two remain inseparable; the **Bapak Rajah** is the **Kepala Desa** and vice versa.

According to principles of State administration, the **Kepala Desa** is also the head of the State-sponsored local government body in the village known as **Lembaga Musyawarat Desa** ("village consultative committee"), commonly referred to by the acronym LMD. In theory, this committee consists of an elected secretary, treasurer and a dozen or so representatives from the *desa* population. However, in practice this is not always the case. In *Amaya*, the village consultative committee (LMD) is comprised of the **Bapak Rajah**, the seven *Uma* heads, the heads of the four territorial aggregates known as *ono* (or *soa* in Ambonese-Malay) and the **Marinyo** or "village crier". The members of this committee are not democratically elected by the residents of the village. Rather, the positions are either inherited by *mahno* men, as is the case for the **Bapak Rajah**, the seven *Uma* heads and the **Marinyo**, or nominated by the **Bapak Rajah** himself, as is the situation with the four *ono* heads, who are also affiliated with *mahno* "houses". This system of selection effectively precludes immigrants, *uhro* and *ota* persons from holding these positions and consequently they are marginalized within the local political domain.

It is this body of men who largely define the temporal, spatial and practical limits of *desa* life. The demarcation of time in *Amaya* reflects the degree of local identification with and participation in the village or *desa* constructed as a cohesive community. In *Amaya*, Mondays and Tuesdays are designated as community work days and all able-bodies adult residents of the village are required to participate in the State-funded village development project at hand. The State-coined community development ethic of *gotong royang* or "mutual assistance" is frequently cited as the logic which informs many of these community based activities. **Gotong royang** is seen as reflecting cultural ethics of generosity, generated by kinship relations and shared residence. In this context, the principles and logic of the State and local culture are conflated in the social and political articulation of community and national identity.

The LMD oversees the working of the next level of local government known as the **Lembaga Ketahanan Masyarakat Desa** (LKMD) ("village community's maintenance committee"). This body consists of a number of officers, including chairman, deputy chairman, secretary and treasurer, with the entire population of the village comprising the general members of this institution. The LKMD is divided into ten sections, with a leader appointed to each section. The sections within LKMD are concerned with such things as religion, education, family planning, women's development and life style, to name but a few.

The institution of LKMD is a recent phenomenon in *Amaya*, having been formed in late 1984. The **Bapak Rajah** is the chairman of the LKMD. The office-holders of this committee are delegated by him and consist of *mahno* men, two of whom are also members of the LMD. This executive body appoints the leaders of each of the ten sections which make up the formal structure of LKMD. Three of the executive officers were nominated to be section leaders. Interestingly in this instance, one of the section leaders is a woman and another, an *uhro* man. Notwithstanding these recent appointments, in practice the LKMD is a nominal government structure. Meetings of the LKMD, which in principle should include all adult members of the community but in practice usually only involve the male members of the village, are called when the LMD wish to inform the residents of new directives. At each meeting, there is a session in which the executive answers questions from the general audience. Only a handful of men ever use this opportunity to voice their opinion about the matters at hand. While these meetings and the LKMD in general may appear to operate along democratic lines, the views of the members have little political weight in influencing the outcome of any meeting. The majority of issues have already been decided prior to the convening of the meeting.

In *Amaya*, it can be seen that it is the decision-making body *ryesro viti mahnoni po viya* cum LMD, and not the LKMD, which wields power and influence in the community. In short, this body has taken on the role of the State at the local level of village government. The "body politic" in this context refers to more than just a particular structure of political organization or the individual as a politicized subject. It delineates a systematic and coherent constellation of strategies, mechanisms and modes for the communication and integration of relations of power and identity, as witnessed in the following incident.

In the 1989/85 financial year, the LMD submitted plans for a new community hall (**Balai desa**) to the **Camat's** office in Kisar and received a subsidy of one million **rupiah** towards the estimated total costs of three and half million **rupiah**.

The LMD decided that the new community hall would be built on the site occupied by the "ancestral house" (*umtuvtuvcha*) of the **Bapak Rajah**. So on a Monday morning late in June 1986, the men of the village tore down the bamboo and sago leaf constructed ancestral house. In its place they would erect a new concrete, zinc-roofed community hall which would also continue to function as the ancestral house of *Uma Surlialy*.

In November of that year, the wooden frame of the building was erected. The erection of the main posts in the construction of a house is an important ritual event in *Amaya* and is usually celebrated according to local *adat* practices. However, on this occasion, the day set aside for the erection of the posts was proclaimed a holiday for the 100 or so school-age children and the entire village assembled at the house site. The local representatives of the Indonesian government, the **Kepala Desa**, and members of the LMD and LKMD committees, wore their official State uniforms on this occasion. Before the frame was erected, the origin "histories" of each of the seven founding *Uma* were narrated in order of their arrival at *Amaya*. According to **adat**, this task is the prerogative of the village orator, a man traditionally selected from the *uhro* "house" of *Surlia*. However, on this occasion, it was decreed by the **Bapak Rajah** that the orator would only narrate the "history" concerning the origins of the first "house" to arrive at *Amaya*; that is, the narrative for *Uma Surlialy*. The "histories" of the six other founding "houses" were consequently narrated by the respective *ryesro* for these "houses". No reference was made to the origin "histories" of the numerous immigrant residents in the village or to the ancestry of those "houses" classified as *uhro* and *ota*.

Afterwards, the **Bapak Rajah** spoke at length to those assembled in front of the **Balai Desa**/*Umtuvtuvcha* about the shared "historical" traditions of the *mahno, uhro* and *ota* members of the village and reminded all those present (both "indigenous" and "immigrant" residents) of their community responsibilities and obligations as members of both the *desa* of *Amaya* and the nation of Indonesia. "Today", he concluded,

> we have **adat** together with LMD and LKMD. In *Amaya* we do not separate government from the seven leaders, the *ryesro*, they walk together. We speak Indonesian and we refer to the government but we still live in our own land and we still own the tradition of seven *ryesro*. Those leaders hold **adat** from before until this day. Previously, the *adat* of the original inhabitants of *Amaya* were separate. Then they taught each other their customs and they formed one body of custom which is called **adat** *Amaya*. The **adat** of *Amaya* teach people so that they can live together with their kinsmen in *Amaya*. The customs of *Amaya* are appropriate for the people here, for all people to live by, so that people can live in a humble and modest way. With these customs we can finish things together, like when we thatch the roofs of houses in the village or sit down together and feast. We open coconut fronds and sit down on the ground together and together we eat and drink. We who live in *Amaya* have to follow these customs, we cannot copy other **adat**. We

people of *Amaya* are very different from others, we are very humble. We cannot elevate ourselves above others.

The founders of this village were two men and two women. The men were called *Luane* and *Harmei* and the women were called *Achleli* and *Rarlairo*. The people who are referred to as the founders of this village are the ancestors of *Surlialy*. Their ancestral house has recently been renewed. The section below is called the *Balai Desa* ["community hall"] and is the office while above is the ancestral "house". They will finish this building soon. People who are young don't you forget this history, carry it with you everyday. If you are far away, you remember, don't you forget at all.

With the conclusion of this speech, the men then proceeded to erect the wooden frame of the new ***Balai Desa**/umtuvtuvcha*.

There are a number of interesting points to emerge from this event. The construction of the new State-subsidized community hall on the site of the ancestral house of *Surlialy* affirms, in a most concrete manner, the position and authority of the ***Bapak Rajah*** and his "house" in the political order of the village. On this occasion, he simultaneously wears the hat of the official representative of the national government and that of *adat* head. The two positions are effectively homogenized into a single identity.

The actions of the ***Bapak Rajah*** and others in this incident are not seen for the political strategies they are. For many people, the ***Bapak Rajah*** and the members of his *Uma* have given their ancestral house for the benefit and good of the community. Such an act is viewed as an honourable gesture made by a virtuous man. By acting in "good faith" towards the other members of the community, the ***Bapak Rajah*** secures the misrecognition of the community and amasses the symbolic capital necessary for the reproduction of these strategies of integration (cf. Bourdieu 1977). The decision, in the above incident, to prevent the orator, an *uhro* man, from demonstrating his knowledge of the narratives is an act which consciously shifts the accent of power away from him to those already inculcated in the apparatus of authority. This subterfuge on the part of the ***Bapak Rajah*** and the seven *Uma* heads is part of an on-going process of political consolidation and denotes the continual tension that exists between their claims of authority and the belief offered by the members of the community.

At another level, the conflation of this event with elements of the central *Mayawo* origin narrative by the ***Kepala Desa*** not only serves to further legitimate his own authority and that of his "house" but also ensures the status of this event as an historical and immutable truth. In this incident, the hierarchical possibilities disseminated in local narratives are spatially and politically given expression. In turn, the event is injected back into the narrative to produce a dialectical interplay of meaning and form.

In *Amaya*, the thematic logic inscribed in local "histories" of origin circumscribes the parameters of what is constructed as *hnulcho/**adat*** and, in so doing, informs the content and context of social and political action in the village. The themes of siblingship, unity and diversity, which structure social and political relations in *Amaya*, are represented as corresponding with the logic which pervades and organizes the political anatomy of the State. The symbols, rites and administrative structures of the State are thus interpreted and represented in terms of the categories and meanings which also inform local *hnulcho/**adat*** practices. This ideological appropriation further serves to legitimate what are already regarded as historically verified forms and practices. Within these ideological horizons, strategies of integration are dissimulated and "naturalized", the diverse interests of the non-indigenous and disenfranchised members of the population are homogenized and the objectified classifications of rank, age and gender operating within the community are given a semblance of orthodoxy (cf. Bourdieu 1977). Within this context, local origin narratives produce the "naturalization of their own arbitrariness" (Bourdieu 1977:164) because no cultural distinction is made between the ideal and the real. The logic which "history" produces in this context is also that which mediates social reality.

In *Amaya*, the consent and cooperation of the residents which empowers local strategies of integration arises from the sharing of a common ontological ground and the transformation of relations of power into symbolic relations, articulated in an idiom of good faith (cf. Bourdieu 1977). In this process, the mechanisms of power are masked in order for it to operate (cf. Foucault 1978:86). When harnessed to the administrative structures of the State, this process of mythic seduction ultimately distorts the ideological foundations of the body politic.

Concluding Remarks

In the preceding sections, I have attempted to outline the discursive framework within and against which the people of *Amaya* articulate and reproduce their social and cultural identity. The version of indigenous "history" presented here represents more than just a chronological ordering of the past. Like any construction presented as "history", local narratives conjoin and refract themes of cosmological, ontological and ideological significance and, in this sense, they render culturally meaningful people's experiences of the world. These origin narratives also provide a readily accessible field of possible forms and logic for the articulation of power, the legitimation of identity and the expression of difference.

As I pointed out at the beginning of this paper, local expressions of knowledge do not exist as independent narratives but are influenced by and connected to wider structures. In this respect, local origin narratives also serve to "open up new spaces" (Bruner 1986:152) for the hegemonic practices of the Indonesian State. The State, in this context, is able to empower and legitimate its own order, which is shot through with its own logic of opposition and syncretic symbolism, through its dissimulation within local structures of differentiation and segmentation.[17] In the engulfing practices of nationalism, however disparate social histories and cultural beliefs are often flattened out or distorted to form a unified narrative of political consensus and social experience. What is *different* about local cultures is often objectified and ossified to the point where culture becomes a spectacular procession of simulacra (cf. Baudrillard 1983).

References

Adorno, T.W.

1973   *The jargon of authenticity*. Trans. Knut Tarnowski and Frederic Will. London: Routledge and Kegan Paul.

Barraud, Cecile

1985   The sailing boat: circulation and values in the Kei Islands, Indonesia. In R.H. Barnes, Daniel de Coppet and R.J. Parkin (eds) *Contexts and levels — anthropological essays on hierarchy*, pp.119-130. Oxford: JASO Occasional Papers No. 4.

Baudrillard, Jean

1983   *Simulations*. New York: Semiotext(e).

Bourdieu, P.

1977   *Outline of a theory of practice*. London: Cambridge University Press.

Bruner, Edward

1986   Ethnography as narrative. In Victor Turner and Edward Bruner (eds) *The anthropology of experience*. Urbana and Chicago: University of Illinois Press.

Clifford, James

1988   *The predicament of culture: twentieth-century ethnography, literature and art*. Cambridge, MA: Harvard University Press.

Dumont, Louis

1970   *Homo hierarchicus: the caste system and its implications*. Chicago: The University of Chicago Press.

Forth, Gregory L.

1981   *Rindi: an ethnographic study of a traditional domain in eastern Sumba.* Verhandelingen van het Koninklijk Instituut voor Taal-, Land- en Volkenkunde, No. 93. The Hague: Martinus Nijhoff.

Foucault, M.

1978   *The history of sexuality,* Vol. 1: *An introduction.* Trans. Robert Hurley. Harmondsworth, Middlesex: Penguin Books Ltd.

Fox, James J.

1971   A Rotinese dynastic genealogy: structure and event. In T. Beidelman (ed.) *The translation of culture,* pp.37-77. London: Tavistock Press.

1979 Standing in time and place: the structure of Rotinese historical narratives. In Anthony Reid and David Marr (eds) *Perceptions of the past in Southeast Asia.* Singapore: Heinemann Educational Books (Asia) Ltd.

1989   Category and complement: binary ideologies and the organization of dualism in Eastern Indonesia. In David Maybury-Lewis and Uri Almagor (eds) *The attraction of opposites: thought and society in the dualistic mode.* Ann Arbor: The University of Michigan Press.

Fox, James J. (ed.)

1980   *The flow of life: essays on Eastern Indonesia.* Cambridge, MA: Cambridge University Press.

Geertz, Clifford

1980   *Negara: the theatre state in nineteenth-century Bali.* Princeton, NJ: Princeton University Press.

Hicks, David

1974   The Tetum folktale as a sociological, cosmological and logical model (Timor). *Anthropos* 69:57-67.

Hoskins, Janet

1983   Spirit worship and feasting in Kodi, West Sumba: paths to riches and renown. PhD thesis, Harvard University.

Josselin de Jong, J.P.B. de

1937   *Studies in Indonesian cultures: Oirata, a Timorese settlement on Kisar.* Amsterdam: North Holland. [Verhandelingen Koninklijk Akademie van Wetenschappen, Afd, Letterkunde, nieuwe Reeks deel 39.]

Josselin de Jong, P.E. de

1980 *Ruler and realm: political myths in western Indonesia.* Amsterdam: North-Holland Publishing Co.

Kapferer, Bruce

1988   *Legends of people, myths of state: violence, intolerance and political culture in Sri Lanka and Australia*. Washington and London: Smithsonian Institution Press.

Kolff, D.H.

1840   *Voyages of the Dutch brig of war* **Dourga** *through the southern and little-known parts of the Moluccan archipelago and along the previously unknown south coast of New Guinea performed during the years 1825 and 1826*. London: James Madden and Co.

Lattas, Andrew

n.d. Sexuality and cargo cults: the politics of gender and procreation in West New Britain. Seminar paper, The University of Adelaide.

Lebar, Frank M.

1972   *Ethnic groups of Insular Southeast Asia*, volume 1: *Indonesia, Andaman Islands and Madagascar*. New Haven: Human Relations Area Files Press.

Lewis, E. Douglas

1988   *People of the source: the social and ceremonial order of Tana Wai Brama on Flores*. Dordrecht and Providence: Foris Publications.

McKinnon, Susan M.

1983   Hierarchy, alliance and exchange in the Tanimbar Islands. PhD thesis, University of Chicago.

Malinowski, Bronislav

1926   *Myth in primitive psychology*. London: Psyche Miniatures General Series no. 6.

Pannell, Sandra

1989   Carving the palm: the role of metaphor in Mayawo marriage rituals. *Mankind* 19(3):December.

Pauwels, Simone

1985   Some important implications of marriage alliance: Tanimbar, Indonesia. In R.H. Barnes, Daniel de Coppett and R.J. Parkin (eds) *Contexts and levels: anthropological essays on hierarchy*, pp.131-138. Oxford: JASO Occasional Papers No. 4.

Platenkamp, J.D.M.

1988   Myths of life and image in Northern Halmahera. In Henri J.M. Claessen and David Moyer (eds) *Time past, time present, time future: perspectives on Indonesian culture. Essays in honour of Professor P.E. de Josselin de Jong*. Dordrecht and Providence: Foris Publications.

Renes, P.B.

1977   Circular connublum in the Leti Archipelago. In P.E. de Josselin de Jong
        (ed.) *Structural anthropology in the Netherlands: a reader*. Koninklijk In-
        stituut voor Taal-, Land- en Volkenkunde. Translation series 17. The
        Hague: Martinus Nijhoff.

Ricoeur, Paul

1985   *Time and narrative*. Vol. 2. Chicago and London: The University of
        Chicago Press.

1988   *Time and narrative*. Vol. 3. Chicago and London: The University of
        Chicago Press.

Sahlins, Marshall

1981   *Historical metaphors and mythical realities: structure in the early history
        of the Sandwich Islands Kingdom*. Ann Arbor: The University of Michigan
        Press.

1985   *Islands of history*. London and New York: Tavistock Publications.

Schulte Nordholt, H.G.

1971   *The political system of the Atoni of Timor*. Verhandelingen van het
        Koninklijk Instituut voor Taal-, Land- en Volkenkunde, No. 60. The
        Hague: Martinus Nijhoff.

Traube, Elizabeth G.

1986   *Cosmology and social life: ritual exchange among the Mambai of East
        Timor*. Chicago and London: The University of Chicago Press.

Visser, Leontine E.

1984   Who are the Sahu and what do they belong to? In P.E. de Josselin de
        Jong (ed.) *Unity in diversity: Indonesia as a field of anthropological study*.
        Dordrecht/Cinnaminson: Foris Publications.

1988   The elder and the younger: dual opposition and a hierarchy of values.
        In Henri J.M. Claessen and David Moyer (eds) *Time past, time present,
        time future: perspectives on Indonesian culture*. Essays *in honour of Profess-
        or P.E. de Josselin de Jong*. Dordrecht and Providence: Foris Publications.

Wouden, F.A.E. van

1968   *Types of social structure in Eastern Indonesia*. Trans. R. Needham.
        Koninklijk Instituut voor Taal-, Land- en Volkenkunde Translation
        Series, vol. 2. The Hague: Martinus Nijhoff.

Notes

[1] The research on which this paper is based was supported by a Research Scholarship from the University of Adelaide and was conducted in Indonesia during the period 1986-87 under the auspices of **Lembaga Ilmu Pengetahuan Indonesia** ("Indonesian Institute of Science") and **Universitas Hasanuddin**. In preparing the final draft of this paper I benefited from the editorial contributions of Geoffrey Bagshaw.

[2] For recent works on the legitimating role of "myth" in "eastern Indonesian" societies see, among others, Fox (1971, 1980); Schulte Nordholt (1971); Hicks (1974); Visser (1984, 1988); Barraud (1985); Pauwels (1985); Traube (1986) and Platenkamp (1988).

[3] While many of the authors of the anthropological literature on so-called "eastern" Indonesian societies have chosen to refer to local accounts of the past as "myths" (for example see Barraud 1985; Hicks 1974; Pauwels 1985; Platenkamp 1988; Schulte Nordholt 1971; Traube 1986; van Wouden 1968; Visser 1984 and 1988) I have elected, for reasons outlined in the text, to speak of these constructions as "historical narratives" (cf. Fox 1979).

[4] The appellation "Eastern Indonesia" is widely used by anthropologists to generally refer to the numerous islands and cultural groups located in the area bounded by the island of Bali in the west and Irian Jaya in the east. The term "Eastern Indonesia" constitutes, I would argue, an arbitrary field of reference and does not correspond with any known culturally or linguistically demarcated area except that constructed, as a matter of convenience and coherence, by western ethnographers. In this situation, to quote Jean Baudrillard, "it is the map that engenders the territory" (1983:2) and not the territory which precedes or survives the map.

[5] For the purposes of clarity and ease of reference, throughout this paper I will italicize words derived from the indigenous language *Vnyola Mayawo*, which is spoken by inhabitants on the western side of the island of Damer (as opposed to the other language spoken on Damer which is confined to the eastern half of the island), and bold italicize both Indonesian and Ambonese-Malay words. A note on orthography and pronunciation, the phoneme *ch* is pronounced as in the gaelic word "loch".

[6] Throughout this paper, I will use a capital "U" to distinguish *Uma* as descent-based social groups from the other signification of the term.

[7] James Fox (1979), in his discussion of Rotinese historical narratives, also points out that similar distinctions are made between various local oral accounts.

[8] In the more detailed version of the narrative, from which this account has been extracted, this part of the narrative is somewhat reminiscent of the story recounted in the Bible concerning Noah's journey in the ark and his eventual arrival on the peak of Mt Ararat. It is not altogether unlikely, given the history of Christian proselytization in the region, that elements of Christian narratives have been incorporated within local accounts. Van Wouden (1968), referring to a Timorese narrative, also suggests that it is possible to ascribe certain aspects of the story to "Christian influences" (*ibid.*:120).

[9] According to one member of *Uma Surlialy*, his ancestors originated from the top of the mountain *Lumtuni* in the centre of the island and are therefore autochthonous. However, according to the version presented by the village orator, *Surlialy* are immigrants and not the original inhabitants of the island as the members of the orator's "house" claim to be.

[10] This paradigm of the enterprising and knowledgeable younger sibling and the subordinate elder sibling is also discussed in the works of Forth (1981), Hoskins (1983), Josselin de Jong, de P.E. (1980), van Wouden (1968), and Visser (1984, 1988), to name but a few. In contrast to this view, McKinnon (1983) and Fox (1989) discuss other situations where the category of "elder" is considered "superior" to that of the "younger".

[11] The "war" referred to here is said by local people to have been waged between the villages located on the western side of Damer and the invaders from Seram. Interestingly, the Dutch naval officer D.H. Kolff (1840:84) reports that one of the villages on the nearby island of Romang [Roma] was forced to relocate further inland as a result of attacks by Seramese "pirates". Some people in *Amaya*, however, have suggested that the phrase "the invaders from Seram" refers to the fact that the invading forces came from the north and were not necessarily from the island of Seram. Other people have suggested that the invading fleet referred to in the narrative belonged to the Majapahit empire.

[12] My understanding of what is meant by ontology is primarily informed by the works of Theodor Adorno (1973) and Bruce Kapferer (1988). According to Kapferer, ontology refers to "those constitutive principles of being that locate and orient human beings within their existential realities" (*ibid.*:220). Furthermore, I would argue (as does Adorno) that these constitutive presuppositions of human subjectivity are linked to the historical setting in which a human being is formed. Such a view of ontology rejects the "essence-mythology" (Adorno 1973:xvi) view of being exemplified in the works

of Heidegger and Buber. For Adorno, the existential philosophy of Heidegger represents a jargon which pretends to make present an idealized form of human subjectivity that is devoid of content and discounts the historical development of human consciousness.

[13] In *Amaya*, the classifications *mahno, uhro* and *ota* are also referred to with the respective Ambonese-Malay terms, **Marna, Bur** and **Stam**. Throughout the region of Maluku Tenggara, similar systems of social classification are invoked by local people with slight variations to the Ambonese-Malay terms employed. In the literature (see de Josselin de Jong 1937; Lebar 1972; and Renes 1977), these terms are respectively glossed as "aristocrats", "commoners" and "slaves". These appellations, I would argue, do not adequately, if they do so at all, convey the meanings and relationships associated with these categories of social identity nor do they take into account the shifting and contextual dimensions of that identity.

[14] In a field census conducted in *Amaya* in late 1986 I recorded 100 people (or approximately 17 per cent of the residential population) whose socially recognized family name was one of the 33 different immigrant family names represented in the village. More than a third (39 or 37 per cent) of the 105 residential dwellings in *Amaya* are associated with and occupied by individuals who are locally regarded as *pendatang* or "immigrants".

[15] In *Amaya*, **adat**, or *hnulcho* as it is known in the vernacular, refers to all beliefs, relations, discourses, practices and classifications which are locally regarded as constitutive of a distinct *Mayawo* cultural identity. Within the context of contemporary Mayawo society, *hnulcho/**adat*** encompasses local expressions of Christianity, local interpretations of State ideology, local translations of the regional economy and local manifestations of population diversity. *Hnulcho* thus represents a synthesis of the historical and the contemporary, the traditional and the novel, the continuous and the transformative aspects of the experienced world. Important here is the realization that *hnulcho/adat* constitutes a particular way of thinking and doing which is regarded by many people in *Amaya*, as the only "natural" way to act (Bourdieu 1977).

[16] The founding principles of the Indonesian Republic referred to as *Panca Sila* delineate the five fundamental aspirations of the Nation-State. They are as follows:

—	*Ketuhanan yang Maha Esa*	"Belief in one God"
—	*Kemanusiaan yang adil dan berab*	"A just and civilized humanity"
—	*Persatuan Indonesia*	"The unity of Indonesia"
—	*Kerakyatan yang dipimpin oleh hikmat kebijaksaan dalam permusyawaratan/perwakilan*	"Democracy guided by the wisdom generated by social consultation/representation"
—	*Keadilan sosial bagi seluruh rakyat Indonesia*	"Social justice for all the Indonesian people".

[17] The national motto of Indonesia **Bhinneka Tunggal Ika**, which is commonly glossed as "Unity in Diversity", together with the official emblem of the Republic, which consists of the **Garuda** (the mythical bird carrier of the God Vishnu) and the associated icons of **bintang emas** ("golden star"), **kepala banteng** ("head of a wild buffalo"), **pohon beringin** ("Banyan tree"), **rantai** ("chain") and **setangkai padi, setangkai kapas** ("one stalk of rice, one stalk of cotton"), symbolically express and epitomize both the political anatomy of the Nation and State strategies of encapsulation.

Chapter 12. Rivals and Wives: Affinal Politics and the Tongan Ramage

Aletta Biersack

Tongan *ha'a* are agnatically grouped clusters of titles that are ranked according to a rule of historical — and, in the case of the apical ancestor, mythical — emergence or precedence (cf. Fox 1994, 1995). Since elder brother outranks younger brother and father outranks son, "elder brother" or "father" titles outrank "younger brother" or "son" titles, the "branches" (*va'ava'a*) of the Tongan ramage or "origin structure" (Fox 1988) being graded according to relative proximity to an original "root" (*tefito*). Mythically, if not historically, this root is the Tu'i Tonga or high chief of Tonga (Figure 1) (Sahlins 1958:ch.1). While these botanic idioms suggest a centred, self-totalizing, and self-generating "origin structure" (Fox 1995), they are as important for what they conceal as for what they reveal. Precedence may reflect affinity and the dynamics of the system rather than descent and the statics of the system (cf. *ibid.*:12-13).[1]

In any effort to explore the mobilities and instabilities of Polynesian systems, Irving Goldman's *Ancient Polynesian Society* offers some crucial insights. There Goldman places "status rivalry" — a jockeying for position at the top motivated by a *systemic* "ambiguity of rank" (Goldman 1970:24) — at the heart of these societies. Ambiguity of rank is created by the complexity of the ranking system. "Hereditary rank ... is no single factor, but a compound of multiple genealogical criteria ..." (*ibid.*:5).

In Tonga (but also elsewhere in Polynesia), senior and junior brothers, senior and junior dynasties, typically contended for top honours. "It was ... a frequent theme that younger brothers and junior lines of descent, although lower in rank, came to be greater in de facto political power and eventually 'upstaged' the senior line" (Bott 1982:62). The competition often (though not always) aligns matrilateral half-brothers, who do not compete for the same titles, against patrilateral half-brothers, who do (Bott 1981:17; Rogers 1977:171-173). The great secular trend of Tongan history is driven by this rivalry. According to oral tradition, when the 23rd Tu'i Tonga was assassinated in the fifteenth century, his son retained the divine privileges of the Tu'i Tonga but surrendered the effective governance of his kingdom to his younger brother, Takalaua. From that time the government was divided between a "working chief" (*tu'i* or '*eiki ngāue*) associated with the Kauhalalalo cluster of titles and a "most sacred chief" (*tu'i* or '*eiki toputapu*) associated with the Kauhala'uta cluster of titles (Figure 1). The term *kauhala'uta* means the "bush" side of the road and the term *kauhalalalo* means the "lower" side of the road, most scholars interpreting this as a symboliccum-geographical division between land and sea. While the "sacred chief" enjoyed a great many privileges, the "working chief" was the effective leader, a governor of the people and the land (Ve'ehala, pers.comm.).

The initial "working chief" was the Tu'i Ha'atakalaua (Figure 1). However, by the seventeenth century, the Tu'i Kanokupolu had displaced the Tu'i Ha'atakalaua as the "working chief", the Tu'i Tonga continuing as the "most sacred chief". These diarchic arrangements (Biersack 1990a; Valeri 1989, 1990a) were superseded in the nineteenth century, when Tāufa'āhau, a usurper,[2] unified the archipelago, took the name King George Tupou, and substituted for the diarchy of the past a constitutional monarchy. Since Tāufa'āhau was heir to the Tu'i Kanokupolu title, the Kauhalalalo had in effect displaced the Kauhala'uta.

As I shall argue here, these hierarchical transformations were underwritten by the complexity of Tongan ranking. A person acquires political status through his or her father but personal status through his or her mother and is thus complexly and often contradictorily positioned within a social and political field. Over against a *ha'a* system of titles, egocentric kindreds or *kāinga* (Kaeppler 1971) have their own social and political force. Considering such complexity, Goldman argues that though the "structure is stable" in the sense that its "two coordinates" endure over time (*ibid.*:304), the "points on the coordinates" — that is, the rank order of particular historical actors — "are unstable" (*ibid.*). "… persons who are ambitious cannot change the absolute laws of genealogical rank …. The structure does, however, allow for shifts in power relationships, offering several leverage points for such shifts" (*ibid.*:304-305).

Together with Bott's *Tonga at the Time of Captain Cook's Visits,* Goldman's analysis offers a basis for rethinking Tongan society in historical terms, albeit without precluding structural analysis. Here I develop a post-Durkheimian sociology of Tonga based on a combination of structural analysis and historical investigation. The first section provides the structural analysis. The remainder of the paper exploits this analysis as an instrument of diachronic investigation. In the concluding section I draw the lessons that Tongan history has to teach about the relationship between structure and event, the synchronic and the diachronic. My main claim is that Tongan structure becomes operational only in and through Tongan élite marriage practices and that the Tongan ramage is a product of these practices and their dynamics. In the course of developing the argument, I take up the issue of women's status and position in Tonga — a topic that is unavoidable given the array of synchronic and diachronic material this paper surveys and the importance assigned to marriage in it.[3]

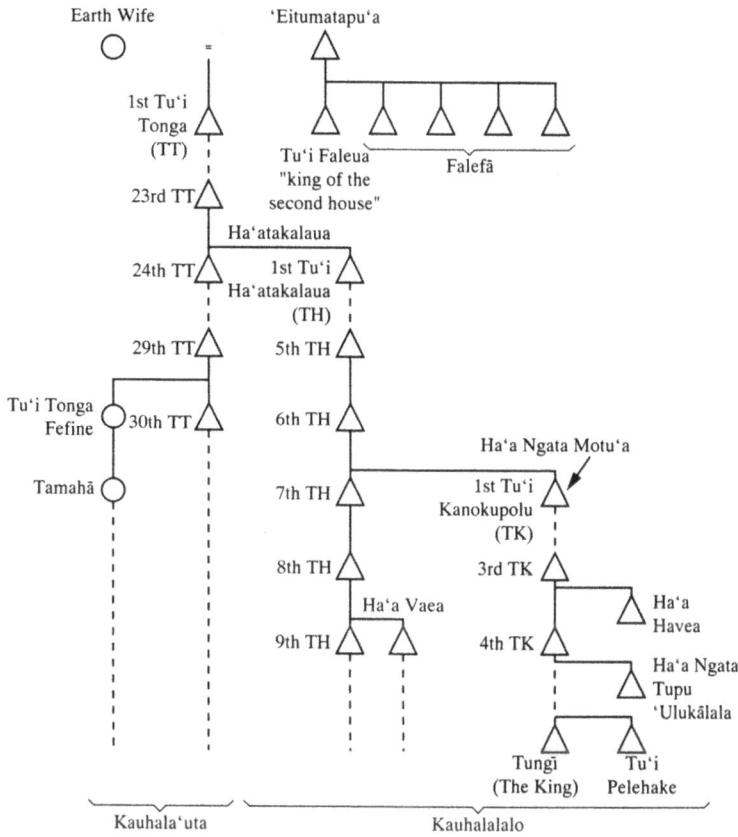

Figure 1. A simplified representation of the Tongan title system (adapted from Biersack 1982 [1974]:197 [Figure 1]).

Complexities of Rank: Blood and Garland

Traditionally and still today, Tonga sustains two ranking systems (Biersack 1982 [1974], 1990b, 1991a; Bott 1981, 1982; Goldman 1970:449-459; Kaeppler 1971; Rogers 1977), each operating in its own context and cultural domain. The *kāinga* (kinship, kindred) system rank orders persons as persons and as they participate in kindreds, while the *ha'a* system rank orders titles and their holders according to an agnatic calculus: elder brother:younger brother: *'eiki* [or chiefly rank]:*tu'a* [or commoner rank]::high:low.[4] Within the title system, at least in theory, the consanguineal relationship among actual titleholders is immaterial. What matters is the genealogical proximity of eponymous ancestors to an apical ancestor: 'Aho'eitu, the father of the first Tu'i Tonga (Sahlins 1958:ch.1). Also, whereas eligibility for office is unilineally conferred, personal rank is not only unique but is *bilaterally* rather than unilaterally and unilineally determined.

Within the context of the *kāinga*, sister and sister's children outrank brother and brother's children. Thus, in life crisis ceremonies women and their children are the ranking figures (Biersack 1982 [1974]; Bott 1972, 1981:18-20; Kaeppler 1971; Rogers 1977). The highest position in such ceremonies is the *fahu* position, which is usually occupied by a sister's child or a father's sister's child. A position of honour, the *fahu* receives the best of the valuables distributed in such ceremonies.

In the past sororal hegemony had its most dramatic expression in the extraordinary status accorded the sister of the Tu'i Tonga as the "female" Tu'i Tonga or Tu'i Tonga Fefine. The status of the Tu'i Tonga Fefine and that of her eldest daughter, the Tamahā, were conferred within the *kāinga* of the Tu'i Tonga rather than within the *ha'a* system. Of the Tu'i Tonga Fefine, John Thomas, the first continuing Methodist missionary in Tonga, wrote that the position gave "her no power or authority, but she is raised by it, and greatly honoured" (Thomas 1879:15). The Tu'i Tonga Fefine was married to a chief of the Ha'a Fale Fisi, the "*ha'a* of the house of Fiji", a line of foreign provenience (Figure 1). The foreign paternity of the Tamahā or eldest daughter of the Tu'i Tonga Fefine meant that, although the Tu'i Tonga Fefine's children had the highest possible personal rank through their mother and outranked their mother's brother, the Tu'i Tonga, their rank in the *ha'a* or title system was inferior to his. Chiefs of a *foreign* line, they constituted no serious political threat to the paramount (cf. Sahlins 1976:42).

In an idiom of "garland" (*kakala*) (or "name" [*hingoa*]) and "blood" (*toto*), Tongans themselves distinguish between the person and his or her rank *vis-à-vis* kin, on the one hand, the title and its rank, on the other. The title is metaphorically a "garland" the titleholder wears. In contrast, personal rank is "blood" rank, the rank of the "body". A key aspect of the blood/garland distinction concerns the kind of power associated with each kind of rank. The sister and her children, *vis-à-vis* the brother and his children, exercised power over individual and biological life (*ibid.*), while the power of the titleholder was a public power exercised over macrosocial geopolitical units, the village and the estate (*tofi'a*) on which a village or multiple villages formed. Sororal power was manifested most dramatically in a father's sister's cursing power, which placed organic life at risk, while the latter was manifested in the juridical authority of a chief.

The distinction between *ha'a* and *kāinga* rank, "garland" and "blood", is gendered. The rank acquired through women is personal while the rank acquired through men is the impersonal public rank of title and office (Biersack 1982 [1974], 1991a; Rogers 1977). Thus, while paternal rank is a factor in determining a child's personal rank, the blood of the mother is more important than the blood of the father (Bott 1981:19; Gifford 1929:113; Marcus 1977:227, n.8, 1980:89; Spillius n.d., ch.5, BSP 4/3/31[5]). "If an aristocratic woman and an aristocratic man of roughly equivalent rank marry commoners of low rank, the children of the aristocratic woman will have much higher rank than the children of the aristocratic man" (Spillius, "Kinship and Ha'a in Tonga", BSP 5/6/5-6). It follows that the fount of aristocratic blood is feminine. "To be 'aristocratic' ... means to be descended from the Tu'i Tonga Fefine or the Tu'i Tonga" (Bott 1982:61) or the Tamahā (Bott 1981:36; see Rogers 1977:170-173). Of a child whose high rank depends primarily on the mother it is said that the child is *tama tu'u he fa'*, "child standing on the mother" (BSP 17/6/n.p.) or "child standing in the mother" (Collocott and Havea 1922:118).

Whereas women and their children effectively dominate the contexts governed by personal rank (life crisis ceremonies), "their ascendancy was supposed to be confined to the realm of rank" (Bott 1982:76). Titleholders, however, assumed the command of particular villages and districts and all the people living therein; and it is men rather than women who are associated with the title system. Except in rare cases, titleholders were and are male.

> Men have authority (*pule*) over their younger brothers and over their children — also over their wives. They control access to land and titles; they control and organise economic affairs. Reciprocally, men owe allegiance, subservience, respect, and tribute to their fathers and older brothers, real and classificatory. Sisters, however, have higher rank than brothers, even though they have no secular authority over them. They are more '*eiki* than brothers, but have no *pule* over them (Bott 1982:58).

Similarly, Garth Rogers refers to "the ideology that the 'father's side' of the family has the *pule* over the children and not *kāinga 'i fa'* 'the mother and her immediate relatives' ... 'father' is normally considered the head of the household with *pule* over its members ..." (1977:159). He goes on to observe — drawing on remarks made by Tupou Posesi Fanua, a well-known authority on Tongan culture — that the "rights of a *fahu* at a wedding, first-birthday, or funeral are symbolic and decorative but not political; in fact, Tupou Posesi said that "the *fahu* have no say in anything; they are not the *pule*" (*ibid.*:168).[6] Moreover, the idioms in which the relationship between and among titles is couched — as father and son or older and younger brother (Biersack 1982:196) — is agnatic. It is said, I am told ('Okusitino Māhina, pers.comm.), that "from women blood flows" ("*ko e fefine ko e fakahokohoko toto*") but "from men titles flow" ("*ko e tangata ko e fakahokohoko hingoa*"). This is not to deny that men no less than women had personal rank and that men no less than women functioned as *fahu* on particular occasions. Since sister's children outrank brother's children, men outrank their mother's brother and his children and have the same *kāinga* or kinship superiority toward them that the sister enjoys *vis-à-vis* the brother or the father's sister enjoys *vis-à-vis* the brother's children.

Public authority is acquired through titleholding; and no matter how high the rank of a particular person, rank could not be translated into command without the bestowal of a title. Elaborating upon Bott's (1981, 1982), Rogers' (1977) and Kaeppler's (1971) work, as well as my own early work (Biersack 1982 [1974]), I have argued that title and the authority that attaches to it are inherently impersonal — authority emanates from the office rather than the person and all titleholders are the same — while rank is inherently personal, an attribute of bodies (Biersack 1990b, 1991a). Thus, the Tu'i Tonga Fefine, second in rank only to her own children, had no heir. Instead of being succeeded, the Tu'i Tonga Fefine was transcended — by a daughter who outranked her: the Tamahā or "most sacred child". A daughter of a chief of the Ha'a Fale Fisi (Figure 1) and the Tu'i Tonga Fefine, the Tamahā was *fahu* to the Tu'i Tonga.

In distinguishing the two ranking systems, Bott dwells in particular on one Lātūnipulu, who as Tu'i Lakepa of the Ha'a Fale Fisi (Figure 1) had a relatively low status within the title system but who as sister's son or *fahu* of the Tu'i Tonga had exceptionally high personal status. In meeting Lātūnipulu in 1773, Captain Cook was immediately impressed with his apparent power and prestige. Cook "saw that he was a man of some consequence by the extraordinary respect paid him, some when they approached him fell on their faces and put their heads between his feet and what was still more no one durst pass him till he gave them leave" (from Cook's journals; quoted in Bott 1982:16-17). Lātūnipulu's prestige, a matter of blood and not title, stemmed from his mother, the Tu'i Tonga Fefine;[7] and in this was feminized. It was (and still is) possible for a man to have high personal rank but no title; a man could be, in the local idiom, "chiefly in body" (*sino 'i 'eiki* [Bott 1981:10-11] or an aristocrat without being appointed to title (*'eiki fakanofo,* "chief who has been installed") (*ibid.*).

There is a sense in which title rank is inferior to blood rank, the rank being an attribute of the title but not the person. A titleholder having no royal blood is said *merely* to wear a garland ("Discussions with Queen Sālote" 1:50; hereafter referred to as "Discussions"). "The title [or] 'garland' (*kakala*) can be taken away [but the] 'blood' (*toto*) is one's own for ever" (Bott 1981:38; see also "Discussions" 1:50; Marcus 1980:18-19). "It was typical for titles to be disdained", Marcus observes (*ibid.*:61). High ranking chiefs "frequently passed them on to younger siblings, adopted children, or other persons of lower kin rank" (*ibid.*); and James Spillius writes that "very high ranking [male] aristocrats considered it lowering to have a title, and were known by their personal names rather than the name of their titles. Some had no titles. Titles meant political obligations; high rank meant deference from everyone" (Spillius, "Kinship and Ha'a in Tonga", BSP 5/6/6). Even though Lātūnipulu was Tu'i Lakepa, "he rarely used the title; ... the very great ' *eiki* (like Lātūnipulu) were scornful of titles, which they considered to be appropriate to lesser ... chiefs" (Bott 1982:60).

Affinal Politics

Although commoners may marry willy nilly for romantic reasons, élite marriage is regulated. Partners marry class endogamously and by way of assuming public responsibilities. Among aristocrats there is a preference for aligning the two kinds of status. Through mother's brother's daughter marriage, a man could reinforce his title status with *fahu* status. From the fifteenth century on, the leader of the Kauhala'uta side of the title system took the eldest sister of the chief directly inferior to him as his *moheofo* or principal wife, each Tu'i Tonga being at once holder of an "older brother" or "father" title and *fahu* to the holder of a "younger brother" or "son" title (Biersack 1982 [1974]; Bott 1981:55-58, 1982:59, Fusitu'a 1976:10; Lātūkefu 1974:3). Among high aristocrats who succeed to title, the preference for status congruity is clear. Heirs have occasionally declined a title because they believed themselves to be insufficiently aristocratic in blood to merit it. Agnatic heirs may step aside to enable sisters' sons to succeed lest their inferior blood tarnish the title ("Discussions" 1:57). Conversely, if their personal rank was too high for the title, as already discussed, they might spurn it and remain untitled.

A well-known example of this preference for congruity across the two status fields concerns the Tuita title. Tuita Kahomovailahi had two wives. The ranking one, Tamahā Lātūfuipeka, gave her cousin Naukovi, of much lower blood, to Tuita Kahomovailahi as a secondary wife.[8] Naukovi bore Po'oi Niutupu'ivaha, while the Tamahā bore Makahokovalu. As the first-born son of the principal wife, Makahokovalu was the clear heir to the Tuita title. Yet this title was relatively low — not even a chiefly title but a *matāpule* or ceremonial attendant title. Through his mother, Makahokovalu had access to the Tu'i Lakepa title. The previous Tu'i Lakepa had been the son of Lātūnipulu mentioned earlier (Bott 1982:73). This son had died without issue, placing the title at risk. Makahokovalu rescued the situation by assuming the Tu'i Lakepa title as Lātūnipulu's daughter's son and *fahu* ("Discussions" 2:285; see also *ibid.* 1:175). "None of the patrilineal heirs [those who were from agnatic collateral branches] could compare to him in rank, and he just went and had himself appointed without even having a meeting of the male heirs" (Bott 1982:73) (see Figure 2).[9]

Personal rank was among the criteria employed in making succession decisions. It came into play again in the next generation, with the appointment of a new Tuita. Makahokovalu's failure to assume the Tuita title opened the door to Po'oi, the son of the secondary wife, to succeed — which he did (Figure 2). Po'oi's son was then heir apparent. Yet it was not Kahomovailahi but Makahokovalu's son who succeeded to the Tuita title. Makahokovalu had married the daughter of Laufilitonga, the last Tu'i Tonga ("Discussions" 2:285; see also *ibid.* 1:175). In view of the exceptionally high rank of the resulting son, 'Ulukivaiola, Po'oi's son stepped aside to let 'Ulukivaiola succeed (Figure 2)

(Tupou Posesi Fanua, pers.comm.; see also Fanua, n.d., and "Notes on the Pongipongi of Tu'i Vakanō, 4th July 1958", BSP 13/4/3).

It was in the interest of those at the margins of the political system to use marriage to elevate their status in a bid for public recognition and prestige. As Bott has observed, junior lines agitated against their seniors by marrying the women of the senior line (Bott 1982:62), appropriating for themselves, for example, the very sororal blood that the Tu'i Tongas preferred to bestow upon foreign chiefs to avoid empowering rivals. Such practices are sometimes described in terms of theft or seizure, suggesting the agonistic character of the practice. "Wives of high rank were sometimes seized by other men who wanted suitable mothers for their children" (Spillius n.d.: ch.5, BSP 4/3/84).

Tāufa'āhau, the usurper who dominated the nineteenth century, was himself "only a little tiny bit *'eiki* [or chiefly]" ("Re Feudalism", BSP 22/3). Laufilitonga, heir apparent to the Tu'i Tonga title, though not by any means Tāufa'āhau's only adversary, was the most prestigious one. A woman could not be *moheofo* or principal wife of the Tu'i Tonga unless she was a virgin (Ve'ehala, pers.comm.). Wanting to deprive the Tu'i Tonga of an heir, Tāufa'āhau found a pretext for sending his sister, Halaevalu Mata'aho, to another chief — the Tu'i Ha'ateiho of the Ha'a Fale Fisi ("Discussions" 1:53), who, like the Tu'i Tonga, was on the Kauhala'uta side — to whom she bore a child. When she was finally sent to the Tu'i Tonga, she was no longer suitable as *moheofo* and could not produce an heir.[10]

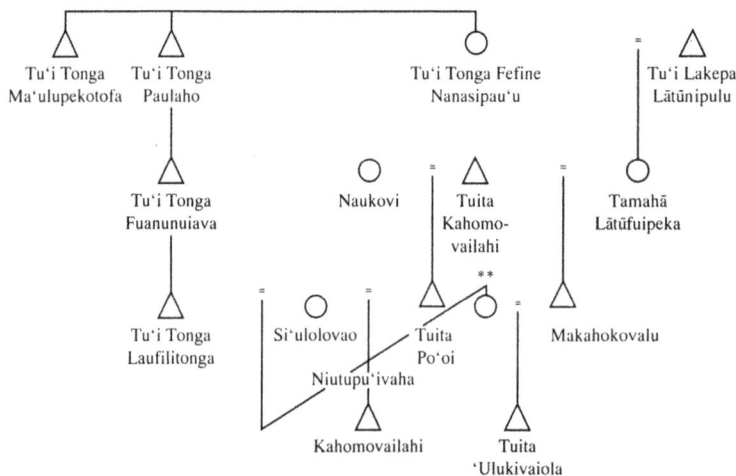

Figure 2. Succession to the Tuita title.[*]

[*] Compiled from Bott (1982:12) (Figure 1), *ibid.*:32 (Figure 4), *ibid.*:74 (Figure 9), and *ibid.*:154 (Figure 31(b); BSP 13/4/3; Fanua (n.d.).

[**] Bott (1982:74) (Figure 74) lists this woman as Fatafehi Fangaafa. However, she is listed as Fatafeni Fanga'ofa in Bott, "Notes on the Pongipongi of Tu'i Vakano, 4 July 1958, BSP 13/4/3.

The withholding of Halaevalu was part of a larger initiative that culminated in the Constitution of 1875, with its renovation of the title system and related developments. Though the Tuʻi Tonga title was never abrogated, after the death of Laufilitonga it was not reappointed and effectively lapsed (Lātūkefu 1974:90; Marcus 1980:38). When Halaevalu Mataʻaho was finally released to Laufilitonga, she bore him twins, the one Lavinia Veiongo, a woman who subsequently became an important source of Tuʻi Tonga blood for the Tupou Dynasty, and the other Kalaniuvalu. Kalaniuvalu was made a *nōpele* by the 1875 Constitution as a representative of the Tuʻi Tonga line (Ellem 1981:66; Marcus 1980:38-39). Since the Kalaniuvalu title was created by Tupou I and is appointed by the Tuʻi Kanokupolu cum King, it is *ipso facto* inferior to these two titles, as the Tuʻi Tonga title was not ("Discussions" 2:351). As a result, Kalaniuvalu cannot be buried in the special tombs or *langi* reserved to the Tuʻi Tonga (*ibid.*). The marriage between Halaevalu and Laufilitonga was therefore crucial to producing an heir for a title that could not be vested with authority in the old system but that took its place in a Tupou-dominated constitutional monarchy. It was also crucial for setting the stage for an appropriation of Kauhalaʻuta blood by the Tupou Dynasty later, when Tupou II married, a chapter of Tongan history reviewed below.

Tāufaʻāhau made the complementary move of capturing as his own wife one of the Tuʻi Tonga's wives, Lupepauʻu (Cummins 1980:41, 74; "Discussions" 1:61; Queen Sālote, "*Ko e Ngaahi Haʻa ʻo Tonga*", BSP 11/2/15; cf. Ellem 1981:66). Tāufaʻāhau was to have married Lupepauʻu's younger sister; but when Lupepauʻu attended a wedding in Tāufaʻāhau's area, he claimed her for himself (Collocott Papers, MS 1058:1, 19). There was no retaliation — either because Laufilitonga was no match for Tāufaʻāhau (he had already lost the decisive Battle of Velata to him) or because it was considered "beneath the dignity of a chief to quarrel over women" (Bott 1982:139).

Marriage was not just a status game. It could be and was used to develop political resources through the prerogatives of blood. A brother owes his sister and her children support.

> The mother's side consists of a set of brothers and brother's children to whom she and her children are superior. This principle was of great importance in the traditional political system. It meant that a leader could always expect support from the groups of his mother and his wives, also from the group of his mother's mother. It meant that he had to give support to the groups into which his sister, his sister's daughter, and his father's sister married, always assuming they had children (Bott 1981:19; see also Bott 1982:62-63).

Typically this support consisted in provisioning the sister and her husband with food, which meant that a leader could acquire the wherewithal to support a large retinue through his affinal and matrilateral ties. These ties, moreover, could be used to augment this retinue. Since "[t]raditionally the main basis of political power was the ability to build up and lead a local group" (Bott 1981:9), a polygamist could encourage his wives and relatives to live with him, thus expanding his group (Spillius, "Kinship and Ha'a in Tonga", BSP 5/6/17) and its labour resources. The kinspeople of a woman who married a chief were often committed supporters of the woman's son by that chief (Bott 1982:132).

Then again, if the wife-giver were himself high in rank but bereft of resources, land, labour, and people could flow in the opposite direction, from wife-taker to wife-giver. For example, when Fusipala, the daughter of the fourth Tu'i Kanokupolu Mataeleha'amea, was given by her brother to an untitled Pelehake leader who controlled a lot of people and land in eastern Tongatapu and was thus powerful, "even though he was not of high rank" (Bott 1982:138), the sister's husband shared his resources with his wife's people and not vice versa. Queen Sālote elaborated upon the husband's reasoning:

> The brothers knew that the very fact he was not 'eiki would make him keen to marry a king's daughter, and they wanted to get his support. Normally it is the woman's people who feed and support the husband's people. But in a case of this sort, where the man was powerful but had no title and was not 'eiki whereas the woman was the daughter of a king, the husband's people would support the wife's people and particularly the king (ibid.).

Land no less than labour could be acquired through marriage. As Spillius has written:

> There were many cases of inheritance of land through women before the Constitution [1875], when the daughter of a title-holder married a king or some other important title-holder, her father gave her a piece of land to support her and her children. After her death it might be kept by her children or it might be returned, depending on circumstances. In other cases a prominent man, usually the brother or son of a king, married a woman whose father was rich in land but lower in rank. The children of such a marriage inherited the land of his mother's father (Spillius, "Kinship and Ha'a in Tonga", BSP 5/6/8).

Since transfers of land implied transfers of people, titles could be inherited matrilaterally as well as patrilineally. For all "working chiefs" — and all chiefs except the Tu'i Tonga of the diarchic era have been working chiefs (Biersack 1990b) — primogeniture has never been the only discriminator in matters of succession. Multiple criteria were employed in choosing a successor: not only birth order but the rank of the mother and the power of matrilateral support, age, experience, and ability — all were factors (Bott 1982:72, 123-124; "Discussions" 1:176). Under these circumstances, it was possible for sister's sons to succeed, particularly if the mother was of very high rank (*ibid.* 1:177, 180). Sister's son could also succeed if the male line lapsed — as, for example, in the case of Makaholovalu's accession to the Tu'i Lakepa title.

In the resulting shifts in effective control from senior to junior lines, affinity and *fahu* successions played an important role. In the case of both the Tu'i Ha'atakalaua and the Tu'i Kanokupolu, younger brothers were sent, often without title, to outlying districts, where they married in. In a generation or two, these cadet lines would capture the land and titles of these districts, subordinating these to their senior, who now held the paramount title of a growing *ha'a* or cluster of titles. In regard to the growth of the Ha'atakalaua in the sixteenth century, Bott tells us that the titles thus accruing to that *ha'a* were "often named after the original son or younger brother of the Tu'i Ha'atakalaua who was sent out in the first place" (Bott 1982:63), the land and the title being absorbed as subsidiary units within that *ha'a*. "... local titles used to get swallowed up or forgotten" as new centres emerged, expanded, and were consolidated (Bott 1981:51).[11] After these cadets had secured local support, land, and title, they intermarried with the national élite to upgrade the rank of their heir, providing a double anchorage for their dynasty, local and national (*ibid.*:48).

Marriage was also the key to upgrading the title that a line already controlled. Again, Tuita provides an example, for 'Ulukivaiola reverted to the Tuita title to raise the rank of that title ("Discussions" 2:296; Figure 2). Traditionally the Tuita title was a "specialised *matāpule*" title (Marcus 1980:41, n.27) — a *matāpule* of the navigator kind; Gifford placed the title somewhere between *matāpule* and '*eiki* in its rank (Gifford 1929:109).[12] In 1880 Tuita was reclassified as a *nōpele* or "noble" title, the post-Constitutional equivalent of the chiefly titles of the past (*ibid.*). In recent years Tuita has held one of the more important ministries of the Tongan government and his son is the husband of the King's only daughter, bestower of the highest ranking blood in contemporary Tonga.

The same is true of the Tu'i Pelehake title. The title is related to a mythic one: the title Tu'i Faleua or "King of the Second House", which a sky god bestowed upon the older brother of the first Tu'i Tonga, 'Aho'eitu (Figure 1). 'Aho'eitu ascended to the sky to find his father, this god 'Eitumatupu'a, whom he had never seen. For various reasons, his older brothers were jealous of him and killed him. 'Eitumatupu'a brought 'Aho'eitu back to life and punished the older brothers by sending them back to earth as 'Aho'eitu's subordinates (Biersack 1991a; Bott 1972; Valeri 1989). Just when the Tu'i Pelehake title originated is not clear; but its origin is related to the marriage between Fusipala, daughter and sister of a Tu'i Kanokupolu and the powerful leader of the Pelehake district on Tongatapu mentioned before. Presumably from that time on, the Pelehake line became a close satellite of the Ha'a Ngata Motu'a, the Tu'i Kanokupolu's line; and the Tu'i Pelehake title was "lifted up" (*ibid.*). Later a Tu'i Pelehake married a daughter of a Tu'i Tonga Fefine ("Discussions" 2:282; see Figure 3). This "lifting" through marriage was symbolically reinforced in the nineteenth century, when the Tu'i Tonga's kava privileges were transferred to the Tu'i Pelehake and the Tu'i Tonga title was allowed to lapse.[13]

Politically crucial, women became the focus of a dynamic factional politics. If a woman married a chief and her brother or father was ambitious, her people would rally around her son as a pretender to the title, even without his being a clear heir apparent to the position ("Discussions" 1:46). The gift of a woman could seal a political and military alliance. For example, when Tākai, a famous warrior, decided to settle his differences with the seventeenth Tu'i Kanokupolu, father of the man who would become King George Tupou I, he offered his daughter in marriage to him. He also supplied Tupouto'a with troops upon request and lobbied the chiefs of the Ha'a Ngata Motu'a and Ha'a Havea (Figure 1) to elect him Tu'i Kanokupolu (Gifford 1929:208; Lātūkefu 1974:21). Furthermore, as the episodes of Tongan history soon to be recounted illustrate, an enemy could be co-opted through marriage.

Twentieth-Century Foundations

The Tupou Dynasty and Its Early Opponents

The Ha'a Ngata chiefs (Figure 1) initially dominated the western end of Tongatapu and some of them (Ata, for example, or Ve'ehala) continued to be associated with western (*hihifo*) Tongatapu (Map 1). The children of the fourth Tu'i Kanokupolu became geographically split, however. Mumui and his descendants were associated with central Tongatapu and the shoreline rather than the lagoon (Ellem 1981:60). Meanwhile, Maealiuaki and his descendants operated out of Hahake, the eastern district (*ibid.*:62). Historically Hahake is associated with the Tu'i Tonga and the Tu'i Ha'atakalaua (Figure 1), titles that are superior to the Tu'i Kanokupolu title. Hahake's ranking town was Mu'a,[14] the seat of the Tu'i Tonga. With respect to Hihifo, then, Hahake was a rival centre. Its chiefs "were traditionally opposed to the people of Hihifo … and regarded the assumption of kingship by the Tu'i Kanokupolu, a Hihifo chief, as an usurpation of the rights of the Hahake chiefs, Tu'i Ha'atakalaua and Tu'i Tonga" (Rutherford 1971:14). Compounding this east-west split on Tongatapu was the north-south split between Vava'u, referred to in poetic texts as *tokelau* or "north", and Tongatapu, literally "sacred south". Ellem dates the hostilities between the northern group and the southern island from the end of the eighteenth century (1981:62). In the nineteenth century, the principal chiefly name associated with the north was 'Ulukālala (Figure 4) of the Ha'a Ngata Tupu (Figure 1). Over the course of the history summarized in this section, the east of Tongatapu (Map 1) entered into alliance with the north of the archipelago (Map 2) and together east and north opposed the centre of Tongatapu. Herein follows a summary of this history.

The close of the eighteenth century was a turbulent era. Maealiuaki had been the 8th Tu'i Kanokupolu, and some alleged he also held the Tu'i Ha'atakalaua title (Bott 1982:14, Figure 3; Campbell 1982:186-187; Ellem 1981:451, Figure 2; see Figure 4). Maealiuaki and his son Mulikiha'amea were associated with the eastern district of Tongatapu, Hahake (Map 1). Mulikiha'amea was also a Tu'i Kanokupolu, though sources disagree about whether he succeeded his father directly and whether he also held the Tu'i Ha'atakalaua title, as his father apparently had.[15] The principal rivals of the Maealiuaki line would come from central Tongatapu in the person of the chiefs of the Tupou Dynasty, beginning with Mumui (Figure 4). Mumui, the founder, was the 13th Tu'i Kanokupolu (Bott 1982:14, Figure 3) and according to Bott he died two years before Mulikiha'amea died. How did Mumui acquire the Tu'i Kanokupolu title? The answer to this question concerns in part the exploits of one of the best known Tongan women, Tupoumoheofo.

Tupoumoheofo was the main wife or *moheofo* of the Tu'i Tonga Paulaho and daughter of the seventh Tu'i Kanokupolu and full sister of the ninth Tu'i Kanokupolu. She was also father's sister of an heir to the title (see Figure 4; Bott 1982:14, Figure 3; Gifford 1929:88; Herda 1987:203). There are many accounts of how Tupoumoheofo captured the Tu'i Kanokupolu title. Some claim that Tupoumoheofo secured the Tu'i Ha'atakalaua title for Mulikiha'amea so that she herself could assume the Tu'i Kanokupolu title ("Tonga: A Brief History", BSP 4/5/8-9; "Discussions" 1:44). Still others report that it was Mumui and Tuku'aho (Figure 4) who pressed for Mulikiha'amea's installation as Tu'i Ha'atakalaua so that one or the other could assume the Tu'i Kanokupolu title once he had vacated it (Herda 1987:205, 1988:100) (but see n.15). Gunson, meanwhile, envisions Tupoumoheofo as assuming the title after her brother Tu'i Halafatai, the "effectual ruler" (Gunson 1979:39; see n.18), "retreat[ed] from political life and ... retired to Fiji and Samoa" (Gunson 1979:40; see also "Discussions" 1:44).[16] However the title became vacant, once it was vacant Tupoumoheofo named herself the successor and installed herself as Tu'i Kanokupolu by sitting with her back against the *koka* tree in Hihifo that the Tu'i Kanokupolu traditionally leaned against when being installed (Gifford 1929:88).

'ATA

'NUKU
'FUKAVE

'EUEIKI

MOTUTAPU
'ONEVAI
'ONEVAO

VELITOA
FAFA
MONU'AFE

MAKAHA'A
MANIMA
'ONEATA

PANGAIMOTU

Nuku'alofa

ALAKIPEAU
POLO'A

Muifonua Point

ATATA

TOKETOKE 'TUFAKA

Niu'aunofo Point

To
Hakautapu
Reef

Ha'atafu
Kanokupolu
Ha'akili
'Ahau
Kolovai
Neiafu
Ha'avakatolo
Te'utu

Monotapu
Beach

Hingavele
Beach

Kala'au
Fahefa
Maholfa
Vaotu'u

Masilamea
Matahau
Ha'autu
Te'ekiu

HIHIFO 6

Nukunuku
Fatai
Lakepa
Houma
Ha'alalo
Ha'akame
Ulutau
Utulau
Tokomololo
Pea

7

Pake
Hofoa
Hihifo Road
Lou Road
Liku Road
Totoa
KANATEA
Kolonga
Fanga'Ula Lagoon
Ha'ateiho
Veitongo
Longoteme
Folaha
Lokoha'apai
Puke

2
1
PANGAIMOTU
Havelulolo

Fanga kakau
Kakau

3

Vaini
Tapuhia
Pelehake
Toloa
Malapo
Holonga

VAHE LOTO

DISTRICTS
1 Kolomotu'a
2 Kolofo'ou
3 Vaini
4 Lapaha
5 Takakamotonga
6 Nukunuku
7 Kolovai
District boundary

TALAKITE
MATA'AHO
Talasiu
Mu'a
Tatakamotonga
MOUNGA

NUKUNUKUMOTU 4

Kolonga
Afa
Heketa
Niutoua
Makaunga
Talafo'ou
Niutao
Navutoka
Manuka
Nukuleka
Alakifonua

HA'AKAME 5

Havelikiku
Fatumu
Lavengatonga
Ha'asini
Hamula
Fua'amotu
Nukolefi

Ahononou
Beach

Fua'amotu Beach

Houma Toloa (Cook Point)
TU'ALIKUTONGA BEACH

TU'ALIKUTAPU BEACH

'EUA
16 km

HOUMA-'UTULAU BEACH

ATA
155 km

N

'ATA ISLAND

'EUA ISLAND

Nafanua Harbour

'Ohonua

Topuva'e-'a-Maui
Tongamamao
Matalanga-'a-Maui

Li'angahuo-'a-Maui

10 km

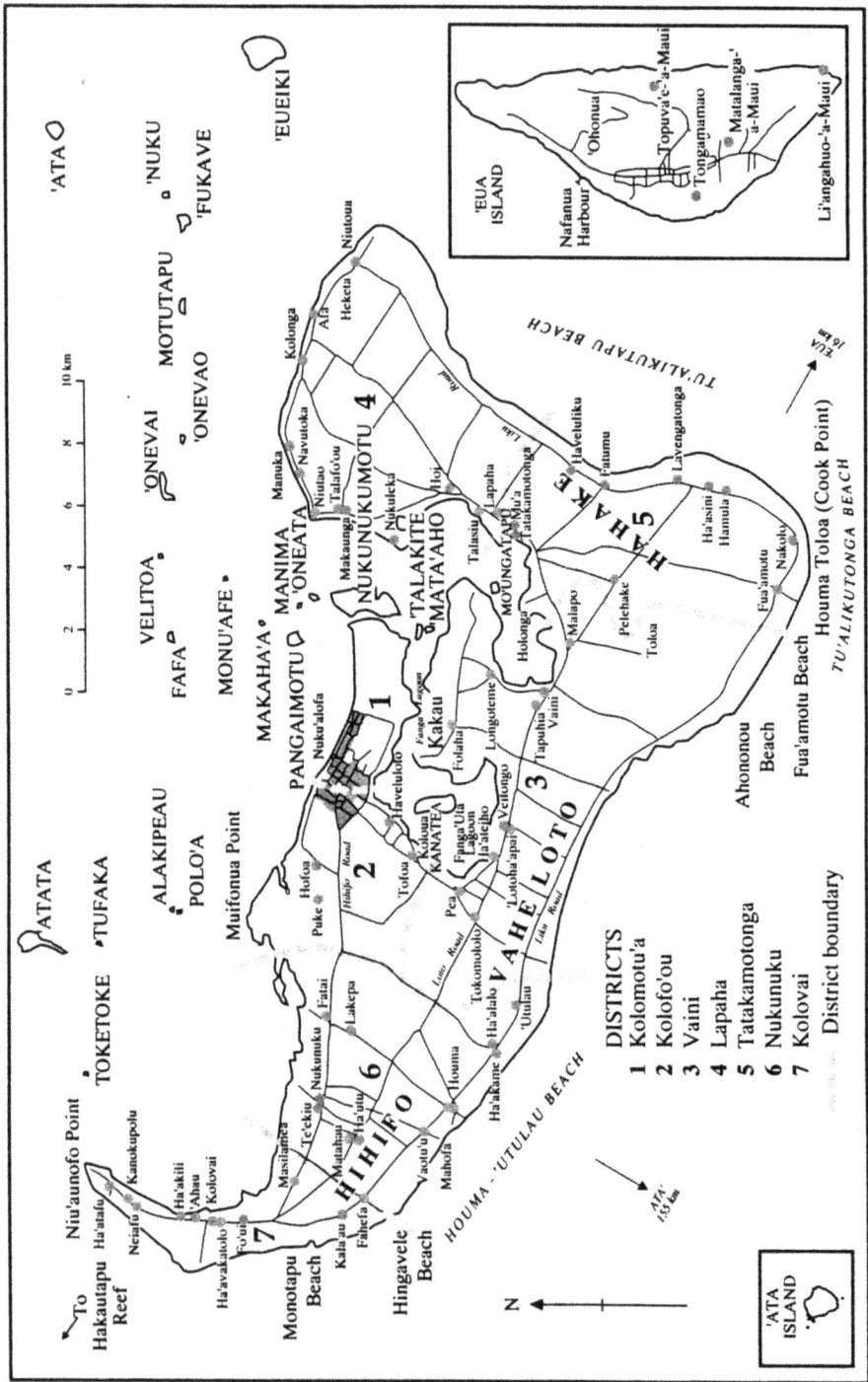

Map 1. Tongatapu.

What her intentions were is a matter of conjecture. Ellem suggests that her goal in becoming Tuʻi Kanokupolu was to pass this title on to her son, Fuanunuiava (Ellem 1981:61), who would eventually contend (Ellem claims [*ibid*.:62]) for the Tuʻi Kanokupolu title in 1797, when Mumui died (see, for example, Dumont D'Urville, 1989:114). Others speculate that Tupoumoheofo hoped to restrain the Tuʻi Kanokupolu by uniting the country under the Tuʻi Tonga again ("Discussions" 1:60). She could have been responding, among other things, to the failure of Maealiuaki to send his daughters to the Tuʻi Tonga but, rather, to send them to men of the Tuʻi Kanokupolu line instead (*ibid.* 1:69) and to the fact of the recent doubling of titles on the Kauhalalalo side, a single person holding both the Tuʻi Haʻatakalaua and the. Tuʻi Kanokupolu titles (Figure 1). In fact, some claim that she attempted to install her son Fatafehi Fuanunuiava as Tuʻi Tonga while her husband was still alive. This occurred, according to Bott and Queen Sālote, at the *ʻinasi* ceremony witnessed by Captain Cook (*ibid.* 1:44). (*ʻInasi* was the ceremony in which the annual prestation of tribute [also called *ʻinasi*] was made.)[17] That would have been a victory for the Kauhalaʻuta side, although Tupoumoheofo could as well have unified the country under the Tuʻi Kanokupolu, thus favouring the Kauhalalalo side (Figure 1).[18] As *moheofo* of the Tuʻi Tonga and full sister to a Tuʻi Kanokupolu, Tupoumoheofo was capable of operating across the divide between Kauhalaʻuta and Kauhalalalo. Whatever her ambitions, Tupoumoheofo's power and office were short-lived, for Tukuʻaho, Mumui's son, mobilized an army on Tongatapu and defeated her and her supporters (*ibid.*); and he followed up this victory by naming his own father, Mumui, Tuʻi Kanokupolu.

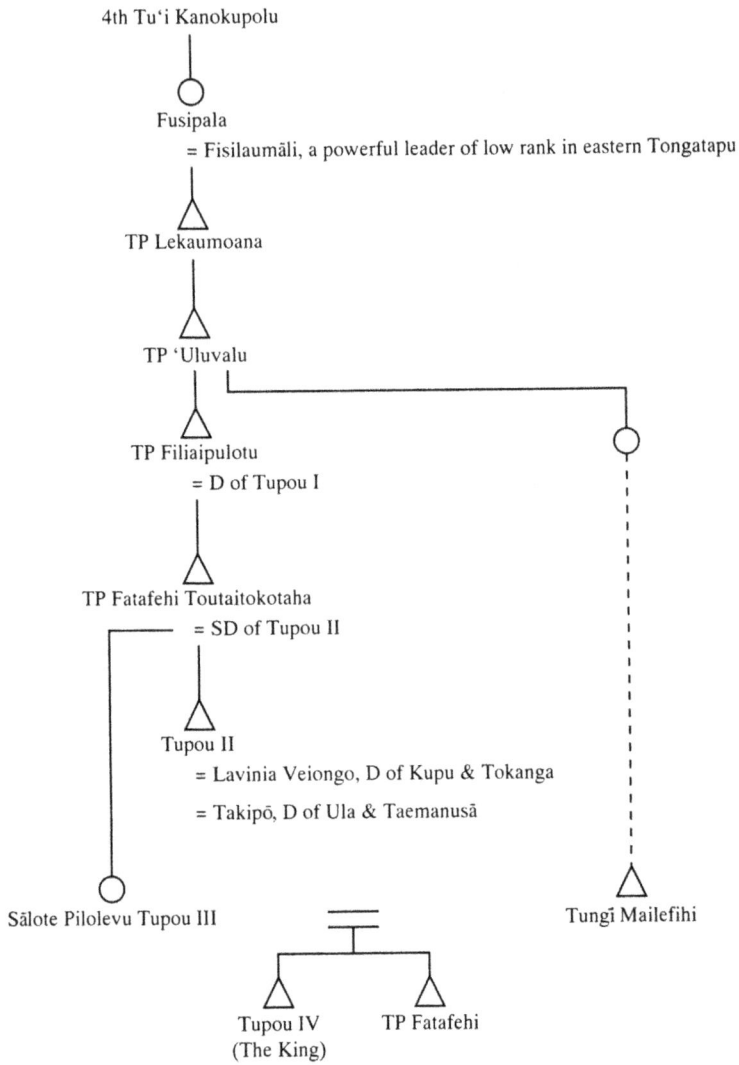

Figure 3. Fusipala and the elevation of the Tu'i Pelehake (TP) title (adapted from Bott 1982:147 [Figure 24]).

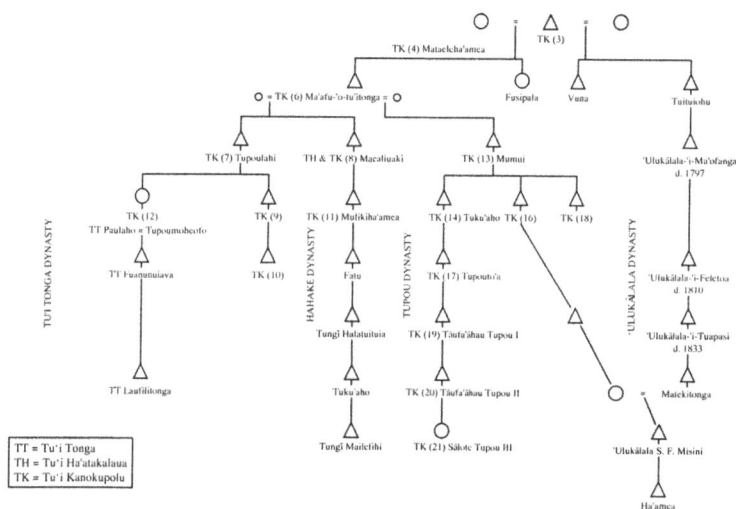

Figure 4 Rival dynastic lines 1780-1938 (adapted from Ellem 1981:451 [Figure 2]).

However short-lived her term as Tu'i Kanokupolu, Tupoumoheofo managed to overturn an achievement of another powerful chiefess, Fusipala. Fusipala has been mentioned before, as the wife of Fisilaumāli, the chief in eastern Tongatapu who was low in rank but powerful. Fusipala was the daughter of the fourth Tu'i Kanokupolu and half-sister of Tuituiohu, founding ancestor of the Ha'a Ngata Tupu, with which the 'Ulukālala title of today is associated (Figure 4) (Bott 1982:140). She was also possibly the wife of the fourteenth Tu'i Ha'atakalua and mother of the fifteenth Tu'i Ha'atakalaua (Bott 1982:138, *ibid.*:Figure 2, p.13, and Figure 23, p.138). Her son by Fisilaumāli was the first known Tu'i Pelehake (Figure 3). Fusipala was therefore powerful (Herda 1988:93) — so powerful that she was able to depose Vuna Ngata, the Tu'i Vava'u (*ibid.*; Bott 1982:76; Map 2) and son of the fifth Tu'i Kanokupolu. After deposing him, Fusipala installed Tuituiohu as Tu'i Vava'u, "establish[ing] herself as virtual ruler of Vava'u" (Gunson 1987:159) in the process, though officially the Tu'i Vava'u was Tuituiohu (*ibid.*; also Bott 1982:76; Herda 1988:93, 110). Since Fusipala could count on the support of her full brother, the sixth Tu'i Kanokupolu, "there were few in Tonga willing to cross her" (Herda 1988:93).

In this initiative, Fusipala was thwarted by Tupoumoheofo, now forced into exile in Vava'u as a result of Tuku'aho's recapture of the Tu'i Kanokupolu title. Tupoumoheofo apparently viewed Tuituiohu's son Fīnau-'i-Ma'ofanga as a rival; and when she assumed the Tu'i Kanokupolu title, she deposed him, restoring the Tu'i Vava'u title to her daughter's husband in the Vuna line (Spillius n.d.; BSP 4/5/9; Gunson 1979:40). She thus overturned the work of Fusipala, who had at least momentarily succeeded in shifting the Tu'i Vava'u title from the Vuna to the 'Ulukālala line. It was this daughter's husband that gave her refuge in Vava'u when she was first exiled there (Campbell 1989:153; Gunson 1979:41; Herda 1988:112, 114).[19]

With Mumui's accession, the Tu'i Kanokupolu title was transferred to the Tupou Dynasty and incidentally from eastern to central Tongatapu. When Mumui died in 1797, Tuku'aho despite his reputation for cruelty, was elected to replace him. Some claim that Mumui nominated Maealiuaki's son Mulikiha'amea (Figure 4) rather than his own son Tuku'aho as his successor (Campbell 1982:187, 1989:153; Herda 1988:107), thus tacitly endorsing Hahake or eastern precedence. Bott attributes Tuku'aho's success to the support he received from his matrikin, for his mother was the daughter of Ata, ranking chief of the Ha'a Ngata Motu'a and effective ruler of the Hihifo district ("Discussions" 1:42; Bott 1982:146; see also Herda 1988:108-109; see Map 1).

The deposed Tu'i Vava'u, Fīnau 'Ulukālala-'i-Ma'ofanga (Figure 4), was matrilateral half-brother of Tuku'aho (Bott 1982:142, Figure 29; Gunson 1977: 99-100); and he supported Tuku'aho for the Tu'i Kanokupolu title with the expectation of receiving the Tu'i Vava'u title his father had briefly held. But once Tuku'aho had achieved his goal, he confirmed the Vuna line in that office (Campbell 1989:153; Herda 1988:112), despite the kinship tie. 'Ulukālala-'i-Ma'ofanga died several weeks after Tuku'aho's accession — of disappointment, some claim (Campbell 1989:153; Herda 1988:112) — but not without extracting a pledge from his son 'Ulukālala-'i-Feletoa to avenge Tuku'aho's insult (Campbell 1989:154).

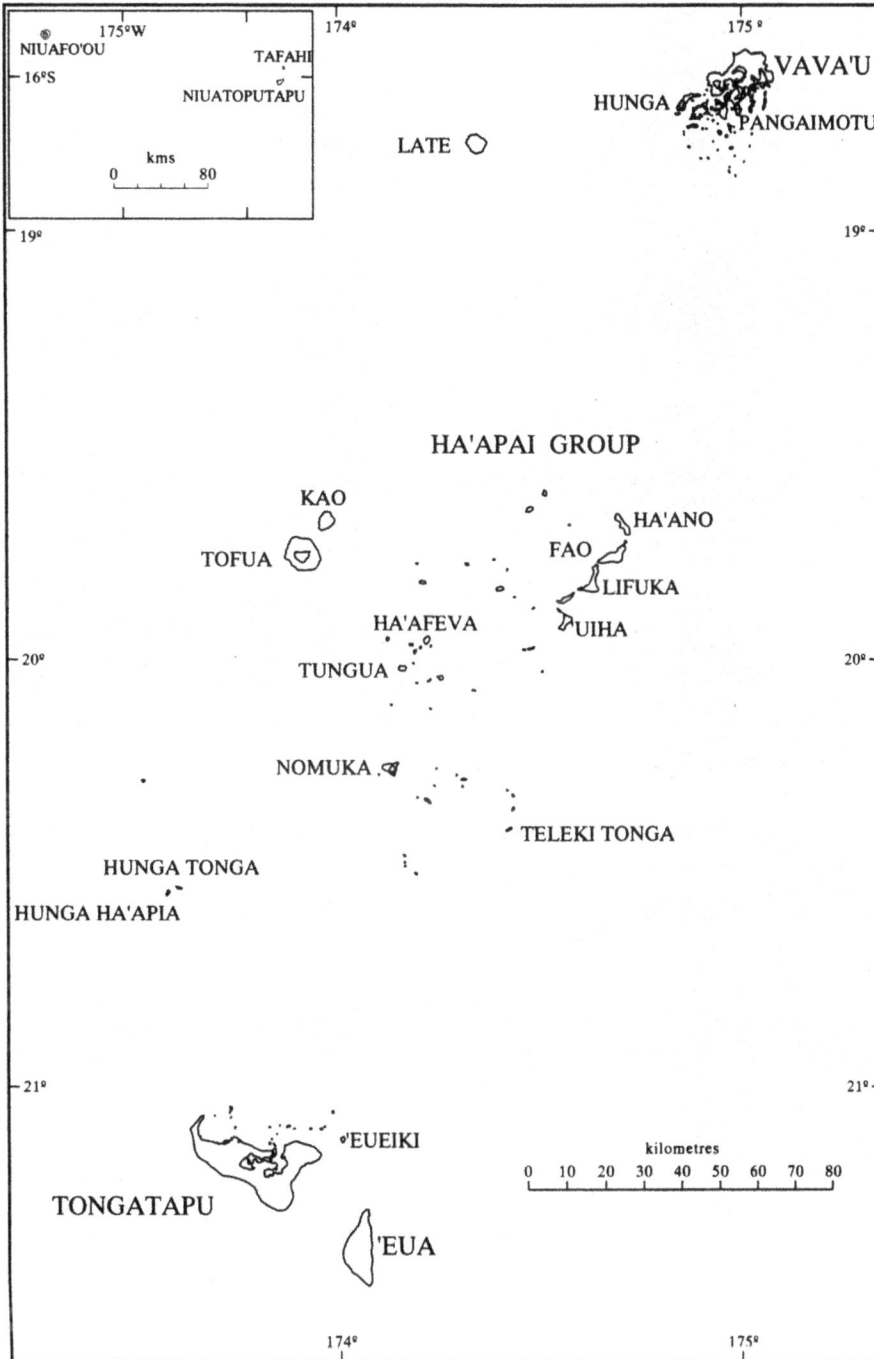

Map 2. Tonga.

Ostensibly because of his cruelty, though issues of revenge and rivalry unmistakably figured, Tuku'aho was assassinated within two years of his accession. The principal conspirators and their supporters[20] came from rival branches: Mulikiha'amea from the Hahake Dynasty and 'Ulukālala-'i-Feletoa and his half-brother (Figure 4) (Bott 1982:112, 143; Martin [Mariner] 1981). The matter of Hahake control of the Tu'i Kanokupolu title appears to have had some saliency (Campbell 1989:154; Herda 1988:113-114), yet the anti-Tuku'aho faction was in fact led by 'Ulukālala-'i-Feletoa. In this venture, Mulikiha'amea had two other important allies. One was Fuanunuiava, Tupoumoheofo's son. Mulikiha'amea and Fuanunuiava jointly directed troops marshalled to fend off the expected revenge attack (Campbell 1989:155; Thomas n.d.:2, Book 4, p.256). Tupoumoheofo was herself an ally. Though in Vava'u, Tupoumoheofo was 'Ulukālala's enemy, she was sufficiently outraged by Tuku'aho's appropriation of the Tu'i Kanokupolu title that she was willing to make common cause with 'Ulukālala — some even claim, actively instigating the assassination of Tuku'aho (Lātūkefu 1974:15; Gunson 1979:29; Herda 1987:206). In the civil war that followed the assassination, Tonga was split along geographical as well as dynastic lines: seeking revenge for Tuku'aho's death, Hihifo and central Tongatapu opposed Hahake, Mu'a, elements of the Ha'a Fale Fisi (Figure 1), and the 'Ulukālala Dynasty of the north v. the south (Maps 1 and 2; Herda 1988: 114). There appears then to have been a three-way alliance among those the Tupou Dynasty had in one way or another displaced: the Hahake Dynasty, the 'Ulukālala line, and the Tu'i Tonga.[21]

As the nineteenth century wore on, the schism between Hahake and northern groups, on the one hand, the Tupou Dynasty, on the other, would be played out as a confrontation between Tāufa'āhau, Tuku'aho's son's son, and Tungī Halatuituia, Mulikiha'amea's son's son (Figure 4); and the 'Ulukālalas would continue to demand a Vava'u title.

Tungī Halatuituia

Though the Tu'i Kanokupolu title was retained by the Tupou Dynasty, and the Tu'i Ha'atakalaua title was no longer appointed, the Hahake Dynasty continued to aggrandize power in eastern Tongatapu. Mulikiha'amea's son, Fatukimotulalo, who based himself at Mu'a, was an ally of Fīnau 'Ulukālala-'i-Feletoa (Gunson 1979:44) and was also the host of the first Wesleyan Methodist missionary in the archipelago, Reverend Walter Lawry (Lātūkefu 1977:115). Despite Fatu's early association with missionaries, he resisted conversion, dying "an unrepentant pagan" ("Tonga: A Brief History", BSP 4/5/36). Fatu settled down in Mu'a, where he was recognized as a local leader, despite the fact that he held no title.[22] His first wife was the daughter of Tu'i Kanokupolu Mumui and the patrilateral half-sister of Tuku'aho (Bott 1982:88). The mother of this half-sister outranked

Tuku'aho's mother; and this, together with the fact that sisters always outrank brothers, meant that her child outranked Tuku'aho's son's son, Tāufa'āhau ("Re Feudalism", BSP 22/3).

Tungī Halatuituia was the son's son of a Tu'i Kanokupolu, and he was the son's son's son (if not the son's son [see n.15]) of a Tu'i Ha'atakalaua. As discussed in the previous section, his father's father, Mulikiha'amea, had made common cause with 'Ulukālala in assassinating Tuku'aho, Tāufa'āhau's father's father. However, the Tu'i Ha'atakalaua title had now lapsed and a collateral branch of the descendants of the fourth Tu'i Kanokupolu had captured the Tu'i Kanokupolu title (Figure 4). Through his father's marriages Tungī garnered resources and strengthened his claims to high title. Tungī would eventually base his claim not only to the Tu'i Kanokupolu title but to kingship itself on his descent from Tuku'aho's half-sister, for Tungī's strongest claim to these titles was arguably through his mother's mother ("Re Feudalism", BSP 22/3; Fusitu'a 1976:17). Fusitu'a speculates that it was Tungī's high birth as a *hako'i fefine* or descendant of a woman that encouraged Tāufa'āhau, now King George Tupou I, to bestow 'Ana Seini, the daughter of his half-sister Halaevalu Mata'aho, on Tungī in 1853 (*ibid.*), thus reinforcing existing ties between the Hahake and the Tupou dynasties (see Ellem 1981:67). But Tungī was never firmly in Tāufa'āhau's camp. According to one missionary observer, Tungī nurtured "very lively expectations" of a reversal of fortunes and a coming to power as the descendant of the last Tu'i Ha'atakalaua (Cummins 1980:118).

Tupou I ruled as the first constitutional monarch and as author of a number of codes, one of the most important being the Emancipation Edict of 1862. In effect, the Edict, promulgated by Tāufa'āhau in a plenary meeting of chiefs and to some degree against their will, released commoners from traditional obligations. In theory chiefs could no longer require that their people work for them. Tungī was among those chiefs who opposed the reforms, viewing the Emancipation Edict "as but another move to strip the chiefs of their privilege, and of their source of labour and livelihood" (Fusitu'a 1976:18).

He also led the opposition in Parliament to Tupou I's choice of successor (Ellem 1981:84; Fusitu'a 1976:18). Everything that made Tungī eligible to succeed to the Tu'i Kanokupolu title also made his heir eligible. Not only was Tungī the son's son of a Tu'i Kanokupolu but his mother's mother was the sister of the assassinated Tuku'aho (Fusitu'a 1976:17), and his personal or "blood" status was therefore high. When Tupou I bestowed upon him his adopted daughter 'Ana Seini Tupou Veihola in 1853, he elevated Tungī even further in importance if not status. 'Ana Seini was the great granddaughter of the Tamahā Lātūfuipeka and much higher in status than Tāufa'āhau himself ("Re Feudalism", BSP 22/3), and with this marriage the superiority of Tungī Halatuituia's heir to any heir that Tāufaʻāhau could produce was assured (Fusituʻa 1976:17-18). Tungī also had symbolically significant holdings: "the powerful and second part of the ancient town of Muʻa, Tatakamotonga, as well as a great part of the more populous district of Hahake" (*ibid.*:18; see Map 1); and despite Tungī's father's lack of title Bott refers to Tungī's father, Fatu, as "the ruler of Muʻa" ("Re Feudalism", BSP 22/3).

Despite Tungī's credentials, the Constitution of 1875 named as Tupou I's heir a son by a secondary wife. Furthermore, Maʻafu, the son of the eighteenth Tuʻi Kanokupolu, and his heirs, not Tungī and his heirs, were named to succeed Tupou I in the event that his own line should fail. The same legislation awarded him the newly created title Tungī, which supplanted the Tuʻi Haʻatakalaua title (Bott 1981:22; Gifford 1929:84; Marcus 1980). The Constitution had replaced the Tuʻi Tonga with the Kalaniuvalu title, a title that was appointed by the King and that was *ipso facto* inferior to the royal title. By the same token, whereas the Tuʻi Haʻatakalaua title was superior to the Tuʻi Kanokupolu title, Tungī, a position created by monarchical fiat, was inferior to the royal title (Gifford 1929:84). When Maʻafu died in the early 1880s, Tupou I attempted to mollify Tungī by replacing Maʻafu with Tungī and his heirs (Ellem 1981:94; Fusituʻa and Rutherford 1977:175, Rutherford 1971:139-140).[23] But, as events were to show, Tungī was hardly appeased.

The focus of Tungī's opposition became an expatriate named Shirley Waldemar Baker, principal architect of King George's constitutional monarchy, at least as it existed on paper. As if to add insult to injury, Tungī was passed over for the Premiership and Baker was named Premier instead in 1880 (Rutherford 1971:111). In my reading of the events of this period, opposition to the King was often masked as opposition to the white *papālangi* foreigner; and agitation against Baker was simultaneously, though unspokenly, agitation against the King. Baker's arch *papālangi* rival, the Reverend J. Egan Moulton, attracted elements of the antiroyal faction (see Cummins 1980), thus marking the other end of a field that was largely polarized through national contestations.

The 1880s offered several dramatic settings for Tungī's opposition; and in these contexts, the coalition that was already in place at the end of the eighteenth century resurfaced. The first was the series of events stemming from the actions of a group of minor chiefs and *matāpule* who stood to lose most from Tupou I's reforms (Rutherford 1977:165). Though Baker was the particular target of the group that convened at Muʻa to oppose recent legislation failing to honour the customary land rights of this group, opposition to Baker was inseparable from opposition to the King. Tupou I certainly seems to have seen things that way, for he viewed every anti-Baker initiative, including those associated with what Baker pejoratively dubbed the Muʻa Parliament, as acts of rebellion.

The Mu'a group entered into coalition with *nōpele* titleholders who had their own reasons for opposing Tāufa'āhau — in particular with Tungī and the Tu'i Pelehake. Though Tupou I ordered Tungī to suppress the activities of the Mu'a group, Tungī defied him and sided with the dissidents, most of whom were either Tungā's relatives or his dependant minor chiefs (Rutherford 1971:111; see also Fusitu'a 1976:18-19). The Mu'a group petitioned first the King and when that did not work Queen Victoria herself to have Baker removed. Even though the Constitution had granted rights of petition, the King considered these actions seditious and brought the petitioners to trial.

Meanwhile, even though the bulk of the population, commoners, stood to gain from the Tupou-Baker reforms, the issues were more complicated than they seemed. Tupou I had unified the archipelago, but only precariously. Regional loyalties persisted, and in the eyes of many, Tupou I represented the oppressive military might of Ha'apai and Vava'u (Map 2) in the "north's" attempt to dominate Tongatapu, the "sacred south". Tāufa'āhau rose to the Tu'i Kanokupolu and eventually the royal titles as Tu'i Ha'apai and Tu'i Vava'u (Lātūkefu 1974:65-66); his helper in these campaigns was 'Ulukālala Tuapasi (Figure 4). In the wake of these accomplishments, a united and centralized north confronted a still fragmented Tongatapu (*ibid*.:22). Based at Mu'a in Tongatapu, Tungī represented not only the *ancien regime*, not only the insurgency of a senior line against its junior yet politically dominant branch, but Tongatapu resistance to Tāufa'āhau-instigated northern hegemony (Rutherford 1971:116-117).

When in 1885 Tupou I announced his intention to establish a Free Church of Tonga independent of the parent Conference of New South Wales (Ellem 1983:170), civil war all but broke out. A rallying point for "Old" Wesleyans was Baker's *papālangi* rival, the Reverend J. Egan Moulton, a staunch opponent of secession and also the person who had translated the petition the Mu'a group had sent to Queen Victoria from Tongan to English. But the political landscape these two men divided was split by other tensions and rivalries. Whereas the north quickly embraced the "King's Church", resistance developed on Tongatapu. Among the Old Wesleyan sympathizers were Tungī and the Tu'i Pelehake (Ellem 1981:132; Fusitu'a 1976:27, 46). Tupou I's own daughter, Sālote, who was married to the Tu'i Pelehake (Figure 3), refused to convert and became a Wesleyan, joining others in exile in Fiji. In Hahake spokespeople for the Wesleyans included one Tōpui, a cousin of Tungī who had been the ringleader of the Mu'a group. Other Mu'a veterans were Wesleyans as well (Rutherford 1971:130).

Matters came to a head when an effort was made on Baker's life. The plot was hatched in Mu'a. Tungī's cousin was among the would-be assassins. Rutherford thinks it probable that Tungī, his son Tuku'aho, Tu'i Pelehake, and even the Crown Prince were operating behind the scenes (*ibid*.:140; Rutherford

1977:169) — presumably as a shadow government awaiting its opportunity to usurp the key positions, Baker's and the King's included. Though the attempt aborted, the perpetrators were brutally punished. To teach Tongatapu a lesson, Tupou I unleashed his northern warriors on Tongatapu, where they ransacked Wesleyan holdings and killed rapaciously (ibid.).

As a result, the British High Commissioner, Sir John Thurston, intervened and decided to deport Baker, a British subject, in part on the basis of affidavits signed by Tungī, his son, and the Tu'i Pelehake "declaring Baker to have been the sole source of Tonga's troubles" (Fusitu'a 1976:40). The new ministry Thurston established was stacked with opposition chiefs, including Tungī as chairman of Parliament and Minister of Lands, the Tu'i Pelehake as Governor of Ha'apai, and Tuku'aho, Tungī's heir, as Premier and Minister for Foreign Affairs (ibid.:42). This move would undermine the entire position of Tupou II (Fusitu'a and Rutherford 1977:174; see Campbell 1992:ch. 7).

The Affinal Politics of the Twentieth Century

When Tupou I finally died in 1893 — in his 10th or, some even say, his 11th decade — the matter of succession was far from settled. All his heirs save one, a son's daughter's son named George Tāufa'āhau, had already died,[24] and by traditional standards this descendant was not the only possible successor. Others had strong claims: Tungī, Tuku'aho, and the Tu'i Pelehake (see Figure 5), for example. Though another title was created to substitute for the Tu'i Tonga title, the Tu'i Pelehake had and still has the strongest symbolic associations with the Tu'i Tonga title. This particular Tu'i Pelehake, moreover, had married Tupou I's son's daughter and was the father of Tupou II (Ellem 1987:213; see Figure 5). Tungī was now quite old and was not eager to press his claim; but Tungī's son, Tuku'aho, son of 'Ana Seini, the great granddaughter of the Tamahā Lātūfuipeka who Tupou I had bestowed upon Tungī Halatuituia, was a viable contender.[25] Siaosi Tuku'aho grew up "feeling that he had higher rank and a better claim to the throne than Tupou I's descendants" (Fusitu'a 1976:18); and he married a woman of such exceptional rank that she was fahu at the funeral of the Tu'i Pelehake in 1912 (Ellem 1981:100, n.36). So manifest were Tuku'aho's ambitions that Tupou II suspected Tuku'aho of trying to supplant him (Ellem 1981:95). Moreover, his wife, according to Ellem, was the highest ranking Old Wesleyan in the first decade of this century (Ellem 1981:111); and Tuku'aho himself was Old Wesleyan rather than Free Church in his sympathies (Fusitu'a 1976:46, 95).

To mollify Tungī Halatuituia still further, Tupou I had a "tacit" understanding with him (Fusitu'a 1976:99) that his successor would marry 'Ofaki-Vava'u, Tungī's sister's daughter's daughter and his fahu (Ellem 1981:96; see also Ellem 1987:213; Fusitu'a 1976:99; see also Seddon 1900:21). Through both her mother and her father, 'Ofa's blood rank was "exceedingly high" (Ellem 1981:96). Along with Tungī, she was supported by her father, Mā'atu, chief of the northern island Niuatoputapu, and 'Ulukālala Siaosi Fīnau Misini, her classificatory uncle (*ibid.*; see Figure 4). Since Mā'atu is a chief of the Kauhala'uta, this faction replicated the 'Ulukālala-Mulikiha'amea (Hahake Dynasty)-Tu'i Tonga faction of the end of the eighteenth century.

Misini's father's mother had been a daughter of Mā'atu (Bott 1982:151, Figure 28), and Misini carried into the twentieth century the same grudge that had set 'Ulukālala against Tupou Tu'i Kanokupolus throughout much of the nineteenth century and that had played a role in the assassination of Tuku'aho in 1799. Misini's father's father, 'Ulukālala Tuapasi (Figure 4), had opposed Tāufa'āhau's father, Tupouto'a, because Tupouto'a had failed to bestow the title of Tu'i Vava'u upon him (Figure 4). Tuapasi had eventually won that title himself; but he had failed to retain it for his line. He had combined forces with Tāufa'āhau, then Tu'i Ha'apai, with the expectation that Tāufa'āhau would name him Tu'i Vava'u once he attained the Tu'i Kanokupolu title. On his deathbed, 'Ulukālala Tuapasi is alleged to have granted Tāufa'āhau the Tu'i Vava'u title (Cummins 1980:41; Lātūkefu 1974:66, 93), presumably with the understanding that the title would revert to his heir once his heir was of age to hold it.[26] But when his son later requested the title, Tāufa'āhau, now King George Tupou I, refused to bestow it upon him. Instead he appointed as governor 'Osaiasi Veikune, one of the leading chiefs of Vava'u. According to Lātūkefu, Tāufa'āhau "deliberately side-stepped Fīnau 'Ulukālala's son, Matekitonga, who was now of age, anticipating that he would try to restore himself as ruler of Vava'u if he were placed in such a position. Thus he forestalled a potential rival" (Lātūkefu 1974:94) — or at least tried to. According to Ellem, "The 'Ulukālala chiefs claimed that Tāufa'āhau ... had usurped their title of Tu'i Vava'u in 1833; and they had never ceased in their attempts to reclaim that title" (Ellem 1987:216). So it was that Matekitonga fought alongside the rebels at Pea in 1852 against Tupou I (Lātūkefu 1974:97) and was exiled for it to 'Eua ("Discussions" 1:181).

Had Tupou II married 'Ofa, he would have appeased Matekitonga's son, Misini, as well as the entire Tungī line. The alternative was Lavinia, the great granddaughter of Laufilitonga, the last Tu'i Tonga (*ibid.*; see Figure 5). Her father's mother's mother had been Halaevalu Mata'aho, the sister Tāufa'āhau had refused to give as *moheofo* to Laufilitonga. Her father's father's father was 'Osaiasi Veikune, Tupou I's appointee as Tu'i Vava'u. Though Tu'i Tonga blood flowed in her veins (Marcus 1977:286), neither parent was "of truly aristocratic descent" (Fusitu'a 1976:98).[27]

To decide between these two women, Tupou II convened his chiefs. They hotly debated whom the King should marry. At night "the supporters of the two factions fought in the streets and burned down each other's houses", Ellem reports (1981:98). In the end they voted 17 to 7 in favour of 'Ofa. However, Tupou II chose to marry Lavinia. Visiting Tonga at the time of the decision, the then premier of New Zealand accounted for the King's choice in terms of his fear of being outranked by his wife. Though 'Ofa was "prepossessing" enough (Seddon 1900:21),

> it happened that when negotiations were proceeding the unfortunate remark was made to the King that he would strengthen his position by marrying Ofa, because she was of better blood than himself. The pride of the monarch was aroused. "There is no one in Tonga who would not be honoured in being raised to share the throne of Tonga", he said, and conceived strong animus against the marriage. For a year the struggle went on, as to whether Ofa or the King's new choice, Lavinia, should be Queen. It ended in the King calling for the advice of his chiefs, and when they counselled his marriage with Ofa he did what it is said he had made up his mind a year before to do — viz., reject both the advice and the girl. He married Lavinia, the present Queen (*ibid.*:18-21; see also Ellem 1981:97).

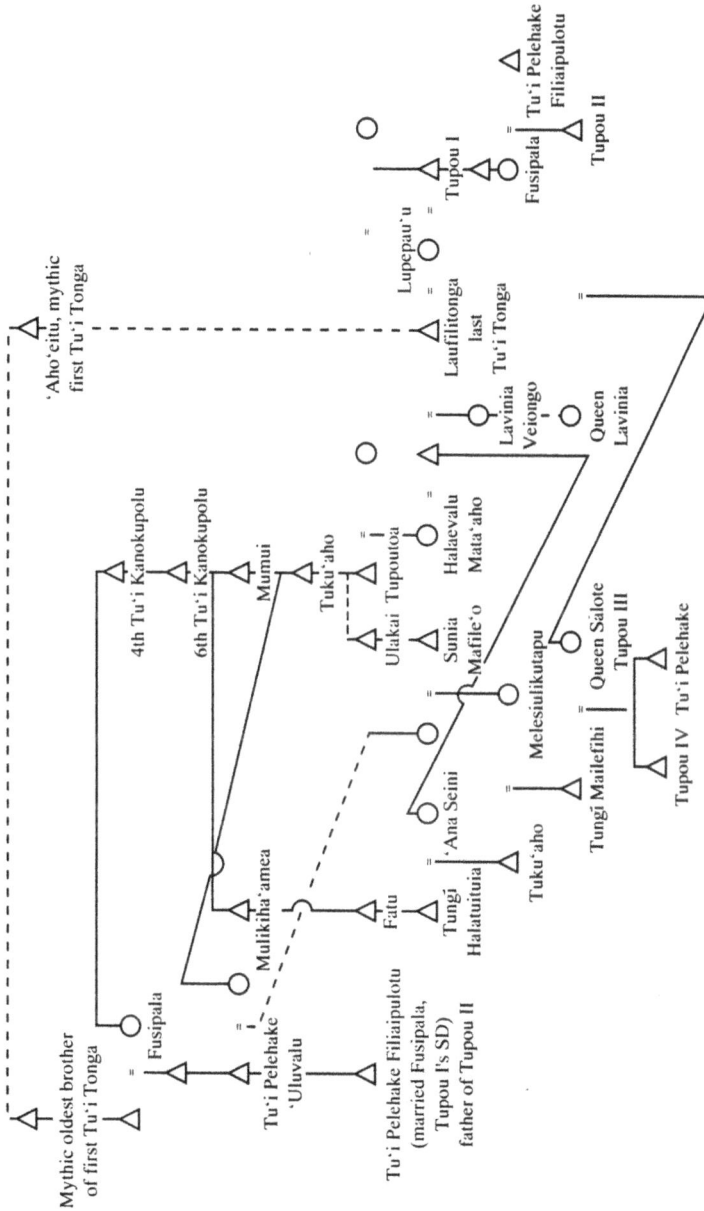

Figure 5. Genealogy of the present King (synthesized from materials in Bott (1982) and Ellem 1981)).

In the wake of the King's decision to marry Lavinia, the situation continued to be volatile.

On the day of the King's wedding, the supporters of 'Ofa carried her through the streets dressed as a bride, and they shouted the *tu* of marriage processions. For nearly a year afterwards the King and his new Queen dared not leave the grounds of the Palace for fear of personal attack. Public demonstrations occurred whenever the two factions met. The funeral of 'Ofa in 1901 was marked by rioting in the streets (Ellem 1987:214).

Opposition remained vehement. The hostility toward the King and the Queen was so strong that the King placed guards around the Palace, and the couple rarely left the Palace grounds. The houses of supporters on either side were burned. "When Lavinia died in the following year, the King buried her in the royal cemetery. Her grave was marked by a costly and ostentatious monument" (*ibid.*).

After Lavinia died, Tupou II erratically married 'Ofa's matrilateral half-sister Takip , thereby binding to himself the opposition faction, soon to be known as the King's Party. Since Sālote was Lavinia's child, once she ascended the throne her father's supporters became her enemies; and her father's daughter by this second wife, 'Elisiva Fusipala Tauki'onetuku (known as Fusipala or Fusi [Ellem 1987:215]) became her rival.

These alignments were very much intact when it came time to choosing a husband for Sālote. The person she would marry was the son's son of Tungī Halatuituia and the son of Tuku'aho: Tungī Mailefihi, who was also related to Takipō. Tungī Mailefihi's mother was Melesiu'ilikutapu, son's son's daughter of Aleamotu'a, the eighteenth Tu'i Kanokupolu. The name *mailefihi* — literally "tangled myrtle" (Gifford 1929:232) or "entwined myrtle" (Ellem 1981:129; Churchward glosses *fihi* as "tangled; figuratively, intricate, complicated, or problematical" [1959:188]) — refers to Tungī's complex genealogy (Gifford 1929:232; see Figure 5). In his person he combined the blood of the Tupou Dynasty, the Hahake Dynasty, and the Tu'i Ha'atakalaua. The marriage was arranged, some say at Sālote's birth, to compensate Tungī Halatuituia for Tupou II's not having married 'Ofa (see Ellem 1981:131; Fusitu'a 1976:99). "On hearing the 13-gun salute … that announced Sālote's birth on 13 March 1900, old Tungī had claimed her as the future bride of his twelve-year-old grandson Mailefihi" (Ellem 1981:101; see also *ibid.*:131).

The fact that Tungī Mailefihi had been Governor of Vava'u since 1912 (Ellem 1987:216) was perhaps a stumbling block to his acceptance by the 'Ulukālala Dynasty, which continued to covet that title. The King's Party had supported 'Ofa and therefore Fusipala over Sālote; and now it favoured Tungī's rival, Ha'amea, the son of 'Ulukālala Misini. 'Ulukālala Misini's supporters included those petty chiefs and *matāpule* who had been dispossessed of their customary rights by the Tupou-Baker reforms (Gunson 1979:48-49), and in this the issue of whether Sālote would marry Tungī or Ha'amea revived the contestations of the 1880s. To choose Haʻamea over Tungī would mend some fences (Ellem 1987:216). Yet this would strengthen a rival without necessarily pacifying him. And this the King did not want to do, even though he had enjoyed ʻUlukālala's support ever since having married Takipō.

When Sālote married Tungī, she strove to rejoin what had been historically rent asunder. The rift between the Hahake and Tupou dynasties had dominated much of the politics of the nineteenth century. A gesture in the direction of healing that rift had been made in 1853, when Tupou I bestowed his sister's daughter upon Tungī Halatuituia. At the time this had "placated" Tungī (Ellem 1981:68), though it did not in the long run quell his opposition to the King, as I have shown. Like his father, Tukuʻaho, Tungī Mailefihi had strong claims to the throne. (Ellem reckons that he was third in line at the time of his marriage [*ibid.*].) In choosing Lavinia over ʻOfa, Tupou II had chosen against uniting the Hahake and the Tupou dynasties, perhaps out of fear of empowering a Hahake-based opposition. The marriage of Sālote and Tungī Mailefihi was designed to effect this reconciliation. Since Tungī represented the Tuʻi Haʻatakalaua while Sālote's mother carried the Tuʻi Tonga blood (Figure 5), the fractures of the eighteenth century that had deepened in the nineteenth century would finally be healed (see Ellem 1981:59). In the 1880s, the north-south rift had been exacerbated by the controversy over Tupou I's establishment of an independent Wesleyan Church. As of 1921, Haʻapai and Vavaʻu were overwhelmingly Free Wesleyan Church while Tongatapu contained most of the Old Wesleyans (Ellem 1983:166, n.10). At the time of their marriage, Sālote "was the temporal head of one church [the Free Church], and [Tungī] the highest ranking chief in another [the Wesleyan Church]" (Ellem 1983:166). In her speech to Parliament in 1925, the year following reunion, she said: "let us give our best to unite Tonga into one happy and contented people. It is my earnest wish ..." (Ellem 1987:182).

Yet unification remained elusive. An opposition crystallized around issues of church and (state) marriage and included those who had supported ʻOfa, Fusipala, and Sālote's marriage to Haʻamea. ʻUlukālala Misini was its leader (Figure 4). As in the Muʻa Parliament affair, the antiroyal party included minor chiefs and *matāpule* whose customary land rights were denied by the Tupou-Baker reforms (Ellem 1983; 1987:217). Sālote and Tungī's attempt to merge the two churches in 1924 was opposed by Misini, who "demonstrated his continued alliance with the dispossessed chiefs by heading the dissident Free Church ..." (Gunson 1979:49). A way of dispensing with this opposition was to dispense with the title. Accordingly, the ʻUlukālala title was vacant from 1960 to 1989, when the King appointed his second-born son to the title.

The King's Body

While scholars such as Bott and Marcus have insisted upon the importance of conceptually distinguishing power from authority (Bott 1981, 1982; Marcus 1980), this distinction is effectively blurred in Phyllis Herda's "Gender, rank and power in Tonga".

> Much has been made in the literature of the lack of *pule* (authority) of the sister and the father's sister, it being claimed that, at most, she influenced her brothers and their children in their rule, but did not effectively control or influence affairs [here she cites Kaeppler 1971, Rogers 1977, and Bott 1981]. This appears, in many respects, to be an anachronistic understanding of the extent of 'influence' in traditional Tonga. Before the advent of fixed hereditary title succession which was initiated by the Constitution of 1875, title succession was fiercely competitive; in such a situation, the power to influence the choice of successor would be great (Herda 1987:197).

She goes on to elide the distinction between specifically feminine powers, the powers a woman exercises over her brother and his children, on the one hand, and the jurisdiction a chiefly titleholder exercises over people and land, arguing that "some Tongan women held politically active titles distinct from those which emphasized their sacred sister role" (*ibid.*:198-199) and concluding therefore that "chiefly women were not, categorically, denied titles or legitimate access to political power" (*ibid.*:198). Herda's test case is Tupoumoheofo.

> Tupoumoheofo's actions have been explained away by foreign observers as 'subversive', 'tyrannical' and 'odious in the extreme' and Tupoumoheofo herself described as an 'extremely ambitious, scheming woman', a 'meddling wife' and 'nothing at all to the credit of her sex'. However, it will be argued that *Tupoumoheofo's actions were in accordance with her position* and, more importantly, her rank in Tongan society and that her negative portrayal represents the European misunderstanding of female roles in pre-Christian Tonga, particularly as they related to the political sphere, rather than denoting unfeminine Tongan behaviour (*ibid.*:195; emphasis added).

I would agree with Herda that the father's sister's power to curse and a woman's ability to choose her brother's children's marriage partners are substantial powers (*ibid.*:197), and I would also concur that some women did indeed aggrandize significant power in the political arena itself. But I would have to insist upon the *transgressive* nature of Tupoumoheofo's deeds. According to the model if not the reality, in the pre-Constitutional era titleholders were not women. (This does not detract, of course, from Herda's point that Western observers judged events ethnocentrically.) Tupoumoheofo's actions were entirely transgressive — not only in terms of what she did but in terms of how she did it. Installation to the Tu'i Kanokupolu title occurs within the context of a kava ceremony attended by subordinate chiefs, who thereby display their fealty and essentially elect the titleholder on the basis of attributes such as seniority, blood rank, suitability (Biersack 1991a; Bott 1972; Valeri 1989). Though Tupoumoheofo placed her back against the *koka* tree that all Tu'i Kanokupolus placed their back against when they were installed, she could not thereby appoint herself. Herda knows this, for she writes: "No individual could simply appropriate the title, he had to be called to it" (Herda 1987:100). If indeed Tupoumoheofo did install her son as Tu'i Tonga while Tu'i Tonga Paulaho was still alive (see n.17), this act also was transgressive ("Discussions" 1:44; Bott 1982:41-42). Similarly, if her intention was to reunify the Kauhala'uta and the Kauhalalalo, the "sacred" and "working" titles, this too constituted a major violation (see Ellem 1981:61; see n.18). In fact, it could be argued that the transgressions as such were appropriate to Tupoumoheofo's position, for as *moheofo* she could operate *across* and not just within categorical boundaries (Biersack 1982 [1974]).

When King George Tāufa'āhau Tupou IV, the present king (Figure 1), ascended the throne, he was hailed as the long-awaited embodiment of the blood of all three ancient lines. Through his mother, daughter of Lavinia Veiongo, he traced descent from Laufilitonga, the last Tu'i Tonga, the Tamahā Lātūfuipeka, and the half-sister of Tāufa'āhau; through his father he traced descent from the last Tu'i Ha'atakalaua and the Tu'i Pelehake, in whom the Tu'i Tonga's kava privileges were vested and who symbolized the Tu'i Tonga and the Kauhala'uta side (*Ko e Kalonika Tonga*, June 30, 1967; see Figure 5). The title he held prior to his accession and still holds is his father's title, Tungī. His younger brother was made the Tu'i Pelehake. Now at the "summit" (*tumutumu*) of a transformed Tongan society, the present King, descendant of a nineteenth-century usurper, is the living emblem of a unity that was historically achieved through a weaving together of bloodlines.

The King's body is emblematic of the fact that in Tonga centralization is achieved historically and horizontally, through marriage, rather than structurally and vertically, through descent. This contravenes the divisions rehearsed herein: blood and garland, marriage and descent, a domain of feminine empowerment and a domain of masculine empowerment. If the present King governs *as the embodiment of the blood of the three branches* (Figure 1), then the distinction between these domains is effectively collapsed, and transgression assumes the status of an "organizing principle". My account is far more replete with examples of male transgressions than it is with examples of female transgressions. For example, whereas the father's sister theoretically chooses her brother's children's spouses, it is clear enough from this history that men exploit marriage in pursuit of their own political ambitions. As usurper, Tāufa'āhau's career was largely transgressive.

Normative sociology places structure and event in causal relationship. As a result, it can explain conformity and reproduction but not transgression and transformation. Is there a sociology consistent with the Tongan historical record?

The Tongan title system is part of an encompassing totality that turns on an axis of blood and garland. Formal analysis is thus centred upon this axis. A rule of matrilateral cross-cousin marriage would integrate and align blood and garland statuses, allowing the system as such to be operationalized. However, as Kaeppler has emphatically stated, élite marriage is a matter of choice. Matrilateral cross-cousin marriage "was not prescribed, proscribed, or preferred, but was occasionally practiced among the highest chiefs to prevent social repercussions that might result if a Tu'i were outranked by a collateral line" (Kaeppler 1971:192-193, n.25). It is therefore impossible to construe élite marriage as the mere "execution" of a rule (Bourdieu 1977:24) or as an "instantiation" of structure. Rather, Tongan élite marriage must be construed as a political tool for positioning actors across status fields. Élite marriage is always strategic — a matter of consolidating or upgrading rank and of mobilizing resources and labour in the pursuit of chosen ends. As Bott observed more than twenty years ago: "In the traditional system the object of the social and political game was to use one's standing in one system [kāinga] to increase one's standing in the other's [ha'a], marriage being one of the main devices for doing so. The process took several generations" (Bott 1972:219).

Whether a line rises or falls, élite marriage is therefore always a *practice*. But it is a practice in which the blood/garland system is fully implicated, as the ground of the practice's pragmatics and politics. Rather than suppressing time, blood/garland creates a number of *possible* futures. These futures are conservative or radical, depending upon the goals of the players and the strategies they employ. The *moheofo* institution, for example, resolves the uncertainties of the blood-garland relationship conservatively, by way of reinforcing existing status asymmetries in the title system. Thus, until a certain point, the Tu'i Ha'atakalaua, directly subordinate to the Tu'i Tonga, supplied the Tu'i Tonga with his principal wife or *moheofo* (Figure 1). Yet juniors could also withhold a sister from a senior or appropriate the senior's wife, thus altering the *status quo*. As the Tu'i Tonga title began to decline in effective power, the Tu'i Kanokupolu began sending wives to the Tu'i Tonga, just as other chiefs began sending women to the Tu'i Kanokupolu (Biersack 1982 [1974]; Bott 1981, 1982; Fusitu'a 1976:10).

Sahlins has defined the event as "a *relation* between a happening and a structure (or structures)" (1985:xiv). For Tonga the word *happening* is problematic, since it implies happenstance rather than the motivated political entrepreneurship that is so much in evidence in the Tongan historical record. I would reformulate Sahlins' definition of an event as follows: an event is a relation between a *practice* — motivated and intentional — and a system — in this case, the blood/garland system. Regardless of whether conjugal practices result in reproduction or transformation, since the system is always fully implicated in the practice as the ground of its pragmatics and its politics, practice remains "internal" but without being determined by the system.

If the relationship between practice and system is thus redefined, formal analysis acquires new powers and also new limitations. Since there is no direct, causal relationship between system and practice, formal analysis alone cannot explain behaviour. However, since the system is the ground of the pragmatics and the politics of practice, formal analysis becomes a preliminary step in understanding the field of historical action and historical action itself. Actors act out of their interests as their position stipulates these interests and by way of exploiting the possibilities for empowerment the system opens up. Historical analysis thus centres on the relation between the system and (rather than the happening) the *practice* — that is, on the event, construed as a relation between the two (cf. Sahlins 1985:vii). The resulting theory of Tongan history is at once event-centred (Biersack 1991b) and highly political. It understands actual events in terms of an actor's *possible* moves and their *political* consequences, and it is as equipped to explain moments of transformation as it is to explain moments of reproduction. This is precisely the strength, it seems to me, of Goldman's theory of status rivalry. As he argued in *Ancient Polynesian Society,* "structure … allows for shifts in power relationships, offering several leverage points for such shifts" (Goldman 1970:304-305). Structure energizes (to use Goldman's figure of speech) or motivates a field of political actors and informs their initiatives. What becomes characteristic, therefore, is *a range of practices, a historical culture* (cf. Sahlins 1985).

Attention thus shifts from structure to structuring (Giddens 1979) in the very strongest sense of the word: to activities of making and remaking. Tongans themselves speak of such activities in terms of *fa'u*. As a verb the word means "to bring into existence; to make, construct, put together; to build …; to found, institute; to formulate, draw up, making, bring in (a law, etc.) …" (Churchward 1959:147); and as a noun the word means "bringing into existence, constructing, etc.; plan, measure, or institution; thing formed or constructed" (*ibid.*). These words accent the activity of construction rather than its product; they call attention to a certain kind of agency. Integrating blood and garland in such a way as to uphold the *status quo,* the *moheofo* institution was one such *fa'u*: not a structure of alliance so much as a structuring through alliance. Whether the action maintains the *status quo* or encourages change, in either case the hierarchy of titles is generated through marriage as a *fa'u* or artefact of historical practices. The Constitution of 1875 is itself the much celebrated *fa'u* of King George Tupou I. It retained some titles, dropped others, and strategically added new ones —

the Tungī title, for example — erecting a new order of *nōpele* titles upon the ancient foundations (Biersack 1990a).

The rank of the body is a personal rank, the rank of the historical individual. The present King's body represents the totality in terms of a historical genealogy: the many acts of structuring and restructuring that the last two hundred years have witnessed. It is a *fa'u*. In and of itself it signifies the historicality of political life (cf. Valeri 1985, 1990b) and the historicity of the Tongan ramage.

References

Biersack, Aletta

1982   Tongan exchange structures: beyond descent and alliance. *Journal of the*

[1974] *Polynesian Society* 91(2):181-212. (Revision of "Matrilaterality in patrilineal systems: the Tongan case", Curl Bequest Prize Essay, R.A.I., 1974.)

1990a   Under the *toa* tree: the genealogy of the Tongan chiefs. In Jukka Siikala (ed.) *Culture and history in the Pacific*. Helsinki: Finnish Anthropological Society.

1990b   Blood and garland: duality in Tongan history. In P. Herda, J. Terrell and N. Gunson (eds) *Tongan culture and history*. Canberra: Target Oceania and the Department of Pacific and Southeast Asian History, Research School of Pacific Studies, The Australian National University.

1991a   Kava'onau and the Tongan chiefs. *Journal of the Polynesian Society* 100(3):231-268.

1991b   History and theory in anthropology. In Aletta Biersack (ed.) *Clio in Oceania: toward a historical anthropology*. Washington, DC: Smithsonian Institution Press.

Bott, Elizabeth

1958/59   Discussions with Queen Sālote. 2 vols. BSP 25.

1972   Psychoanalysis and ceremony. In J.S. La Fontaine (ed.) *The interpretation of ritual: essays in honour of A.I. Richards*, pp.205-237. London: Tavistock Publications.

1981 Power and rank in the kingdom of Tonga. *Journal of the Polynesian Society* 90(1):7-81.

Bott, Elizabeth, with the assistance of Tavi

1982   Tongan society at the time of Captain Cook's visits: discussions with Her Majesty Queen Sālote. Memoir No. 44. Wellington: The Polynesian Society.

Bott Spillius Papers (BSP)

Manuscripts and Archives Collection, New Zealand and Pacific Collection, The Library, University of Auckland, New Zealand.

Bourdieu, Pierre

1977   *Outline of a theory of practice*. Cambridge: Cambridge University Press.

Campbell, Ian

1982   The Tuʻi Haʻa Takalaua and the ancient constitution of Tonga. *Journal of Pacific History* 17:178-194.

1989   The demise of the Tuʻi Kanokupolu. *Journal of Pacific History* 24(2): 150-163.

1992   *Island kingdom: Tonga ancient and modern*. Christchurch: Canterbury University Press.

Churchward, C. Maxwell

1959   *Tongan dictionary*. Nukuʻalofa: Tonga Government Printing Press.

Collocott, Rev. E.E.V.

Miscellaneous Papers 1922-62. MS 1058:1, p.19. Alexander Turnbull Library.

Collocott, Rev. E.E.V. and Sione Havea

1922   *Proverbial sayings of the Tongans*. Occasional Paper No. 8. Honolulu: Bernice P. Bishop Museum.

Cummins, H.G.

1980   Missionary chieftain. PhD thesis, The Australian National University, Canberra.

Dumont D'Urville, J.M.

1989   *Voyage pittoresque autor du monde*. Papeete: Editions Haere Po.

Ellem, Elizabeth Wood

1981   Queen Sālote Tupou III and Tungī Mailefihi: A Study of Leadership in Twentieth Century Tonga (1918-1949). PhD thesis, Department of History, University of Melbourne.

1983   Sālote of Tonga and the problem of national unity. *Journal of Pacific History* 18(3):163-182.

1987   Queen Sālote Tupou of Tonga as Tuʻi Fefine. *Journal of Pacific History* 22(4):209-277.

Fanua, Tupou Posesi

n.d. Wistful thoughts of the past and the future, with explanatory notes (*fakamatala*) by Tupou Posesi Fanua and Wendy Pond. (Typescript in the possession of the author.)

Fox, James J.

1988   Origin, descent and precedence in the study of Austronesian societies. Public Lecture in connection with De Wisselleerstoel Indonesische Studien, given on 17th March 1988. Published, Leiden University.

1994   Reflections on "hierarchy" and "precedence". In M. Jolly and M. Mosko (eds) *Special Issue of History and Anthropology. Transformations of hierarchy: structure, history and horizon in the Austronesian world,* 7(1-4): 87-108. Chur and Reading: Harwood Academic Publishers.

1995   Austronesian societies and their transformations. In P. Bellwood, James J. Fox and D. Tryon (eds) *The Austronesians: historical and comparative perspectives*, pp.214-228. Canberra: Department of Anthropology, Research School of Pacific and Asian Studies, The Australian National University.

Fusitu'a, Eseta

1976   King George Tupou II and the government of Tonga. MA thesis, The Australian National University, Canberra.

Fusitu'a, Eseta and Noel Rutherford

1977   George Tupou II and the British Protectorate. In N. Rutherford (ed.) *Friendly Islands: a history*. Melbourne: Oxford University Press.

Giddens, Anthony

1979 *Central problems in social theory*. Berkeley: University of California Press.

Gifford, Edward Winslow

1929   *Tongan society*. Bernice P. Bishop Museum Bulletin 61. The Museum, Honolulu.

Goldman, Irving

1970   *Ancient Polynesian society*. Chicago: University of Chicago Press.

Gunson, Niel

1977   The coming of foreigners. In N. Rutherford (ed.) *Friendly Islands: a history*. Melbourne: Oxford University Press.

1979   The *Hau* concept of leadership in Western Polynesia. *Journal of Pacific History* 14:28-49.

1987   Sacred women chiefs and female "headmen" in Polynesian history. In C. Ralston and N. Thomas (eds) *Sanctity and power: gender in Polynesian history*. Special issue of *Journal of Pacific History* 22(3-4): 139-171.

Herda, Phyllis S.

1987   Gender, rank and power in 18th century Tonga: the case of Tupoumoheofo. *Journal of Pacific History* 22(4):195-208.

1988   The transformation of the traditional Tongan polity: a genealogical consideration of Tonga's past. PhD thesis, Department of Pacific and Southeast Asian History, Research School of Pacific Studies, The Australian National University, Canberra.

James, Kerry

1991   The female presence in heavenly places: myth and sovereignty in Tonga. *Oceania* 61:287-308.

1992   Tongan rank revisited: religious hierarchy, social stratification, and gender in the ancient Tongan polity. *Social Analysis* 31:79-102.

Kaeppler, A.L.

1971   Rank in Tonga. *Ethnology* 10:174-193.

Lātūkefu, Sione

1974   *Church and state in Tonga*. Canberra: Australian National University Press.

1975   *The Tongan Constitution: a brief history to celebrate its centenary*. Nuku'alofa: Tonga Traditions Committee Publications.

1977   The Wesleyan mission. In N. Rutherford (ed.) *Friendly Islands: a history*. Melbourne: Oxford University Press.

1980   The definition of authentic Oceanic cultures with particular reference to Tongan culture. *Pacific Studies* 4:60-81.

Linnekin, Jocelyn

1990   *Sacred queens and women of consequence*. Ann Arbor: The University of Michigan Press.

Māhina, 'Okusitino

1986   Religion, politics and the Tu'i Tonga empire. MA thesis, University of Auckland.

Marcus, George

1977   Succession disputes and the position of the nobility in modern Tonga. *Oceania* 47(3, 4):220-241, 284-299.

1980   *The nobility and the chiefly traditions in the modern kingdom of Tonga.* Memoir No. 42. Wellington: The Polynesian Society.

Martin, John [William Mariner]

1981   *Tonga islands: William Mariner's account*, 4th ed. [1st published London, 1817.] Tonga: Vava'u Press.

Rogers, Garth

1977   "The father's sister is black": a consideration of female rank and power in Tonga. *Journal of the Polynesian Society* 86(2):157-182.

Rutherford, Noel

1971   *Shirley Baker and the King of Tonga.* Melbourne: Oxford University Press.

1977 George Tupou I and Shirley Baker. In N. Rutherford (ed.) *Friendly Islands: a history*. Melbourne: Oxford University Press.

Sahlins, Marshall

1958   *Social stratification in Polynesia.* Seattle: University of Washington Press.

1976   *Culture and practical reason.* Chicago: Chicago University Press.

1981   *Historical metaphors and mythical realities: structure in the early history of the Sandwich Islands kingdom.* Association of Social Anthropologists of Oceania Special Publication No. 1. Ann Arbor: The University of Michigan Press.

1985   *Islands of history.* Chicago: University of Chicago Press.

Seddon, The Right Hon. R.J. (Premier of New Zealand)

1900   *Visit to Tonga, Fiji, Savage, and the Cook Islands, May 1900.* Wellington: Government Printer.

Spillius, James

n.d. Unnamed PhD thesis concerning Tonga, Samoa, and Tikopia. BSP, Box 4.

Thomas, John

1879   History of the Friendly Islands. CY Reel 446; ML A 1961, frames 92-323.

n.d. Journals.

Thomson, Basil

1894   *The diversions of a Prime Minister: life in the Friendly Islands, 1887-1891.* Edinburgh: Blackwood.

Valeri, Valerio

1972   Le fonctionnement du systéme des rangs á Hawaii. *L'Homme* 12:29-66.

1985   The conqueror becomes king: a political analysis of the Hawaiian legend of 'Umi. In Antony Hooper and Judith Huntsman (eds) *Transformations of Polynesian culture*. Memoir No. 45. Auckland: The Polynesian Society.

1989   Death in heaven: myths and rites of kinship in Tongan kingship. *History and Anthropology* 4:209-247.

1990a   Diarchy and history in Hawaii and Tonga. In Jukka Siikala (ed.) *Culture and history in the Pacific*. Helsinki: Finland Anthropological Society.

1990b   Constitutive history: genealogy and narrative in the legitimation of Hawaiian kingship. In Emiko Ohnuki-Tierney (ed.) *Culture through time: anthropological approaches*, pp. 154-192. Stanford: Stanford University Press.

1994   On female presences and absences in heavenly places. *Oceania* 65:75-93.

Wood, A.H.

1932   *A history and geography of Tonga*. Nuku'alofa: Government Printer.

Notes

[1] This paper was initially drafted while I held a grant-in-aid from the American Philosophical Society and was a Visiting Fellow with the Comparative Austronesian Project, Research School of Pacific and Asian Studies, The Australian National University. It was revised for publication in light of further research while I held a NEH Travel to Collections grant. Dr James Fox was the convener of the project. It is based in part on research I completed under grants-in-aid from the Wenner-Gren Foundation for Anthropological Research and the American Council of Learned Societies and a summer research award from the University of Oregon, all in 1986. I thank also Dr Niel Gunson and the Department of Pacific and Southeast Asian History, Research School of Pacific Studies, for a visiting fellowship in that department in January 1987. Others have also been encouraging and helpful: Tupou Posesi Fanua, Futa Helu, Adrienne Kaeppler, Sione Lātūkefu, "Okusitino Māhina, George Marcus, the late Garth Rogers, Tavi, 'Ofa Tulimaiau, Takapu, Pohiva Vaimo'unga, Valerio Valeri, and the late honourable Ve'ehala. I am indebted to Drs Fox and Sather and especially to Drs Ian Campbell and Niel Gunson for their thoughtful critiques of a prior version. I also wish to thank Richard Brown, Suzanna Layton and Clive Moore, all of The University of Queensland, for assistance in locating a key text in the eleventh hour of preparing this article for publication. Any errors of fact or interpretation remain my own.

[2] I use the word *usurper* in a rather loose sense. I do not mean to imply that Tāufa'āhau appropriated a title that another person by rights should have succeeded to. Tāufa'āhau rightly claimed the Tu'i Kanokupolu title; and since the royal title, King, was of his invention, it is impossible to argue that he illegitimately held that title. However, the King title in effect displaced the Tu'i Tonga title and it placed Tāufa'āhau, as King George Tupou I, at the top of the title system. Since Tāufa'āhau had no birth right to the "summit" (*tumutumu*) of Tongan society, in the broad sense of the word he was a usurper.

[3] The literature on ancient Hawai'i similarly emphasizes the political uses of marriage. Valeri's "Le fonctionnement du systéme des rangs á Hawaii" was the first to discuss this matter. The topic has been pursued by Sahlins (1981 and 1985), Valeri (1985, 1991) and Linnekin (1990).

[4] I hope I do not misrepresent her argument in saying that Kerry James envisions the source of status — "rank", in her terminology — as ultimately feminine (James 1992). While the Tongan polity (traditionally and yet today) is clearly religious, as James claims, to emphasize blood- and female-derived status over title, with its masculine associations, is to miss the crucial distinction between blood and garland that Tongans themselves seem to draw and which informs my argument. After all, the first Tu'i Tonga was 'Aho'eitu, a male; he was killed by his heavenly older brothers; to reward him 'Aho'eitu's father, 'Eitumatupu'a, sent him back home on earth and installed him as the first Tu'i Tonga; and to punish the brothers, the same father sent them with 'Aho'eitu to serve as his assistants and subordinates (Biersack 1991a; Bott 1972; Māhina 1986; Valeri 1989). The charter of the political system as a religious

system could be neither more patriarchal nor more focused on fraternal rivalry (see also the exchange between James (1991) and Valeri (1994)).

[5] BSP refers to the Bott Spillius Papers in the New Zealand and Pacific Collection of The Library, University of Auckland. The tripartite number scheme refers to box number, file number, and page number, respectively. These papers are a compilation of the work of three authors: primarily Elizabeth Bott (then Elizabeth Spillius), James Spillius and Queen Sālote Tupou III. During the period 1958-1960, when Bott was in the employ of the Tonga Traditions Committee, Bott interviewed Queen Sālote as their principal informant on Tongan history and culture; and Spillius did so as well, although to a lesser extent. In the two-volume compilation of interviews with Queen Sālote called "Discussions with Queen Sālote", Bott records the answers Queen Sālote principally, but also occasionally Ve'ehala, gave to her questions, as well as the questions themselves. In citing documents from this collection, where no author is designated, the author of the cited document is Bott.

[6] While Bott here associates *pule* with the juridical power of the chiefs, the power they exercised over land and people, *pule* or "authority" may refer to the authority of the father's sister as well (Lātūkefu, pers.comm.). Similarly, whereas I have distinguished the *ha'a* from the *kāinga* system, the idiom of the chief-villager relationship was an idiom of kinship (Lātūkefu, pers.comm.; 1975:9, 1980:65-66), an idiom that reflects the moral character of governance in Tonga (Biersack 1990b, 1991a; Valeri 1989, 1990a).

[7] Bott notes that Lātūnipulu is sometimes described as a male Tamahā, but dismisses the possibility. "What seems most probable is that the actual title of Tamahā was bestowed only on ... three women ..., but that there was also a less precise usage by which all the people who stood in the right relationship were called Tamahā even if the actual title had not been specifically granted to them. The evidence of Cook strongly suggests that this was so. In any case, it is clear from Cook's account that Lātūnipulu and his sisters, as well as their mother, were of higher rank than the Tu'i Tonga" (Bott 1982:35).

[8] A woman who was given as a secondary wife by her kinswoman, the primary wife of her husband, was called *fokonofo* (Bott 1982:77).

[9] However, according to Bott (1982:74, Figure 9), Makahokovalu died before succeeding to either.

[10] Ellem expresses serious reservations about the story of Tāufa'āhau withholding Halaevalu Mata'aho from Laufilitonga. She writes that this legend "presupposes that the heir of the Tu'i Tonga could only be the son of the *moheofo*, and that the Tupou Dynasty could provide the *moheofo*, although Tupouto'a [Tāufa'āhau's father] was dead" (Ellem 1981:66) and Tāufa'āhau was not yet Tu'i Kanokupolu (*ibid.*). Regardless of whether it is true, the story reveals a recognized strategy for besting a rival. According to Gunson, Tāufa'āhau's refusal to send his sister to the Tu'i Tonga was the official cause of the famed Battle of Velata (Gunson 1979:47), where Tāufa'āhau trounced Laufilitonga. It was only after Tāufa'āhau defeated the Tu'i Tonga at Velata and Tāufa'āhau was recognized as a "conqueror" or *hau* that Laufilitonga was installed as Tu'i Tonga (in 1827) and Halaevalu Mata'aho was transferred as his *moheofo* (*ibid.*).

[11] For example, the 'Ahome'e title of the Ha'a Ngata Motu'a appears to have been incorporated within the Ha'a Ngata through marriage, since the first Tu'i Kanokupolu married the daughter of 'Ahome'e, who was then a chief in the Hihifo district of Tongatapu appointed, presumably, by some other chief, the title having been transferred from one *ha'a* to another with the Tu'i Kanokupolu's acquisition of the right to appoint it (see Bott 1982:13).

[12] Writing in 1929, Gifford stated that "the late chief Tuita was spoken of as *mua 'eiki*, because his father as a navigator (*toutai*) was *matapule* and his mother, the daughter of the Tamahā Amelia, was of chiefly rank" (1929:109). Queen Sālote reinforced the perception, speaking of the Tuita title as an '*eiki matāpule* in 1958/59 ("Discussions" 2:296).

[13] Though the Tu'i Pelehake was given the special kava *tapus* of the Tu'i Tonga, he was not the titular representative of that title. That honour fell to Kalaniuvalu.

[14] *Mu'a* implies both spatial and temporal precedence; it means "front, space or place in front or further forward" and also "earlier time or period" (Churchward 1959:372). It opposes *mui*, "to be or go behind" and "back, rear, hind" and also "young, immature" and "later, second" (*ibid.*:370).

[15] Ellem merely lists Mulikiha'amea as Tu'i Kanokupolu (1981:451, Figure 2), and Bott places a question mark over the possibility of Mulikiha'amea's holding the Tu'i Ha'atakalaua title (1982:13, Figure 2). However, in a piece labelled "Tonga a Brief History" and written in Bott's hand as an appendix of a chapter to the dissertation her then husband James Spillius was writing on Tonga, Samoa, and Tikopia, Bott writes that "Mulikihaamea was the last Tu'i Ha'a Takalaua" (BSP 4/5/36). In yet another piece, "Re Feudalism", Bott speaks of Maealiuaki as the "last certain Tu'i Ha'atakalaua" (BSP 22/3), as do Fusitu'a

(1976:17), Gifford (1929:86), Gunson (1977:99, 1979:40-41 and 1987:18), and Lātūkefu (1977:115). However, Gifford also refers to Mulikiha'amea as "the last Tu'i Ha'a Takalaua" (1929:84); and Bott equivocates in her publications: "According to Tungī, husband of Queen Sālote, Maealiuaki was the last Tu'i Ha'a Takalaua, though some sources say that his son Mulikiha'amea became Tu'i Ha'a Takalaua too" (Bott 1982:64). Queen Sālote herself equivocated ("Discussions" 1:60). It has also been proposed that Mumui was at one point named Tu'i Ha'atakalaua, though Campbell does not agree (Campbell 1982:188). Herda is noncommittal on the question of whether Mulikiha'amea was ever Tu'i Ha'atakalaua (1987:203).

[16] Campbell (1989) does not acknowledge that Tu'i Halafatai, Tupoumoheofo's full brother, ever became Tu'i Kanokupolu; and he does not list his son as having succeeded either. According to Gifford (1929:88) and Wood (1932:26), Tu'i Halafatai actually was Tu'i Kanokupolu for a time but gave up the title and went to Fiji in 1782 (see also "Discussions" 1:44).

[17] Interpretations of Tupoumoheofo's apparent attempt to install her son as Tu'i Tonga while his father was still alive also vary. Herda claims that it was Paulaho himself who wished to assure the accession of his son because his own position was precarious, and Gunson now agrees that the initiative was Paulaho's, not Tupoumoheofo's (pers. comm.). Meanwhile, Campbell claims that Fuanunuiava was fully appointed Tu'i Tonga in 1795 by Mumui himself, in the interest of stabilizing the situation (Campbell 1982:186; see also Campbell 1992:39-40).

Much remains unclear about this episode. Fuanunuiava was not the first-born son and he appears not to have had his father's *moheofo* as his mother's (Herda 1987:202-203, *ibid*.:n.31; 1988:97). Herda bases this conclusion on a genealogy Niel Gunson collected in Vava'u (Herda 1988:9, n.80). Gunson tells us much more about this genealogy in his own paper "Sacred Women Chiefs and Female 'Headmen' in Polynesian History". It is "a genealogy of the descendants of [Tu'i Tonga] 'Uluakimata recorded or copied by a member of the family of the Hon. Ma'afu Tupou, governor of Vava'u" (Gunson 1987:142, n.16). He vouches for the accuracy of this genealogy in the following way: "The accuracy of this elaborate record has been confirmed by a number of tests involving cross referencing with other genealogies and with obscure documentary references for the period before 1822" (*ibid*.); but, as he also tells us, this is the only genealogy in which the name Inumofalefā, a secondary wife, rather than Tupoumoheofo is given as the mother of Fuanunuiava (*ibid*.:162, n.86). Since this "well-authenticated genealogy" (*ibid*.) agrees with no other known genealogy on this point, and it appears to disagree with all known oral tradition, perhaps its evidence, at least in this regard, is to be set aside. If, as Gunson suggests, Fuanunuiava was adopted and raised as Tupoumoheofo's own, thus accounting for the ubiquitous impression that Tupoumoheofo was his mother (*ibid*.), whether Tupoumoheofo was Fuanunuiava's biological mother becomes immaterial anyway. What Herda leaves unexplained, assuming that Tupoumoheofo was not the mother of Fuanunuiava, however, is why Tupoumoheofo's own son was not acceptable. If Paulaho had legitimacy problems, surely he would have wanted to avoid compounding them through an irregular succession in the next generation. Also, if, as Herda tells us, there was "no specific installation ceremony for the Tu'i Tonga" (Herda 1988:98), it is not clear what Paulaho accomplished in subjecting himself to the humiliation of having his own son breach the *tapus* on eating in the presence of the father.

Herda also claims that the title, presumably the Tu'i Tonga title, passed to Ma'ulupekotofa's full sister, Nanasipau'u, upon his death, Fuanunuiava acquiring the title only after his *mehekitanga* died (Herda 1987:203). Yet Bott lists Nanasipau'u as the Tu'i Tonga Fefine and not as the Tu'i Tonga (Bott 1982:33). Indeed, no other scholar has suggested that there was ever a female Tu'i Tonga, and, as I have explained, the Tu'i Tonga Fefine was not a title in the *ha'a* system.

For her part, Bott expresses confusion about the irregularity of Paulaho's succession, for his higher ranking brother, Ma'ulupekotofa, whose mother was a Tamahā and who appears to have been older, does not precede Paulaho but assumes the title only upon Paulaho's death (Bott 1982:99-100).

[18] One casualty of Tupoumoheofo's machinations was her husband, the Tu'i Tonga Paulaho. Accounts of Pau's demise vary. Some say that he was deposed because of his wife's outlandish behaviour (Gifford 1929:50; Wood 1932:26). Queen Sālote believed that Pau had voluntarily retired from the Tu'i Tongaship because Tupoumoheofo had installed her son, Fuanunuiava, while his father was still alive and this made a mockery of the title ("Discussions" 1:60; cf. Herda's interpretation 1987:201-202). Others envision Tupoumoheofo as agitating against her husband. Herda claims that she conspired with Mumui and Vuna, the Tu'i Vava'u and her son-in-law, against Paulaho (Herda 1987:206; Herda 1988:99; see also Ellem 1981:60, n.22); and Gunson also supports a conspiracy theory (1979:29, 40). Others attribute the decline of the Tu'i Tonga to Paulaho's and his son's penchant for meddling in secular affairs (Spillius n.d.: ch.5, BSP 4/3/46). Theoretically the Tu'i Tonga was a ritual rather than a political leader, the "most

sacred chief" and not the "working chief" (Biersack 1990a; Valeri 1989, 1990a); and this meddling was a clear breach of the division of labour between the sacred and the working chiefs.

[19] He also (at least in some accounts) made common cause with Tupoumoheofo and Mumui, Tuku'aho's father, in overthrowing Tupoumoheofo's husband, Paulaho (Gunson 1979:40; Herda 1987:206).

[20] These included Tuku'aho's own patrilateral half-brother Tangata-'i-Lakepa (Bott 1982:146), who apparently backed Mulikiha'amea as the next Tu'i Kanokupolu (Herda 1988:114).

[21] The 'Ulukālalas nonetheless undercut any residual power or status the Tu'i Tonga had. Fīnau 'Ulukālala-'i-Feletoa's short-lived son Moengangongo decreed after the death of Fuanunuiava in 1809 or 1810 that the Tu'i Tonga title would not be reappointed (Herda 1988:131); and Fuanunuiava was buried in an ordinary grave, a *fa'itoka* rather than a royal tomb or *langi* ("sky") (*ibid.*:131-132). Moreover, he abolished the payment of first fruits or *'inasi* to the Tu'i Tonga (*ibid.*). For historical reasons, the 'Ulukālalas did not propose to make common cause with the Vuna line either. "Rather than open conflict, Tu'i Vava'u Vuna instigated secret attacks and raids on 'Ulukālala and his supporters, while publicly entertaining them as visiting dignitaries. His intention appears to have been to undermine 'Ulukālala's ambitions by constantly reminding him of Vava'u's resistance to his rule" (Herda 1988:117).

[22] According to Queen Sālote, this is how Fatu became ensconced at Mu'a: Originally he was located in Fua'amota with his mother's people. But Tāufa'āhau sent him to Mu'a after he had defeated Laufilitonga. Fatu was appointed to guard Laufilitonga and to curb any counter-insurgency ("Discussions" 1:197).

[23] According to Fusitu'a, the naming of Tungī and heirs as being in line to succeed occurred in 1888 (Fusitu'a 1976:17-18) while according to Ellem (1987) this took place in 1885.

[24] Vuna, Tāufa'āhau's only legitimate son by Lupepau'u, had died in January 1862 (Campbell, pers.comm.); T vita 'Unga, his illegitimate son, had died in 1878; Uelingatoni Ngu Tupou Mālohi, T vita 'Unga's legitimate son, had died a bachelor in 1885; Laifone had died married but childless in 1889; and Fusipala, his daughter, had died in 1889 (Fusitu'a 1976:30).

[25] Also a possible contender was a grandson of Tupou I by a secondary wife, Mateialona. He was Tupou II's classificatory father (Ellem 1981:96). Together with the Tu'i Pelehake and Sāteki Tonga (later Veikune), also associated with the Kauhala'uta, he encouraged Tupou II to marry Lavinia.

[26] Herda questions the accuracy of the story about Tuapasi's bequest of the Tu'i Vava'u title on his deathbed. "In 1833, Tāufa'āhau assumed the rule of Vava'u claiming that on his deathbed. Tuapasi had passed his authority to his *uho taha* ... until his own son was of a ruling age. Interestingly, Tuapasi's last testament was not recorded by any of the European missionaries present at his death, but did appear in the papers of Thomas who was a staunch supporter of Tāufa'āhau. Significantly, Tuapasi's son was never named as Tu'i Vava'u nor as Fīnau 'Ulukālala" (1988:134).

[27] According to Queen Sālote, the original marriage plans for Uelingatoni Ngu Tupou Mālohi, first-born son of Tupou I's son by Fusima Taliti and who was Tupou I's lawful successor after T vita 'Unga died in 1879 — was to have married the daughter of Lavinia Veiongo and 'Inoke, so that the original intention was to merge Tu'i Kanokupolu and Tu'i Tonga blood, but these plans aborted because Ngu died in 1885; and even though his younger brother married Lavinia Veiongo's daughter, there were no offspring ("Discussions" 1:164).

Chapter 13. The Politics of Marriage and the Marriage of Polities in Gowa, South Sula Wesi, During the 16th and 17th Centuries

F. David Bulbeck

The Wider Background

The traditional political systems of the Malay and Bugis worlds, northern Sumatra and Java, produced a high frequency of female rulers by world standards (Reid 1988:169-172). Nonetheless the élite titles in these systems still tended to be inherited patrilineally even though very different descent principles, usually bilateral but even matrilineal, operated within society as a whole (e.g. Gullick 1958; Palmier 1969; de Josselin de Jong 1980:10; Millar 1989:25). Fox observes that élite patrilinealism within a bilateral system is only one variant, albeit the most common, of a widespread tendency for Austronesian élites to claim a separate origin from commoners and follow a distinct and socially exclusive descent system. These devices allow the élite to maintain precedence over restricted resources, and characterize societies which have undergone consolidation after an earlier phase of lateral expansion (Fox 1995). Moreover, as this paper will show in the case of the Makassar state of Gowa, the élite were further advantaged by a selective adoption of the kinship system prevalent in society as a whole. So even though the highest Makassar posts were held almost exclusively by patrilineal descendants, bilateral kinship principles (notably the real or symbolic transfer of authority through related women) underpinned the central position of the highest status individuals within society, and guaranteed the resilience of the system as a political entity.

As recorded ethnographically the Makassar and the Bugis, South Sulawesi's two main ethnic groups, share a very similar social organization. Both are organized into overlapping sets of bilateral kindreds rather than sharply demarcated descent groups. Individuals can choose their particular affiliation, resulting in the crystallization of discrete networks of (usually) related individuals. Postmarital residence can be either virilocal or (more usually) uxorilocal, the spouses retain membership within their natal group, and the children enjoy homologous relationships with the families of both parents. While the flexibility allows the ready incorporation of newcomers, the communities maintain their stability through physical and occupational propinquity and some measure of endogamy. An individual's behaviour is also strongly constrained by his or her status which is largely ascriptive, especially for women who, in the rôle of (principal) wife, mark the status attained by the more socially mobile men (Chabot 1950; Millar 1989; Acciaioli 1989).

The ascription of status is best described with reference to traditional, pre-twentieth century Bugis-Makassar society, since some of the social divisions have been formally abolished even if the effects still persist in more conservative areas (Röttger-Rössler 1989:28 ff.). Society was traditionally stratified into aristocrats, commoners and slaves. The aristocracy and its various ranks consisted of those who could trace their origins to the supposed founders of the Bugis-Makassar kingdoms, the white-blooded *Tomanurung*. In theory aristocrats were ranked by the degree to which their white blood, as traced through both parents, remained undiluted by the red blood of commoners; access to titles depended on nobility of birth, and only pure descendants reserved the right to rule a kingdom (Friedericy 1933; Mukhlis 1975; Acciaioli 1989). Despite the essentially bilateral manner of ascribing status, a patrilateral bias clearly existed, at least among the Makassar (Röttger-Rössler 1989:42-43; Mukhlis 1975:37-38).

Now, bilateral descent principles can readily generate a nobility through marriages between royalty and commoners, but clearly the origins of the white-blooded royalty must stand outside the bilateral network — hence *Tomanurung*, the descended one(s). In some cases this external derivation indeed occurred, as for example recorded with the Konjo Makassar living at Kasepekang in the Gowa highlands. In the late nineteenth century a lowland Gowa aristocrat called Daeng Bunding married into the Kasepekang nobility and was installed as *Karaeng*. The Kasepekang *Karaeng* and other prominent nobles now trace a real or fictional genealogical closeness to Daeng Bunding through his three official wives (Röttger-Rössler 1989:38-40). The observation by Rössler (1987:66), that the Kasepekang *Karaeng* descent group traces itself to a heavenly princess comparable to the *Tomanurung* who supposedly began the Gowa royal line, presumably hinges on this Daeng Bunding.

Moreover, the existence of pure white-blooded royals presupposes either a quantity of original *Tomanurung* amounting to a breeding population or massive inbreeding within the royalty. But neither was true of the Makassar rulers who instead clearly referred to their patriline as the critical pedigree defining purity of descent. The relevant ethnographic analogy comes from the Kasepekang Konjo whose élite regulate their membership through bilateral descent groups (*pattola*) consisting of the descendants of the ancestral holder of a hereditary title. Theoretically eligible candidates for the title, in practice men, are individuals either belonging to the *pattola* or married to a woman within the *pattola*. However, at any point in time, the core of the *pattola* lodges with the title holder and his sons (Rössler 1987:64-66). The prerogative of the noblest Kasepekang Konjo, to apply the strictest criteria for admission into the pure nobility

(Röttger-Rössler 1989:43), combined with the patrilateral bias in the ascription of status, would appear to legitimize the usual patrilineal succession of noble titles.

Nonetheless the principle of bilateral descent is an equally intrinsic part of the Kasepekang system. It provides the flexibility which has allowed occasional lateral movements of titles in response to political machinations and individual aptitudes. We have already mentioned the case of Daeng Bunding who, as a prominent outsider, cemented his central position by marrying widely into the Kasepekang nobility (Röttger-Rössler 1989). The bilateral ideology also encourages potential title holders to strengthen their eligibility by marrying women close to the core, generating the endogamy towards the core which maintains the distinctiveness of the lineage. Marriages between equals belonging to different *pattola* are also sanctioned, reinforcing the social distance between nobles and commoners, and the attachments of the lesser *pattola* to the central *pattola* associated with the highest title of *Karaeng*. Last but not least the bilateral ideology retards the fissioning of descent groups so that the nobility in general, and each *pattola* according to its prestige, hold a central position within the social network (Rössler 1987:66-67).

Gullick (1958) documented a similar organization on a larger scale for the Malay peninsula states, leading him to coin the description "status lineages" in contradistinction to the classical patrilineal "segmentary lineages" of the Nuer. As Fox (1971) demonstrates for the Rotinese, a patrilineal society combining deep genealogical knowledge among the nobility and "genealogical amnesia" among the commoners can also generate status lineages which place individuals within an overarching social hierarchy. Fox (1995) generalizes further by noting that Austronesian societies ruled by a high élite typically present "apical demotion systems". These systems continually reassess the comparative status of lines and their members depending on which line, and ultimately which member, holds the most prestigious title. This individual represents the apical point against which other lines (and their members) automatically lose status unless they can curtail their genealogical distance (Fox 1995). In the Kasepekang system, patrilineal descent acts as the usual criterion for succession to the apex, while bilateral descent both holds the other lines to the apex and allows movement towards (or even usurpation of) the apical point.

The present paper summarizes my analysis (Bulbeck 1992) of the Makassar texts, covering the sixteenth and seventeenth centuries, which describe the rise and fall of the Gowa empire. The analysis shows that Gowa's sociopolitical organization was elaborated on the basic principles described for the Kasepekang Konjo. The elaborations concern Gowa's annexation of previously autonomous territories, the development of an overarching hierarchy incorporating sets of titles of distinct origins, and the creation of a high royalty both distinct from but binding the lesser social echelons. All in all, expanding political power was associated with the ability to attract well-born brides, absorb previously independent titles and assure patrilineal succession of the lineage's own titles, while decreasing political power was associated with the reverse. Furthermore the system showed a remarkable ability to legitimize political change.

Background to Gowa

The people generically called the Makassar occupy the far south of South Sulawesi (Sulawesi's southwest peninsula). They speak three related languages — Konjo and Selayar in the east, and Makassar proper in the west (Grimes and Grimes 1987). The lowlands support generally denser populations than those found in the Bugis heartland to the immediate north, even though the latter region contains South Sulawesi's most extensive wet rice lands. Indeed, South Sulawesi's southwest corner between Gowa and Sanrabone (see Map 1) holds rural population densities comparable to those in Java and Bali. The coastal strip, rich in maritime and littoral resources, backs against extensive alluvial plains which are ideal for *sawah*. Irrigation schemes first developed by the Dutch permit double cropping and hence higher populations in favoured areas. Nonetheless the traditional annual *sawah* cultivation, based on the very pronounced monsoon, also supported hundreds of thousands of people by the seventeenth century, with densities apparently reaching towards 1000 people per square kilometre (Bulbeck 1992).

Two major trade routes from Java lay along the south coast by at least the fourteenth century. One route extended via Selayar to the spice islands, and the other extended to Luwuk with its nickeliferous iron and other valuable primary produce (Caldwell 1988). Selayer, Luwuk, plus Bantaeng and Makassar along the south coast, are the only identifiable South Sulawesi toponyms mentioned in the Majapahit literature. Selayer, Luwuk and the south coast are also the parts of South Sulawesi evincing the strongest Javanese influence (Reid 1983; Bulbeck 1992). The origins of the Bugis kingdom of Luwuk specifically invoke Majapahit (Caldwell 1988), while the founder of the Makassar kingdom of Sanrabone was reportedly an immigrant from north Majapahit (Bulbeck 1992).

The Bugis agrarian kingdoms show the reverse constellation of traits — absence from the Majapahit literature, little direct Javanese influence, and *Tomanurung* with explicitly local, Bugis origins. However, far from having been a cultural backwater, by c. 1400 AD this area had apparently developed the first South Sulawesi scripts. The resulting texts show that the Bugis heartland supported the largest fourteenth-century kingdoms in South Sulawesi, and probably the oldest kingdoms as well (original study by Caldwell [1988] as interpreted by Bulbeck [1992]).

Map 1. "Lineage groups" (capitalized) and other key places.

Granted the general dichotomy between maritime kingdoms with their external orientation and occasional claims to foreign origins, and the locally oriented agrarian kingdoms, Gowa combines the two. Gowa's origins are ascribed to the marriage between a mortal called Karaeng Bayo or the "Bajau King", and a heavenly nymph who descended on a hill within Gowa's rice fields (Reid 1983). Although dressed up as legend the origin story appears to reflect a real historical memory, to judge from the concordance between the archaeological and genealogical data. At c. 1300 AD a Bajau chief, based at the river mouth port which later became Sanrabone, apparently married a Katangka (pre-Gowa) princess of Makassar ethnicity to give rise to Gowa's royal line (Bulbeck 1992).

By around 1500, when a detailed picture emerges of South Sulawesi's southwest corner (see Map 1), the near-coastal agrarian kingdoms dominated the small trading communities based at the river mouths. For instance, after a succession dispute within Gowa the defeated faction moved to the mouth of the Tallok River, overpowered the local inhabitants and established the kingdom of Tallok. In the same vein Gowa, Tallok and Siang successively conquered Garassik, then a small port-polity named after Gresik (north Java) but containing a significant Bajau component. After finally wrestling back Garassik by the 1540s, Gowa developed its demographic and geographical advantages to dominate South Sulawesi's long distance trade. In a series of sweeping military campaigns, Gowa raided other polities throughout the peninsula, and directly conquered the kingdoms from Maros in the north to Bajeng and Katingang in the south (Bulbeck 1992).

In 1593 Tallok instigated a palace revolution whereby the area conquered by Gowa now supported a confederation of powerful status lineages. While the Gowa royalty formally headed the larger political umbrella, which I call "greater Gowa", leadership often resided with Tallok. For instance it was the Tallok raja who adopted Islam in 1605 and established political hegemony throughout the South Sulawesi peninsula under the banner of Islam. The individual in question, Sultan Abdullah, also developed the *entrepôt* of Makassar to the point where greater Gowa rivalled the Dutch East India Company (VOC) for control over the Moluccan spice trade (Andaya 1981). Makassar grew so large during the mid-seventeenth century that its population can be estimated at 100,000 inhabitants, and its status as a major rice exporter during the early seventeenth century changed to one of major rice importer (Reid 1987).

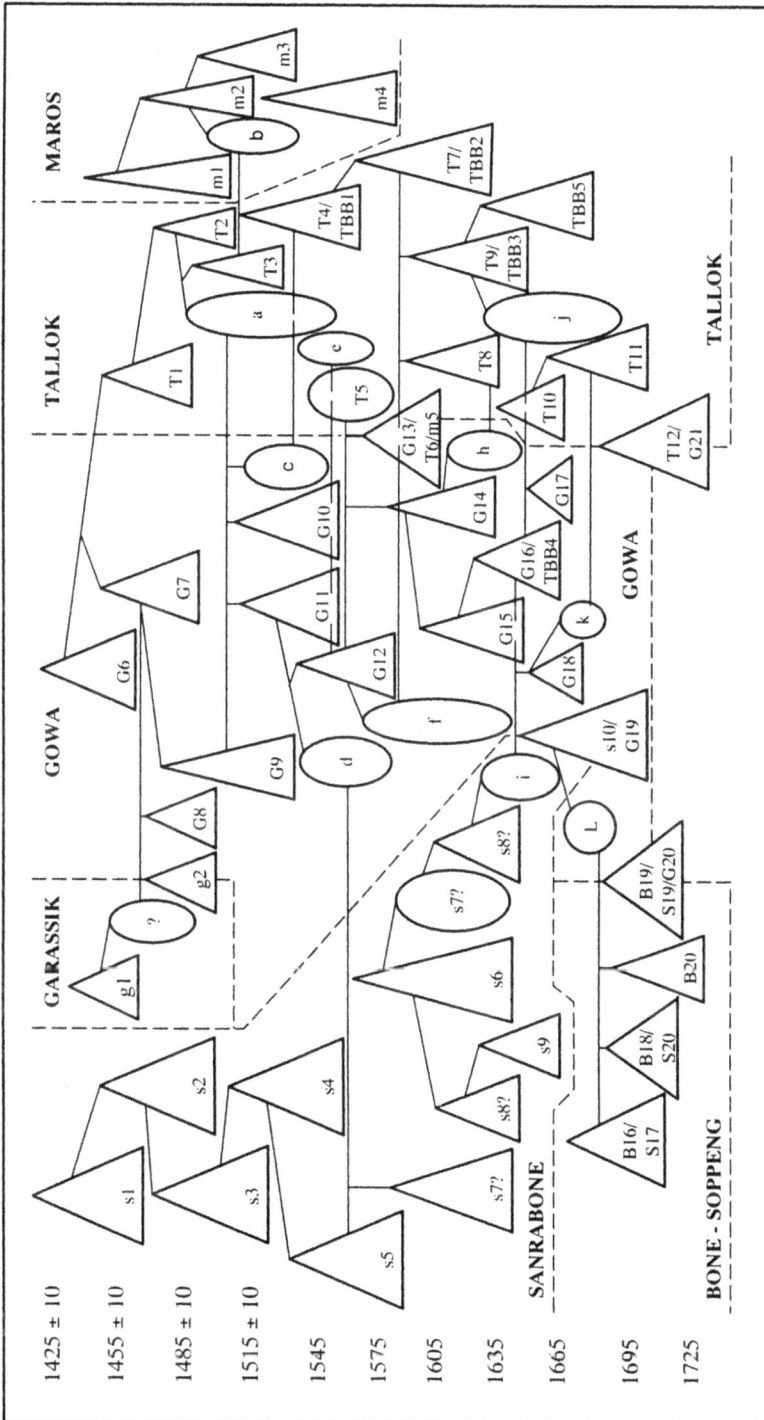

Figure 1. Skeletal genealogical outline of royal Makassar history.

SANRABONE:

s1 = Karaeng Pancabelong; s2 = Tunijallok ri Pakrasana; s3 = Karaeng Massewaya; s4 = Tonibasara; s5 = Tumenanga ri Parallekkena; s6 = Tumenanga ri Campagana; s7?(left) = Karaeng Bambanga; s7?(right) = Karaenga I Pucu; s8?(left) = Tumenanga ri Buttana; s8?(right) = Karaeng Banyuanyarak; s9 = Puanna Jenalak; i = Petak Daeng Nisali.

BONE-SOPPENG:

B16/S17 = Alimuddin; B18/S20 = Sulaiman; B20 = Abdullah Mansyur; B19/S19/G20 = Ismail.

GARRASIK:

g1 = Somba Garassik.

GOWA:

G6 = Tunatangkaklopi; G7 = Batara Gowa; G8 = Tunijallok ri Passukik; g2 = Karaeng Barataua Karaeng Garassik; G9 = Tumapakrisik Kallona; G10 = Tunipalangga; c = Karaenga Somba Opu; G11 = Tunibatta; G12 = Tunijallok; d = Karaeng Mapekdaka; f = Tuniawanga ri Kalassakanna; G13/T6/m5 = Tunipasuluk; G14 = Alauddin; G15 = Malikussaid; G16/TBB4 = Hasanuddin; G17 = Amir Hamzah; G18 = Muhammad Ali; s10/G19 = Abdul Jalil; k = Karaeng Parang-Parang; l = Karaeng Pattukangang.

TALLOK:

T1 = Karaengloe di Sero; T2 = Tunilabu di Suriwa; T3 = Tunipasuru; a = Karaengloe Bainea; T4/TBB1 = Tumenanga ri Makkoayang; T5 = Karaeng Bainea; e = Karaeng Batu-Batu; T7/TBB2 = Abdullah; T8 = Mudhaffar; T9/TBB3 = Mahmud; TBB5 = Karaeng Karunrung; j = Raja Perempuan; T10 = Harrunarasyid; T11 = Abdul Kadir; T12/G21 = Sirajuddin.

MAROS:

m1 = Karaengloe ri Pakerek; m2 = Karaeng Loeya; m3 = Tuamenanga ri Bulukduaya; b = Tumamaliang ri Tallok; m4 = Tunikakassang.

Legend to Figure 1

In 1667 the Bone noble Arung Palakka (later Sultan Sahaduddin) and his Bone and Soppeng Bugis rebels joined forces with the VOC and defeated greater Gowa during the battle known as the Makassar War. The new overlords then divided up greater Gowa's empire while retaining Makassar as South Sulawesi's effective capital. In this new arrangement the VOC superintended Makassar's trade, while Sahaduddin settled in Makassar to rule South Sulawesi's internal affairs (Andaya 1981; Bulbeck 1990).

Methodology

My primary database consists of five texts, available as translations into Indonesian, which stemmed from the development of a Makassar literary tradition during the early sixteenth century. These texts are called *lontarak* after the palm-leaf strips on which the first texts were composed and copied, a name which persists despite the adoption of paper by at least the seventeenth century (Cense 1966). They include the "chronicles" of Gowa (Wolhoff and Abdurrahim n.d.) and Tallok (Rahim and Ridwan 1975) which describe the succession of Gowa and Tallok rulers. A royal diary (Kamaruddin *et al*. 1985-86) has sporadic entries up to 1630 and numerous entries thereafter. Finally, two short texts (Bulbeck 1992) chart the Maros and Sanrabone dynasties.

While these texts do not always provide self-explanatory information, ambiguities could generally be resolved as a result of earlier research on the Makassar texts (e.g. Mukhlis 1975), scholarly studies of the coeval Bugis (e.g. Caldwell 1988) and European records (e.g. Andaya 1981), and my archaeological survey of Gowa (Bulbeck 1986-87, 1992). A very detailed picture emerges of the "Who's Who" of the Makassar world during the sixteenth and seventeenth centuries, allowing the analysis of social organization through statistically demonstrable associations. This paper presents only the most important results and accordingly I restrict the methodological discussion to the main points.

To start with, many individuals accumulated titles during life or even received a posthumous name, making it necessary to collapse the recorded names into the minimum number of clearly discrete individuals. E.g. if a person was named "Daeng x Karaeng y", and the "Daeng x" who carried out certain acts could not be clearly distinguished from the "Karaeng y" who carried out other acts, then I assigned both sets of acts to the one life history of "Daeng x Karaeng y". This procedure was facilitated by constructing genealogical diagrams which attempted to situate individuals and their marriages in real time (e.g. Figure 1). For statistical purposes the only relevant individuals are adults, here defined as those individuals who cannot be shown to have died before reaching marriageable age. Definite sub-adults were excluded, firstly because they would not normally have attained their expectable titulation, and secondly because Gowa's "bureaucratic" posts were held only by adults. I then extracted those individuals who could be paired with some adult next-of-kin of known sex and title —

whether as spouses, full siblings or parent-offspring. To these 545 individuals I added a further 14 individuals, of unknown genealogical links, who held a "bureaucratic" post (Bulbeck 1992). Various subsets of these 559 individuals can then be employed according to the topic under review.

The skeletal royal genealogy shown here (Figure 1) is incomprehensible unless the reader takes the time to understand my conventions. The symbols for individuals are stretched between upper and lower points which represent dates of birth and death. Marriages are shown by horizontal lines whose vertical position marks when the marriage occurred. (Note that Figure 1 does not distinguish between recorded dates and my estimates.) Sometimes the spouses could not be juxtaposed and so the "lines of marriage" cross symbols standing for other individuals, as indicated by the horizontal lines which intrude into a symbol from either side. Individuals resulting from a depicted marriage are joined by a vertical line to the line of marriage. When only one parent is depicted, descent is shown by slanting lines, including slanted bifurcations for full siblings.

Secondly, my analysis relating marriage strategies to political change will use the concept "lineage group" (see Map 1). These "lineage groups" constitute a heuristic device for dividing up the world of socially significant individuals as seen from the vantage of the Makassar royalty. The term is deliberately ambiguous to accommodate status lineages within a descent group, descent groups, and aggregates of descent groups.

Makassar Titles and Their Wider Equivalents

To understand greater Gowa's socio-political organization we should first describe the Makassar titulation system (Bulbeck 1992; cf. Mukhlis 1975 and Röttger-Rössler 1989:45-46).

A. *Areng kale* — the personal name or birth name.
B. *Areng padaengang* — the "Daeng" title, virtually the highest title which a commoner could receive but bestowed on aristocrats at an early age. Rarer variants denoting a comparable status include the "Kare", "Lokmok" and "Gelarang" titles.
C. *Areng pakkaraengang* — the "Karaeng" title. This distinctly aristocratic title could be translated as "chief". Bugis equivalents included the "Arung" and "Datu" titles.
D. Lesser raja titles. I use the term "raja" to distinguish the main chiefs who exercised authority over a body of lesser chiefs. Even the lesser rajas (or petty royalty) were recognized, at least theoretically, as independent white-blooded rulers by the major kingdoms. Some lesser rajas were distinguished by their titles, e.g. the Bugis *Ratu* who ruled Bulo-Bulo, and the sixteenth century Makassar entitled *Karaengloe* ("great chief"), *Somba* and *Tumakgauka*. Other lesser rajas belonged to historical dynasties, e.g.

Sanrabone, Maros (Bulbeck 1992), Siang (Pelras 1977), Agongnionjok (Kallupa 1984), the "Limae Ajattappareng" confederation (Caldwell 1988), and Laikang (cf. Kamaruddin *et al*. 1985-86:169; Andaya 1981:128, 137).

E. Greater raja titles. Three royal families — Luwuk, Gowa and Tallok — became formal sultanates after voluntarily embracing Islam at the beginning of the seventeenth century. Gowa's lesser allies, Sanrabone and Bulo-Bulo, did not become sultanates, indicating a distinction between the major and the lesser pro-Gowa royalty. As for the three major Bugis agrarian kingdoms — Bone, Soppeng and Wajok — they initially eschewed the title of sultan for their ruler, presumably as a reaction to their forced conversion to Islam. But the Bone and Soppeng rulers were undoubtedly on a par with the sultans as shown by their triumph in the Makassar War.

Prior to Islamization, great Makassar rulers were distinguished by a nickname ("Tu-" or "person", followed by a passive verbal form) commemorating some highlight of their reign. All of the late fifteenth to late sixteenth Gowa rulers received such a nickname (apart from the deified Batara Gowa), as did some Tallok, Maros and Sanrabone rulers (Figure 1). Analogously the Makassar royal diary nicknames Bone's Sultan Sahaduddin as "Tunisombaya" (Kamaruddin *et al*. 1985-86). The only other person remembered by a nickname was Tuniawanga ri Kalassakanna, the main wife of Sultan Abdullah, the latter arguably the highest status Makassar man who ever lived.

The greater rajas, then, are the sultans, the rulers of Bone and Soppeng, and the nicknamed individuals. The sultans also include, further afield, the seventeenth century rulers of Bima and Sumbawa (Noorduyn 1987).

F. *Tumenanga* — the posthumous name. From at least the sixteenth century various prominent Makassar individuals received a posthumous name which usually indicated where they had died. These posthumous names reflect historical prominence rather than socially sanctioned status (Bulbeck 1992) and are not relevant here.

The Makassar titles were incremental, with duplications of titles as well as higher titles reflecting enhanced status. E.g. Sultan Abdullah's full name was "Palakkaya I Malingkaeng I Daeng Mannyori Karaeng Matoaya Karaeng Kanjilo Karaeng Segeri Sultan Abdullah Awalul Islam Tumenanga ri Agama Tumenanga ri Bonto Biraeng" (Rahim and Ridwan 1975:14-15; Wolhoff and Abdurrahim n.d.:70). To take a Bugis example, Sahaduddin's full name was "La Tenritatta Datu Mario ri Wawo Daeng Serang Arung Palakka Petta Malampéké Gemmekna Tounruk [Tunisombaya] Sultan Sahaduddin Matinroe ri Bontoalak" (Andaya 1981:43-44).

The Makassar titles were often associated with place names within or near my archaeological survey based in Gowa. Only one individual occupied any toponymic title at any time, apart from occasional instances of husbands and wives holding the same title. The frequency of toponymic association helps to elucidate the titles, as can be shown by taking every title associated with every Makassar individual within my database (see "Methodology", p.288) — e.g. Abdullah (Daeng Mannyori Karaeng Matoaya Karaeng Kanjilo Karaeng Segeri Sultan Tallok) counts as five titles. The "Gelarang" title is idiosyncratic, so we first consider the other titles shown in Table 1.

Table 1. Percentages of Makassar titles linked with toponyms

	Males	Females	Both Sexes
Gelarang (6,0,6)	100.0	-	100.0
Kare (11,17,28)	0.0	5.9	3.6
Daeng (95,106,201)	14.7	22.6	19.9
Lokmok (0,23,23)	-	26.1	26.1
Karaeng (138,91,229)	86.2	80.2	83.8
Lesser Raja (26,5,31)	100.0	60.0	93.5
Greater Raja (23,1,24)	100.0	0.0	95.8

N.B.   The first figure inside the brackets shows the number of male titles, the second figure shows the number of female titles, and the third figure shows the total cases. The Gelarang title departs from the usual pattern (see text).

Several associated trends emerge. The higher the title, the greater the proportion of male titulars, and the more frequent the association with a toponym. Analogously, whereas women held lesser titles in association with a toponym more frequently than men did, this relationship was reversed with the Karaengs. Not only that, but all of the male rajas ruled a kingdom while half the female rajas were honorary recipients.

Essentially, a lesser toponymic title merely linked the individual with some community. Take for instance the "Lokmok" title, which was typically associated with women of common origin who had acquired status as the secondary wife of a raja and other high status man. All but one of the six associated toponyms (cf. Table 1) refers to some wife of a Tallok raja and falls within the area which he ruled (Bulbeck 1992). (Male Lokmok are not relevant here, because their next-of-kin were never recorded and none held a "bureaucratic" post.)

Toponymic karaengships, on the other hand, identified the chiefs of land-holding communities in the most densely populated areas. Thus Mukhlis (1975:42-44, 64) states that the community was required to provide its Karaeng with a suitable residence, manpower and the necessities of life. While the number of female Karaengs rivalled the number of male Karaengs, the former were associated with smaller karaengships such as places within palace centres, and never with the largest and most populous karaengships such as Garassik and Galesong (Bulbeck 1992).

The Gelarang present a complementary pattern. Originally these were the nine district headmen who represented the Gowa populace in its dealings with the raja, and constituted Gowa's highest council of customary law (Mukhlis 1975). However, by the mid-sixteenth century a distinction had emerged between the "inner Gelarang" (Mangasa and Tombolok) and the "outer Gelarang". The former were important officials who represented districts which also supported Karaengs, while the latter represented the wider area which provided Gowa's surplus produce and deepest reservoir of manpower (Bulbeck 1992).

During the mid-sixteenth century Gowa also developed an exclusively male "bureaucracy" of non-territorial posts, as detailed by Mukhlis (1975) and Bulbeck (1992). The most important was the regency or *Tumabicara Butta* (TBB in Figure 1). Several regents were also rajas, and the long-serving regents all became greater Gowa's real authority. The other posts were originally held by prominent commoners, but over time tended to be occupied by Karaengs. The *Tumailalang* or Ministers for Internal Affairs were members of the central court who mediated between Gowa's council of customary law and the central court. The *Tumakkajannangngang* or guildmaster headed the guilds which were responsible for specialist crafts (e.g. construction and weaponry) and certain designated duties. The harbourmaster was responsible for maintaining the security of the Makassar *entrepôt* and collecting port duties.

Gowa (and later greater Gowa) thus had a male-dominated socio-political structure linked across four substructures. The Gelarang represented a system of agrarian administration which was in place before Gowa's expansion. The "bureaucrats" belonged to a state-sponsored administration postdating Gowa's initial expansion. The lesser territorial chiefs (toponymic Karaengs) managed greater Gowa's ongoing manpower requirements, usually but not necessarily under the immediate jurisdiction of a raja. Individuals belonging to one or more substructures were ranked within a single status hierarchy by means of the Makassar titulatory system.

This status hierarchy could be extended to titled individuals from non-Makassar polities by recognizing where they would rank within the Makassar system. Accordingly foreign dignitaries could be received properly and suitable marriages arranged with non-Makassar élite individuals.

Correlations in Titulation Across Next-Of-Kin

The interrelationship between nobility of birth and access to titles can be explored by comparing titulation across next-of-kin. Here we consider the 545 Makassar and non-Makassar adults who could be paired with some next-of-kin of known sex and title (see "Methodology"). After ranking the individuals according to the highest title accredited to them in the records, we have 264 males and 281 females distributed across the titulatory ranks as shown in Table 2. The systematic bias against women in the titulatory stakes is even clearer here than in Table 1.

Table 2. Cross-tabulation of titles against sex

		Males	Females	Both Sexes
Rank 1	(Greater Rajas)	44	1	45
Rank 2	(Lesser Rajas)	35	6	41
Rank 3	(Karengs)	119	87	206
	/ Daengs + Gelarang	39	79	118
Rank 4	— Kare	9	13	22
	\ Lokmok	0	18	18
Rank 5	(Untitled)	18	77	95
Total		264	281	545

To compare titles across next-of-kin, we could use those shown in Table 2. But to avoid the unnecessary multiplicity of categories, we pool the titles into the broader ranks of rajas, Karaengs and non-chiefs (Tables 3-1 to 3-8). Ten main points result.

1. Sons attained the rank of their father or a lesser rank, but a higher rank in only 4/155 cases (Table 3-1).

2. Therefore the great majority of rajas belonged to unbroken royal patrilines (see Figure 1), and the great majority of male Karaengs were sons of rajas or male Karaengs.

3. Daughters generally attained a rank lower than their father's (115/138 cases), and attained a higher rank in only one case (Table 3-2).

4. Therefore the great majority of female Karaengs were daughters of rajas (Table 3-2).

5. Sons usually attained the rank of their mother or a higher rank, and a lower rank in only 10/103 cases (Table 3-3).

6. Ranks were equally distributed across mothers and daughters, with a weak tendency for mothers and daughters to hold the same rank (Table 3-4).

7. Brothers' ranks show virtually no correlation (Table 3-5).

Table 3. Comparisons of titulation across next-of-kin

		Raja	Karaeng	Non-chief	Sum
3-1. FATHER IS					
S					
O	Raja	54	2	0	56
N	Karaeng	30	36	2	68
	Non-chief	17	12	2	31
I					
S	Sum	101	50	4	155
D	**3-2. FATHER IS**				
A		Raja	Karaeng	Non-chief	Sum
U					
G	Raja	5	1	0	6
H	Karaeng	54	10	0	64
T	Non-chief	27	34	7	68
E					
R	Sum	86	45	7	138
	3-3. MOTHER IS				
		Raja	Karaeng	Non-chief	Sum
S					
O	Raja	8	13	13	34
N	Karaeng	4	12	30	46
	Non-chief	2	4	17	23
I					
S	Sum	14	29	60	103
D	**3-4. MOTHER IS**				
A		Raja	Karaeng	Non-chief	Sum
U					
G	Raja	0	2	2	4
H	Karaeng	7	26	19	52
T	Non-chief	0	14	29	43
E					
R	Sum	7	42	50	99
	3-5. BROTHER IS				
B		Raja	Karaeng	Non-chief	Sum
R					
O	Raja	18	19	7	44
T	Karaeng	19	18	12	49
H	Non-chief	7	12	10	29
E					
R	Sum	44	49	29	122
	3-6. BROTHER IS				
		Raja	Karaeng	Non-chief	Sum
S					
I	Raja	1	0	0	1
S	Karaeng	30	22	12	64
T	Non-chief	3	25	10	38
E					
R	Sum	34	4 /	22	103

		3-7. SISTER IS			
S		Raja	Karaeng	Non-chief	Sum
I	Raja	0	1	0	1
S	Karaeng	1	30	8	39
T	Non-chief	0	8	24	32
E					
R	Sum	1	39	32	72
		3-8. HUSBAND IS			
W		Raja	Karaeng	Non-chief	Sum
I					
F	Raja	7	2	0	9
E	Karaeng	49	50	2	101
	Non-chief	76	76	43	185
I					
S	Sum	132	128	45	305

N.B. In these tables the summed figures show the number of cases of reconstructible relationships, not the number of individuals involved in the comparison. The latter figure is less than the former except for offspring who of course could have no more than one parent of any sex (Tables 3-1 to 3-4).

8. Sisters mostly attained a rank lower than their brothers', and a higher rank in only 12/103 cases (Table 3-6).

9. Sisters tended to attain the same rank (Table 3-7); indeed, as can be demonstrated through formal statistical analysis (Bulbeck 1992), no other next-of-kin showed such strong titular correlation.

10. Wives were either ranked below or at the same level as their husband, and in only 4/305 cases did women marry a lower ranked man (Table 3-8). This holds despite the high divorce rate which, along with the frequency of marriages noted in the royal diary (Kamaruddin et al. 1985-86) between individuals who are otherwise absent from the records, and the practice of élite polygyny, explains why so many marriages are on record. (While Tables 3-1 and 3-8 suggest 132 wives for 56 male rajas, and 128 wives for 68 male Karaengs, these totals understate the level of élite polygyny. This is especially true for the rajas, many of whose wives went unnamed or were even noted as too numerous to list.)

It is formally impossible that Tables 3-1 to 3-8 could describe a closed system. As fathers, and to a lesser degree as husbands, rajas figure prominently, Karaengs figure less prominently, and non-chiefs hardly at all. Yet as sons and as brothers these three categories are similarly represented. This paradox rests on two points. Rajas usually had many more wives (often of common origin) than the male Karaengs did, and hence more offspring. Undoubtedly, also, male Karaengs had more wives and offspring than male non-chiefs did. But the supporting evidence is unavailable because the genealogical records hardly mention male non-chiefs except in their capacity as sons of high status men. This brings us to the second point; regardless of their birth, men who did not attain karaengships exited beyond the pale of genealogical significance. And many well born sons failed to earn high titles, explaining the lack of correlation between brothers' titles.

The strong correlation between sisters' titles agrees with the ethnographic observation that women's titles were strongly ascribed by birth. This might appear to support the idea that women (as principal wives) tended to mark the status which the husband attained, and that individuals inherited their nobility (and hence their access to titles) fairly equally from both parents. But the highest status, royal titles were usually restricted to patrilineal descendants, even if the mother's birth helped to rank candidates' chances. Furthermore women were systematically demoted compared to their male next-of-kin, so an equality of titles between sisters had only loose implications for their husbands' or sons' titles. All in all, statistical analysis shows that the father's title was between two to three times more influential than the mother's, regardless of the sex of the offspring (Bulbeck 1992).

Horizontal Links Between the Royal Cores

While marriages were closely linked with political solidarity and alliance, political considerations often changed rapidly and flexible marriage strategies had to be followed. One component of this flexibility derived from the systematic demotion of women's status, so that even princesses could marry a wide range of aristocrats. The other component stemmed from the Makassar's eschewal of prescriptive or preferential marriage, as indicated by the enormous sweep of consanguineal relationships which, from my database, can be reconstructed between wives and their related husbands.

Far more relationships trace their closest common ancestor through step siblings born of a single polygynous man (Table 5) than to a conjugal pair (Table 4). Since divorces occurred frequently, we might expect that some of the consanguineal spouses shared, as their single closest common ancestor, a woman who mothered children to different men; but I could not find any examples. Both points emphasize the structural importance of noble and especially royal polygyny.

Because almost all male rajas belonged to an unbroken royal patriline, a mala raja rarely married a related woman unless their closest common ancestry involved one of the raja's royal forefathers. 28/55 of the marriages between recorded relations were of this type. The royal forefather was two generations back on both sides in 13 cases and no more than three generations back on either side in 23 cases. That is, the royal lines frequently intermarried (Figure 1) to maintain their position as the ruling class distinct from the nobility. Men removed from a royal core could strive to marry a raja's daughter, but the enhancement of their own prospects then became dependent on the authority of the daughter's royal core. The Malay ruling class maintained its central position in the same way (Gullick 1958).

Table 4. Relationship of wife to her related husband (where a conjugal pair forms the closest common ancestors)

HUSBAND IS WIFE IS	Raja Raja	Raja Karaeng	Raja Daeng	Raja Untitled	Karaeng Karaeng	Karaeng Daeng	Karaeng Untitled	Sum
FZD & MBD		2						2
FZD	1	2					1	4
MBD		1		1				2
FBD		1	1		2	1		5
FBSD	1							1
FFBD		1						1
FFBSSD		1						1
MFMBSD			1					1
FFFZSDSD			1					1
Sum	2	8	3	1	2	1	1	18

N.B.   The "FZD & MBD" relationship involved three common grandparents.

Table 5. Relationship of wife to her related husband (closest ancestry traced via step siblings)

HUSBAND IS WIFE IS	Raja Raja	Raja Karaeng	Karaeng Raja	Raja Daeng	Raja Untitled	Karaeng Karaeng	Karaeng Daeng	Karaeng Untitled	Sum
FFDD & MFSD						1			1
FFDD						1			1
MFSD		1		1		2		1	5
FFSD				1		1		1	3
MFDD				1					1
FFFSD							1		1
FFSDD							1		1
FFSSD	1								1
FFDSD		1				1			2
FFDDD		1							1
FMFSD				1			1		2
FFFSSD						1			1
FFFSDD						1			1
FFFDSD	1			1					2
FFFDDD		1			1				2
FMFSSD						1			1
FMFSDD				1				1	2
FFFSSSD			1						1
FMFSSSD		1							1
MFFDSSD						1			1
FFMFSSSD						2			2
FFMFSSDD				1				1	2
FMFFDSSD						1			1
FMFFDSSSD						1			1
Sum	2	5	1	7	1	14	3	4	37

N.B.   "FS" stands for father's son's, i.e. step-brother's, and "FD" stands for father's daughter's, i.e. step-sister's. The "FFDD & MFSD" relationship involved two polygynous grandfathers as the equally closest common ancestors.

Makassar Status Lineages

To summarize the foregoing, male patrilines constituted the vertical structure within Makassar aristocratic genealogical space. Women of various origins entered into the structure with increasing frequency towards the top. The superfluous proportion of well-born sons were banished from contention. The daughters generally entered into élite marriages, creating horizontal links within the genealogical space. But these horizontal links supported rather than bound the men at the top of the hierarchy.

Table 6. Status and patrilineality of male-dominated posts

| | TITLE HOLDER IS: | | | | % WHO WERE SONS OF TITLE-HOLDING FATHER |
	Greater Raja (%)	Lesser Raja (%)	Karaeng (%)	Nonlord (%)	
Gowa Raja (n = 15)	100	0	0	0	86.7
Tallok Raja (n = 11)	81.8	18.2	0	0	81.8
Maros Raja (n = 4)	50.0	50.0	0	0	75.0
Sanrabone Raja (n = 9)	27.3	72.7	0	0	88.9 or 55.6 (see below)
Regent (n = 7)	42.9	0	57.1	0	42.8
Tumailalang (n = 14)	0	0	85.7	14.3	26.7
Guildmaster (n = 4)	0	0	50.0	50.0	25.0
Harbourmaster (n = 12)	0	0	16.7	83.3	0

N.B.   These figures ignore inaugural occupants who obviously could not have inherited the post from their father. Statistics for the Makassar thrones are taken from Figure 1, and count Batara Gowa (G7) as a "greater raja". The last three seventeenth century regents, and Gowa's other non-territorial administrators, are not shown in Figure 1 but are documented elsewhere (Bulbeck 1992).

Thus the Makassar élite practised a type of apical demotion which depended structurally on patrilinealism and polygyny as élite privileges. To see how privileged this patrilinealism was, consider the very strong association between the status of a title (as measured by the status of the title holders) and the degree to which the title was inherited patrilineally (Table 6). Far from being a principle which included related individuals within a descent group, patrilineal descent was used by a higher status lineage specifically to exclude related men whose father belonged to a lesser lineage.

Just because a man was barred from membership within status lineages higher than his father's, this did not guarantee him automatic membership within his father's status lineage. On the contrary, apical demotion involves the continual reassessment of "ascribed status" depending on achievement. A man who failed to earn the required status lost his (potential) natal membership and either started a new status lineage or married into a lesser status lineage.

To take the example of the sons of a Gowa (or other Makassar) raja, any son who failed in the succession concurrently lost any direct claim on the title for his sons, and so began a new patriline. Therefore the only men included in a royal status lineage are those belonging to the patriline of rajas, including all the installed brothers.

Furthermore, any man who failed to attain a karaengship virtually guaranteed that his descendants would be banished to genealogical insignificance. So the only men included in a noble status lineage linked to the Gowa royal line are those who can trace a direct line of male Karaengs back to the son of a Gowa raja. They could also have traced an ambilineal line of ancestry into other lineages, but this would have been pointless since the Gowa royalty constituted the highest status Makassar lineage. We would also expect the Gowa nobility to exclude from their ranks any nobles directly descended from lines inferior to Gowa's, and this expectation is confirmed by the genealogical distribution of the major noble titles (Figure 2).

Where do women fit into a genealogical system based essentially on men's titles? For two reasons I assign women to their father's status lineage even if the mother's was higher. Firstly, the father's title was the major influence on the offspring's title irrespective of gender, and the systematic demotion observed in the opposite-sex next-of-kin comparisons held true between brothers and sisters. Secondly, the notion that women should marry at their own level or upwards implies that the husband enjoyed either equal or greater authority.

It is not even necessary to assume that daughters left their father's status lineage upon marriage. Indeed the frequency of divorces, and the occasional instances of women marrying within their own status lineage (Bulbeck 1992), suggest that many women never did. However, the offspring were born within their father's status lineage, either as potential members in the case of boys, or as members to be strategically married in the case of girls. This and the other points discussed above will become clearer during the description of my 17 "lineage groups" (see Map 1) and the associated status lineages.

Makassar Lineage Groups

Gowa Core. All of the sixteenth and seventeenth century Gowa rajas (plus their daughters).

Gowa Nobility. All of the Karaengs (plus their daughters) patrilineally descended from a Gowa raja. Whether we consider them a single status lineage or a group of closely related status lineages is irrelevant. The important point is that their fortunes closely followed those of the Gowa royalty (see below).

Tallok Core. All of the sixteenth and seventeenth century male Tallok rajas, plus their daughters (including Tallok's only queen), but excluding Tunipasuluk (G13/T6/m5 in Figure 1) who belonged to the Gowa core. Tallok's origins would make Tallok a branch within the Gowa nobility (Figure 1) except that the Tallok core constituted an independent line of rajas.

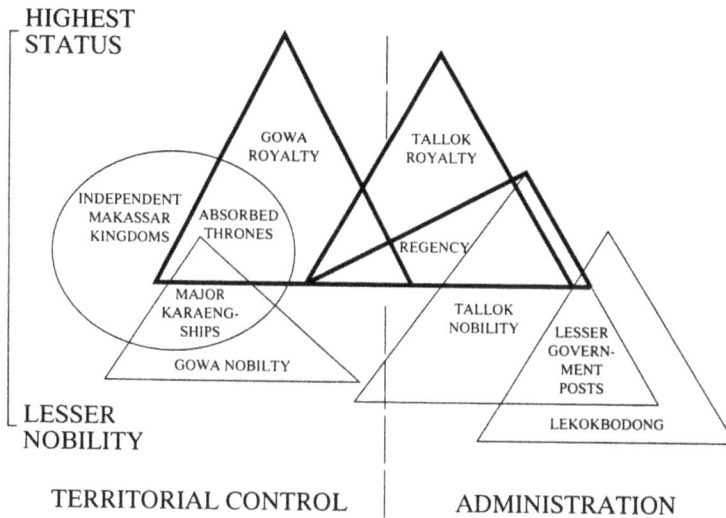

Figure 2. Schematic representation of Greater Gowa's organization.

Tallok Nobility. See "Gowa Nobility" above.

Gelarang. Previously I had discussed the Gelarang in relation to Gowa, but a similar arrangement also existed in Tallok. The texts occasionally mention marriages involving the families of the Gowa or Tallok Gelarang. These are pooled into a "Gelarang" group for convenience since I have no data on their descent principles.

Garassik. The earliest detailed Makassar historical accounts identify Garassik as a former port-polity which had been reduced to a patch of prime real estate by the early sixteenth century (see "Background to Gowa"). Garassik first lost its independence after an unnamed daughter ("?" in Figure 1) of Somba Garassik (g1) married Batara Gowa (G7) and gave birth to a Gowa noble who later ruled Garassik (g2, i.e. Karaeng Barataua Karaeng Garassik). Before losing its independence Garassik was also involved in some other marriage exchanges (Table 7). After the late sixteenth century the Garassik karaengship came to be held by one Tallok noble and various Gowa nobles.

Polombangkeng. Polombangkeng had consisted of an umbrella of seven "brother kings" headed by Bajeng and including Jamarang, Mandallek, Katingang, Jipang, Sanrabone and Lengkesek. The west Polombangkeng members — Katingang, Jipang, Sanrabone and Lengkesek — were punished by Gowa during the mid-sixteenth century for having earlier assisted Tallok's unsuccessful attempt to retake Garassik from Gowa (Bulbeck 1992). At around this juncture Jamarang, Mandallek and Katingang were also involved in documented marriages with Gowa and with certain local Makassar karaengships. Circumstantial evidence suggests that these three Polombangkeng polities then supported patrilineal cores, even if they were also attached to Bajeng as their central royal line (Bulbeck 1992).

Sanrabone. Although originally one of the west Polombangkeng polities humiliated by Gowa in the mid-sixteenth century, in the late sixteenth century Sanrabone rose to fill the power vacuum created by the demise of Bajeng. Sanrabone retained its prominence until the death of Tumenanga ri Campagana (s6 in Figure 1) in 1642. The next two Sanrabone rulers died within five years, amidst such chaos that two quite different successions appear equally possible from the records (Bulbeck 1992). In one interpretation, rulership first passed to Campagana's full brother Karaeng Bambanga (s7?), and then patrilineally from Campagana to his son Tumenanga ri Buttana (s8?) and grandson Puanna Jenalak (s9). In the other interpretation rulership passed to Campagana's daughter Karaenga Pucu (s7?) and to her son Karaeng Banyuanyarak (s8?) before passing back to Puanna Jenalak (s9). Anyway, Puanna Jenalak was expelled in 1658. After an interregnum lasting a decade, Karaeng Campagaya (later Sultan Abdul Jalil), the son of Gowa's Sultan Hasanuddin (G16/TBB4) by the daughter of Karaeng Banyuanyarak, was installed as Sanrabone's raja (Figure 1). Hitherto Sanrabone had supported a royal patrilineal core, even if chaos in the 1640s conceivably led to some irregular appointments and ultimately to Sanrabone's absorption by Gowa.

Minor Makassar. The records are dotted with references to marriages involving local Makassar nobility or petty Makassar royalty not descended from the major lines (Bulbeck 1992). These include Anak Sappuk, Bangkala, Kasuarrang, Bungaya, Beroanging, Laikang, Batu-Batu, Pattung and seventeenth century Mandallek (Map 1), as well as three which cannot be unambiguously located (Paria, Pabolik and Bontomanaik). I have only the sketchiest data on the succession to these karaengships, none of which forms a cohesive unit of analysis by itself. They can be pooled for present purposes.

Pattekne. The title of Karaeng Pattekne recurs throughout the records and so Pattekne stands apart from the other minor noble Makassar lines. From the late sixteenth century the title was held by men, apparently not descended from the major lines, who furthermore held one stream of the *Tumailalang* posts until the mid-seventeenth century (Bulbeck 1992).

Maros. The short dynasty of autonomous Maros rulers, plus their daughters (Figure 1). The last of the dynasty, Tunikakassang (m4), reportedly had no offspring. He died an old man and so probably outlived anyone else within the core. When the Gowa king Tunijallok defeated Maros during Tunikakassang's reign, he struck a treaty whereby Tunijallok's descendants would rule Maros while Tunikakassang's "descendants" (presumably his nephews and their descendants) would hold the post of Gowa *Tumailalang*. Tunijallok's son

Tunipasuluk (G13/T6/m5) briefly occupied the Maros throne before Tallok's palace revolution expelled him in 1593 (Bulbeck 1992).

Lekokbodong. After Tunipasuluk, Maros failed to recover its former status as an independent kingdom. But a status lineage or group of related lineages based in Maros apparently gained major factional status within greater Gowa. A clutch of men held the recurring karaengships of Cenrana and Lekokbodong, as well as one and later two streams of the *Tumailalang* posts. Where it can be followed, the succession of these titles resembles the succession of the Kasepekang titles (cf. Rössler 1987 and Röttger-Rössler 1989). Kamaruddin *et al.* (1985-86) retain the name "Maros" for this noble house, but I prefer "Lekokbodong" to distinguish it from its predecessor.

Minor Bugis. Various minor Bugis kingdoms were fleetingly involved in marital exchanges recorded in the Makassar texts (Bulbeck 1992). They are Siang (c.1500), Suppak and Lamuru (sixteenth century), Segeri (early seventeenth century) later called Agongnionjok (late seventeenth century), and Siang, Barru, Sawitto and Sidenreng (late seventeenth century).

Bulo-Bulo. Also a minor Bugis kingdom, Bulo-Bulo had a special status owing to its location due south of Bone. Greater Gowa and its allies propped up Bulo-Bulo as a means of containing any southward expansion by Bone (Bulbeck 1992).

Luwuk. During greater Gowa's period of hegemony in South Sulawesi affairs, two of the major Bugis kingdoms, Luwuk and Wajok, were allied with Gowa. Only Luwuk is considered here because Wajok fails to appear in the genealogical records (Bulbeck 1992).

Soppeng/Bone-Soppeng. Prior to 1667 Gowa took a few wives from Soppeng (Bulbeck 1992). Bone and Soppeng jointly spearheaded the 1667 assault on Makassar, after which point Bone set about absorbing the Soppeng rulership (Bulbeck 1990). So for our purposes Bone and Soppeng can be grouped for the period after 1667, and made to include the major Bone "Arung" (Maroanging, Tanete and Teko) and Soppeng "Datu" (Belo).

Eastern Indonesia. Bima and Sumbawa, as well as some nearby kingdoms, were defeated at various times by greater Gowa between 1616 and 1626. After some revolts in the early 1630s, Bima and Sumbawa entered into regular marriages with the various factions of greater Gowa from 1646 onwards. The only recorded bride exchange involving Ternate occurred in 1672 when I Asseng, a daughter of Malikussaid (G15), married the Ternate sultan (Bulbeck 1992). All of these data are here grouped into "Eastern Indonesia".

Having defined our lineage groups, we can now relate the politics of élite marriage to (greater) Gowa's political history. While the categories "wife givers" and "wife takers" are inappropriate for the Makassar system (Fox pers.comm.), nonetheless we are still dealing with groups of related men who perpetuated their status lineage by attracting wives from other groups of related men. Marriage strategies can therefore be shown by cross-tabulating the father's and husband's lineage groups. Chronologically the marriages can be grouped according to the three major phases of Gowa's history during the sixteenth and seventeenth centuries (Tables 7 to 9).

Gowa's Initial Expansion (c.1500-1593)

In the early sixteenth century Gowa was merely one of the chiefdoms located in South Sulawesi's southwest corner. After the mid-sixteenth century Gowa expanded southwards to incorporate the northern two-thirds of Polombangkeng. When Tunipasuluk (G13/T6/m5) briefly occupied the Tallok and Maros thrones between 1590 and 1593, he commanded the largest area ever directly ruled by Gowa.

Until 1593 the great majority of the recorded marriages involved Makassar polities, and one Bugis polity (Siang), located within the southwest corner of South Sulawesi. The notable rôle played by the (Gowa) Gelarang highlights the restricted geographical range of the marriages (Table 7). True, four royal and noble women from Bugis kingdoms north of Siang married Gowa royalty (Table 7), but no offspring resulted (Bulbeck 1992).

Most of the marriages which I recorded between close relatives descended from a conjugal pair (Table 4) resulted from the series of royal marriages between Gowa and Tallok during the early to middle sixteenth century (see Figure 1). These marriages bound the fortunes of the Gowa and Tallok royalty, but at Tallok's peril since the number of princesses provided by Tallok was not reciprocated by Gowa (Table 7). When the Tallok raja Tumenanga ri Makkoayang (T4/TBB1) died in 1577, his only adult descendants were two daughters both married to the Gowa raja Tunijallok (G12). (One of the daughters, Karaeng Batu-Batu [e], may have already died, but this does not affect the argument.) Unless Tallok were to install an immature incumbent, the throne had to pass to a wife of Tunijallok. The woman appointed, Karaeng Bainea (T5), produced nine offspring but little evidence of government independent from her husband (Bulbeck 1992). Tallok was no longer in the position to exclude these offspring from the Tallok core on the basis of lacking patrilineal membership, because Tallok had become a lesser status lineage compared to Gowa. Consequently the first born son of Tunijallok and Karaeng Bainea, Tunipasuluk, claimed the Tallok throne while patrilineally inheriting the Gowa throne.

The growing status of the Gowa royalty compared to Tallok is clear from the number of brides taken by the Gowa royalty, accounting for over half of the marriages between lineage groups (Table 7). Moreover the Makassar lineage groups which produced rather than attracted wives came to fall within Gowa's domain. These include Garassik, an early source of brides; and Jamarang and Katingang (here included within Polombangkeng) which had provided Gowa with several royal brides. In contrast Sanrabone and Pattekne attracted wives and survived as status lineages into the seventeenth century (Tables 7 to 9).

The Golden Period of Greater Gowa (1593-1667)

Greater Gowa's heyday began in 1593 when Karaeng Matoaya (T7/TBB2), or Abdullah as he was later called, instigated the palace revolution which expelled Tunipasuluk. Because his father had been Gowa regent as well as king of Tallok (Figure 1), Abdullah had a direct claim both on Tallok and the regency. His fellow conspirators also joined the confederated power structure which blossomed particularly during the mid-seventeenth century reigns of Malikussaid and Hasanuddin (Reid 1987; Bulbeck 1992).

During the period, marriages involved a wide geographical range of lineage groups (Table 8), reflecting greater Gowa's expanded sphere of political influence. Included are Gowa's eastern Indonesian allies of Bima and Sumbawa, and Gowa's Bugis allies on the east coast, Bulo-Bulo and Luwuk. The Gelarang now hardly figured at all.

Greater Gowa's decentralized power structure is clearly reflected in the marriage patterns. The Gowa, Tallok and Lekokbodong nobilities now took a prominent part, while the frequency of daughter exchanges between the Gowa royalty and other lineage groups was reciprocal overall. Indeed the Tallok royalty provided rather than attracted wives; and by the end of the period the rulers of Gowa (Hasanuddin) and Tallok (Harrunarasyid) both had mothers whose common origin is revealed by their "Lokmok" title.

Sanrabone lost its independence during this period. Sanrabone had attracted wives during the reigns of Parallekkena (s5) and Campagana (s6), but then provided wives leading up to and during the period of chaotic succession in Sanrabone discussed above. This change is not apparent from the figures in Table 8 which are aggregated to reflect the political situation in greater Gowa rather than Sanrabone. Note that the Gowa prince who absorbed the Sanrabone throne, s10/G19 (later Sultan Abdul Jalil), was either the matrilateral grandson or matrilateral great grandson of a Sanrabone raja (depending on how we interpret Sanrabone's mid-seventeenth century succession). He could claim the Sanrabone throne based on his descent from a woman either right within or one step removed from the royal Sanrabone core.

The Survivors (Post-1667)

Our third period began when Bone and Soppeng, the two important Bugis kingdoms which suffered most under greater Gowa, joined forces with the VOC. The allies occupied Makassar in 1667 and destroyed Gowa's *entrepôt* palace of

Somba Opu in 1669. In 1677 the Bone leader Sultan Sahaduddin finally snuffed out all resistance when he occupied Gowa itself. Until his death in 1696, he continued to combine diplomacy and thuggery in monopolizing power within South Sulawesi affairs to an unprecedented degree. Sahaduddin himself was childless but before his death chose a successor in his nephew Alimuddin, who along with his offspring maintained Bone's pre-eminence in local politics until the mid-eighteenth century (Andaya 1981; Bulbeck 1990).

After the Makassar War, greater Gowa virtually ceased attracting women from external status lineages and instead provided wives (Table 9). Greater Gowa's Bugis ally, Bulo-Bulo, which was immediately absorbed by Bone after the Makassar War (Andaya 1981), falls in the same pattern. The Bugis kingdoms which greater Gowa had previously dominated, some of whom had also provided greater Gowa with wives, now married greater Gowa's daughters (Table 9). In accordance with Sahaduddin's pre-eminence, Bone was dominant, but Soppeng, Siang, Agongnionjok, Sawitto and Sidenreng also drew wives from greater Gowa. So did the eastern Indonesian sultanates, now including Ternate.

Marriage patterns within greater Gowa reflect the reorganization of its internal power structure. The Gowa royalty and nobility provided wives while the Tallok royalty and especially Lekokbodong attracted wives. The Tallok nobility was especially active in both spheres (Table 9). The last point identifies the Tallok nobility as greater Gowa's "power broker", a rôle centred on Karaeng Karunrung (TBB6 in Figure 1) who was then the regent and the single most powerful Makassar man. Thus after the Tallok sultan Harrunarasyid fled in the wake of Gowa's 1677 military debâcle, Karaeng Karunrung managed to maintain the royal Tallok patriline by installing the boy sultan Abdul Kadir (Andaya 1981; Patunru 1983).

Gowa's eclipse and the rise of Tallok and Lekokbodong reflect the specializations of the various factions within greater Gowa. As detailed elsewhere (Bulbeck 1992) territorial control was primarily the province of Gowa, whereas the noble administrative posts were mostly vested in Tallok and Lekokbodong (Figure 2). The Makassar War and its aftermath grievously diminished the area under greater Gowa's jurisdiction, but without simplifying greater Gowa's administration (Bulbeck 1992). Consequently Gowa had become largely redundant to the survival of an organization whose strength now lay in its capacity to accommodate the new territorial overlords, Bone and the VOC.

Table 7. Sixteenth Century Marriages Between Lineage Groups

Father's Lineage Group	Gowa Core	Gowa Nobles	Tallok Core	Garassik	Gelarang	Polombankeng	Sanrabone	Minor Makassar	Pattekne	Maros	Minor Bugis	Soppeng	TOTAL
						Husband's Lineage Group							
Gowa Core	2	2	3	0	0	1	1	1	0	1	0	0	11
Gowa Nobility	0	0	0	0	0	0	0	0	0	0	0	0	0
Tallok Core	7	0	0	0	0	0	0	0	0	0	0	0	7
Garassik	1	0	1	0	1	0	0	0	0	0	0	0	3
Gelarang	2	1	2	0	0	0	0	0	0	0	0	0	5
Polombangkeng	6	0	1	0	0	0	0	3	1	0	0	0	11
Sanrabone	0	0	0	0	0	0	0	0	0	0	0	0	0
Minor Makassar	1	0	0	0	0	1	0	0	0	0	0	0	2
Pattekne	0	0	0	0	0	0	0	0	0	0	0	0	0
Maros	0	0	1	0	0	0	0	0	0	0	0	0	1
Minor Bugis	2	0	1	0	0	0	0	0	0	0	0	0	3
Soppeng	2	0	0	0	0	0	0	0	0	0	0	0	2
TOTAL	23	3	9	0	1	2	1	4	1	1	0	0	45

Table 8. Marriages Between Lineage Groups c.1593-1667

Father's Lineage Group	Husband's Lineage Group														
	Gowa Core	Gowa Nobles	Tallok Core	Tallok Nobles	Gelarang	Pattekne	Lekokbodong	Sanrabone	Minor Makassar	Bulo-Bulo	Luwuk	Minor Bugis	Soppeng	Eastern Indonesia	TOTAL
Gowa Core	0	2	1	3	0	1	1	1	2	1	0	0	0	2	14
Gowa Nobility	1	0	0	0	0	0	0	0	0	0	0	0	0	0	1
Tallok Core	4	0	0	0	0	0	2	1	1	0	0	0	0	1	9
Tallok Nobility	1	1	1	1	0	0	0	0	0	1	1	0	0	0	6
Gelarang	1	0	0	1	0	0	0	0	0	0	0	0	0	0	2
Pattekne	0	1	0	0	0	0	0	0	0	0	0	0	0	1	2
Lekokbodong	1	1	0	2	0	0	0	0	1	0	0	0	0	0	5
Sanrabone	2	0	1	0	0	0	0	0	0	1	0	0	0	0	4
Minor Makassar	3	0	0	1	0	0	0	0	0	0	0	0	0	0	4
Bulo-Bulo	0	0	0	0	0	0	0	0	0	0	0	0	0	0	0
Luwuk	0	1	0	0	0	0	0	0	0	0	0	0	0	0	1
Minor Bugis	0	0	0	0	0	0	0	1	0	0	0	0	0	0	1
Soppeng	0	1	0	0	0	0	0	0	0	0	0	0	0	0	1
Eastern Indo.	1	0	0	1	1	0	0	0	0	1	0	0	0	0	4
TOTAL	14	7	3	9	1	1	3	3	4	4	1	0	0	4	54

Table 9. Post-1667 Marriages Between Lineage Groups

Father's Lineage Group	Husband's Lineage Group											
	Gowa Core	Gowa Nobles	Tallok Core	Tallok Nobles	Lekokbodong	Minor Makassar	Bulo-Bulo	Luwuk	Minor Bugis	Bone-Soppeng	Eastern Indonesia	TOTAL
Gowa Core	0	0	1	2	2	2	0	0	3	4	2	16
Gowa Nobility	0	0	0	1	1	0	0	0	1	0	0	3
Tallok Core	0	0	0	0	1	0	0	0	1	1	1	4
Tallok Nobility	2	0	1	4	2	1	0	0	2	5	0	17
Lekokbodong	0	1	1	0	0	0	0	0	0	2	1	5
Minor Makassar	1	1	0	1	1	1	0	0	0	1	0	5
Bulo-Bulo	0	0	0	0	0	0	0	0	0	0	0	1
Luwuk	0	0	0	0	0	0	0	0	0	0	0	0
Minor Bugis	0	0	0	0	0	0	0	1	0	0	0	0
Bone-Soppeng	0	0	0	0	0	0	0	0	0	1	0	1
Eastern Indo.	0	0	1	0	0	0	0	0	0	0	0	1
TOTAL	3	2	4	8	7	4	0	1	7	14	4	54

The rot set in Gowa's succession when Hasanuddin (G16/TBB4) abdicated after the destruction of Somba Opu. His chosen successor, Amir Hamzah (G17), died in 1674. Amir Hamzah's half brother, Muhammad Ali (G18), was expelled following Sahaduddin's occupation of Gowa in 1677. Stability was restored only when Muhammad Ali's full brother, Abdul Jalil (s10/G19), accepted Gowa's reduced status as the necessary price (Bulbeck 1990).

Furthermore, Hasanuddin's three successors either died as young adults or were constrained from taking many wives. They produced few children, none of them a son who survived to maturity (Figure 1). Amir Hamzah was childless. Muhammad Ali left two daughters, one of whom (Karaeng Parang-Parang, "k") married the Tallok Sultan Abdul Kadir (T11) and gave birth to Tallok's Sultan Sirajuddin (T12/G21). Abdul Jalil's only mature child, Karaeng Pattukangang (1), married Sahaduddin's chosen successor Alimuddin (B16/S17). As the (adopted) son of a Soppeng female raja, Alimuddin later absorbed the Soppeng rule. His three sons by Karaeng Pattukangang serially ruled Bone, and two also came to rule Soppeng (Bulbeck 1990).

When Abdul Jalil died in 1709, Hasanuddin's other sons were either dead or close to death, and Gowa's surviving princesses were aged (Bulbeck 1992). The Gowa royalty was vanquished as a patrilineal core and had to include princesses' sons. As South Sulawesi's most powerful lineage, Bone-Soppeng forced its claims, and Sultan Ismail (B19/S19/G20) ruled Gowa as the first of his three royal titles. But Bone-Soppeng's authority waned with the approaching death of Alimuddin. In 1714 Ismail was forced to abdicate in favour of Karaeng Parang-Parang's daughter, Sirajuddin (T12/G21). Thus the Tallok Sultan Sirajuddin, as a matrilateral grandson within the Gowa royal core from a higher status lineage, ultimately absorbed the Gowa rulership within the Tallok royalty (Bulbeck 1992).

Sirajuddin was preferred over Ismail because a Makassar royal constituted a far more palatable ruler of Gowa than a Bugis royal did (Patunru 1983:76). A fuller explanation notes the depth of Sirajuddin's ties with the Gowa royalty, compared to Ismail's which extended back only a generation (Figure 1). Further, very many Makassar nobles were related one way or another to Sirajuddin, and the late seventeenth century flurry of marriages between Bone-Soppeng and greater Gowa was inadequate to repair the difference. This point highlights a key strength of the bilateral component of élite Makassar kinship. Usurpation of a royal title from above could be briefly successful, but it could only be sustained if the appropriate breadth and depth of relationships with the subjects were also established.

Conclusions

Statistical analysis of the data clarifies the nature and transmission of élite Makassar titles during the sixteenth and seventeenth centuries. The results strikingly resemble those obtained by Palmier (1969) for traditional Java and Gullick (1958) for the western Malaysian states. But the closest parallel comes from the system documented by Rössler (1987) and Röttger-Rössler (1989) for the Kasepekang Konjo. Moreover our sparser data sets, such as those pertaining to Polombangkeng and Lekokboding, invoke the Konjo model, even if the available details are inadequate for rigorous comparisons.

The key institutions were the bilateral descent groups composed of descendants of the inaugurators of hereditary titles. The most powerful of these were associated with a royal title closely guarded by a patrilineal core. Royal polygyny at the centre generated a bank of potential princes who ensured uninterrupted patrilineal passage of the title. *Ipso facto* it also generated unsuccessful candidates who, along with their patrilineal descendants, maintained a recognized place within the bilateral descent group if they achieved a karaengship. The more powerful the patrilineal royalty, the larger its following of attached noble patrilines. In short, securing the patrilineal succession stimulated political expansion, to such a degree that the power of any monarch was closely related to his number of wives.

Royal polygyny also generated a bank of princesses who tended to marry other royal lines and entrench the royalty's genealogical distinctiveness. Yet because these daughters' status was systematically downgraded, they could also marry nobles either attached to some royal patriline or descended from local status lineages. This did not create any dangers for the royal patriline as long as it kept its position of power. The offspring from these marriages were simply not admitted into the royal core.

If the system excluded by patrilineal descent towards the centre, it also included by bilateral descent towards the peripheries. Men from a higher status lineage could attach themselves to a wife from a lower status lineage, and the offspring could then belong to the wife's group. (Hence the indigenous view which derives the nobility from the marriage between commoners and descendants of the *Tomanurung*.) This privilege allowed the powerful lineages to dump their superfluous proportion of well-born men towards the margins. The men then held exalted positions within their group (witness Daeng Bunding in Kasepekang) which enjoyed greater prestige because of its attachment towards the centre. The privilege also allowed a powerful royal patriline to absorb territorial titles previously belonging to autonomous patrilines. The powerful royal retained his membership within his natal group while his wife, as the princess from the weaker line, transmitted the right of office to her husband through marriage, or to their sons through bilateral descent. (Note that the Konjo did not permit men this right of affiliation or membership within two cores [Rössler 1987:65], but the Gowa royalty did not observe this nicety during their territorial expansion.)

In a very practical sense the king was the husband of his realm (cf. Jordaan and de Josselin de Jong 1985). The legitimacy of his control derived from his marriages, or those of his direct ancestors, to princesses within the cores of the subjugated domains. So during 1500-1593 the Gowa royalty attracted status wives from those areas which Gowa came to rule. The territorial ambitions of the Gowa royalty, and its ability to draw status wives, were then contained until the mid-seventeenth century when Gowa legitimately absorbed Sanrabone. With the loss of Gowa's subjugated lands after 1667, Gowa now became "wife" to the two powerful royal lineages in Makassar, Bone-Soppeng and Tallok.

Makassar remained as South Sulawesi's effective capital after the eclipse of the Gowa patriline. The most prestigious title, the rulership of Gowa, was absorbed by Tallok as the most powerful Makassar line. Sirajuddin's ascendancy, which bequeathed a disputed succession until his direct descendants finally monopolized the Gowa rulership late in the nineteenth century (see Patunru 1983:76-99), is not conventionally registered as a dynastic change (e.g. Patunru 1983). In the sense that the disputed succession involved closely related Makassar lineages, and that Tallok's origins are ultimately one with Gowa's (Figure 1), there was indeed no dynastic change. Thus the principle of bilateral membership not only allowed the legitimate passage of authority between peer patrilines, it also tended to ensure continuity of social organization by resisting unrelated factions. Analysis along these lines may help to explain why western Indonesian (and Southeast Asian) political history suggests a multiplicity of "dynasties" centred in comparatively few heartlands and often showing strong cross-dynasty continuity.

Acknowledgments

Campbell Macknight and Peter Bellwood have unstintingly provided incisive supervision. P.E. de Josselin de Jong, Tony Reid, Jos Platenkamp and Ian Caldwell have assisted me with their comments, contacts, and copies of relevant papers. In particular I thank Jim Fox and Clifford Sather who perceived the potential of my initial analysis and guided it towards a product which (I hope) qualifies as sound anthropology.

References

Acciaioli, Gregory L.

1989   Searching for good fortune: the making of a Bugis shore community at Lake Lindu, Central Sulawesi. PhD thesis, The Australian National University.

Andaya, Leonard Y.

1981   *The heritage of Arung Palakka. A history of South Sulawesi (Celebes) in the seventeenth century*. The Hague: Martinus Nijhoff.

Bulbeck, F. David

1986-87   Survey of open archaeological sites in South Sulawesi 1986-1987. *Bulletin of the Indo-Pacific Prehistory Association* 7:36-50.

1990   The landscape of the Makassar War. *Canberra Anthropology* 13(1):78-99.

1992   A tale of two kingdoms. The historical archaeology of Gowa and Tallok, South Sulawesi, Indonesia. PhD thesis, The Australian National University.

Caldwell, Ian A.

1988 South Sulawesi AD 1300-1600: ten Bugis texts. PhD thesis, The Australian National University.

Cense, A.A.

1966   Old Buginese and Macassarese diaries. *Bijdragen van het Koninklijk Instituut* 122:416-428.

Chabot, Henri T.

1950   *Verwantschap, stand en sexe in Zuid-Celebes*. Groningen: J.B. Wolters. English translation by R. Neuse (1960) *Kinship, status and sex in South Celebes*. New Haven: Human Relations Area Files.

Fox, James J.

1971   A Rotinese dynastic genealogy: structure and event. In T.O. Beidelman (ed.) *The translation of culture*. London: Tavistock.

1995   Austronesian societies and their transformations. In Peter Bellwood, James J. Fox and Darrell Tryon (eds) *The Austronesians: historical and comparative perspectives,* pp.214-228. Canberra: Research School of Pacific and Asian Studies, The Australian National University.

Friedericy, H.J.

1933   De standen bij de Boegineezen en Makassaren. *Bijdragen tot de Taal-, Land- en Volkenkunde van Nederlandsch Indiè* 90:447-602.

Grimes, Charles E. and Barbara D. Grimes

1987 *Languages of South Sulawesi*. Pacific Linguistics Series D No. 78. Canberra: Department of Linguistics, Research School of Pacific Studies, The Australian National University.

Gullick, J.M.

1958   *Indigenous political systems of western Malaya*. Revised edition 1988. London: Athlone Press.

Jordaan, R.E. and P.E. de Josselin de Jong

1985   Sickness as a metaphor in Indonesian political myths. *Bijdragen tot de Taal-, Land- en Volkenkunde* 141:253-274.

Josselin de Jong, P.E. de

1980   Ruler and realm: political myths in western Indonesia. *Mededelingen der Koninklijke Nederlandse Akademie van Wetenschappen, afd. Letterkunde n.s.* 43(1):3-19.

Kallupa, Bahru

1984 *Laporan pengumpulan data peninggalan sejarah dan purbakala di Kabupaten Barru*. Ujung Pandang: Suaka Peninggalan Sejarah dan Purbakala Sulawesi Selatan.

Kamaruddin, H.D. Mangemba, P. Parawansa and M. Mappaseleng

1985-86   *Lontarak Bilang raja Gowa dan Tallok (naskah Makassar)*. Ujung Pandang: Proyek Penelitian dan Pengkajian Kebudayaan Sulawesi Selatan LaGaligo.

Millar, S.B.

1989   *Bugis weddings. Rituals of social location in modern Indonesia*. University of California at Berkeley Monograph Series No. 29. Berkeley: Center for South and Southeast Asian Studies.

Mukhlis

1975 Struktur birokrasi kerajaan Gowa jaman pemerintahan Sultan Hasanuddin (1653-1669). Yogyakarta: Sarjana thesis, Universitas Gadjah Mada.

Noorduyn, J.

1987   *Bima en Sumbawa*. Bijdragen tot de geschiedenis van de sultanaten Bima en Sumbawa door A. Ligtvoet en G.P. Rouffaer. Dordrecht: Foris Publications.

Palmier, Leslie H.

1969   *Social status and power in Java* (corrected edition). London: Athlone Press.

Patunru, Abd Razak Daeng

1983   *Sejarah Gowa*. Ujung Pandang: Yayasan Kebudayaan Sulawesi Selatan di Makassar.

Pelras, Christian

1977   Les premières données occidentales concernant Célèbes-sud. *Bijdragen tot de Taal-, Land- en Volkenkunde* 133:227-260.

Rahim, A. and B. Ridwan

1975   *Sejarah kerajaan Tallo' (suatu transkripsi lontara')*. Ujung Pandang: Kantor Cabang II Lembaga Sejarah dan Antropologi.

Reid, Anthony

1983   The rise of Makassar. *Review of Indonesian and Malaysian Affairs* 17:117-160.

1987   Pluralism and progress in seventeenth century Makassar. Paper presented at the Leiden workshop "Trade, society and belief in South Sulawesi". MS.

1988   *Southeast Asia in the age of commerce*. Vol. 1: *The lands below the winds*. New Haven: Yale University Press.

Rössler, Martin

1987   *Die soziale Realität des Rituals. Kontinuität und Wandel bei den Makassar von Gowa (Süd-Sulawesi/Indonesien)*. Berlin: Dietrich Reimer Verlag.

Röttger-Rössler, Birgitt

1989   *Rang und Ansehen bei den Makassar von Gowa (Süd-Sulawesi/Indonesien)*. Berlin: Dietrich Reimer Verlag.

Wolhoff, G.J. and Abdurrahim

n.d.

c.1959 *Sedjarah Goa*. Makassar (Ujung Pandang): Jajasan Kebudayaan Sulawesi Selatan dan Tenggara.

Chapter 14. The Cultural Construction of Rank, Identity and Ethnic Origins in the Sulu Archipelago[1]

Charles O. Frake

Hierarchy is a feature of social systems whereby a ranking is attributed to socially-defined subjects of discourse. Ordinarily we think of these ranked subjects as individuals. But the rank of an individual as a subject *vis-à-vis* some other individual must be defined in terms of a field of scope of that rank. Thus I might rank very high within my department but, because of my department's low rank within the university, I am scorned by the dean and ignored by the provost. Yet because of my university's high rank among universities, I am accorded deference by my colleagues elsewhere in academia who are, fortunately, unaware of my dean's contempt. Whether it is better to be a big fish in a little pond or a little fish in a big pond depends on the waters in which one aspires to swim. In either case, our aspirations must take account of the rank of our pond in the field of ponds. Ponds, the social fields encompassing individuals, are also subjects of attributed rank. Where do these attributions come from? How does it come to be decided whether my pond, my department, my university, my profession, my country, is better than yours. This paper argues that, however the ranking of ponds comes about in the historical particulars of a given case, that process is constitutive of the very ponds it ranks. If it were not for the differentiation of social fields that social hierarchy requires, we would perhaps all be swimming in a common ocean.

It is with the cultural construction of the social fields of hierarchy that this study is concerned. I examine this process among Moslem Filipinos in the region of the Sulu Archipelago and the Zamboanga Peninsula of southwestern Mindanao in the Philippines. To make the topic manageable, I ignore the region's important links with Borneo to the west and with central Mindanao to the east.[2] Even more seriously, I will largely ignore the parallel social system of Christian Filipinos in the same region, recognizing that the violent conflict between these two systems over the past 400 years has done much, and at this very moment is doing much, to shape each of them.

A prominent attribute of the ethnology of the Sulu region is that it is very "ethnic". Ethnologists happily find that their "tribes" for the most part come already equipped with well accepted names, distinct languages, colourful costumes, varied settlement patterns, contrasting roof slopes, distinctive dance styles, and so on. The ranking of ethnonyms, names for ethnic groups, and their attribution to specific persons and communities are prominent themes in the discourse of Sulu's Moslems. This ranking provides a convenient place to begin our examination. Table 1 presents a list some of the Sulu ethnonyms in rough rank order — rough because the order is subject to local negotiation and reinterpretation. The table also attempts to display some the complexities of ethnic naming, simplifying greatly in order to avoid even clumsier graphic devices. A fundamental distinction, shown in the table by italics, separates names used in self-identification (*deutsch*) from names attributed by outsiders ("German"). Terms of self-identification may show a further distinction, not marked in the table, of inclusive self naming ("my fellow Americans") as opposed to exclusive self naming ("Unlike you Mexicans, we North Americans ..."). Among attributed terms one must distinguish between those internal to the local system of discourse from those externally imposed by outsiders, in this case central government authorities, journalists, movie producers, missionaries, and, of course, anthropologists. Internal attributed naming may vary depending on whether the naming is being done face to face ("You Germans ...") or not ("Those Krauts ..."). The use of some ethnic names, however, can be free of these complexities. These unproblematic names do not vary with user or context.

We begin our examination of ethnic naming in Sulu with the several unproblematic names listed in Table 1. Not uninterestingly, they occur at the top and the bottom of this display of ethnic hierarchy. The heights to which one can aspire as well as the depths beyond which no one fear sink are well marked. It is the more muddled middle grounds that provide room for manœuvre. At the top we find the Tausug, a people remarkably well demarcated from all those about and below them. We can best see what sets them apart as people of high rank by comparing them with the people at the bottom of heap, the Subanun of the mountainous interior of Zamboanga. (The Subanun are actually at the bottom of two heaps: that of the Christian as well as of the Moslem social orders.) The most obvious contrast, both to locals and to outside investigators, is that of religion. The Tausug have religion in the form of official Islam with all its accoutrements: mosques, Mecca pilgrims, religious teachers, religious tracts in Arabic script, pig-free homesteads, and toddy-free markets. True, in purity of faith, they rank, even in their hardly humble eyes, below the Malay to the east in *singapura*, and, of course, to the Arab still further to the east in *makka*. But within Sulu, no one else can challenge their religious credentials. The Subanun, by contrast, have, in local eyes, no religion at all. They are pagans (or, even worse, recently converted Christian protestants), pork eaters, and rice-wine imbibers. The Tausug are linked by name to the economic and political centre of Sulu, the island of Jolo. That island has been an *entrepôt* linking the tropical sources of spices, forest products, and maritime delicacies to China since well before the coming of Islam. Wherever a Tausug might live, he or she "comes from" the historic central place of Sulu. He or she is a person (*tau*) of Jolo (*su(l)ug*).[3] A Subanun's place, on the other had, is simply *suba'* 'upstream.' The name, meaning upstream person, or hick, is of external origin. It is an ethnonym of a type common in Island Southeast Asia, lumping all the people of the interior, the mountains, and the upstream regions in one category as opposed to the more civilized people of the coasts and lowlands. Yet it is a distinctive name and, fortuitously in this case, it does denote a cultural and linguistic entity.[4] Unlike the Tausug language, which is remarkably homogeneous throughout its range, Subanun exhibits sufficient dialectal diversity that its extreme variants border on mutual unintelligibility. Compounding the markers of Subanun low status is their reputation for pacifism which stands in marked contrast to the notorious fierceness of the Tausug. This reputation which seems by all accounts, historic and contemporary, to be well merited, cannot be explained simply as a result of Subanun marginality to the centres of power and wealth. Other marginal pagans of the islands, the Ifugao, the Ilongot and the Iban have firmly established reputations as headhunting savages.

Table 1. Some ethnonyms of Sulu and Zamboanga (in rough rank order)

Tausug
Yakan
(sama) balangingiq *sama* + 'place name' "Samal" "'floater"'
sama + 'true' *sama* + 'sea' "Sama(l) 'to be spit on"' "Bajao"
sama + 'land' " " "Kalibugan" kalibugan
Subanun

Key: Unproblematic ethnonym
        self identification
        "Attributed identification"
        'English gloss of local term'
        "'English gloss of local attributed identification"'

Both the Subanun and the Tausug share in their lexicon a full inventory of Austronesian, Sanskrit, Persian and Arabic titles. Both groups can easily people their stories with timu'ays, panglimas, datus, rajas, maharajas, nakuras, sarifs and sultans. But only the Tausug can ordinarily confront such characters in their daily lives. The Tausug see themselves, and are viewed by others (including their ethnographers), as a stratified society with a hereditary titled nobility headed by a ruling sultan. Western scholarship typically reflects the Tausug view of a system of named titles as actors: "A Tausug *datu* would authorize a *panglima* to conduct a raid ... The *panglima* then selected the *nakhoda* or captain, who recruited his own crew. The crew members consisted of ... *Balangingi*" (Gibson 1990:6). In ideology the Tausug are masters of a single political state, ruling over all the peoples of the archipelago. Actual political structure is much more chaotic and contested, but there is a structure to discern in practice as well as in discourse (see Kiefer 1969). The Subanun, on the other hand, have never had any pretensions at political unity (Frake 1980:83-103). Economic centrality, militancy, internal stratification and a semblance of political unity mark the Tausug as high rank; marginality, pacifism, egalitarianism and absence of political coherence reveal the low position of the Subanun.

Both groups, the highest and the lowest, are, however, marked off by clear ethnic distinctiveness. No account of Philippine "tribes", from the sixteenth century to the present, fails to list both the Subanun and the Tausug and to note their relative worth.[5] It is in the middle ranks of the ethnic hierarchy that the distinctiveness of peoples becomes obscure and their ranking contested.

Located both geographically and socially between the Tausug of Jolo island and the Subanun of the mountains of Zamboanga are peoples variously sorted out from a pool of speakers of a distinct set of closely related languages and dialects here labelled "Samalan". The linguistic diversity within this group is considerable, but the boundaries between a Samalan language and Tausug on the one hand or Subanun on the other are quite apparent to locals as well as to investigators. Most Samalan speakers identify themselves as *sama*. I will use the name "Sama" for those who so identify themselves and the term "Samalan" for the language group.[6] Whether or not a Samalan speaker is ethnically a "Sama" is a matter of local negotiation. To the Tausug, and in the ethnographic literature, most are "Samal". To Combés, the seventeenth century Jesuit historian of Mindanao, they were "Lutao", literally "floaters" (Combés 1897).

The Sama, unlike the Tausug and the Subanun are associated with the sea. They live along the shores of the islands of the archipelago and on the peninsula. In spite of the alleged romance of maritime life, making one's living from the sea does not confer high rank in Sulu no more than anywhere else in the modern world. Most Sama augment fishing and marine-gathering with commercial coconut cultivation and some subsistence agriculture. Many engage in trade, including quite profitable smuggling. There is considerable diversity among them in economic standing and political power. Amongst themselves, the Sama differentiate ethnic identity according to provenance — where one can claim to "come from". There are *sama tagtabun, sama ubian* and even, near a gasoline storage facility on the outskirts of Zamboanga City, *sama mobilgas*. Some locales rank higher than others, proximity to economic and political centres being a factor but, even more important, is something that might be called place-name notoriety. One of the highest ranking places in all the archipelago is, in fact, an uninhabited stretch of coral between Jolo and Basilan called Balangingi'. That is a name which, to judge from nineteenth century Spanish, Dutch and English accounts, struck terror in the hearts of all who ventured near the Sulu Sea. The Balangingi' were the most notorious pirates of Sulu. Their island base was finally demolished by the Spanish and the power of the pirates broken. But the notoriety and prestige of the name has continued. Most Sama in Eastern Sulu and Zamboanga who are not obviously from somewhere else, claim to be *sama balangingi'*. During the nineteenth century their notoriety was such that they were "Balangingi'" pure and simple. They had, by military prowess and fierce reputation climbed out of Sama status. Now they are clearly Sama again, but they are at least Sama of high rank among Sama: big fish in a lesser pond (Geoghegan 1975; Rutter 1986; Barrantes 1878; Montero y Vidal 1888; Warren 1981; Pallesen 1985).

Another group of Samalan speakers did, in fact succeed in climbing out of Sama status. In seventeenth century records the Samalan speakers of Basilan Island, off the tip of the Zamboanga Peninsula, are identified as "Sameacan", i.e. *sama yakan* (Combés 1897). Shortly thereafter, and down to this day, they have been known simply as "Yakan". The Yakan have worked hard at not being Sama. Like the Balangingi' they built a reputation for fierceness — but on land rather than at sea. The Yakan, in early accounts are recorded not as pirates, but as notorious bandits. The Yakan have shunned the sea, changed their costumes, altered their roof slope, rescored their music, and stopped dancing. They have fought off Sama pirates, Tausug raiders, and Christian settlers.[7] In spite of the obvious Samalan affinities of their language, the Yakan are everywhere acknowledged to be a distinct ethnic group with distinct origins from the Sama. The Yakan have climbed above Sama identity but still fall below the Tausug. Their notoriety is geographically restricted, their political integration more feeble, their claim to titles on shakier grounds. Most of all, the markedness of their ethnicity casts suspicion on the purity of their Islam (Frake 1980:175-252).

One can not only climb out of Sama identity, one can fall out. Some Samalan-speakers have been so identified with the sea that they are considered to be boat-dwelling sea nomads with no local provenance. Having no Mosques, their Islam status becomes suspect. They are poor and powerless enough to border on being outcasts in the Sulu hierarchical system. Although they call themselves "true" Sama (*sama to'ongan*), outsiders call them a variety of derogatory terms such as "Sama to be spit upon". In the ethnographic literature, as well as among local Christians, they have a distinctive label: they are the "Bajao", a term also applied by outsiders to Samalan speaking communities scattered along the Borneo and Eastern Indonesian coasts. The use of "Bajao" in the Philippines represents an unusual case of over-differentiation by outsiders. One expects outsiders to overlook internally recognized boundaries. Among Sulu Moslems, these maritime Sama, called Bajao by Christian and academic outsiders, are everywhere acknowledged to be Sama or "Samal", albeit of the lowest sort.

Finally, there are Samalan speakers who have disappeared altogether as an ethnic identity. These are swidden agriculturists, living much as the Subanun, in the mountains of the southern Zamboanga Peninsula. They are nowhere listed in any inventory of named ethnic groups, thus the "empty string" symbol (" ") that represents their externally attributed ethnonym in Table 1. They consider themselves *sama*, but outsiders typically confuse them with Islamicized Subanun, the "Kalibugan".[8] Essentially they are nobodies, a status not without adaptive merits in the political and military arena of the southwestern Philippines (Pallesen 1985; Frake 1980:325).

How did the Tausug achieve their position of ethnic distinctiveness at the top of the Sulu hierarchy? Their own story is that they were the original inhabitants of Jolo island. The Sama came in later from Johore, accepting subservient status in turn for the right to settle among the islands. The Tausug gave religion and civilization to these sea nomads. This myth of Sama origins as external migrants wandering in by sea from Johore has a firm place not only in local ethnohistory but also in the historical literature (Saleeby 1908). Here is a recent version presented as history by a Western scholar: "One recurrent pattern in Southeast Asian history was an alliance between ethnic Bajau, or sea nomads, and a dominant ethnic group such as Malays, Bugis, or Tausug. The Bajau were originally fishers and gatherers occupying the Riau archipelago off the east coast of Sumatra, who lived their lives on boats. In the course of time, they spread up the west coast of Thailand, to the southern Philippines, and perhaps even as far as southern China" (Gibson 1990:7). It is easy to show on linguistic grounds that this myth inverts historical fact. The Tausug language is clearly intrusive to Sulu, whereas the locally well diversified Samalan languages first differentiated within the Sulu archipelago and then spread outward from there to Borneo, eastern Indonesia, and to one island in the central Philippines. Tausug closely affiliates with the languages spoken geographically far away on the northeast coast of Mindanao. It is very obviously a member of the closely-related Bisayan group of central Philippine languages, all of whose speakers are today Christian Filipinos. The linguist Kemp Pallesen (1985) has presented a well documented argument that before the appearance of the Tausug language, Samalan-speaking traders of Jolo had established trading stations in northeast Mindanao where they had intermarried with women speaking Bisayan languages. Enough of these women came back to Jolo that their language was established as a second language there. As the people of Jolo became more prosperous and powerful they created an identity for themselves that separated them from their Samalan-speaking kin. The new language provided a clear marker of that identity. It became the distinctive language of the Tausug. Whether or not one accepts this particular account of the formation of Tausug identity, one cannot deny that the identity was constructed and maintained locally as part of a struggle by individuals and groups to affirm and maintain high rank in a region-wide discourse of hierarchy (cf. Brown 1973).

Figure 1 presents a display of the dimensions of this discourse. The subject of the discourse is the ranking of ethnonyms, names for peoples. The attribution of these names to specific individuals and communities and the use of these names as self-identification asserts that these individuals and communities display the characteristics appropriate to the name. The Tausug display the attributes of high status: Islam, centrality in the political-economic systems; militancy; and a distinctive non-Samalan language of their own. At the bottom the Subanun are pagan, peripheral, docile, are linguistically distinct from the Samalan speakers above them. Samalan-speakers can raise their status by displays of militancy and economic power. They fall in status by being seen as geographically peripheral to the centres of power, either on land or at sea, and by displaying in behaviour the docility appropriate to a marginal people. Adherence to Islam, however, provides a firm bottom line to the descent of any Samalan-speaker and warrants, for self-identification at any rate, the ethnonym *sama*.

Before ending our story, note should be taken of the ethnic labelling that marks the Moslem-Christian boundary in the southern Philippines. Since the first Spanish encounters with them, the Philippine Moslems have been known to Philippine Christians as "Moros". That term has been used as an ethnic group label not only by local Christians but by outside officials and scholars down to the present. A US Department of Army poster commemorating an attack by US Troops on a Jolo bastion in 1913 thus describes the Tausug defenders whose slaughter is graphically depicted:

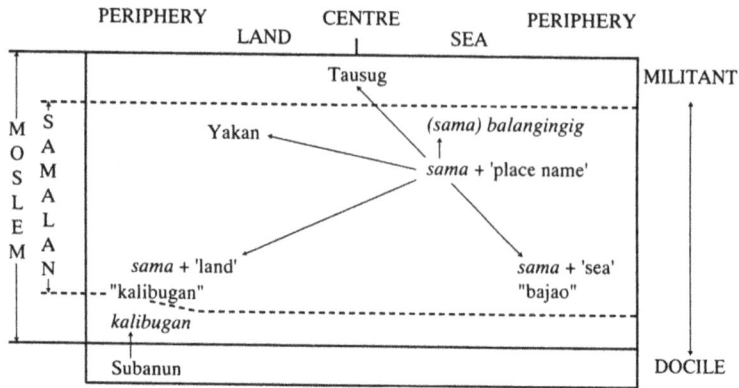

Figure 1. Dimensions of hierarchy in Sulu and Zamboanga.

Knocking out the Moros, the U.S. Army in Action: The four-day battle of Bagsak Mountain on Jolo Island in the Philippines took place from 11 to 15 July 1913. Americans of the 8th Infantry and the Philippine Scouts, personally led by Brigadier General John J. Pershing, brought to an end years of bitter struggle against the Moro pirates. These Jolo men, outlaws of great physical endurance and savage fighting ability were well organized under their Datus or chiefs ... The U.S. Army .45-caliber pistol was developed to meet the need for a weapon with enough striking power to stop fanatical charges of lawless Moro tribesmen in hand-to-hand fighting (Department of the Army 1963).[9]

The traditional use of "Moro" by outsiders, apart from carrying derogatory connotations, served to obscure the very real cultural and linguistic differences among Philippine Moslems (Frake 1980:314-318). The Moslems of course reciprocated with an epitaph of their own: *bisaya'*, a term which Moslems take to mean both Filipino Christian and "slave".

With the escalation of conflict between Moslems and the Philippine government in recent decades, Moslem political and military leaders have adopted a strategy now familiar in ethnic conflict. They have taken an externally applied slur as their own self-identification, a tactic aimed on emphasizing the common historical experience of all Philippine Moslems as victims of the slurrers. The "Moro National Liberation Front" (MNLF) was formed in the 1970s by a Tausug intellectual. Its military arm titled itself the "Bangsa Moro Army" (BMA) ("Bangsa", from Malay, means "nation", "identity", "rank" in all "Moro" languages.) As a symbol of unity, however, "Moro" has had questionable success. The word has, in fact, fostered a whole new set of divisive ethnonyms. Along with the MNLF and the BMA, there arose the MILF, MNLFR, MIM, BMLO, MRO and MNRDF. All of these acronyms contain "M" for "Moro" and are based on English (MNRDF, for example is the "Moro National Revolutionary Democratic

Front"), the only common language of the "Moros" (the southern Philippines is outside the scope of the use of Malay as a *lingua franca*). These divisions reflect conflicts along ethnic lines, especially between Tausug and Central Mindanao Moslems, along ideological lines between Communist and Islamicist, and along lines of political orientation between traditionalist and modernist (Cayongcat 1986; George 1980). The game of labelling and thereby constituting identities in the discourse of political practice is still very much alive among the Moslems of the southern Philippines.

The history of hierarchy peculiar to Sulu has something in general to tell us about the interconnections between horizontal and vertical social differentiation in human society. But I tell this story on this occasion on the grounds that all its actors speak Austronesian languages. Does that make any difference? In talking about hierarchy in our various Austronesian-speaking societies, are we saying anything "Austronesian"? Certainly the fact that members of two societies speak languages of the same family says nothing, *per se*, about the forms of their society. After all the Hindus and the Western Europeans, by conventional anthropological wisdom, are supposed to have diametrically opposed ideologies of hierarchy — yet they both speak languages of a common family. It is true that, among language families, there is something historically unique about Austronesian. The wide, purely insular, distribution of these languages as well as the parallel distribution of a distinctive agricultural complex both point to a shared cultural heritage among Austronesian-speakers that goes beyond linguistic affiliation. But is that heritage likely to lie behind any contemporary commonalities in systems of social hierarchy? If that is to be our argument, we must show the common historical experiences relevant to the shaping of hierarchical systems that Austronesian-speakers shared. I do not think that can be done. It is not enough to point out how the hierarchical system of one Austronesian-speaking society shares similarities with another Austronesian-speaking society at the other end of the Pacific. (Comparisons are in fact usually made between Island Southeast Asia and Polynesia, ignoring all that lies inbetween, both geographically and temporally.) One could just as easily pick out utterly dissimilar cases within the Austronesian-speaking world. Alternatively, by judicious selection of cases — focusing on the Subanuns and Hanunóos of the Austronesian world — one could just as easily argue that the fundamental Austronesian ethos has been egalitarian rather than hierarchical, diffuse rather than centric, and pluralistic rather than dualistic. Hierarchy, whatever one means by it, is not a simple, contextually arbitrary form transmitted across generations like the word *mata* for "eye"; it is a complex socio-cultural arrangement, constantly changing in adaptation to local socio-cultural contexts. One word for "eye" works as well as another in any context — so why not call it *mata*? — but one system of hierarchy definitely does not work as well as another in any circumstance. Changing social, political and ecological circumstances, in other words, "history" shapes hierarchical forms. The historical experiences of the western Austronesian world, peoples taking over islands already inhabited, replacing all existing languages, and then becoming enmeshed in the vortex of trade and conflict among old world civilizations, were opposed in almost every respect to those of the isolated eastern islands of Polynesia, as free of outside contact as any communities could be. If there are similarities between the hierarchical systems of Polynesia and those of Island Southeast Asia, as have been commonly proposed, then they can only be convergences of form arising from utterly dissimilar causes. It is difficult to see how sharing an Austronesian language could have anything to do with it.

References

Barrantes, Vincente

1878   *Guerras piráticas de Filipinas contra mindanaos y joloanos*. Madrid: M.G. Hernandez.

Brown, D.E.

1973 Hereditary rank and ethnic history: an analysis of Brunei historiography. *Journal of Anthropological Research* 19:113-122.

Cayongcat, Al-Rashid I.

1986   *Bangsa Moro people in search of peace*. Manila: GRAPHICOM.

Combés, Francisco

1897   *Historia de Mindanao y Jolo (1667)*. W.E. Retana (ed.). Madrid: Viuda de M. Minuesa.

Department of the Army

1963 *Knocking out the Moros: the U.S. Army in action*. Department of the Army Poster No. 21-48. Washington, DC: U.S. Government Printing Office.

Frake, Charles

1980   *Language and cultural description*. Stanford: Stanford University Press.

Geoghegan, William

1975   *Balangingi*. In Frank M. LeBar (ed.) *Ethnic groups of insular Southeast Asia*. vol. 2, *Philippines and Formosa*. New Haven: Human Relations Area Files Press.

George, T.J.S.

1980 *Revolt in Mindanao: the rise of Islam in Philippine politics*. Kuala Lumpur: Oxford University Press.

Gibson, Thomas

1990   *On predatory states in Island Southeast Asia*. Canberra: Department of Anthropology Comparative Austronesian Project, Research School of Pacific Studies, The Australian National University.

Kiefer, Thomas M.

1969 *Tausug armed conflict: the military activity in a Philippine Moslem society*. Chicago: University of Chicago Department of Anthropology.

1972   *The Tausug: violence and law in a Philippine Moslem society*. New York: Holt, Rinehart & Winston.

Montero y Vidal, Jose

1888   *Historia de la piraterí a malayo-mahometana en Mindanao, Joló y Borneo.*
2 vols. Madrid: M. Tello.

Pallesen, Kemp A.

1985   *Culture contact and language convergence.* Manila: Linguistic Society of
the Philippines.

Rutter, Owen

1986   *The pirate wind: tales of the sea-robbers of Malaya.* Singapore: Oxford
University Press [reprint of 1930 edition].

Saleeby, Najeeb M.

1908   *The history of Sulu.* Manila. Bureau of Science.

Sather, Clifford

1984   Sea and shore people: ethnicity and ethnic interaction in Southeastern
Sabah. *Contributions to Southeast Asian Ethnography* 3:3-27.

Verschuer, F.H. van

1883   De Badjo's. *Tijdschrift van het Aardijkskundig Genootschap* 7:1-7.

Warren, James F.

1981   *The Sulu zone, 1768-1898.* Singapore: Singapore University Press.

Notes

[1] This paper represents a reworking of an earlier study (Frake 1980) rethought, updated, and oriented toward issues of hierarchy. It depends ultimately on field work conducted in the region from 1953 to 1972, ending with the year of the imposition of martial law in the Philippines. New information is forthcoming thanks to the just completed study of the Sama of westernmost Sulu by Patricia Horvatich of Stanford University. I have benefited by her work, as well as by comments from participants in the conference on hierarchy in the Austronesian-speaking world held at the Research School of Pacific Studies, Australian National University and from audiences of presentations of this material at the University of the Philippines and Cornell University. Clifford Sather, an expert on the peoples of the wider region of this study, has provided especially useful suggestions.

[2] Sather (1984) provides a comparable discussion of ethnicity among related and interconnected peoples to the west in Sabah.

[3] "Jolo" is a hispanicization of *sulug* (or Sama *suluk*) dating from when Philippine Spanish "j" represented a sound closer to [s] than to [h], its current pronunciation in the Philippines. The contrast between "Sulu" as the name for the archipelago, and "Jolo" as the name for the island and its city is an artifact of that sound change. The dropping of intervocalic /l/ (*sulug* vs. *suug*) marks stylistic and dialectical variants throughout the region.

[4] The same is not true of comparable ethnonyms, such as Bukid(non), Igorot, Mangyan, Dayak and Toraja used elsewhere for interior peoples of Southeast Asian Islands.

[5] Outsiders, the Spanish, Americans and Christian Filipinos have frequently labelled the Tausug as "Joloano" (see note 1).

[6] Pallesen, and others following him, label the linguistic group "Sama-Bajaw". Since it is necessary here carefully to distinguish the linguistic group both from the ethnic self-identification of *sama* and from the externally imposed and variously applied identity of "Bajao" (a spelling with "w" does not seem to do the job), I use "Samalan" for the language group, albeit with misgivings about perpetuating the form of a Tausug ethnonym *samal*, which they impose on the *sama*. The possible term "Samaan" for the language group strikes me as infelicitous.

[7] In conflicts with the Philippine military since the imposition of martial law by Marcos in 1972, the Yakan have not fared so well. The consequences for their ethnic viability are not yet clear.

[8] "Kalibugan", literally in Tausug and Cebuano Bisayan "mixed, or half-breed, especially of cocks", is an attributed ethnonym loosely applied to Moslems who live in the interior of Zamboanga and practice swidden agriculture like the Subanun. Those who speak Subanun accept the ethnonym as their own in preference to local forms of "Subanun" (*subanon, suban'un*). Those who speak Samalan call themselves *sama*. Table 1 reflects these usages.

[9] I am grateful to my colleague Karl Heider who found this poster for me.

Contributors

Peter Bellwood

(PhD, Cambridge, 1980), Reader, Department of Archaeology & Anthropology, The Faculties, The Australian National University, Canberra, ACT 0200, Australia.

Aletta Biersack

(PhD, Michigan, 1980), Professor, Department of Anthropology, University of Oregon, Eugene, Oregon 97403, USA.

F. David Bulbeck

(PhD, ANU, 1992), Lecturer, Centre for Archaeology, The University of Western Australia, Perth, Western Australia 6009, Australia.

James J. Fox

(D.Phil, Oxford, 1968), Professor and Head, Department of Anthropology, Research School of Pacific and Asian Studies, The Australian National University, Canberra, ACT 0200, Australia. (Convenor of the Comparative Austronesian Project.)

Charles O. Frake

(PhD, Yale, 1955), Professor, Department of Anthropology, State University of New York at Buffalo, Buffalo, New York 14261, USA.

Barbara Dix Grimes

(PhD, ANU, 1995), Visiting Lecturer, Centre for Regional Studies, Universitas Kristen Artha Wacana, P.O. Box 147, Jl Adisucipto, Oesapa, Kupang, NTT, Indonesia.

E. Douglas Lewis

(PhD, ANU, 1983), Senior Lecturer, Anthropology Program, Faculty of Arts, The University of Melbourne, Parkville, Victoria 3052, Australia.

Sandra Pannell

(PhD, Adelaide, 1991), Lecturer, Department of Anthropology & Archaeology, James Cook University, Townsville, Queensland 4811, Australia.

Clifford Sather

(PhD, Harvard, 1971), Associate Professor of Anthropology, Department of Anthropology, Reed College, Portland, Oregon 97202-8199, USA; and Research Editor, Tun Jugah Foundation, Iban Oral Literature Project.

Jukka Siikala

(PhD, Turku, 1982), Professor, Department of Social Anthropology, University of Helsinki, FIN-00014 Helsinki, Finland.

Ken-Ichi Sudo

(D.Litt., Tokyo Metropolitan University, 1986), Professor, Faculty of Intercultural Studies, Kobe University, 1-2-1 Tsurukabuto, Nada-ku, Kobe, Japan 657.

Michael P. Vischer

(PhD, ANU, 1993), Research Fellow, International Institute for Asian Studies, Leiden, 2300 RA Leiden, The Netherlands.

Aram A. Yengoyan

(PhD, Chicago, 1964), Professor, Department of Anthropology, University of California at Davis, Davis, California 95616, USA.